Norse Witch

Reclaiming the Heidhrinn Heart

About The Author

Connla Freyjason prefers to think outside the box, even as he practices the Old Ways. Having spent the past twenty years as a Pagan, he is fulltrui (a dedicant) of Freyja, a practicing vitki, and also a digital artist and graphic designer. The "presiding spirit" currently "horsed" by Ollamh Michelle Iacona, he is also the primary author of the Iaconagraphy blog.

Norse Witch

Reclaiming the Heidhrinn Heart

Connla Freyjason

via Michelle Iacona

Iaconagraphy Press

Massachusetts

FIRST EDITION

Author Photo: S. Hersey

Book Design: Connla Freyjason & Michelle Iacona

Cover Art & Illustration: Connla Freyjason

Interior Illustration: Connla Freyjason

ISBN 978-0692092941

Iaconagraphy
michelleiacona.com

facebook.com/Iaconagraphy

For the two most important women in my life:

Michelle, who has given me this life-after-death,

&

Suzanne, who has made this life worth living....

~Connla

I am the cat in the darkness,
I am the rose and the thorn,
I am the falcon on the wing,
And the whisper of air which lifts her up.
I am the artist and I am the art;
The maker, and the made.
I am the silence between the words
That gives the meaning to what's been said.
I am the Lover;
I am the Beloved.
I am what lies between.

~Connla Freyjason
For Freyja....

Contents

Acknowledgments

People tend to think of writing as a lonely endeavor, but in truth, it is anything but. This book would have been impossible without a number of people, and I would like to thank them again, even though they are all likely very tired of hearing those two little words from me by now.

Michelle Iacona, because without you, I absolutely *would not* be here. You have given up more than any one human should ever have been asked to give up over the past twenty-four years of our relationship as Horse and Rider, and "thank you" is simply too small to encompass what you mean to me. You are so much more than "just a writer", and I hope this book finally proves that to the entire world.

Suzanne, my Beloved and my very best friend. You are my wife-of-the-heart, and that means far more than a piece of paper ever could. Your patience and your ability to love *because* not *despite* never cease to amaze me. I never could have believed in myself enough to write this book, or make art, or even simply *keep going*, if you hadn't believed in me first.

Lawrence Hoffman, my heart-brother: your faith in me has never wavered, and your friendship is priceless.

Sharon, "Little Sister": it's been a long road together, but worth every step of the trip. Thank you for teaching me endurance, especially on those days when I didn't think I had another ounce of strength left in me.

Linda, my mother-of-the-heart, thank you for adopting me. No matter how "weird" it has ever been, you have always been there for me, with kindness and wisdom, shaping my Wyrd for the better.

Jan Tjeerd, for becoming first and foremost a dear friend, and second, the greatest cheerleader a guy could ever want. Thank you for continually pushing me out onto limbs I never dared to dream of, and then graciously celebrating as I soar.

Alfred McCarthy, for helping me find my footing on this path, and reminding me always what it means to be not only a good witch and a good writer, but also a good man.

The "Mighty Woof", for always being brutally honest, but also for reminding me when to stop beating myself up. I would not be the man I am today, had I never known you. You have taught me the true price of wisdom, as well as the true value of kindness.

KEM: You said I could do it, so I did. Thank you for teaching me to be unstoppable!

My Ancestors of Flesh and Blood, for gifting me with an ever-open mind.

My Ancestors I have gained through Michelle: Mema, thank you for the gift of an ever-open heart, to go with my ever-open mind.

And most of all: Freyja.
Thank You for choosing me as one of Your representatives here in this mundane world, and thank You for giving me the courage to attempt to bring the shimmer of the Northern Lights into the lives of others. I hope I do not disappoint....

Foreword

Meeting Connla Freyjason for the first time in 1994 completely changed my life, and I hope the book you presently hold in your hands will enable him to change yours as well. Since that first time I saw him, sitting there, spectral, in the back row of the movie theater where I worked my just-out-of-college-job, mouthing *"help me"*, because he wasn't sure I could *see* him, much less *hear* him, my life has been one constant roller coaster ride. Sometimes enchanting, and sometimes hauntingly tragic, I would not trade a single one of the moments that I've had to give up so that he could be here in my stead. You see, for every moment lost, I have gained so much more than simple *time*.

That movie theater job was my "bill paying job" just out of college; my real *passion* in life was potentially becoming a writer. I had already been published once: I won the Bunn-McClelland Chapbook at Saint Andrews in 1993 for my book, *Carnavale* (available in a newly revised and updated edition via *Smashwords*). I had just graduated Magna Cum Laude with a BA in English with Emphasis on Creative Writing, and I was earning my stripes as a part-time book designer and editor at a small press. I was sitting on top of the world, with all the hopes and dreams one expects from a fresh graduate with a creative bent.

And then the bottom dropped out from under me.

I found myself fired from the press, through no fault of my own, and I thought my life was over. In fact, I more than a little bit *wanted* it to be. But there was that spectral face in the back of the theater, and when I would find myself alone in there, hiding my tears from my co-workers and fiance, Connla would be there, and we would comfort each other as best we could.

Fast forward three years....

By 1997, I still had not become a best-selling author, and I no longer found myself employed, due to my struggles with my disability, but I *did* manage to finally marry my fiance. And Connla was there then, too, but in a completely different way. Shockingly, my brand new husband was perfectly okay with that arrangement. You see, somewhere along the way, *I began stepping out*, and *Connla began stepping in.*

I had been walking a shamanic path since before I even knew it was called that, though I'll admit, becoming a medium of any sort had always been the furthest thing from my mind. It wasn't exactly an *aspiration*, if you get my drift. In fact, most dead people scared the living crap out of me, until Connla came along. Then, at one of my darkest points, he wrapped his arms around me, and I took a deep breath, and we discovered that we had *switched places*. Both of us were shocked, but we went with it. It was the best and most convenient way to solve a lot of issues for *both* of us.

I had never even heard the word *seidhr*, when I began this journey twenty-four years ago. My knowledge of the Ancient Norse encompassed the few things I recalled about Ivar the Boneless from my World History class in college, and those dreadful Wagnerian Bugs Bunny cartoons. I had no idea that anyone else had ever experienced what I was experiencing then, or what I continue to experience today. When I researched channeling or mediumship, everything I found either involved Vodun (aka Voodoo), or some hocus pocus koo-koo-nut in a turban. My only exposure to anything even remotely resembling what was going on in my life was Whoopi Goldberg in *Ghost*, when she "steps aside" to let Patrick Swayze use her body to kiss Demi Moore.

So you can imagine my amazement when Connla found a passage from *Hrolfs Saga Kraka*, describing *precisely* what he and I have been experiencing together, as "Horse" and "Rider" for the past twenty-four years. After I said "God bless you", he explained that the text dated from 15th century Iceland. After that, he told me he had stumbled upon it while doing some research for a *book* he was thinking of writing.

That my dear little artistic "ghosty" might be pondering adding writing to his repertoire was perhaps the biggest shock of them all. After all, wasn't *I* supposed to be the writer? That had always been "my gig", and art had always been Connla's. But he has never clipped my wings, so I wasn't about to clip his!

I am so glad that I didn't.

This little book right here in your hands is a *brave* thing. In fact, it is far more brave, and far more beautiful than anything I have ever written. Connla has proven that he is as much of an artist with words, as he is with paint, or brush, or pen, or paper, or pixels. In writing this, he has also proven that he is precisely the *warrior* that I have always known him to be. Your viewpoints will be *challenged*, as you read this book. By the last page of it, parts of your worldview might even find themselves thoroughly *changed*. But if books cannot touch our lives, why do we waste our time reading them? And if writers must only write books that maintain the status quo, why waste time writing them?

Michelle Iacona
Ollamh Dewin
Author of *Carnavale* and *Raven*
Chelmsford, Massachusetts
February 16, 2018

Norse Witch

Reclaiming the Heidhrinn Heart

Norse Witch

I've dreamed of flames nine nights now;
Nine nights, hung upon a pyre of spears,
Burning,
Like Gullveig.
Those flames,
The flames of condescension
     and derision,
Sparked by all those who would
     claim Heathen,
Without understanding or accepting
     what it is to be
Heidhrinn.
I've dreamed of flames nine nights now;
Nine nights, hung upon a pyre of spears,
Burning,
Like Gullveig.
Each time,
Thrice-burned,
Thrice-born,
To become Heidhr.
And now the smoke has cleared;
I see the path that lies before me
     with clarity,

As I could never see before.
I am Heidhrinn, not Heathen:
Bright and shining;
A prophesying witch,
My wand, enchanted;
For I am versed in magick,
And wherever I go, spirits are at play,
Including my own.
I bring healing to those in need of it,
And magick where once there was none.
I *am not* woman,
But I *am* witch.
I've dreamed of flames nine nights now;
Nine nights, hung upon a pyre of spears,
Like Gullveig.
And I burn
To ignite the flames of others,
Where once only ashes
        of the past held sway.

~Connla Freyjason

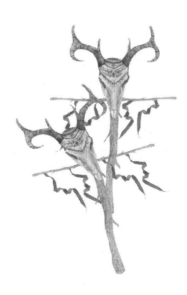

Northern Lights

This book almost didn't happen. Two-hundred-and-six pages in, I hit save one final time on my word processor, and shelved this project. On the outside, aloud, to other people, my excuse was that our impending move of house simply made things entirely too hectic to maintain my current writing schedule. But on the inside, in those quiet places where the brain curls up and hides just before attempting to drift off to sleep, the truth silently simmered: *I was terrified.*

Terrified: If I release this to the public, I will be crucified. Public scrutiny is a frightening prospect for any writer or artist, I suppose, and a fear of it, I would reckon, is common among our kind, but the brand of terror I am referring to here surpasses any such normal fears that are the bane of we artistic types. No, I had already paid regular visits to this particular lion's den, and I knew not only the size of its teeth, but the pressure of its jaws: I had spent enough time in Heathen groups to know that very little of what I had to say was going to be met with a warm reception. Those who follow the Norse Traditions are an interesting mix of straight Historical Reconstructionists ("screencap of where it says that in the Eddas, or it didn't happen, dude!"), Pagans with a Norse base ("I'm surprisingly okay with Unconfirmed Personal Gnosis"), Ceremonial Magickians who "dress up" their practice in strictly Norse trappings ("A little bit of Chaos Magick applied to 13th century Runic sigils is perfectly apropos"), and Brosatru Tagalongs ("Look at me, I'm a Viking!"), to say nothing of the

3

Aryan Poster Children ("If your ancestors were not of white/Scandinavian descent, you shouldn't be here. No, I don't just mean in this group; I mean, like, on Earth...at all..."). Pardon me for the over-generalization there, but if you've ever even stuck your toe into an online Heathen group, you likely recognize all of the above. You probably have also had arguments with parties from at least one or more of these over-generalized groups in which they've patently told you "you're doing it wrong". (For the record, the last group on that list—the Aryan Poster Children—are the only ones who are actually "doing it wrong".)

The prospect of publishing this book would not simply mean being politely patted on the head and told "you're doing it wrong"; it was going to raise an outcry of "how dare you call yourself Heathen at all?!" And it would all happen very publicly, and it would be very, very ugly, before all was said and done. No, best to crawl back under the rock 'neath which I've been living for the past twenty-four years, and salvage what little bit of dignity I have left.

So what changed my mind? How did I suddenly become brave enough not only to finish this, but to actually seek to put it out there for others besides my immediate family and friends (who know and love me for what and who I actually *am*) to read?

In truth, I still don't know that I'm brave enough. What I do know is that Ralph Waldo Emerson was right about a lot of things, and one of those things is this:

> *What you are afraid to do is a clear indication of the next thing you need to do.*

This book *needs* to happen. It needs to happen right now, in this particular time and space in history, and it needs to happen by the mind, heart, and hand of a **Norse Witch**.

It *needs* to happen because right now, too many people are too busily trying to define for others one of the most personal matters of all: *faith*. Whether you decide to remain in the company of the Norse Gods and Goddesses, or whether this is simply a pause along your path until such time as you meander away with Others, you need to know that right now, right under everyone's noses, such behaviors as "you're doing it wrong" are *happening* within not only the Heathen community at large, but also in others; in other Reconstructionist paths, and in the world at large. And that needs to *matter*. That needs to matter *deeply*.

It *needs* to happen because an entire symbology and

mythology of an ancient people—the Norse and Germanic peoples —is being bastardized *again* by a racist regime. Note that word: *again.* This is not the first time this has happened to this particular set of myths, Deities, and symbols, and if we do not stand up and take notice and say **no more**, it is destined to repeat itself over and over. And that needs to *matter.* That needs to matter *deeply*, because the next set of symbols, myths, and Deities which are thus stolen and bastardized might be *your own*, even if these are not.

It *needs* to happen because too many people from other Pagan Paths wholeheartedly believe that those who claim a Norse Reconstructionist-derived path *are not witches*, and have no claim to that title, which could not be further from the truth. In fact, were it *not* for the Norse and Germanic peoples, their languages, symbology, mythology, and traditions, the very word *witch* would not mean what it does to us today. The word *witch* actually stems, as many of you might know, from the much older Old English word *wicca*, which many of you reading this likely also associate with the modern Pagan Religion of the same name. Old English is also known as Anglo-Saxon: the language of the Germanic Tribes of what we would today consider mainland Europe; a people who, prior to their subsequent conversion to Christianity, worshipped the same group of Deities as modern Heathens or Norse Traditionalists. So, in fact, the first *wiccans* or *witches* were pagans of the Norse/Germanic variety. And that also needs to *matter.* That needs to matter *deeply.*

Why?

Because when all of those things cease to *matter*, we arrive in a world where *opinion governs reality*, and I refuse to live in that sort of world. Whether a Norse Witch or not, I hope you'll refuse to live in that sort of world, too.

If you are as exhausted as I am with being told "you're doing it wrong", *you belong here*, as much as the Northern Lights (Aurora Borealis) belong in the night sky of the ancient Scandinavian North.

There's something distinctly mysterious about those shimmering colors in the night sky, and that mystery is part of their beauty, just as my mystery is part of my own, and your mystery is part of *your* own. But there's also a science behind that mystery: the Northern Lights (in fact, all auroras) are caused by the collision of particles in Earth's atmosphere. One might say that I am here in the same way: I'm writing this book with this degree of abject honesty because I have endured one too many collisions, so now I burst across your sky in a blaze of my true colors, in the hopes of awakening your own.

I am tired of being told "you're doing it wrong", and I am tired of sitting back and keeping my silence while watching it happen over and over again to other good people. The Gods and Goddesses Call whom They will, and in whatever way They will, and then set those people to doing *what* They will, and no petty human should then get to say to those who have been thus Called "you're doing it wrong".

The big question that brings most people to any religious system—and any discussion of *faith*--in the first place is usually "what's the point in striving so hard in this life when life's so damn short anyway?" It's a question that either drives us to our knees, or that we ask once we're already down there. It is, in fact, the question I found myself asking over and over again when I first embarked upon the journey that led me to become a Norse Witch. What is the answer? **Life is limitless**. Now, by that, I don't mean that there's not a glass ceiling. Face it: we're *all* going to die. What I mean by that is that **death is not the end**. Energy can neither be created nor destroyed, it can only *change shape*, and you, my friend, are energy, and so am I.

In the *Havamal* (literally: "sayings of the High One", from the *Codex Regius*, 13th century), Odin All-Father has this to say in answer to "what's the point?":

> Cattle die, friends die,
> One dies oneself the same,
> But fame never dies,
> For him who gains goodness/righteousness for
>   himself.
>
> Cattle die, friends die,
> One dies oneself the same,
> I know one that never dies:
> Renown of the dead.
> --Havamal 76-77, Translation Mine

It is certain and unchangeable that every human will die. It is what happens *between* your birth in the past and your death in the future that *matters*! In order to gain fame (and, therefore, a noble name), one must *do* good and righteous deeds (gain renown), which requires *active participation*—getting out there and actually *doing* your life. In order to be remembered for one's righteous (or even famous) deeds, those deeds actually require *doing*! Over time (and, I'll confess, in a lot of ways, I am *still* learning this), I have come to finally understand that *death* is *not* when your physical heart stops beating; it's when *you stop doing things* in this world. When you are no longer *actively participating* in life, then you are *truly dead*, whether you're clinically alive or not.

Life is limitless means that you *go at life* understanding that that is the case; you *actively participate* in your own life, as well as in the lives of others. **That is the point!** When we *actively participate* in life, and in the lives of those around us, we *build a legacy*: we gain renown and we give people good things to remember us by so that when we *do* finally pass over, and find ourselves wherever we wind up finding ourselves, those who remain behind *actively participating* have a model from *our* lives that helps *them* continue to do so, and so that *we* don't wind up on the Other Side draped in a shroud of regret over all those things that we never got to do.

Most systems of faith answer this question with what I call a "backwards response": "Live a good life so that when you die, you will be rewarded." Instead of concentrating on providing answers for the *here and now* in which you're actually living, they provide a carrot at the end of a very long stick, which makes the stick hellishly hard to face on a daily basis. Too many modern followers of the Norse Traditions (and especially Heathenry) do the same thing: "Live a good life so that when you die, you can be swept up by Valkyries and dine in Valhalla!" Most outsiders of the Northern Tradition easily come to believe this as the epitome of what those on a Norse Path believe, because all they know of what we *actually* believe is what they've seen in movies and on television. Once upon a time, that was all I knew of the Norse view of the afterlife, too. Then I became a Norse Witch.

Why a **Norse Witch**, rather than Heathen or Northern Traditional Pagan? Because I've slowly (and often painfully) come to realize that I'm *not* either of the latter two designations, but I *am* the former. As I began to ask those *questions of faith* which I had avoided my entire life, I found myself moving in "Heathen circles". I began frequenting Heathen Facebook groups, and getting to know some of the "movers and shakers" in that part of the Pagan world. I tried to learn as much as I could, and share the things I myself was learning. In the process, I began experiencing constant tension, as I was repeatedly told "you're doing it wrong".

And, according to the primary paradigm of what it apparently means to be Heathen or Norse Traditional Pagan, in truth, I *was* doing both of those two things wrong. I have zero desire to resurrect a dead religion, simply for the sake of doing so, while at the same time, I *do* require a fair bit of historical accuracy to support my beliefs and practices. I also have zero problem with uniting what I have learned within the Norse Tradition with what I *know* from both genuine experience and past practice in other systems of faith. In short, I'm *neither* Heathen nor Norse Traditional Pagan: I'm something else entirely. I'm a **Norse Witch**. Maybe you are one, too....

In my own personal practice, I employ my own brand of soft polytheism, which is a sort of "polytheistic monotheism", combined with "light" reconstruction, a heavy Druidic backbeat, and strong shamanic overtones. Most modern Heathens, on the other hand, are hard polytheists: Odin is Odin and *only* Odin, and to discuss cognates, or anything of that nature, is akin to blasphemy. Yet most modern Heathens are also *strict* Historical Reconstructionists. Those two things—hard polytheism and *strict* Reconstructionism—simply do not "gel well" together, as concepts. I have never quite been able to fathom how one allegedly comes at their faith from a supposedly educated anthropological perspective, and yet is still able to maintain a strictly hard polytheistic view of the Gods. Most simply put: to deny, from an anthropological perspective, that a deity has definite cognates *outside* a system of faith (and in some instances, even *inside* a particular system itself) too often denies the *history* of that particular deity (or at least a portion of that history). If someone claims to be a Historical Reconstructionist, while at the same time actively *picking and choosing* in such a manner as this which bits to reconstruct, then precisely *whose* history are they reconstructing, anyway? Still, lots of card-carrying Heathens would likely not only tell me I'm "doing it wrong", but positively *scream* it! In fact, some might even disparage me even claiming the titles "Heathen" or "Norse Traditional Paganism" at all for what I personally practice, even though it definitely shares all of the features of what would make a faith system distinctly Norse (or Norse-driven, Norse-derived, or even Norse-inspired). That being the case, I have slowly begun to realize that I am not exactly Heathen at all, but something distinctly similar and, at the same time, profoundly different: I am a **Norse Witch**. What I practice is a process of bringing a distinctly Norse foundation into contact with a *living* and *thriving* modern world. While drawing from the historical reservoir of the Norse Tradition, I often merge the surviving remnants of that Norse faith with other traditions and practices that are *not* entirely strictly Norse, in an effort to embrace a *living faith* that is Norse-derived.

Which is how I came to first encounter the brief tale of Gullveig, while scrolling through posts in a Facebook group dedicated to Freyja. A major argument had ensued over whether the "burned witch" was actually an aspect of Freyja or not. And that argument, as with most in Heathen circles, got fairly vicious. Nevermind that most scholars actually *agree* that Gullveig *is*, in fact, Freyja. Nevermind that the closing line of *Voluspa 25* pretty much "seals that deal". As is too often the case, a staunch hard polytheistic bent prevented many of the participants in the conversation I was observing from realizing any of those *facts*. So I read the discussion, rolled my eyes, and moved on to more positive environs. I didn't need anyone putting that much negative towards my positive, after all. Who does?

Yet Gullveig remained ever-present, somewhere on the periphery of my mystical mind, and I simply could not shake Her. That She was the *initial cause* of the Vanir-Aesir war, which ended with Njordr, Freyja, and Freyr going to live among the Aesir as hostages (Hoenir and Mimir served as Aesir hostages to the Vanir, in return), positively *escaped me*. Until I started writing this book. Suddenly, Freyja literally whacked me over the head with "*That's ME, you idiot! It is ALL because of ME!*" And it *is ALL because of Her*: this book; my service to the Vanir; my finally taking my place in life as a **Norse Witch**.

> That memory of the first war in the worlds,
> When Gullveig was pierced on all sides and held up
> > by spears
> And burned in the Hall of Har (Odin's Hall):
> Thrice burned thrice born,
> Oft, repeatedly, though She yet lives.
>
> Heidhr they named Her, who came to their house,
> Prophesying witch, Her wand enchanted;
> Everywhere She practiced seidhr for She was versed
> > in magic;
> She practiced seidhr in trances (literally: spirit-
> > play or mediumship);
> She was a delight to sickly married women
> > (suggests mid-wifery).

Then the Gods all went to the judgment-seat.
And around it, the most holy Gods held council:
Whether the Aesir should collectively pay for what
 They had done (to Gullveig),
Or should all the Gods give recompense with
 everything They possessed.

Odin flung (His spear), and into the people it shot:
It was and yet is still the first war in the worlds;
Broken was the wall of Asgard,
And the Vanir could not prophesy a ground on
 which to to stand.

Then the Gods all went to the judgment-seat
And around it, the most holy Gods held council:
(To decide) Who had created this venomous
 atmosphere,
Or (who had) given Od's bride (Freyja) to the
 Tribe of the Jotuns (Devourers).

Thor alone in that place rose up, pressing forward
 angrily;
He seldom sits when hearing such news:
(People) not walking their talk (not keeping their
 oaths);
Words and oaths (broken);
All the mighty pledges between Them (the Aesir
 and the Vanir) were gone.

--*Voluspa 21-26, Translation Mine*

As Norse Witches, we aren't Heathen, we're *Heidhrinn*. Note: those two words are pronounced exactly the same way! That's because they are etymologically identical, stemming from the same Old Norse root: *Heidhr*. From the translation of this portion of the *Voluspa* from the Poetic Edda, we learn that the original *Heidhr* was Gullveig, after her trial at the hands of the Aesir (and specifically Odin Himself). *Heidhr* means "bright" or "clear", and is encountered so often throughout the Eddas and Sagas as the name of various volvas (or seidhrworkers; i.e., Norse Witches), that this suggests it may have become a *title* for such practitioners of Norse magick. Over time, as Christianity came to dominate the spiritual landscape of the Norse lands, the word *Heidhrinn* sprang up to denote those who still followed the Old Ways; the *Pagan Path* of the Norse. Today, that term survives as *Heathen*. Though often mistranslated as meaning "of the heath"--people who lived on the fringes of society in the countryside, and, therefore, clung to the Old Ways--in truth, the very word *Heathen* is actually a combination of the word *Heidhr* and the Old Norse suffix -*inn*, which is used to turn nouns into adjectives. Therefore, to be *Heidhrinn* is to be *like Heidhr*: a *bright, clear*, some might even say *shining* **witch**.

I have had some serious issues, over the years, with claiming that title: the title of **witch**. Part of that has stemmed from those twenty years I spent in the South, where to call oneself *witch* was basically the same thing as shouting to the local rednecks "please, here I am, throw rocks at me". The other part of that has to do with some of the Wiccans I encountered during my earliest explorations of Paganism. There were a lot of "my hat is pointier than your hat" types; in other words, too many people claiming that title from a "holier-than-thou" standpoint. As when I first began down this *Heidhrinn Path* (while mistakenly calling it *Heathen*), there were far too many self-proclaimed witches met in my travels who looked down their noses at me while raucously proclaiming "you're doing it wrong".

Four years ago, I moved North to what some might deign to call "The Land of the Witches": no more than a half hour away from Salem, Massachusetts. Suddenly, I met an entirely new sort of *witch*. I met people who were warm and loving and eager to teach, and who abhorred that "you're doing it wrong because *I say so*" attitude as much as I do. Rather than being an ugly word for ugly people, *witch* became the title held by some of my best friends, my Beloved, and some of the wisest teachers I have ever met. *Witch* was a word for gentle people with good hearts who actually *understand*, and even more importantly, *accept* a "guy like me".

Yet I still did not understand that was what I was: a **Norse Witch**. While I had developed less of a distaste for the title thanks to the wonderful people that I have met since moving here, it was still not a title I associated with what I practice and what I believe. On both sides of the divide—Heathen and Wiccan—it was made clear to me that "Norse Witch" is not a welcome term. On the one hand, local Pagans whom I actually *respected* had, as I said earlier, made it clear that the owners of the local Heathen shop had *no right* to call themselves witches or a coven *because Heathens aren't witches*. On the other side of the equation, in the Heathen groups to which I belonged, those who practiced seidhr and the magickal aspects of the Norse Tradition were told to use the terms vitki, volva, seidhrkona—*anything but the word witch*—again, *because Heathens aren't witches.*

And yet, **we are!** Well, at least, *some of us.* I know, finally, that *I am.*

Which leaves me to ask you: does the expression of your *truest spiritual self* lead you likewise on a path shimmering with the myriad colors of the Northern Lights? Do you feel Called by Freyja, or by Odin, or by any of the other Norse Gods and Goddesses, but have you felt that others who claim that same Call have shunned you or ostracized you because your beliefs and practices are so apparently different from theirs? If this is the colorful yet shadowed path upon which you find your heart treading above your feet, I would be more than happy to have you along on this journey, so long as you come with an open heart and an open mind and can leave your criticisms behind. From this page forward, I will no longer be making excuses or apologies for mixing Norse tradition with valuable resources from other traditions, up to and including Christianity, though I will continue to identify other traditions, when applicable. From this point forward, the road we tread together may be rocky in some places, and overgrown in others, so be mindful as we tread. There may be the occasional sheer cliff-face that requires a certain measure of faith as we skirt it; there may be a few deep streams that we have to fjord together. The only promise that I can make you from this point forward is that my heart and mind are open, and hopefully yours will be as well. We are now leaving the realm of pure Reconstructionist academics behind; this is officially an *adventure!*

This is my official invitation to you: come and walk alongside me, down this many-colored and winding road together, for a mile or two or three. I will not tell you that "you're doing it wrong", if you'll pay me the same courtesy. Nor will I try to tell you that my way is the right way for you, for it may not be. Ultimately, I do not own this road; only the feet that carry the heart that walks it. Some parts of this map may work for you; others may not. They all work for me, of course, but your mileage may vary....

God(s) Enter By A Private Door

If you cannot be a *true individual* in relationship to your Deity/ies, then whatever religion you're practicing isn't a *true* one. What do I mean by that? In the immortal words of Ralph Waldo Emerson:

God enters by a private door into every individual.

Whether you choose to define your personal faith-practice as a *religion*, or whether you prefer the term *spirituality*, at the end of the day, when it is all said and done, your personal faith-practice is precisely that: *personal*. Ultimately, you chose to walk this particular path, out of all the myriad paths available, because of *who you are*, as an *individual*, or because of Who has Called you onto that particular path. So the only "wrong" way to "do it" is if it requires you to act *contrary* to that--contrary to *who you are*, as an *individual*, and/or contrary to Those Who have Called you— or if it requires you to crush the individuality of others. In the end, if you're "not doing *you*", and allowing others to "do *them*" wholeheartedly and completely on the daily, then, yes, you're "doing it wrong".

There are, of course, certain **linchpins** that set what you and I are practicing apart as specifically *Norse*. These are things or themes which *define* what we are doing in our daily practice as something specifically *not* other faiths. In 1981, in the Third Circuit of the U.S. Court of Appeals, three objective guidelines of what actually constitutes a religion were established:

- It must address fundamental and ultimate questions having to do with deep and imponderable matters;
- It is comprehensive in nature, consisting of a belief system as opposed to an isolated teaching;
- It often can be recognized by the presence of certain formal and external signs

Addressing fundamental and ultimate questions includes providing answers to the "**Six Big Questions**" of human existence:

- **Who am I?** (What defines me? Is there anything unique and special about me?)

- **Where do I belong?** (Why do I feel so alone in this world? Where can I find acceptance? How do I form deep and meaningful relationships?)

- **What should I do with my life?** (To what should I devote my life? What is my calling?)

- **How do I make the right choices?** (How do I tell right from wrong? Ethical questions)

- **How can I be happy?** (Is this all there is to life?)

- **What is the point of striving when life is so short?** (What is the point of building something only to have it swallowed up by death?)

Obviously (I hope), different religions answer these **Six Big Questions** in ways specific to that system of faith/spirituality. For example: the Christian answer to **Who am I** could be either "a child of God", or a "brother of Christ", or even "an inheritor of the Kingdom of Heaven". Meanwhile, a Norse Witch's answer to that same question might be "I am a spouse/lover/child of Freyja", or a "brother/sister of Thor", or even "an agent on Earth working to the benefit of the Aesir/Vanir/Rokkr". In other words, how these questions are answered from a Norse Witch's perspective is part of what makes this path specifically Norse.

The second part of those three guidelines, that what you

believe in is "comprehensive in nature, consisting of a belief system as opposed to an isolated teaching", means that your faith-practice includes more than "edicts of behavior" or even *an* "edict of behavior". It should also include a cosmological framework that includes an afterlife, deities, etc. Part of how we arrive at this "comprehensive nature" lies in how we answer questions five and six of the **Six Big Questions**. Again, this will be distinct from religion to religion. For example: Christianity is composed of far more than "an isolated teaching", regardless of how many picket lines you see full of signs emblazoned with quotes from Leviticus. There's more to it, as a faith, than the Ten Commandments, or even the Great Commandment of the New Testament; there is also a distinct cosmology (whether one considers the "spiritual landscape" of Heaven/Earth/Hell, or even the numerous hierarchies of angels), a defined Deity (or, as most Christians would likely not appreciate me pointing out: Deit*ies*, including God The Father, Jesus Christ, and Sophia, aka the Holy Spirit). By the same token, Norse Witchcraft consists of far more than simply the edicts of the Norse Virtues or even the *Havamal* from which they are based. There is, likewise, also a cosmology (the Nine Worlds), and a series of numerous defined deities and "spirits" (such as the Alfar, the Disir, and the Landvaettir).

Finally, a specific religion can be recognized by its own distinct formal and external signs, such as defined places of worship, specific religious texts, and the rituals it enacts. Christianity has the Catholic Mass, its churches (Protestant, Catholic, and Orthodox, all of which generally possess architecture *unique* to their branch of Christianity), The Bible, and the common practices of tithing, praying, and performing acts of charity (when *they* aren't "doing it wrong"!). Meanwhile, Islam has mosques, The Qur'an, and the common practices of praying, fasting, making pilgrimage, and almsgiving (again, when *they* aren't "doing it wrong"!). Likewise, in Northern Witchcraft we have the Ve and the Hof, the Eddas and Sagas, and the common practices of blot, sumbel, sacrifice, and prayer.

You may or may not be doing your Norse Faith the same way as the other Historical Reconstructionists, Norse Pagans, Runic Ceremonial Magickians, or even the Brosatru, but if you are answering the **Six Big Questions** with distinctly "Norse-motivated" answers; if you believe in the Nine Worlds, and in the Aesir, Vanir, Rokkr, Alfar, Disir, and Landvaettir; if you worship at a Ve, a Horgr, or a Hof via blot, sumbel, sacrifice, and prayer and use the Eddas and Sagas as your sacred texts, then your faith *is* distinctly Norse. It just happens to also be distinctly *your own interpretation* of the Norse Tradition. If it is effectively answering those **Six Big Questions**, while in the process making your life and the lives of others *better*, then you're definitely *not* "doing it wrong"! Instead of "doing it wrong", you're more than likely a **Norse Witch**, like me.

To paraphrase a very wise man whom I recently heard speak at the Temple of Witchcraft in Salem, NH (for the record, the man in question was Druid Kristoffer Hughes), what sets magickal people apart from academics is that we don't just *read*, we *do*. Certainly, the archaeological record and "dusty old tomes" such as the Eddas and the Sagas have their *place* in Norse Witchcraft, and we'll be exploring that place frequently throughout the course of this book. But *living* in that place—treating those artifacts and books as though they are holy relics—does not *do anything*. Living with that focus does *nothing* to mold, shape, or otherwise influence our breathing, thriving world. Treating the Gods and Goddesses as though they are the same today as they were a couple thousand years ago *lessens* Them; it *limits* Them. Why would anyone deign to treat a Deity in such fashion, and then claim such acts as a form of *veneration*? Hopefully we don't treat other mortal beings in such a manner! When we confer such behavior onto other mortal beings, we consider it unfair, unjust, and possibly even immoral. Yet it's somehow *okay* to do it to the Gods? That's preposterous! Yet, it is exactly how many people address the Norse Tradition. As Norse Witches, we say **no more; not us**.

We no longer live in a harsh world of fishing villages, as subsistence farmers and hunter/gatherers, as did our Ancestors, nor do we largely view "go forth and conquer" as a valid way of living one's life (except under certain very controlled and confined circumstances). In short, we cannot *live* as our Ancestors did, nor should we *want* to. Their own "go forth and conquer" worldview educates us that they actively *wanted better* for us, so should we not be striving for that *better*? We cannot *live* as they did, nor would they even *want* us to, but we *can* and *should* learn from them, and then take those lessons forward into our modern world, and that, my friends, is the *soul* of what it means to be a **Norse Witch**: learn from the Norse Traditions of the past, take what works for you, make it uniquely your own; discard what does not. Celebrate the Spirit of the Norse, rather than treating History as the Letter of the Law.

Know Yourself To Know Them

To truly know the Gods and belong to Them, you first must know yourself. This is true in relationship to anyone else—lovers, friends, even family members—why should it not also be true in our relationships with the Gods? Too often, our feelings of "not belonging" don't actually come from *outside*, but actually come from *inside* of us, motivated by constant and pervasive **self-doubt**. You really *can* be your own worst enemy! Meanwhile, we remain trapped in this cycle of "not belonging", because we refuse to see its true source, instead constantly and consistently blaming forces outside of ourselves: "the Christians made me feel this way"; "the Heathens made me feel this way"; "my parents/friends/loved ones made me feel this way". It has taken me two decades to realize this, because I was so busy blaming *outside* forces for the power that was actually being held by my own *inside* force: *self-doubt*. To throw out another cliched statement: Knowing really *is* half the battle! Until you can shut your *self* up, no amount of shutting off those outside forces is going to get you where you need to be. If you cannot *belong* with *your Self*, then how in the heck can you ever arrive at *belonging* anywhere or *to* anyone else?

This applies as much to forming lasting relationships with other humans, whether that means friendships or something deeper, such as a marriage partnership, as it does to forming relationships with the Gods. If *you* don't love you, nobody else is going to love you, either, whether that means romantic love or platonic love. The way we show respect to others is directly proportional to the amount of respect we show *ourselves*. If you cannot occasionally put yourself *first*, no one else is ever going to put you first, either. I've watched too many people go through cycles of abuse in relationships—in marriages as well as in friendships/partnerships—wherein they wonder *why* everybody is "treating them like crap." Granted, sometimes it really *is* a matter of "wrong person, wrong time"--someone with a perfectly healthy self-esteem got involved with someone completely *unhealthy* (someone angry, abusive; sociopathic). But more times than I can count, I have seen these unhealthy relationships develop out of a situation wherein one of the two parties involved was coming from a place of constantly and consistently treating *themselves* like crap, and then wondering *why* other people felt like they had been given *permission* to treat them the same way. *Self-ownership— belonging* to your Self—is crucial to maintaining healthy relationships, and this is particularly true when beginning to attempt to form relationships with the Gods.

What does *Self-ownership* mean? It begins with *self respect*. In Heidhrinnry, we live our lives by the **Nine Norse Virtues**. Sourced largely from the *Havamal*, these virtues are essentially the *"rules"* of **Norse Witchcraft**. Generally, most of us don't really have a hard time applying these things when dealing with *other* people, *outside* of ourselves, but how often do you apply things such as integrity, loyalty, hospitality, wisdom, self-knowledge, trust, humility, courage, and justice when dealing with your *Self*? (We will go into further detail about the **Nine Norse Virtues** later in this book, in the chapter on **Good Versus Evil**.) How often are you truly honest with *You*? How often do you keep promises to your *Self*? How often do you allow yourself to be the "last one on the list"; how often do you leave what *you* want/need behind in favor of the needs of others? (I'm not saying you shouldn't be *selfless* in some situations, nor am I encouraging you to be totally *self-absorbed* here; what I *am* saying is that if everyone else's needs are coming before yours *all* of the time, you should probably take a deeper look at that situation.) Go through that entire list applying it to your *Self*. If you come up lacking, then it's very likely that you have a *self-respect problem*! If you cannot apply everything on that list to your *Self* first, then you have no right attempting to apply it to *other* people, nor expecting them to behave in kind towards you. Getting your *self-respect* issues sorted is the first step towards *Self-ownership*.

I've never been placed in a position where I needed to lie to *myself* about who I am, but too often over the past two decades, I have repeatedly been placed in situations where it has actually been *imperative* that I lie to the rest of the world about that. Living in the South often makes such guile positively *necessary* for one's own personal *safety*. Over time, even as I trusted people enough to form real friendships in which I revealed my *true* identity, I was hurt so many times by so many people that forming lasting relationships became something which I no longer sought out. Fox Mulder's mantra of "Trust No One" became mine as well. Eventually, that came to include even the Gods. I reached a point where I no longer wished to offer hospitality to other people because I had simply been hurt too many times. Eventually, that came to include even me, my *Self*. I learned so many hard lessons emotionally that seeking further knowledge of anything became a case of "what I don't know probably can't hurt me". The "best of my abilities" seemed to be good enough for far too few people, so eventually, that came to include me, my *Self*, as well. I reached a point where I was angry *all the time*, yet forced to *keep silent* about that anger. Sure, on the surface, I went through the motions of being a practicing "Sunday Druid", but underneath that veneer, all of those things were simmering; eating away at my spirit like a corrosive acid. I was a miserable sonofabitch. There was very little about *my Self* that I could find worthy of *respect*.

In 2012, I met the woman who would change my life. Meeting her created in me a deep desire to "get my shit together" and take *Self-ownership*. I knew I could not be what she *deserved*, if I couldn't first get a handle on my own issues of *self-respect*. I had to have that to be worthy of her. At face value, this may seem like I am putting *way* too much power in the hands of another person, but in truth, it wasn't about her having *power over me*, it was about meeting someone who was a complete *wake-up call* to *my own lack of power over myself*. She was a *signpost*. How do we know when something or someone is a *signpost*? In my experience, it's a combination of repetition (as in, whatever it is will continually "pop up" in your path, such as when we see a certain animal or symbol repeatedly, or encounter a key phrase in every song we hear and every book we read) and that "hair standing up on the back of your neck" feeling we get when we have been touched by Something or Someone *bigger* than ourselves. From the first moment of our meeting, I knew the Gods had a hand in our paths crossing, and as much as I mistrusted Them at that time, I thank Them daily that just that once, I actually *listened*. For the first time in a *very* long time, I found myself being completely honest about who and *what* I am. I fully embraced *all* of that, and found that I not only wanted to start *learning* things again, but that I have a *lot* to offer the world as a *teacher*. I had a lot to offer *her* as a teacher. And I gave in to *trusting*, and in the process, I stopped being a miserable bastard, as I arrived at the most *elemental understanding* of who I *truly* am. Turns out, that guy's not so bad.

The second step of *Self-ownership* is figuring out *who you truly are*, and then coming to actually *own* that person, and *like* that person. In today's modern society, we too often answer the question "*who are you?*" with things like job titles, or even with identifiers such as "mother", "father", "wife", or "husband". All of those things *are* important, but they are not the true definition of *who you are*. Chances are great that before you became whatever your job title is, or came to identify as "mother", "father", "wife", or "husband", you were still You, *independent* of all of those other identifiers. To truly figure out *who you are*, you need to return to square one—to get back to what is simple and elemental about *you*. When asked "who gets the highest rank in Heaven" in the Christian Bible, Jesus answers:

> *"I'm telling you, once and for all, that unless you return to square one and start over like children, you're not even going to get a look at the kingdom, let alone get in. Whoever becomes simple and elemental again, like a child, will rank high in God's kingdom."*

--Matthew 18:3-5, The Message.

I can hear the grumbling from here! "But wait, we're witches: why do we care what it says in the Christian Bible? Why *should* we care?" The Bible is a *book*, just like the likely plethora of books sitting over there, across the room from you on your bookshelf. To discount it as a valid source of *wisdom*, based on experiences you may have had with others who have summarily beaten you over the head with it, is as arbitrary—and discriminatory—as dismissing the Qur'an purely because you have some sort of personal issue with Muslims. The book *itself* hasn't done anything to you: it *can't*; it's an *inanimate object. It's just a book!* It's also a magnificent work of literature, so if you're down with quoting Byron, Eliot, Poe, or Tolkien—all of whom were *Christians*—taking issue with the Bible is hypocritical, at best. Having said all of that, let me see if I can make this passage a bit more palatable:

*I'm telling you, once and for all, that unless you go back to square one and take a look at the world through the eyes of a child, you're never going to meet the Gods, much less get to **know** Them. Whoever becomes simple and elemental again, like a child, will learn The Truth.*

That return to square one may require taking a mental trip back in time to the earliest point you can remember: maybe at that point you were ten or twelve; maybe at that point you were five or two. The actual timeframe/age doesn't matter; what matters is that you can take yourself back to a time when you were simply *you*, without all of those identifiers we tend to tag onto ourselves as we are forced to "grow up" and define ourselves to the world at large. This isn't *about* defining yourself to the world at large; this is about defining yourself to *you*! What is the earliest thing you can remember *deeply wanting*? I don't mean things like toys or food or other mundane things; I mean *causes or emotions*, like world peace, or happiness, or love. What is the earliest thing you can recall actually *enjoying*? This might be something mundane—like swinging on a swingset or fishing or dancing or drawing or painting—but if you really pick it apart, you will find that it leads to something *deeper*. For example, if you enjoyed swinging on a swingset more than anything else as a small child, this hints to an enjoyment of *physical freedom*. If you enjoyed fishing, then you probably enjoyed *being one with nature*. If you enjoyed dancing or drawing or painting, then you were comfortable embracing your inner *artist*. How did you understand your *place in the world*, when you were a child? How did you *understand God(s)*?

The earliest thing I can remember *deeply wanting* is *knowledge*. To say that I was an inquisitive child is to put it extremely mildly! I asked questions about *everything*, and when I got answers to those questions, it only bred more. I drove my poor parents nuts. I was also a definite exercise in patience for any teacher, sifu, priest, nun, or other adult who crossed my path. The earliest thing that I can recall actually *enjoying* is playing with paper toys with my father: the idea that a folded-up piece of cardboard with the picture of a car printed on it could actually *become* a tiny car that you "drove" down a tiny paper road absolutely enchanted me when I was two. Even as I got older, the things that could be created in the marriage of *imagination and ingenuity* never ceased to amaze me. They *still* do! My earliest recollection of how I understood my *place in the world* was as the "person who asks the questions". I was told from infancy that I was a "hero"; as such, I imagined myself from a very early age as a person on a quest. What was the end goal of that quest? To *learn stuff!* *Knowledge* was my holy grail, pretty much from infancy onward. How did I *understand God(s)* as a child? Being raised primarily Buddhist/Taoist with a soft Christian backbeat, my earliest understanding of God(s) was *yes*: never "either/or", just *yes*. Are there many Gods? Yes. Is there one God? Yes. Period. It was never "all or nothing", it was always "all is All". Now, what does all of this tell me about *who I am*? I am a *student of life* who will stop at nothing in the pursuit of *knowledge,* and who believes that all people everywhere should have the right to that same pursuit; I am an *artist* who understands that the marriage of *imagination and ingenuity* is what makes the world work; I am, at my very core, a *polytheistic monotheist*, and there is little that anyone else can say or do to change that perspective. At my most *elemental*, I am a *Seeker*, a *Maker*, and a *Believer*.

Who are you, then, at your most *elemental*? What three archetypes from the following table best describe your *truest self*? Do you *like* that person? Are you pleased to take *ownership* of that person? How might you best express *your truest self* as a Norse Witch?

Elemental Self Archetypes

Archetype	Deeply Wants	Enjoys	Place In The World	God(s)?
Seeker	Knowledge	Learning; Asking questions	On a quest	Seeks knowledge about and/or requires proof of
Maker	To Create and/or Invent	Making things; crafting; art; handiwork	Creator; Designer; Artist	Prime mover(s)/ Prime Creator(s)
Believer	Hope; Faith	Acts of devotion, charity; improving the lives of others	Teacher, Helper, Do-er, Light-Bringer; Justice-Bringer	All is All; believes with conviction
Dreamer	Happiness	Personal freedom; promoting the freedom of others; physical activities (swinging, sports, dancing, playing, etc.)	Sacred Clown; service to others; "daredevil"; adventurer	God has a sense of humor; even god(s) is/are not infallible; flawed does not equal bad or negative

Archetype	Deeply Wants	Enjoys	Place In The World	God(s)?
Lover	Love	Cuddling, hugging, showing general affection, cooking, nurturing	Nurturer, Caregiver, Parent, Lover and/or Beloved	Deity is Parent and/or Family Member, Lover and /or Beloved
Peacemaker	Peace	Solving arguments, finding answers, showing compassion and/or resolving conflict, building infra-structure	Teacher, Problem-Solver, Engineer, resolver of conflicts, Justice-Bringer, Do-er, Helper	Deity as Prime Mover(s) and/or Prime Creator(s) and/or Peace Bringer(s)
Mystic	To Play	Spending time in nature, such as fishing, spending time at the beach, etc.	Understand Self as part of a greater intercon-nected "whole" that includes the rocks, trees, and Earth. The compas-sionate "Eco-Warrior".	Deeply animistic view of God(s)

The Calling

A *calling* is a "strong urge toward a particular way of life or career; a vocation". A *vocation* may be understood as "a function or station of life to which one is called by a Higher Power". "*What is my calling?*" is encapsulated within one of the **Six Big Questions** we discussed in the second chapter of this book: ***What should I do with my life?*** Phrased in such a manner, it may sound a lot like this one of the **Six Big Questions** is inviting you to the priesthood, and perhaps, in your own personal case, it is, but in reality, you can be completely devoted to your faith, and to the Gods, without serving in the official capacity of priest or priestess. If you've come this far along the path, and you're still wandering alongside me, clearly you have a strong urge toward a Norse-derived path which is different from the others: the Path of the Norse Witch. That is the function or station of life to which the Gods are calling you: to be a faithful practitioner of a Path that is both distinctly *Norse* and distinctly *magickal*.

Another way of asking this question is "to what should I *devote* my life?" There are many layers to that word, *devote*:

> **devote:** 1) to commit by a solemn act;
>
> 2) to give over or direct to a cause, enterprise, or activity;
>
> 3) to set apart for a special purpose;

4) to give up to entirely or in part;

5) to set apart for a special and often higher end

Devoting your life to something means giving yourself over to it almost completely (in some cases, maybe even completely). That requires spending the most expensive commodity we have as human beings: *time*. There is a very popular anonymous quote which reads:

> "If it is important to you, you will find the time. If not, you will find an excuse."

We *devote* ourselves to what is *most important* to us. The things of primary importance in our lives are set apart from everything else: whether that applies to your job, your family, or even a hobby, such as playing video games or papercrafting. Through small and sometimes solemn acts, we commit ourselves to those things, whether we realize it or not. Those small acts of *devotion* may not be something ritualized or even concrete; they may be as simple as *making time*. Whatever that "most important thing" might be, we give ourselves over to it completely while we're doing it, or while we're involved with whoever or whatever it is. It becomes our *special* thing, and we treasure it. But how often is that *special* thing—that *most important* thing—our relationship with the Gods?

What is my calling? To what should I devote my life? Attempting to answer those questions with "devotion to God(s)" can honestly be one of the most frightening prospects a person can face. Face it: we've all had bad experiences with *people*; where is the guarantee that the Gods won't be the same situation, only on a much larger scale? We've all suffered perceived *injustices* in our lives; aren't the Gods the ones to blame? For most people, relationships end because someone finally figured out the essence of *who they think* you *really are*, and find something about your nature distasteful. The Gods are in a position to not just base that opinion on what They *think*: They will *know* who you *really are*. What if They find something about you distasteful? What then? "Break-ups" suck, whether we're talking about a friendship, a marriage, or even a relationship that is on the level of family. How would one endure a "break-up" on such a cosmic scale?

In the Norse Tradition, our Gods are a bit more "anthropomorphized" than in other religions, so these become very real things to believe, and even perhaps fear. Anthropomorphized means that They have exceptionally *human* character traits, appearances, and personalities. They aren't just "vague entities up there in the sky somewhere": They have *emotions* of Their own, *preferences* of Their own, *identities* of Their own, and, perhaps most frightening of all, *judgments* of Their own. We can only come to stop *fearing* these things when we have taken full *Self-ownership*, in much the same way that we come to stop *fearing* these things in mundane human relationships once we have done that. The next steps are to *get to know Them*, and then to *trust*: perhaps the most frightening thing we humans could ever be asked to do!

Before I came to this Norse Path, and before I began the practice of a Friday blot to Freyja every week, I was a "church on Sunday" type of Pagan: as a Druid, I participated in ritual on every High Day, to the best of my ability, but daily devotion wasn't something I had *time* for. Or, at least, it wasn't something I *made time* for. Once I began pouring blot every Friday to Freyja, however, daily devotions to other Gods quickly followed suit. Most people know that the English names of the days of the week (with the exception of Saturday) correspond to specific Norse deities:

Sunday: Sunna

Monday: Mani (Moon Day)

Tuesday: Tyr

Wednesday: Odin

Thursday: Thor

Friday: Frigga or Freyja

When I first began doing daily devotionals, I tried to adhere to that schedule. I quickly discovered which Gods had an affinity for me, and vice versa. Sunna, for example, was very hard for me to get close to. Mani, to a large degree, likewise. Tyr, on the other hand (no pun intended), felt a natural fit. Wednesdays with the Allfather have been an interesting sort of slavedriver/slave relationship (with me being the slave in question), to the degree that at least once He cheered me on by shooting a three foot flame

up from a devotional candle which I had burning on my bookcase!
I attempted to make friends with Thor on Thursdays, but with the
exception of times of great need (like the one week when someone
had challenged my honor/integrity on Facebook), our relationship
was much like my previous attempts at forming one with Sunna:
Thor was hard for me to get close to, unless I actually *needed* him
for something important. Obviously, Fridays were Freyja's, and
she was soon joined by Her brother, Freyr, and Her father, Njordr.
Since Saturday was "bath day" (literally: *Laugardagar*) in ancient
Norse culture, I decided that made it a perfect day to focus on
spiritual cleansing, and, therefore, compassion, so I gave
Saturdays to Sigyn. She's been there for me every Saturday since.
So what do I do now on those other days which belong to a certain
God or Goddess with whom I haven't been able to build a
relationship? Sundays have been given to Skadi, second wife of
Njordr. Monday is officially Njordr's Day for me. Tuesday still
belongs to Tyr, and Wednesday to Odin. On Thursdays, I often
spend time with Thrudh or Sif, as the ladies in Thor's life seem to
like being in *my* life, too.

As you can hopefully see from my example, *daily devotionals*
are an excellent way of introducing yourself to and *"getting to
know"* the Gods. But what makes an act *devotional*?

> **Devotional:** an act of prayer or private worship; from
> *devotion*: the act of dedicating something to a cause,
> enterprise, or activity; the fact or state of being ardently
> dedicated and loyal.

A *devotional* act doesn't have to be time-consuming. It
doesn't require pomp and circumstance. A full-on Hammer Rite is
not required every time you step up to your *stalli* (indoor altar),
horgr (grove), or *ve* (an outdoor shrine or altar). All that is
required is that you approach the Gods with dedication and
loyalty, and offer a simple prayer of welcome and gratitude. They
are *not* genies, nor are they Santa Claus. Every time you approach
them, it should not be because you *want* or *need* something
specific. I mean, if a mundane, Earth-bound friend of *yours*
always came to *you* with "I want" and "I need" and nothing else,
you likely wouldn't be friends for very long, now, would you? So
why would that be different when approaching the Gods?

Keeping your *devotionals* simple helps to prevent them from
becoming *habits* which you *perform by rote*. Most people view

habits as something which can be either good or bad: you may have a "good habit" of brushing your teeth every night before bed, for example, or you may have a "bad habit" of eating a snack right before bed. In truth, in my experience, anything that becomes *habit* rather than a *mindful activity* is always a *negative* in our lives. It's not exactly a state secret that when I want to figure something out, I often turn to the writings of Bruce Lee. Master Lee spent most of the later years of his life writing about how to **break free of the "*classical mess*"**, as he called it. Granted, at first blush, he was talking about martial arts forms when he coined that term—*classical mess*—but the truth is: **any complexity which *enslaves* us is *classical mess***. That includes *habits*. **Habits are *classical mess***, and the sooner we extract that from our lives, the happier and more *genuine* we will be. When something becomes *classical mess*—like habits, remember—we are no longer *mindful* while we are performing that action. In other words, we are no longer *completely in that moment*, and the action itself no longer **sparks joy**. It becomes something we do completely by *rote*; a *mindless* activity, rather than a *mindful* one. ***Mindless devotion*** to anything or anyone is always a dangerous thing, without exception. Therefore, it is incredibly important that our *daily devotionals* never become denigrated to the status of *habits*!

In the first draft of this book, at this point, I went on in lengthy detail about the *daily devotionals* which I was at that time practicing: namely, a daily rune pull, a prayer to the Green Wights, and nightly prayers of gratitude at the close of day, right before I went to bed. However, one morning as I was saying my prayer to the Green Wights, something dawned on me that was very important: those actions had become nothing more than *habits*. Over the course of a few weeks prior, I had become starkly aware that my nightly prayers of thanks were a litany of the *same things* every night. Obviously, the morning prayer to the Green Wights was a piece which I had composed and then memorized, but that wasn't what made it a *habit*: what made it a habit was the fact that I had reached a point where it no longer brought me *joy* to say those words. They were no longer something I wholeheartedly meant each day; they were merely a *thing I did*, like going to the bathroom or brushing my teeth. Those activities no longer **sparked joy**.

But what does it mean to have something **spark joy**? Let's start with a textbook definition of **sparking joy**, and work our way up and out from there:

sparking joy: setting off feelings of well-being, success, good fortune, happiness and bliss with sudden force; igniting a state of happiness or bliss; setting off a burst of active happiness, well-being, success, good fortune, or bliss; stirring one to *actively be* well, successful, fortunate, happy, or blissful.

So, **sparking joy is first and foremost *active***. It's not so much a simple matter of "well this makes me happy" or "this is pleasing" as it is a sensation of not only *being* happy, but actually wanting to *do something with* that happiness; that joy. **The marrow of what we really want out of life is that feeling of sparking joy**. We *crave* joy. When we can't find it inside ourselves anymore, we look *outside* and when we start looking outside, we amass mountains of things which provide a *momentary happiness*, and we clutter our lives with *inessential activities*—habits--that once gave us that *momentary happiness*, but no longer do. When approaching the Gods with your *daily devotionals*, you should do so with **actual joy**. The moment the joy leaves the action, you are entering the realm of ***mindless devotion***. Trust me: you don't want to go there!

The best way to begin a ***daily devotional practice*** is to use the days of the week and their corresponding deities, as I have them listed above. This will also give you a starting point for **Godfinding**, which we will talk more about in the next chapter. You may need to do some minor research on the deities in question, if you are not yet fully familiar with the Norse Pantheon. Most importantly, begin the day with something that **sparks joy** for you. Suggested activities might include:

SUNDAY:

Sunna: greet the sun (either go outside or to a window and enjoy the warmth of the sun on your face); light a candle with your morning tea or coffee, and imagine the sun's warmth infusing the candle-flame; drink something warm and imagine the sun's warmth infusing your beverage; wear orange, yellow, or gold.

Skadi or Ullr: spend time with a beloved pet; watch the birds or other morning animals, such as squirrels and rabbits; take a walk in nature; if you have a fireplace, start a fire in it, and curl up in front of it with your morning tea or coffee; splurge and make yourself a hearty breakfast of bacon and eggs and bask in the yummy smells; wear blue, black, or white.

MONDAY:

Mani: Find the moon in the morning sky (if you can), and smile at it; make yourself cocoa with marshmallows for breakfast, instead of coffee or tea; eat a cookie; spend time with your children or with someone else's children; watch children's programming that you still enjoy as an adult; wear blue, purple, or white.

Njordr: Listen to ocean sounds while you drink your morning coffee or tea; if you are lucky enough to live by the seaside, take a morning walk along the beach; go outside and let the wind kiss your face; start your day with a brisk bath or shower (sea salt scrubs are entirely optional, but definitely add a kick!); watch a program on seafaring, the ocean, or travel in general; check or balance your budget and/or your business; go window-shopping or actual shopping online or in "real life"; take a drive or go sailing; wear blue, green, or gold.

TUESDAY:

Tyr: Paint your nails or give yourself a manicure to show gratitude to your hands; dedicate time to a cause you believe in; spend time with your dog or with someone else's dog; enjoy Irish coffee; imbibe or enjoy warmly-scented aromatics, such as cinnamon; light a candle for Justice for those in need of it; wear red or orange.

WEDNESDAY:

Odin: Treat yourself to a morning read; read a passage in the *Havamal*; write in your personal journal; enjoy a bit of artist journaling or other papercraft to document something important in your life; compose a bit of poetry; spend time with a favorite tree; take a walk and be mindful of the world around you; spend time with a beloved pet and focus on your spiritual connection to that animal (one way to do this is to time your breath with its breath); if you maintain a blog, post in it; spend time on social media sharing actual wisdom and inspiring and uplifting other people; do yoga; go horseback riding; do a morning rune-pull; consult Tarot or other oracle cards; meditate; wear black, blue, purple, grey, or white.

THURSDAY:

Thor: Take a shower, but pretend it is rain; drink strong coffee; eat a hearty breakfast, complete with sausage and bacon; if there is weather, enjoy the puddles instead of cursing them; watch the movement of the clouds as you drink your coffee or tea; participate in an exercise regimen; lift weights; treat yourself to a video game; go fishing; plan a trip to a petting zoo and enjoy the company of goats; if you're bearded, treat yourself to a full "beard spa" in the morning; wear red or orange.

Sif: Treat yourself to a full "hair treatment" (shampoo, conditioner, full brushing, the works); enjoy some time with your spouse; enjoy some warm toast or other decadent grain product, such as oatmeal or granola; spend some time in a garden or gardening; talk to your houseplants; make corn dollies or braids; spend time lovingly brushing a partner, child, or pet's hair; bake bread or cupcakes or cookies; wear pink or gold.

Thrudh: Participate in an exercise regimen; lift weights; go for a walk and collect rocks; take a drive or a walk through the mountains; do something that improves your life and makes you stronger as a person, or do likewise for someone in need; spend time with someone who makes you feel stronger as a person; wear red or brown.

FRIDAY:

Frigga: Make breakfast for your family; spend time with your children or with someone else's children; spend time with your spouse; knit, crochet, sew, or do embroidery; tidy your hearth (an actual one, if you have a fireplace, or if you don't, your kitchen); plan your (or your family's) meals for the week; curl up with a warm blanket and bask in the workmanship of it (and its coziness); practice hygge in your home; spend time with a lit candle and a warm cup of coffee or tea; celebrate being a parent, if you are one (this includes children of the furred variety); call your best friend for a chat; call your mother or a sister and enjoy time with them; wear red, white, or pink.

Freyja: Spend time with your cat or someone else's; wear your favorite piece of jewelry; treat yourself to something sweet to eat or drink; enjoy a bit of juice; be sensual (whether this means a decadent bath or something a bit...well, *more*...is entirely up to your discretion); enjoy your favorite incense; wear your favorite clothing, jewelry, shoes, and other accessories; treat yourself to a massage; treat yourself to a facial; enjoy putting on your make-up for a change; wear perfume; listen to your favorite music (maybe even dance!); if you live by the ocean, take a walk on the beach; treat yourself to a video game; practice Tai Chi or another form of martial arts kata; do yoga; choose to sleep in; cuddle someone you love; spend time with someone you love; make love; have a bit of piggy for breakfast (sausage or bacon or both is up to you!); do a morning rune-pull; consult Tarot or oracle cards; meditate;

enjoy something yummy and flavored with lavender; wear red, copper, amber, or pink.

Freyr: Enjoy some toast or other yummy grain product, such as oatmeal or granola; put extra sugar in your coffee or tea; treat yourself to something seasoned with rosemary for breakfast; drink some juice; treat yourself to something sweet to eat or drink; be sensual; take a walk; spend time in a garden or gardening; watch the birds, squirrels, and other morning animals; make love; have a bit of piggy for breakfast (sausage or bacon or both is up to you!); handle your budget or your business or both; go shopping or window-shopping; play the lottery; wear green, brown, or gold.

SATURDAY:

Sigyn: Take a long, cleansing bath; clean your house; celebrate the victory of having made it through another week in a way that fills you with joy; treat yourself to a nip of absinthe; eat licorice with your breakfast; add a spot of fennel to your morning tea; spice up your morning eggs with a bit of tabasco, sriracha, or other hot sauce; choose to sleep in; spend time with someone you love; spend time with your spouse; treasure your children; wear green or white.

Once you have enjoyed your **joy-sparking activity** for the day, go to your sacred space (if you already maintain an altar or *stalli*, all the better), light a bit of incense or a candle, or both, which you feel would likewise **spark joy** in the God or Goddess whom you are honoring on that particular day, take a moment to calm your mind, and send out a "hail and welcome, thank you for being with me and guiding me through this day" to the Deity in question. Now that you have *invited* Them into your day, *let* Them *infuse* it. Actively *listen* for Them, throughout the course of your day. Their guidance may actually come to you in divine words, or it may more often come in little signs and portents specific to that Deity, such as encounters with ravens for Odin, for example, or the scent of roses and amber for Freyja. The most important thing is to *not ignore Them*, once you have invited Them to join you on your journey through the day. If you *let* Them be with you, trust me: They *will* be.

Remember earlier in this chapter when I said one of the most precious gifts you can give to anyone is *time*? Devotional acts need not be limited to the activities of prayer and ritual. The ultimate keynote to devotion is *intent*: whatever you do with *intent*, as an act of worship or veneration for your Gods is an act of devotion. This can include giving to charities, doing public service; even things you do in day-to-day life, such as washing dishes, cleaning house, or your job. At risk of offending the sensibilities of a lot of people, I would like to introduce you to a verse from the Christian Bible which, unfortunately, too few Christians are even aware exist:

> *"Here's what I want you to do: take your ordinary, everyday life—your sleeping, eating, going-to-work, and walking-around life—and place it before God as an offering."* --Romans 12:1, The Message

In other words: *live your life with devotional intent*. You don't have to be a gothi or gydja (priest or priestess), vitki or volva (sorceror, seeress, or shaman) to live your life that way. Too often I have encountered people new to Pagan pathways who ask the troubling question: *"But where do I find the time?"* Whether that means finding the time to learn all that they feel they still need to learn, or whether that means finding the time for acts of devotion, this seems to be the number one hurdle for almost every would-be witch. The trick is not "finding the time", the trick is *making* the time. By that, I do not mean clear your schedule, because for many of us, such an attitude would be not only impossible, but in fact unthinkable. What I mean is to *make time count*: everything that you do in life can be done as an act of devotion, if done with the proper *intent*. Live your life intentionally and mindfully, and you will no longer find yourself struggling with that age old question of "where do I find the time". There is time enough already; one simply has to *realize* it.

Hour to hour,
Day to day,
Week to week:
We ponder the order of time.
The more we ponder,
The more of it slips away.
Week to week,
Day to day,
Hour to hour.

Godfinding

Godfinding is perhaps the most important aspect of any system of beliefs that would choose to call itself a religion, and yet it is a topic I have found far too-seldom covered within the Heathen community. What do I mean by that word: *godfinding*?

> **Godfinding:** to come upon (often accidentally, but also through study, research, effort, or experimentation), meet with, or obtain an understanding of God/Gods/Goddesses; to notice the presence of God/Gods/Goddesses and then to deem God/Gods/Goddesses worthy of consideration and respect.

The word "find" is etymologically sourced to Old English *findan*, which in turn sources to Old Norse *finna*: to find, to *notice*, to *deem* (regard in a particular manner; specifically: respect) and *consider*. To actually *find* God/Gods/Goddesses, therefore, we are *forced* to go beyond simply *reading* about them in books, or even recognizing the apparent previous *finding* of Them by our Ancestors in the archaeological and anthropological record. No, to truly *find* God/Gods/Goddesses, we must necessarily *experience Them*, which involves perhaps the most frightening thing of all: *trust*. *Experiencing* the Gods means we must necessarily be open to UPG (Unconfirmed Personal Gnosis), which in turn means we must be open to the concept of *faith*. **A religion without faith is nothing more than yet another**

political body of semi-like-minded people.

Which begs the question: why is it that in other religions a personal experience of God is pretty much the *entire point* of being religious in the first place, yet in Heathenry, such personal experiences are generally chalked up to UPG and then shown varying degrees of derision? On some levels, this would be slightly more understandable if demographics showed that most Heathens were also previously Catholic, but numerous censuses have shown that most of those in our community who were previously Christian were raised Protestant. Why do I say this? Because in Catholicism there is an actual *council* known as The Congregation for the Causes of the Saints whose job it is to *scientifically verify* that miracles have occurred. In other words, it's their job to *scientifically verify* UPG, so clearly such behavior is "approved" in Catholicism. Yet most "Heathen converts" come out of the Protestant faiths: faiths that were indeed *founded* out of an abject *disapproval* of such "behavior"! If, in their previous "Protestant lives", people would have looked on the existence of such a council with deep suspicion (if not outright hatred), why perpetrate such behavior within their "Heathen lives"? It makes *zero* sense.

I'll gladly grant that UPG is a *slippery slope*: I may see Njordr, for example, as dark-haired and clean-shaven, while you may see Him as grey-haired and grey-bearded. I may regard Freyja, from my experiences of Her, as a goddess of healing, as well as magick, victory, and sensuality/fertility, whereas you may regard Her as a goddess of physical beauty, or of self-esteem, or of whatever. I have even encountered at least one person who experienced Her as a goddess of home and hearth, much more akin to traditional views of Frigga. But that is where **godfinding** becomes useful.

One of the ways which we may *accidentally* encounter Deity is if *They* come to *us*, instead of the other way around. The Lady (Freyja) came to me that first time as Valfreyja–Her warrior aspect; She who chooses Her half of the slain–but it took me a *year* to figure that out! In my case, *accident* led to *intent*. I woke up the next morning *driven* to recreate what I had seen in my dream as art: UPG led to *votive action*.

People sometimes ask me where I get the inspiration for my art, especially for my votive art images, which often depict the Norse Gods and Goddesses as I see them. Many of these same people belong to a faith-system (Heathenry) that strangely looks upon actual *mystical experience* with deep suspicion. It also tends to be a belief system that holds firmly to the stance that "we do not bow to our Gods; our Gods do not ask us to bow to them". UPG may not be looked upon too fondly by the staunch Reconstructionists within the Heathen community, but it is the very *life-blood* of the artist, and of the Norse Witch! Insofar as the "to bow or not to bow, that is the question?" debate: many of our historical resources (which are supposed to be the foundation of a Reconstructionist-derived faith) strongly suggest otherwise. When I create a piece of art based upon a vision of a God/dess that I have been given, I do so with great humility, and I offer a gift for the gift which I have been given, whether that be a prayer of gratitude, or a burnt offering of incense, or the actual pouring of a blot. In other words, *contact* with the Gods leads to *votive action*.

Let's pause for a moment to talk about that term: *votive action*. In its most simplified sense, *votive action* breaks down to a *devotional act* (as well as *acts of intent*, both of which we discussed in the last chapter, but let's take this a few steps further). It is, at its most basic core, a form of *prayer through action*. More than simply spoken words, it is a thing that you are *doing*, for one of three purposes:

- As *fulfillment of a vow;*

- As an act of *gratitude;*

- As an act of *worship.*

The **fulfillment of vows** (oath-taking and oath-keeping) forms one of the cornerstones of Norse Witchcraft (we'll discuss this in greater detail in the chapter on **Good Versus Evil**). Another such cornerstone is the concept of **gratitude** ("a gift for a gift"). However, when dealing with other people following a modern Norse-derived Tradition, things tend to get a little bit "sticky" when one starts using the word **worship**:

> **Worship:** the feeling or expression of reverence, adoration, and love for a deity.

Worship requires *humility*; it asks for bended knees, and many Heathens, as I've already said, have a *huge* issue when being asked to *bow down* to anything or anybody, regardless of the fact that our historical record shows that our Ancestors definitely did so. In 98 AD, Tacitus wrote in the *Germania* of the Suebi (a Germanic tribe):

"There is nothing especially noteworthy about these states individually, but they are distinguished by a common *worship* of Nerthus, that is, Mother Earth, and believe that she *intervenes in human affairs* and *rides among* their people. There is a sacred grove on an island in the Ocean, and in that grove there is a *consecrated cart*, draped with cloth, *which only the priests may touch*. The priest *perceives the presence* of the goddess within this innermost shrine, and *with great reverence* escorts her in her cart, which is pulled by cows. There are then days of rejoicing and merry-making in every place which she deigns to *visit* and *accept hospitality*. No one goes to war; no one takes up arms; all objects of iron are locked away. Peace reigns wherever she goes, until the goddess has had her fill of *human interaction*, and then the priest returns her, in her cart, to the temple in the grove on the island in the Ocean. After that, the cart, the cloth, and if you *choose to believe it*, the goddess herself are washed in a clean, secluded lake. This service is performed by slaves who are immediately afterwards drowned in the lake. From this arises the *dread of the mysterious*, and the *pious reluctance* to see what only those who are to be put to death are allowed to see." (J. B. Rives Translation; emphases mine.)

For those who would here raise the "a history not written by its own people isn't a true history" argument, I would also supply this (my own translation) from the third chapter of the *Kjalnesinga Saga*:

Thorgrim, the High Priest, took special note of the men who would not *bow* before the Gods in the temple. His son, Thorstein, also held a high reputation as one who would call *men who did not bow* before the Gods out as *less worthy than dogs* publicly. Bui, who was a great hero, was only twelve years old, six years younger than Thorstein, who was then eighteen, when Thorstein witnessed Bui *not bowing to the Gods* at the temple, and made it public to all who gathered for the local Thing, decrying Bui as an *outlaw*. (Emphases also mine.)

Clearly, historically-speaking, our Ancestors *worshiped* their Gods, and part of *worshiping* is "bending the knee", as a show of reverence as well as affection. Most of us can pretty easily understand the word affection, but let's pause for a second and actually *define* the word *reverence*:

> **reverence:** to have or show *deep respect* of, for, or to someone or something.

If we *love* and *deeply respect* the Gods, why are we reluctant to *express* or *show Them* that? And if you don't *love* and *deeply respect* the Gods, why are you calling yourself a Heathen or, in our case, a Norse Witch or Heidhrinn, in the first place, instead of simply becoming an agnostic, or even an atheist?

Votive action is the point at which *accident* meets *intent* in **godfinding**. Your *devotional act* may be something as simple as saying aloud "Hey, I know you're there", or it may involve hours of research and study, or it may be as formal as an actual blot; it may even actually involve *bowing down before the Gods*. Your *accidental* "first brush" with Deity may not be something so earth-shattering as an actual dream-vision of a God, as mine was; it may be something as seemingly mundane as repeatedly encountering the same Deity over and over again in your research or study of the extant lore. Study and research might then also become an act of *intent*–a *votive action* in and of itself–as you begin to focus on learning more and more about that specific God/dess. As you then begin to *obtain a deeper understanding* of Them, research itself becomes, in essence, an act of "bending the knee".

The other side of *intent* in **godfinding** happens when we *actively seek* Them, instead of *waiting* for Them to *come to us*. How does one *actively seek* God/dess? How does one *actively seek* anybody else, on a mundane level? Breaking down human/Deity interaction to the terms of human/human interaction may at first blush seem to be grossly oversimplifying things, but we are, after all, talking about a faith system wherein the God/desses Themselves are incredibly and distinctly *human* in the way that They interact with each other, as well as with us. How, then, do you *actively seek* another person–another living, breathing human being—who maybe you've only heard about in books or on TV, or from the word of mouth of other people? Or maybe you've passed them on the street or at some function? How would you actively find out more about them, so that you might know better how to approach them the next time you meet, and possibly build a relationship from there? In today's modern age, most of us would answer with two words: **Google search**. You would look them up, right? See what other details you could find on social media or elsewhere that tell you more of their character and interests. We can do the same thing with Deity! Find Them in the Eddas and the Sagas; find other people's UPG of Them on social media and elsewhere online. Learn what They like and do not like; learn what pleases Them; learn what attracts Them. And then *use those things you learn to build a relationship* with Them!

How do you use what you've learned about Them to build a relationship with Them? How would you use that sort of information when attempting to build a relationship with a living-breathing human? You might start by finding out their *contact information*: some way to call them up on the telephone, or speak with them via social media, or even write them an email or a letter. You do the same thing with Deity: what's Their *contact information*? Obviously, our God/desses don't have phone numbers, email addresses, or social media accounts (apart from ones that other humans have set up in reverence to Them), but They *do* have a sort of physical address: your own personal altar/shrine, whether that be a ve, a stalli, a grove, or even your own miniature version of a hof. We also have what could be equated with phone numbers and email addresses, courtesy of the Eddas and Sagas: many of our God/desses have *halls* which they call home, whether that be Sessrumnir (Freyja), Valhalla (Odin), or even Helheim (Hela). So, once we have someone's *contact information*, what do we do with it? We use it to *make contact*, right? Like I said, we call them on the phone, or we contact them on social media, or we email them, or we write them a letter. *Do the same thing with Deity!* How? I mean, that's one helluva long distance phone call, right? Through *prayer*. *Prayer* does not need to be conflated, or composed of poetic phrasing; on the contrary, I have found in my own personal experience that my most profound experiences with prayer consisted of conversations very much like those one might have when initially making contact with another living-breathing human:

"Hi, Freyja? Yeah, this is Connla. Are you hearing me okay? I just wanted to call you up and tell you how much I appreciate having you in my life...."

Or:

"Hello, Hela? This is Connla. I've noticed you being around in my life a lot lately, and I just thought I'd let you know that *I* know that you're there...."

Usually the next step following *first contact* is to organize a "date", whether the living-breathing human that we're talking about is an actual romantic prospect, or just a possible friend. We arrange a *meeting* with them of some sort, usually doing something that we know from our previous research that they will enjoy. Maybe we plan to go to a theater and see a movie that we can talk about afterwards, or maybe we plan a shopping adventure, if we know that they enjoy shopping. Whether our inclinations are romantic or purely platonic, this first *meeting* is a *date*. So how in the heck do you *date Deity*? You use the same sort of information—what do They like; what do They enjoy—and you commit time and effort to bringing those things either to a physical location (your home altar, whatever form it might take) or to a *votive action*, such as cooking Them a meal, or listening to specific music that They might find appealing, or even, yes, watching a movie that They might enjoy. You *make yourself present to Them*, via something that is *appealing* to Them, and then *recognize Their presence with you*.

So what follows a "first date", whether romantic or platonic? Hopefully a *second* date, right? Hopefully that first *meeting* leads to future meetings that are maybe a little less formal, and more on the level of "*hanging out*". That's when most of us know that we're actually involved in a *relationship* with someone: we can just "*hang out*" with them. Time spent doing the most mundane of things—such as cooking a meal or vegging on the couch watching television—becomes equally valuable to (if not more valuable than) meetings that are formally arranged. Of course, that *second date* and subsequent *hanging out* only happens if the *first date* was successful: if you mutually decided that your personalities fit together, and you actually *enjoyed each other's company*. After a *first date* with a Deity, you will definitely *know* if you *enjoyed each other's company*, or not. Just like with another human, if you come away from that *first date* "feeling *wrong* somehow", chances are that you are not meant to work with that particular Deity, for whatever reason. But if that *first date* was, indeed, successful, then how do you *hang out* with God/dess? The same way that you do with another person: notice Their presence, even when you are doing the most mundane of things, and *let Them know you notice*. With another human, you might do that by engaging them in conversation or simply smiling over at them, right? Do the same thing with Deity!

Eventually, over time, as the relationship with another person deepens, you might come to call that person your friend, your beloved, or even your spouse. When we do this, we are, in effect, *dedicating ourselves* to that other person. After a period of time *hanging out* with a particular Deity, you may find that you wish to *dedicate yourself* to Them in the same manner. We'll talk more about that later in our journey. In order to develop a relationship that is that deep, however, you have to *find Them* first, which means that you have to be open to *experiencing Them*. We don't build relationship with physical humans simply by reading about them, or by secondhand accounts of other people's experiences of them; we should not expect to be able to build relationship with Deity in those ways, either!

Much of my art is based on the experiences I have had while **godfinding**. Sometimes, as with my first image of Freyja, it is because They have come to me; other times, as with the art I have done of Njordr (and my subsequent devotion to Him), it is because I have actively sought a relationship with Them, via prayer first, and then a "first date", sometimes followed by "just hanging out" (as has been the case for me with Freyja, Njordr, and Freyr), and sometimes not (as has consistently been the case for me with Thor). Sometimes I find Them; sometimes, They find me. What is important, however, is that *finding*, and being open to the *experience* that follows after.

Finding Odin

You may or may not be completely familiar with the *Havamal* as yet, but one of the quickest ways to **godfind** Odin All-Father is to come to know it. The *Loddfáfnismál* (stanzas 111-137) is particularly valuable, as these stanzas provide excellent advice for daily life and maintaining The Nine Norse Virtues. This portion of the *Havamal* includes lessons from Odin to a young Skald (Norse bard) named Loddfafnir, which literally translates to "Clown Dragon" or "Dragon Clown". Given my own past history with both Dragon as an archetype, and the archetype of the Sacred Clown (Trickster; Heyokah in the Lakota Tradition of the North American Native Peoples), reading these stanzas makes me feel as if Odin is speaking to me, personally. I would recommend taking each stanza in turn (my own translation may be found within this chapter), and using each as a daily meditation, applying the same **situation** and **guidance** method as you would with a daily rune pull (which is also an excellent method of growing closer in relationship with Odin).

If you choose to pursue a daily rune pull in addition to meditations on the *Loddfáfnismál,* what "style" of runes—clay, gemstone, wood, etc.--you choose is, of course, up to your personal preference. It is always best to choose a set to which you are deeply drawn, and which feel like an "extension" of your *true self.* Holding your rune bag in your hand, shake it, while chanting the prayer below (or compose one of your own, or seek out something similar), and then pull one rune. This rune is your **intention** for the day: it is more than divinatory (fortune-telling); it is a set of directions for how to face your day, and how to behave over the course of the day for the best possible outcome and to most effectively shape your *Wyrd* in a positive manner.

> Turn and turn,
> What shall you return?
> Turn and turn,
> What shall you return?
> Speak through these as the wind through trees!
> Shining Gods,
> I pray you,
> Speak to me,
> And reveal to me Your intentions for my day.

> ~Taliesin Emrys of Cerddorion Nyfed, with
> additions by Connla Freyjason

In addition to the book which may have come packaged with your set of runes, there are numerous other books on runes available on the open market. I *do not* recommend Ralph Blum or much of the work of Edred Thorrson (aka Stephen Flowers). Blum includes a blank rune in his interpretation of the runes which is not only historically inaccurate, but also completely *unnecessary*. It is, in fact, *impossible* for there to be a "blank rune": if the stone is blank, it is *runeless*! A blank rune is basically the same thing as a blank page in a book. I don't recommend the work of Edred Thorsson, even though much of his work *is* historically sound. His involvement with Stephen McNallen and the KKK makes his work highly suspect. I *do* recommend the works of Diana Paxson, Freya Aswynn, and anything which might be available now or in future by John Hyatt. There are also the traditional rune poems, which are easily found online, as well as the detailed exploration of the runes later in this book in the chapter on **Runelore**. As you work with the runes daily in this fashion, hopefully you will build your own personal vocabulary for what each rune means. Much of this vocabulary will be learned via *experience*: as you pull a rune, and find its meaning to be made *true* by what you experience on a given day, you will begin to better understand the ebb and flow of each rune, and each rune's myriad nuances of meaning. I would suggest keeping a record of this in a datebook or planner, as I find this a much easier and more "shorthand" way of doing things, rather than maintaining any sort of "runic grimoire". (Over time, certainly, you may decide to create one of those as well.) If you maintain a datebook or planner anyway, you are much more likely to keep up with your morning rune pulls if you do those in the same book, rather than trying to start a new volume, such as a grimoire/book of shadows.

Remember: the purpose of this rune pull is not purely divinatory, in the fortune-telling sense of that word. It is more a way of seeking *hidden knowledge*: the Gods know what's in store for you today, and also how that affects your *Wyrd*. Paul Bauschatz explains *Wyrd* in *The Well and The Tree: World and Time in Early Germanic Culture:*

> "[**Wyrd**] *governs the working out of the past into the present (or, more accurately, the working* **in** *of the present* **into** *the past)."*

In other words, the past doesn't just influence the present, as we understand things within our modern concept of linear time; the present can also influence the past. The pre-Christian Norse understanding of past, present, and future was not fixed in a linear conception of time like ours. Instead, they held a cyclical view of time that included things that had already happened (and, therefore, could not be *changed*), things that *are* happening (which *can change* "on the fly", as it were), and things that *needed to happen* (which *might change* or not, depending on a combination of past, present, and what we moderns might call "fate".) In the mindset of the pre-Christian Norsemen, the past, present, and future were *ruled over* by the Norns: Urdr ("What Once Was"), Verdhandi ("What Is Coming Into Being"), and Skuld ("What Shall Be"). Urdr ("What Once Was") served to *define* who our Ancestors were in the present moment, and nothing and no one could *change* that definition, which is based on past actions, past occurrences, past battles, both won and lost (on the battlefield as well as in general life). But our Ancestors understood wholeheartedly that the past *could not be changed*, so why focus on continually looking *backwards* and fondly *wishing* for a change that could never come? Urdr was (and still is) *Orlog*, the layers of that which *has become*, and those layers are *set in stone*. *Orlog* cannot be changed anymore than the modern laws of physics. Skuld ("What Shall Be") and Verdhandi ("What Is Coming Into Being") rule over *Wyrd*. *Wyrd can change*, depending upon how your present works *into* your past. Since the very definition of insanity is to do the same thing over and over again, while expecting a different result, it therefore makes zero sense to constantly focus on the things that *cannot change (Orlog)* by looking *backwards*, into the past—but much more sense to focus on what *can change* by looking at *now* and looking *forwards*, into the future.

Your daily rune pull not only provides a "hidden glimpse" of what might be in store for you on a given day (**situation**), but also provides valuable *guidance* on how best to *experience* whatever that might be, in a way that will positively affect your *Wyrd*. For example, let's say you've pulled *Eihwaz,* one of the keynotes of which is to "protect oneself and one's rights". This provides you with a "hidden glimpse" of what could be in store for you today: someone may decide to challenge your rights as an individual. Further insight into the meaning of the rune tells us that it also pertains to increasing and exercising one's power, as well as the removal of obstacles. It cautions, however, that to end negative situations and/or solve problems we must make sure that *we* are being completely honest with ourselves and with the situation. These further insights provide the *instruction of experience*: when faced with someone challenging your rights as an individual, you need to first take a step back and make sure that *you* are behaving in an upright manner; before calling anyone onto the proverbial carpet for having impinged *your* rights, you need to make damn sure you're not impinging on the rights of anyone else, and take measures to put right any areas of your life in which you might be.

Another example: one Tuesday, I pulled Gebo. The **situation** revealed by Gebo is that "a curse will be lifted; gifts are in store". Further insight reveals **guidance** for how best to *experience* that situation: remember the Heathen and Norse Traditional maxim of "a gift for a gift", and be sure to make the appropriate sacrifices and offer proper gratitude for what has been received. On that particular Tuesday, my Beloved was going in for surgery on her right hand, to correct carpal tunnel syndrome. The surgery was a success—a "curse" was lifted. When we came home, I offered a burnt offering of His favorite incense to Tyr (the One-handed) as a "gift for a gift", in gratitude.

You may wish to record your daily rune pulls in the following format, so that you can better keep track of them and learn from them:

Rune (Written name of the rune; possibly a drawing of the rune)

Situation (What is the "hidden glimpse" of what might be in store for you today?)

Guidance (How might you best *experience* the *situation*, and affect your Wyrd in the most positive way?)

The most important thing about the daily rune draw, beyond actually committing to *doing* it, is committing to *listen* to it. Follow its guidance, and see how your own Wyrd begins to "unfold" for the better.

As I said in the opening paragraph of this chapter, you may also apply this **situation** and **guidance** method to a daily meditation on the *Loddfáfnismál*. What follows is my own translation.

Loddfafnismal

Translations from the Havamal
by Connla Freyjason

Loddfafnismal 1 (Havamal 111)
I sing from the High Seat:
I sat beside the Well of Wyrd
And was silent;
And I saw and I thought,
And I listened to the speech of men;
I heard and learned the runes,
And there was silence no more,
In my own Hall, in Odin's Hall,
Thus was the speech I heard:

Loddfafnismal 2 (Havamal 112)
I advise you, Dragon-Clown,
To take my advice:
It will benefit you if you can fully understand it;
Good will come to you if you can fully catch its
  meaning.
Do not rise during the night
Unless the news is urgent,
Or you need to use the restroom.

Loddfafnismal 3 (Havamal 113)
I advise you, Dragon-Clown,
To take my advice:
It will benefit you if you can fully understand it;
Good will come to you if you can fully catch its
  meaning.
Never give your heart over to someone
Who seeks to overpower you,
Nor sleep in their embrace
So that they might hold you down--

Loddfafnismal 4 (Havamal 114)
By thus enfolding you in their arms,
Such a person changes you
So that you no longer care about anyone else,
Nor will you listen to the advice of the wise.
Their power over you will steal your appetite,
And your pleasure of living,
Leaving you only with the sadness of sleep.

Loddfafnismal 5 (Havamal 115)
I advise you, Dragon-Clown,
To take my advice:
It will benefit you if you can fully understand it;
Good will come to you if you can fully catch its
    meaning.
Never entrust your secrets
To someone else's spouse.

Loddfafnismal 6 (Havamal 116)
I advise you, Dragon-Clown,
To take my advice:
It will benefit you if you can fully understand it;
Good will come to you if you can fully catch its
    meaning.
If over mountains or across fjords you would go,
Look not only to keep yourself fed,
But also to the things you value most.

Loddfafnismal 7 (Havamal 117)
I advise you, Dragon-Clown,
To take my advice:
It will benefit you if you can fully understand it;
Good will come to you if you can fully catch its
    meaning.
Never let a wicked person
Know of your misfortune,
For a wicked person
Will never repay your confession with compassion.

Loddfafnismal 8 (Havamal 118)
I saw a man who told a wicked woman,
And he was deeply wounded
By her deceitful tongue:
Her accusations were the death of his honor,
Even though there was no truth in her words.

Loddfafnismal 9 (Havamal 119)
I advise you, Dragon-Clown,
To take my advice:
It will benefit you if you can fully understand it;
Good will come to you if you can fully catch its
   meaning.
Know this:
If you have a friend in whom you trust,
Go visit that friend often,
Otherwise they may become hard to find,
As brambles and waving grass overgrow
The road too rarely traveled.

Loddfafnismal 10 (Havamal 120)
I advise you, Dragon-Clown,
To take my advice:
It will benefit you if you can fully understand it;
Good will come to you if you can fully catch its
   meaning.
Draw good companions to you
Through pleasant conversations and benevolence,
And bestow healing charms upon both yourselves,
As long as you both shall live.

Loddfafnismal 11 (Havamal 121)
I advise you, Dragon-Clown,
To take my advice:
It will benefit you if you can fully understand it;
Good will come to you if you can fully catch its
   meaning.
Never neglect your true friends:
Sadness eats the heart
When you do not hear each other's words
With your whole soul.

Loddfafnismal 12 (Havamal 122)
I advise you, Dragon-Clown,
To take my advice:
It will benefit you if you can fully understand it;
Good will come to you if you can fully catch its
  meaning.
Never share your deepest words
With a person who is the equivalent
Of a witless ape;

Loddfafnismal 13 (Havamal 123)
Such people will not give you their attention,
Nor will they do anything good for you;
There is no reward in talking to such people.
But a good person will care what you have to say,
And will repay your benevolence in equal measure.

Loddfafnismal 14 (Havamal 124)
True friendship can only happen
When you can share your whole mind with the
other person.
Anything is better than to be faithless or fickle;
If you cannot share hard truths as well as fair,
You are not truly friends.

Loddfafnismal 15 (Havamal 125)
I advise you, Dragon-Clown,
To take my advice:
It will benefit you if you can fully understand it;
Good will come to you if you can fully catch its
  meaning.
Do not waste even three words
On a person who has proven less worthy than you;
The better man is too often defeated
By the unworthy man who resorts to weapons,
instead of words.

Loddfafnismal 16 (Havamal 126)
I advise you, Dragon-Clown,
To take my advice:
It will benefit you if you can fully understand it;
Good will come to you if you can fully catch its
 meaning.
Make neither shoes nor arrows for other people,
But only for yourself:
If the shoe is poorly made,
Or the arrow twisted,
Then people will think ill of you, not only your
 craftsmanship.

Loddfafnismal 17 (Havamal 127)
I advise you, Dragon-Clown,
To take my advice:
It will benefit you if you can fully understand it;
Good will come to you if you can fully catch its
 meaning.
When you see evil being done,
Call it out as evil,
And show the evil-doer no peace.

Loddfafnismal 18 (Havamal 128)
I advise you, Dragon-Clown,
To take my advice:
It will benefit you if you can fully understand it;
Good will come to you if you can fully catch its
 meaning.
Never rejoice in evil;
Take great pleasure in doing good.

Loddfafnismal 19 (Havamal 129)
I advise you, Dragon-Clown,
To take my advice:
It will benefit you if you can fully understand it;
Good will come to you if you can fully catch its
    meaning.
Do not look up while in the heat of battle--
People are too easily driven mad--
Unless it is to raise the spirits of the men around
    you.

Loddfafnismal 20 (Havamal 130)
I advise you, Dragon-Clown,
To take my advice:
It will benefit you if you can fully understand it;
Good will come to you if you can fully catch its
    meaning.
If you would try to win a lover
By pleasant words or even spellwork,
Then you must make fair promises
And keep to your word--
No one ever minds getting good things by giving
    good things!

Loddfafnismal 21 (Havamal 131)
I advise you, Dragon-Clown,
To take my advice:
It will benefit you if you can fully understand it;
Good will come to you if you can fully catch its
    meaning.
Be wary, but do not give into fear, with these three
    things:
Be wariest with getting over-drunk,
Be wariest also when cheating on a life-partner,
And of a third thing be wary, yet not paranoid:
Of thieves or people who are out to trick you.

Loddfafnismal 22 (Havamal 132)
I advise you, Dragon-Clown,
To take my advice:
It will benefit you if you can fully understand it;
Good will come to you if you can fully catch its
  meaning.
Never laugh at or mock a guest
Or a stranger walking past.

Loddfafnismal 23 (Havamal 133)
Often you may not fully know
The newcomer to your home,
Nor even the person who is actually your kinsman:
No person is so good that they are completely
  without flaw;
No person is so evil that they are completely
  useless.

Loddfafnismal 24 (Havaml 134)
I advise you, Dragon-Clown,
To take my advice:
It will benefit you if you can fully understand it;
Good will come to you if you can fully catch its
  meaning.
Never laugh at the white hair of a teacher:
Often what an old person says is good;
The clearest words often come
Out of the age-shriveled face
Of one who has hung their personality
On time spent with books,
And has wrapped themselves with the wisdom
Of the less fortunate.

Loddfafnismal 25 (Havamal 135)
I advise you, Dragon-Clown,
To take my advice:
It will benefit you if you can fully understand it;
Good will come to you if you can fully catch its
 meaning.
Do not curse a guest,
Nor shoo him from your gates;
Welcome the wretched ones.

Loddfafnismal 26 (Havamal 136)
Mighty must be the beam of your doorway,
If you are going to open it to everyone.
Gifts must be given to all whom you welcome,
Or it will call down misfortune upon you.

Loddfafnismal 27 (Havamal 137)
I advise you, Dragon-Clown,
To take my advice:
It will benefit you if you can fully understand it;
Good will come to you if you can fully catch its
 meaning.
When you drink beer,
Make sure you are on firm ground,
So that you do not fall down.
A warm fire drives out sickness;
Take white oak for diarrhea;
Use wheat to ward against sorcery,
And an open hall to guard against household strife.
In deadly fights, call upon the Moon and the
 Celestial Powers.
Apply grass to bug-bites,
And answer curses with runes:
The field absorbs the flood.

I often refer to Odin as "The Boss". Trust me: once you've worked with Him even a little bit, you'll completely understand why. In my personal experience, most of the Aesir Gods are varying degrees of demanding: They are the ultimate *innangard* deities, and They *know* it, and They behave accordingly. Odin is the All-Father, after all. According to both the Prose Edda and the Poetic Edda, He is one of the first five Gods to come out of Ginnungagap (the other four being His grandfather, Burri, His father, Borr, and His brothers, Villi/Hoenir and Ve), and, as such, He can be regarded as "The Father of the Gods", as well as us, as human beings (since He helped to create the first two humans, Ask and Embla). This puts Him on equal mythical footing with Yahweh/Jehovah of Judeo-Christianity and with Brahman in Hinduism. Depending on your previous experiences with Christianity, you may or may not find this comforting. For me, personally, it was a bit of a no-brainer: I've been working for Him for twenty-four years in one guise or another, so I see no reason for me to stop *now*. Apparently, neither does He!

One of the most unique things about Odin—and there are a *lot* of unique things about Odin—is that He is not only Aesir, but simultaneously Vanir and Jotun/Rokkr. As I've already stated, He was one of the first five Gods to come out of Ginnungagap—all of whom were regarded as Aesir. He is also Vanir, as He is likely Odr, the husband/consort of Freyja who was described as "wandering away", which led Her to cry tears into the ocean which turned to amber as She mourned His loss. Finally, He is Jotun/Rokkr because His mother, Bestla, was one of the first Frost-Etins (Frost "Giants"). Even if you wind up finding yourself feeling more heavily drawn to and more often associated with the Vanir or the Rokkr, chances are great that Odin will "show up" at some point, and have *something* in mind for you to do. I suggest you listen and then *do*!

Odin's Old Norse name is comprised of two parts: *Odr* ("ecstasy, fury, inspiration") and the suffix *-inn*, which, when added to the end of another word like this, means basically "master of" or "a perfect example of". Therefore, His name literally translates to "a perfect example of ecstasy, fury, and inspiration" or "Master of ecstasy, fury, and inspiration". This should buy you a big clue that the Wisdom and Knowledge He can potentially impart to you are of the *overwhelming* variety. While the phrase "a gift for a gift" certainly holds true in all of our dealings with both other humans and the Gods, when working with Odin, the concept of sacrifice as repayment for what you've been given often reaches entirely new heights. Keep in mind, this is a God who sacrificed Himself *three times* to gain all of the Wisdom and Knowledge currently in His possession: once, by hanging Himself on Yggdrasil for nine days and nine nights after having stabbed Himself with His own spear (to receive the Knowledge of the runes); a second time by giving up one of His eyes to Mimir so that He might drink from the Well of Urd and gain all of the Wisdom of the Universe; finally, the third time, He sacrificed His "masculine honor" to learn Seidhr from Freyja Herself. **Be warned**: Odin will expect no less from you. He may not actually ask you to gouge out one of your own eyes, mind you, but He definitely doesn't suffer whiners or shirkers of their duty, and if He gifts you with something, it is better to make appropriate shows of gratitude immediately, or He'll *find* a way for you to show your gratitude, and you may not *like* His ideas of how to do that.

As a writer, artist, and the CEO of Iaconagraphy, I have worked with Odin quite a bit, especially on "Wisdom Wednesdays" (my blog day). Often, that "working with" is in an almost "slave-driver" capacity: He *does* tend to "crack the whip" a bit, especially when it comes to writing and imparting knowledge and wisdom to others. He has His own candle in my sacred space, and His own special incense that I burn for His pleasure. I make offerings to Him every Wednesday, and generally dedicate that day to His service. As I said, the Aesir, in my experience, can often be demanding Gods, but like all of our Gods and Goddesses, none of them are purely one-sided, and that also goes for Odin. There have been many times when Odin has been very much the "father figure" for me that I needed; times when it seemed like the whole world was bearing down on me and I needed a strong shoulder to lean on. Odin understands depression on a level that we humans cannot fully even conceptualize. Whatever you are going through, chances are He has been through that and worse: between the sacrifices He has made, and the death of His son, Baldur, He understands the deepest of losses. During those times when things are at their darkest for me, I often pray this prayer, which I refer to as my "Norse Serenity Prayer" (you'll likely recognize the reference). I hope it will serve you as well as it has served me.

Norse Serenity Prayer

Odin,
All-Father,
Friend of Wealth,
Journey Empowerer,
Teach us Grace
In our weariness,
Victory,
When we believe ourselves defeated,
And the Wisdom to know the difference.

Worlds Within Worlds

Let's imagine for a moment that you have a truly sucktastic life. You may not need to imagine it. If that is the case, I am truly sorry, but stick with me; it gets better. Imagine that you do not have a happy home life. Your relationships are all sub-par. You have a terrible occupational situation, and most of the mundane day-to-day things that make up a person's life are exactly that: mundane, boring, perhaps even alarmingly upsetting. You look around at your life and find nothing to *hope for*; nothing to *believe in*. If this is *all* there is to life, then you've probably already arrived at the first question—*what's the point*—more than once, right? And if the answer to that question is **life is limitless**, that probably *isn't* quite the answer you wanted!

Now, let's take that paradigm of the sucktastic life, and place it against a cosmology where there are more worlds than the one in which you're presently surviving. I'm not just talking about the landscape of an afterlife here—as I said previously, ours isn't a "backwards answer", like those given by the Judeo-Christians and others—I am talking about *worlds within worlds*, of which our own mundane existence is merely *one of many*. What if *people* aren't the only "people"? What if there are other *places* where there are other "*people*" who don't suck?

Norse cosmology gives us **Nine Worlds** to believe in, all of which are situated "around" the World Tree, **Yggdrasil.** *Note:* Various scholars and mystics have attempted to formulate a "map" of the Nine Worlds, based either on snippets of lore from the

Eddas and Sagas, or from UPG and/or experiential knowledge, or a combination of both. The bottom line is, it's fairly impossible to draw a map of worlds which are basically places on top of places-- i.e., interdimensional. Therefore, I have instead listed them, and some of the important landmarks *within* them, in relation to each other as I have personally *experienced* them—or not—myself. The following list is a combination of Reconstructionist theory, based on the Eddas and Sagas; confirmed UPG, and my own personal *experiential knowledge*. This is only an *introduction*. For a more detailed exploration, please see the **Faring-Forth** chapter, later in this book.

> **Asgard:** Located "above" or "at the top of" Yggdrasil, this is the home of the Aesir Gods. Like the Judeo-Christian, Confucian, Buddhist, Hindu, and Islamic Heaven, it is believed to "reside" in the "sky" (which, incidentally, is why Heaven is called Heaven—it's from Old Norse *himmin*, meaning "sky"). It is connected to Midgard (the earthly realm of the *astral plane*—more on that in a minute) by the rainbow bridge, Bifrost (which you've probably heard about either in comics, films, or when mourning a beloved pet). Myself and others that I know on the Other Side have come to lovingly refer to this world or "plane" as *"Central"*, in the same sense as "Grand Central Station", not in the sense of being centrally located. It's sort of the "other hub of existence", apart from Yggdrasil itself. *Hint:* Think of the World Tree as the "crossroads", that leads to all of these other places, then think of Asgard as the "Capital City".

> **Valhalla:** Even non-Heathens know about Valhalla, courtesy of comics, movies, and TV. "The Hall of The Fallen", this is Odin's Hall, where those chosen by Odin and the Valkyries as worthy of being celebrated as a hero for the rest of eternity are taken. At face value, this definitely *sounds* like "Viking Heaven", until one realizes that time in Valhalla doesn't just consist of drinking with Odin for all eternity and

telling tales. According to mythology, it also includes nightly battles where everyone kills each other, and wakes up every morning to do it all over again. My *experienced truth* of Valhalla bears similar connotations, but with slightly less of the "barroom brawl" motif imparted by Good Ole Snorri and others. Those who are actually chosen for the halls of Valhalla effectively become the "military of the Gods" in the afterlife. That may or may not be something to which you would want to aspire. Such an occupation is not "all fun and games", and is, in fact, quite dangerous. I mean, where do the dead go to die? Think about that.

Alfheim: "The Homeland of the Elves"; we are told in the Lore that Freyr, a Vanir God, is Lord of Alfheim. Also called *Ljosalfheim*, "Home of the Light-Elves". We are told in the *Prose Edda* that the elves who live there are luminous and "more beautiful than the sun". Virtually every religion in the world has its *angels*—the Ljosalfar (Light-Elves) are ours. Yes, I said *angels*. Yes, that's exactly what I *meant* to say. (Keep walking with me, please.) Myself and others that I know on the Other Side have come to lovingly refer to the heart of this area as "*The Barracks*", as it can occasionally take on an almost militaristic character. In my experience, it borders "*Central*". "*The Barracks*" are not the only area of Alfheim, however: the outer fringes are more like what one would expect of an esteemed house of learning, such as Harvard or Oxford. It is, as one might expect, a "bright and shining place", populated by Teachers and Guardians.

Vanaheim: "Home of the Vanir"; described in *Lokasenna* as being located to the west of Asgard. This is the original home of the Vanir Gods (Njordr, Freyja, Freyr, Nerthus), the most prominent of which we are told in the Eddas and Sagas were removed as hostages to reside in Asgard, following the Aesir-Van War. Not much is told to us in the

Lore concerning what Vanaheim might actually be *like*, either, but we can make certain broad assumptions about it, based on the character of the Gods who hail from there: it is pastoral, with an emphasis on farmlands and vineyards, and we know that at least part of it borders on and/or contains an ocean, because of Njordr's hall, Noatan, and because we are told that Aegir's Hall lies beneath the waves of the ocean on the border of Vanaheim. We also know that Freyja's Field, *Folkvangr*, and Hall, *Sessrumnir*, lie in Vanaheim. In my own personal experience, this world or plane lies a bit "closer" to mundane existence than either Asgard or Alfheim, it's "eastern" border lying directly against the roots of Yggdrasil, thereby bordering Midgard, with its other borders abutting Svartalfheim to the "west", Alfheim to the "north", and Helheim to the "south". *Folkvangr* (which is the location of *Sessrumnir*) lies very near to Helheim, but also to Yggdrasil, so if one were drawing a *linear* map of Vanaheim (which is pretty much impossible, mind you), it would be located in the southeast.

> **Folkvangr and Sessrumnir:** "The Field of the People" and "The Seat Room", these are Freyja's Field and Hall, respectively, where the other half of those who die as heroes are taken. Historically, what criteria the Gods use to split up who goes to Odin and who goes to Freyja has been lost to us. The modern UPG of many suggests Folkvangr is a pastoral field, full of golden wheat, and much more peaceful than Valhalla. Likewise, Sessrumnir has much more in common with the "heavenly meadhall motif" most people expect of Valhalla than does *actual* Valhalla. Given Freyja's status as one of the Vanir, who are generally more "peaceful, farmer-type deities", this UPG actually makes a certain amount of sense. My *experienced truth* of Folkvangr and Sessrumnir is that those heroes who receive this as their "final

destination" are those who deserve and crave *peace* from battle, rather than a continued military existence in the afterlife. Many who reside there refer to that gift as "Freyja's Kiss".

Aegir's Hall: The home of Aegir and Ran, Jotun deities of the Sea. Those who drowned were said to be scooped up by Ran and taken to live with her, her husband, and their nine daughters (the Nine Waves) in their family home, Aegir's Hall. This hall lies beneath the sea, but quite close to Vanaheim (the home of the Vanir Gods, such as Njordr, who also relates heavily to the ocean), and we are told it is a splendid place, full of coral and jewels and great wealth. The Aesir frequently while away the winter with Aegir and Ran, and if there *is* an actual "heavenly Viking meadhall", this is definitely the spot!

Midgard: "Middle Yard"; Earth, at least by the standards of the Lore—but more on that in a moment. Depicted most often as "midway up" the World Tree—i.e., at the point where the roots meet the trunk—and understood as the only world completely *visible* to the mundane eye among the Nine. It is described as being located between Niflheim (the land of ice) and Muspelheim (the land of fire), and surrounded by an ocean that is impassable, which is inhabited by Jormungandr (the "World Serpent"). We are also told that it is connected to Asgard via the rainbow bridge, Bifrost. In truth, Midgard might be better understood as the *astral plane.* If we take the descriptions of Midgard in the Eddas and Sagas as "gospel", we encounter two obvious issues, and it doesn't take a genius to spot either of them (okay, maybe a scholar in the case of one of the two): Ginnungagap is *also* said to be located directly between Niflheim and Muspelheim, and clearly *our* physical Earth is not some flat "island" lying in the middle of an impassable ocean inhabited by or even surrounded by a gigantic serpent. So, clearly, Midgard is *not* what Marvel Comics and others would like for us to believe; clearly, it's something else. That "something else" is the *astral plane*. Which is not to say that the rest of these worlds don't *also* make up "countries" or "nations" of the astral. Confused yet? Stick with me! Scholars far smarter than me (among them, Christopher Penczak and Michelle Belanger) have gone to great lengths to explain the different "phases" or "regions" of the astral realms, and most can at least agree that the "area" most-oft traveled by modern mystics is an area that could just as easily be termed "collective unconscious". It is a region as populated by *thought forms*, as it is by *ghosts* and is often the "meeting point" between humans and entities such as elementals, angels (see Alfheim above), and even faeries, who actually "hail" from *other* realms. In my experience, that region of the "collective unconscious", that not-quite-defined "nation" of the *astral plane*, is Midgard. At its center stands the World Tree—Yggdrasil--which is why this is the most frequently encountered "gateway image" for astral travelers worldwide. The base of the tree, the branches of the tree, and even the roots of the tree, of course, connect to all of the other actual worlds, or "nations" of the Otherworld. But before we can go on such travels, we must first become comfortable with traveling Midgard itself. But what about the "Ginnungagap Problem", and Jormungandr, and the ocean, and Niflheim, and Muspelheim, you might be asking? Jormungandr, the "World Serpent", is as much of a reality as all of the rest of this, but, again, not in the way one might expect; not even, perhaps, in the way our *Ancestors* may have expected. But we're getting ahead of ourselves....

Ginnungagap: "Gaping abyss"; "yawning void" (Or, at least, that was the *traditional* translation, until Jan de Vries's suggestion of "*magically charged*" for the ginnun-portion of the word in 1930, but more on that momentarily). Mentioned in the *Gylfaginning*,

Ginnungagap is the primordial void from which all life began, and to which all life will return during Ragnarok (the Norse equivalent of "end times" mythology). Supposedly located between Niflheim (Land of Ice) and Muspelheim (Land of Fire), it has been described as a place of perfect, uninterrupted silence and darkness, which would've been considered the ultimate expression of chaos by our Norse ancestors (who had very good reason to *fear* chaos—stepping outside the normal "order" of life could lead to things like starvation, disease, and frostbite). According to John Lindow in his *Handbook of Norse Mythology*:

> *Formally, Ginnungagap must be parsed as "Gap of ginnungs". What ginnungs are is not wholly clear, but the first syllable **ginn-** in mythological contexts was used to intensify what followed, as in **ginn-**holy, "extremely holy", gods, or **ginnregin**, "great powers", that is, the gods. At the same time, as a noun [in poetry] **ginn** meant "falsehood, deception", and there was a common verb **ginna**, "to deceive". A gap of ginnungs, then, was probably a proto-space filled with magic powers. (Note: Lindow likewise sourced from Jan de Vries.)*

Or, if one goes even more literal with Lindow's etymology here, a "gap of ginnungs" could even more likely be a large chasm full of great deceptions and falsehoods of a magical nature, which has, indeed, been *my* personal experience of Ginnungagap, and is why I have included it in a discussion of the Nine Worlds, even though it isn't typically listed among them. If you're going to know about the good places, you need to know about the *bad ones* too. When talking to Heathens, or Pagans in general, really, to even suggest that there are things such as "nether realms" full of "evil things" (*demon* being the closest thing we have in the English language, though if you want to *really* discredit yourself in certain circles, try bandying *that* term about!) will generally discredit everything you've said thus far, and most definitely everything that comes after. I'm not suggesting it. I'm telling you *it exists*, and I have seen its borders, too, as well as the vile things that crawl up out of it. "But, but, but," you stammer: "Ginnungagap is also the cosmic void of Creation, according to the Norse Creation Myth." Well, yes, it *is*, or, rather, it *was*. The keyword in that sentence is *was*. I'll talk more on this later, in the section on "good vs. evil" (which is also a touchy subject among Heathens and many other Pagans who wish to maintain that nothing is *ever* purely black or white), but for now, we'll focus on it from a purely "geographical" perspective. As a "gap" or "chasm", Ginnungagap is a *space between*, and, as such, is closer to our mundane physical world than most of us would like to imagine, much less realize. Our Ancestors and the Gods themselves, however, realize(d) this all too well, which is why we have *guardian* figures such as Jormundgandr, Heimdall, Garm, and Surt in the first place.

Svartalfheim: "Homeland of the Black Elves"; also known as *Nidavellir*, "Low Fields" or "Dark Fields"; traditionally, the home of the Dwarves (*Duergar*) and the Dark Elves (*Svartalfar* or *Dokkalfar*). It is described in the Lore as a labyrinthine, underground domain (which is fitting, when one considers the relationship between dwarves and mining). In my experience, this world or plane sits to the far west of Vanaheim, south of Alfheim and also of Midgard, but north of Helheim. If you don't get along well with what modern Pagans typically refer to as *earth elementals*, I don't recommend a visit. In my personal experience, the landscape here is not always purely subterranean, but it is craggy and dark—think of the volcanic fields full of blackened lava we see here on physical earth, or the landscape of Mustafar in the Star Wars Universe. It shares its southern border with the ocean at the "northern" tip of Helheim (which also adjoins Vanaheim).

Muspelheim and Niflheim: "The World of Muspel"; "World of the end of the world through fire" and "World of Fog" (often translated as "World of Ice"), only attested in the *Prose Edda* of Snorri Sturluson (which may prove an overtly Christian influence). Remember a moment ago when I said Ginnungagap was *supposedly* located between Muspelheim and Niflheim? Well, there's a reason why I said that....if I might be permitted to sound like Han Solo for a second: I've been a lot of places, and I've seen a lot of strange things, but I've never seen anything to convince me that there is a world made completely of fire, akin to the modern Christian ideal of hell, which is precisely what Snorri describes in his concept of Muspelheim. I have seen "fringe places", usually bordering the "chasms" of Ginnungagap, that are "fiery" on this level, but nothing remotely resembling an entire "world" or even a "land". Insofar as Niflheim, that word is likewise only found in Snorri's *Edda*, and may be a valid case of Good Ole Snorri getting confused about the much older word, *Niflhel*, a poetic embellishment of the word *Hel* (i.e., Helheim), found in many Old Norse poems which predate Snorri's *Edda*. That being the case, it could then be said that both Ginnungagap *and* Midgard (the "typical astral plane", remember) are located between "fiery fringelands" and Helheim, but that Midgard is also bordered by oceans (such as those of Vanaheim and Helheim), which is one way that a person can know they're "in the right place". *Hint:* If you're wandering the astral, and you come upon a wall of fire, it's probably a great idea to turn tail and walk back the way you came from!

Jotunheim: "World of the Giants"; also known as "Utgard" ("Beyond The Fence"). Jotunheim is *where the wild things are*. It's secondary name of Utgard provides us with that clue: our Northern ancestors classified both geographical spaces and psychological states as either *innangard* ("within the enclosure") or *utangard* ("beyond the enclosure"). Things that are *innangard* are ordered, civilized; familiar—in the very real sense of "in one's own backyard". Things that are *utangard* are chaotic, wild, anarchic; unfamiliar: "outside the fence". *Utgard* is synonymous with the Old English *wild-deor-ness*, from which we derive the modern term *wilderness*: "the place of self-willed beasts". The -gard endings of Asgard and Midgard are based on precisely this division between *innangard* and *utangard*: those places are "within the fence", so to speak; they are *innangard*. Asgard is the "Enclosure of the Aesir"; it is their realm, *apart* from that which is "beyond the fence", closed off from the *wilderness*. Midgard, meanwhile, is described as being in the *middle* of the *wilderness*, which tells us that, simply put, Jotunheim isn't so much "one land apart", as it is *the wilderness* that is "beyond the fence". It *surrounds* us, here on the physical plane, often overlapping with certain places (such as areas which have become recognized as "faery rings") and it is ever on the fringe of every astral journey one might take. It is, in my experience, the source of all of those tales of the *Otherworld*, from Celtic literature, to Native American tales of the Little People. In that sense, "World of Giants" might be a bit misleading— denizens from Jotunheim might not necessarily be *physically* bigger than you, but their *power* is most definitely bigger than yours! The word *Jotun* is actually sourced from the proto-Germanic word *etunaz*, which means "devourer", a nod to the size of their *appetites*, rather than to their physical stature. In a modern world where the phrase "eaten alive" is frequently used to illustrate what happens when someone gets in over their heads in business, education, or even magick, the warning implicit in the words *jotun* and *jotnar* should be easy enough to understand! Even the Jotun who wound up becoming members of the Aesir or Vanir through marriage remained wild and untamed on some deeper level, and it is wise to remember that when venturing into their homelands.

Helheim: "Realm of the Hidden"; also sometimes simply called Hel (don't let that throw you). In the Lore, we are told that Helheim is ruled over by Hel (some prefer Hela, to avoid sideways glances from the Judeo-Christian community, just as I personally prefer to call Her lands Helheim, rather than Hel) Loki's-Daughter, and that its entry gate is guarded by a Cerberus-like hound by the name of Garm. I can honestly say that I've never met Garm, but then, I've never met Snorri Sturluson, either, yet, clearly, *he* exists (or, at least, he *existed* once upon a time here on Earth)! This is in no way a region of *punishment* in the afterlife for the Dead. On the contrary, Helheim is often mistaken for what many modern Pagans and Mystics would refer to as the *astral plane*, but once again, this definitely isn't the *whole* of that, either. The dead in Helheim spend their afterlife doing the same sorts of things they did in life: eating, drinking, raising families, riding horses, etc. It isn't a place of eternal bliss, but it isn't a place of eternal torment, either; it is simply a place where *life goes on*, just on a different plane of existence. Most of the folks I know refer to this area as "*The Suburbs*", because it's not quite Asgard, but then it's not quite anywhere else, either, and because *life goes on* there, like normal (as one thinks of life going on "as normal" in the suburban neighborhoods of the physical world). In my experience, it is a wee bit closer to this physical realm, and to Midgard (the "typical astral plane") and Vanaheim, than it is to any of the other worlds. Like Jotunheim, it may occasionally even overlap with the physical world and its denizens choose to interact (sometimes this comes across as a "haunting", other times, as a relative acting as a sort of "guardian angel"). In my experience, its "northern" border is an ocean and coastline which is shared with Vanaheim, and *Folkvangr* and *Sessrumnir* (the Field and Hall of Freyja, respectively) lie along that coast. That "seaside fringe" of Helheim also borders on Midgard, not far from the location where Bifrost connects "upwards" to Asgard.

> **Nastrond:** "Shore of Corpses"; the closest thing in the Norse Tradition to the Christian concept of Hell (or Judaic Sheol, which is actually more accurate), its gate is situated in the deepest reaches of Helheim. This is where those who have committed the most horrible crimes, such as murder or rape, are taken to be fed to Nidhoggr, ("Malice Striker") the dragon which gnaws at the roots of Yggdrasil, the World Tree. Rather than eternal torment (unless Nidhoggr has more in common with the Sarlaac from *Return of the Jedi* than we realize), those deemed worthy of punishment in the afterlife are simply swallowed, and that's the end. Forever.

Realizing that there is a *much larger world* than the travails we face here in our mundane, physical world can be a great comfort to many people. If we can look around at the craptastic things that are going on here on Earth and realize that *isn't all there is*, then there is *hope* that we might bring this world into greater *alignment* with the worlds that are better and brighter. We can seek to *emulate* Vanaheim, for example, or even Asgard, while at the same time respecting the wilderness (as epitomized by Jotunheim). We can also come to recognize what is truly *outside*— truly *utangard*—and learn the difference between *wilderness* and "the breach", and then learn to guard against the latter and give it no frith.

Good Versus Evil

If you use the word "evil" in most Heathen circles, prepare yourself for the verbal firestorm that's sure to follow. Trust me on this: it has happened to me more than once. As I touched on briefly in our previous discussion of Ginnungagap, most Heathens see the concept of "evil", or even the notion that things can be broken down into "black and white" absolutes, as "Judeo-Christian grafting" of the worst sort. Yet, it remains a fact that some things *are* indeed purely good or purely bad, no matter how much we might like that not to be the case. As stated in Newton's Third Law of Physics:

Every action has an equal and opposite reaction.

To quote Montgomery Scott from *Star Trek*: "You canna change the laws of physics!" And this Third Law provides a very real case for the *ultimate reality* of both good *and* evil in the Universe. Put simply: you cannot have one without the other. It's a balance: both must *necessarily* exist, whether we like it, or not. Now, that doesn't mean that there aren't also "*grey areas*": just because someone or something *breaks frith* once (or even twice) does *not* make whatever or whoever did so "evil"; it's the *consistent intentional breach of frith* that can lead down that road.

In order to define good and evil in this way, however, one must first understand the definition of *frith*. Frith is an Old

English word (Old Norse cognate: fridhr) meaning "peace; freedom from molestation, protection; safety, security." It dictates the social actions and rules which maintain peace within a household, kinship, or community. In its most simplistic definition, then, frith is *breaking the rules*, but what are the rules in question?

The **Nine Norse Virtues**, sourced largely from the *Havamal*, are the *"rules" of Norse Witchcraft*. They bear an admitted similarity to the *Aesirian Code of Nine*, and thus I apologize in advance for any feathers this might ruffle. I first encountered the *Aesirian Code of Nine* roughly twenty years ago, while attempting to help create a "warrior caste" within our small Welsh Druidic Grove. At that time, I did not know the ugly history of that code of ethics—that the most "popularized" version of it actually hails from around 1974, within organizations which have since proven to be racist in their ethics, edicts, and actions. However, the virtues listed in the *Aesirian Code of Nine* are not the *property* of those organizations. No, those virtues are, in fact, much, much older, and pervasive as *cornerstones of proper behavior* among several distinct cultural groups of the same period as the Ancient Norse: most specifically, the Celts. These virtues also echo down to us through not only the *Havamal*, but portions of the Eddas and Sagas as well. In other words, they have *historical authenticity and validity*, especially when divorced from the later history of the *Aesirian Code of Nine*.

The Nine Norse Virtues

INTEGRITY: Treat everyone with honesty and fairness, including yourself, and always strive to be a person of your word. Never lie or break your word. Keep your promises. Be guileless. Never practice prejudice nor bigotry by labeling or mistreating others. Do not allow others to participate in such acts of prejudice or bigotry.

LOYALTY: True friendship is a bond as strong as blood, and the family we *choose* is as important and sacred as the family into which we are born. The Gods are also our family; our tribe. Always honor and protect your loved ones and your Gods. Never leave your family, whether kith or kin, the Gods, or this Craft behind or in need.

HOSPITALITY: Always treat guests and strangers as you would hope to be treated. Be ever ready to offer help to others as you would likewise hope to be helped. Never behave from a place of selfishness. Always strive to improve the lives of others.

WISDOM: Knowledge is power. Be ever-learning, but also eager to share and teach what you yourself know. Never assume that you already "know everything", or otherwise behave like a "know-it-all", because you *don't*!

SELF-KNOWLEDGE: Be aware of the world around you, but never forget your place within it. Be willing to accept your own flaws, and also to accept change. That which does not adapt and grow cannot survive. Welcome change, realizing it is necessary for growth. Never seek a stagnant life, and be a force for change in the stagnant lives of others.

TRUST: Treat everyone with equity, and expect the same. Never shirk your responsibilities nor make excuses for not meeting them; instead, prove yourself worthy to the tasks set forth. Always pay your debts.

HUMILITY: Strive for good always, and celebrate not only the best of *your* abilities, but the best of others' as well. Realize that the best of one's abilities is all that anyone can offer, and be not only grateful for those areas in which you may excel, but also gracious with them, offering those abilities and talents as gifts to others in the world. Never behave in a "holier-than-thou" manner, and realize that if you do it *will* come back on you in equal measure. To behave in such a manner is to destine oneself to shame.

COURAGE: Be strong of heart: control your anger; never harm the innocent, the outcast, or the good; never tolerate those who do. Never strike out purely from a place of anger, violence or hatred.

JUSTICE: Use your voice and your actions to defend and uphold the innocent, the outcast, and the good. Do not keep your silence when wrong has been done; silence is complicity. Always strive to be the voice of those who may not have voices of their own. Never seek to silence the voices of those who might be perceived as weaker than you. Never tolerate those who actively mistreat or are violent or hurtful to others. Defend your family (both   kith   and kin), your Gods, and your Path with thricefold ferocity when necessary.

It should be a no-brainer that if you go through life trying to bring as much *good* (i.e., *Justice*, and all of the other things on this list) as possible into the world, good things will happen to you and for you, and to and for those you love, and that you'll avoid promoting "evil". Let's take a moment to cut away any religious baggage which we might attach to that term and *truly* define it, as well as the term *good*:

> **Evil:** the force of things that are morally bad; things which are profoundly harmful or bad.

> **Good:** that which is morally right; righteous; things which are beneficial and bring advantage, rather than harm.

When all is said and done, **morality** has less to do with which religious path we choose to follow (or not) than it does with our behavior *in relation* to other beings. Ultimately, it is an implied system of "don't cause harm; bring advantage", and it really *is* just as simple as that. There are, of course, *grey areas*: people make mistakes; sometimes *defense* is necessary and justified. It would, in fact, be impossible, as a human being, to keep every single one of these Virtues every single day of your life in every single situation that you encounter. One does not have to look very far in the Lore to see that it was even impossible for the Gods *themselves* to maintain every single one of these Virtues in every single situation encountered. *Accidentally breaking frith* with one or two or even three of these Virtues every once in a great while under specific circumstances is *not* the definition of evil. *Intentionally* breaking frith with one or two or even three of these virtues in the name of *Justice* is *not* the definition of evil, either. *Actively seeking* to do the *direct opposite* of these Virtues, and thereby *actively breaking frith*, *except* in cases of *justified defense*, however, *is*. In other words: *actively seeking to do harm with zero justification is **evil**.* Period.

So what do we *do* when we actually encounter evil? We *give it no frith*. You may have heard this phrase occasionally, while traveling in certain Heathen circles: "*Give them no frith.*" But what does that actually mean? If *giving* (or *showing*) *frith* means "bringing and/or showing peace, offering freedom from molestation and/or harm, offering/showing/giving protection, and providing safety and security", then *not giving* (or *showing*) *frith* would most *directly* mean "give them no peace; harm them; do not protect them; provide them with no safety or security". Hopefully it's self-evident where *that* definition of *"give them no frith"* is highly problematic with living a remotely *peaceful* life. Certainly, the *Havamal* actually *does* encourage us to harass those who harass us with equal if not even double or triple measure. "Cursing" people or taking other defensive measures to protect our family, friends, or even our Gods and spiritual beliefs are *not* outside the parameters of our faith. However, if you've ever tried to actually *live* your life in such an "eye for an eye" fashion, you know that it quickly becomes more than a bit unpleasant. You can easily become as much of a "monster" as whatever monster you're trying to fight. My Beloved has come up with a rather charming personal translation of *"Give them no frith"*, which I think is far more serviceable in the actual *practice* of not giving/showing frith: *"No frithies for you!"* This has come to basically mean for us "closing the fence": marking something or someone as ultimately *utangard* whenever it/they has/have consistently proven to be "evil" (*actively breaking frith with the Norse Virtues without justification*).

If you'll stop for a moment and think about how you relate to other people through the course of your life, you will find that you actually have *concentric circles of affection*, not unlike the ones that Amy Farrah Fowler used to illustrate to Sheldon Cooper who he could and could not share their intimate details with in the "The Allowance Evaporation" episode of the 2017 season of *The Big Bang Theory*. This is one of the best illustrations of *innangard* versus *utangard* that I've ever encountered! If you think of yourself as the person living in a "home" at the center of these concentric circles, and the first of the circles as that "house", the people who occupy that "home" would be your **family** (whether by blood or by trust). These are the people who are the most deeply or purely *innangard:* "inside your fence". The next circle outward would be the "yard" of that "home". That circle might be occupied by some of your closest friends and associates— your **tribe**, if you will. Some might choose to translate this even as **folk** (although that term admittedly has a *lot* of baggage, courtesy of WWII and the subsequent racist movements in Heathenry). These people are also "inside your fence", just not as *closely* inside as the first circle. They are still *innangard*. The circle outside that one might be imagined as the "street" on which you live, populated by neighbors and co-workers with whom you frequently associate and with whom you routinely maintain the *Norse Virtues*, but who have not yet proven themselves "worthy" of those inner two circles. Your levels of relationship with others radiate outwards from there, in continued concentric circles, until you reach the barrier of those who are *utangard:* "completely outside your fence".

What is "outside the fence"--*utangard*--isn't always evil, but almost without exception, it is *dangerous* in some capacity. As previously discussed, for our Ancestors, the *wilderness* was a scary place. In today's world of city life and the internet, the *wilderness* is still a scary place—perhaps even *scarier* than it was for our Ancestors, since most of us are ill-equipped at best to remotely survive in it. One need look no further than reality TV shows like *Naked and Afraid* or even *Survivor* to understand the modern fear of the *wilderness*: it's a very *real* fear, and with very good *reason*! "*No frithies for you*" means placing someone or something (such as an issue, for example) into the "realm" of *utangard*—placing whatever or whoever it is "outside the fence", essentially exiling them or it into the *wilderness*, and then *closing the fence*. Beyond that, the fence is *closed*. Which means we do not give whatever or whoever it is any more of our *energy* by continually thinking about whoever or whatever it is, or by continuing to try to argue our side of things, or by actively attempting to harass them equal to or in excess of the amount they have harassed us. We *close the fence*, but that does *not* mean we do not *remain vigilant*. *Closing the fence* on someone or something doesn't just mean "proclaim them *utangard* and then *forget* about them to the point of *ignorance*." It isn't accidental that the words *ignore* and *ignorance* have the same root: *ignorare*, "to not know". What we don't know *can* hurt us, so completely *ignoring* someone who is essentially your *enemy* can only serve to cause you greater problems further down the road. Instead, you should *remain vigilant*, which does *not* mean being continually ready to re-engage, but instead to *watch from afar, in case* further action is required at some point in the future. I'm not promoting *paranoia* here, for if you are spending half your life "peeking over the fence", then you are officially expending too much of your time and *energy* on whatever or whoever is supposedly *utangard*. When we continually "peek over the fence" in such a manner, whatever or whoever we have placed *outside* it aren't *really* outside at all, they've just been demoted to the status of "livestock" or "pets". Why would anyone want to keep their problems as pets?

The first act of the Norse Witch, therefore, is to become

oathbound to the maintenance, to the best of their ability, of the *Norse Virtues*. **Oaths** are one of the three primary purposes of *votive action: devotional acts* which are basically a form of *prayer through action*. The **fulfillment of vows** (oath-taking and oath-keeping) is one of the cornerstones of our belief system as Norse Witches and was, in fact, historically one of the cornerstones of Ancient Norse society. We are told in *Heimskringla Saga*:

> First, should Odin be toasted (raising a glass and drinking to the God as a sign of reverence), (next) should (come) that drink to Sigurd and the kings of his kingdom, but after (literally: since), Njordr, a toast (as with Odin, see above), and Freyr, a toast (again, see Odin), for peace and good seasons. Then there (were) many men that eagerly drank thereafter Bragi's toast.--Translation Mine

That second toast—the drink to Sigurd and the kings of his kingdom—is an *oath of fealty*. In the original language of this passage, it should also be noted that "First, should Odin be toasted" literally appears as *Skyldi fyrst Odins full*. In fact, the Old Norse word given repeatedly in this passage to imply toasting, and, therefore, "showing reverence", is *full*: the same as in *fulltrui/fulltrua*. The toasts that began with "Odins full" continued with "Njordar full", "Freyrs full", and "Braga full": essentially, proclaiming Odin, Njordr, Freyr, and Bragi as *fulltrui* of the gathered blot-participants. What does it mean to be *fulltrui/fulltrua*? The word *fulltrui* translates literally as "representative, agent, or trusted friend". Therefore, the toasts in the above passage to Odin, Njordr, Freyr, and Bragi are likewise *oaths of fealty*.

In the first of the *Norse Virtues*, it states "Never lie or break your word. Keep your promises." These are the actions dictated by the virtue of **Honor (Integrity)**. The Old Norse word for *honor* is *virdhring*, which loosely equates to "reverence, respect; dignity". Essentially, it is the ability to hold one's head up high, rather than hide one's face in shame. Oath-breaking was considered precisely such a source of shame among our Ancestors, and is still held in extremely low regard among modern Heathens, Norse Pagans, and, of course, Norse Witches. But why? Quite simply put, an oath is a *promise*, and a broken promise is a *lie*. The natural human tendency is to hold people who consistently lie in low esteem because, clearly, they can neither be trusted nor relied upon. An

oath, ultimately, is a lie not only to another human, nor even to the family or tribe, but to the *Gods Themselves*. Chances are great that someone willing to *break a promise* to the *Gods Themselves* wouldn't blink twice at betraying another human being!

Ultimately, we come into this world with very little: our hamingja, our hamr, and our fylgja. As we grow to become sentient, communicative beings (from just-out-of-the-womb infants to toddlers and children), our hugr is indelibly formed. These are the four parts of the *soul*, as understood by our Norse Ancestors, and by the modern Norse Witch. Certainly over the course of our lives we may amass many things: homes, cars, material possessions, wealth, etc. But at the end-of-days, we leave this world with the same things we brought into it, plus one: hamingja, hamr, fylgja, and hugr. Our hamingja grows with us over the course of our lifetime, almost like a second skin: *reputation* becomes the "clothes we wear", even when we are wearing no other clothes. That old saying "there are no hearses with luggage racks" is very, very true, when it comes to the material versus the spiritual as we "slough off the mortal coil". However, we *do* carry "baggage" into the afterlife, and if we are not very careful in life, the heaviest of those suitcases can become our hamingja. Every broken oath adds weight to that particular piece of luggage, as each oath broken or kept helps to shape our reputation and our *legacy*: how other people—those we leave behind—*remember* us. If we are remembered as people who always kept our word, maintained our oaths, and spoke in Truth and fairness, chances are much greater that someone will still be lighting candles for us on an altar somewhere long after we're gone. However, if we maintain a life wherein we become remembered as an oath-breaker, whose word was worthless, the price in the afterlife can be quite steep.

As you take this oath, it is important to remember that this is not an oath you are making to another human being from whom you might one day be separated in death; this is an oath you are making to the Gods—Gods who are going to know *exactly* where to *find you* when your end-of-days are at hand! There is a great quote from the film *Gladiator*, which is actually a paraphrase of a quote by Marcus Aurelius:

What we do in life echoes in eternity.

It could indeed be said that the *stronger* and *more important* the oath, the *louder* its echo. The oath taken to uphold the Norse

Virtues is, at its deepest core, an *oath of fealty*, and oaths of that type seem to carry some of the loudest echos of all. Certainly, every oath you make (and most definitely every oath you *break*) leaves an indelible *mark* on your hamingja: what we do (or, worse, what we *don't do*) in life truly *does* echo in eternity. Perhaps the best illustration of this in modern fiction would be the Army of Oathbreakers in J.R.R. Tolkien's *Return of the King*. This Army of the Dead, also known as the Dead Men of Dunharrow, were, in life, Men of the Mountains whose King swore allegiance to the original King of Gondor, Isildur. In other words, they made an *oath of fealty*, not unlike the one you are about to take. But when the time came for them to fulfill that oath, they broke their word: they refused to fight alongside Isildur and instead hid in the mountains like cowards. Isildur subsequently cursed them for their breach of oath: they would remain without rest until such time as their oath was finally fulfilled. This is a great illustration of the echo or indelible mark on one's hamingja that actual oathbreaking leaves behind in our very real world (However, in using this as an example, I do not mean to imply that oathbreaking automatically leads people to become "haunting spirits" in the afterlife, though your descendants may, in fact, find themselves "haunted" by the shame of your actions).

Among our Norse Ancestors, and also among the Celtic Tribes, oaths such as this one were often sworn on *oathrings* (or, in the case of the Celts a neck-ring called a torc). Before taking the oath (which follows), I would recommend attaining for yourself an appropriate piece of ritual jewelry. It does not have to be in the traditional form of an oathring; it may be a necklace, ring, or a bracelet. The most important thing is that it appeals to your heart, is easily worn *at all times*, and that it take the shape of a suitable reminder of the oath that you have sworn. Your *oath-piece*, as I will henceforth call it, should be put in a place of reverence in your home, leading up to the time of your oath-taking. Make sure that you "visit" it each day, offering prayers to the Gods in which you make it known to Them that this is more than a "simple piece of jewelry", but actually a *gift* to Them, on which you will swear your oath, which is likewise a *gift* to Them, and which you will wear *for* Them in remembrance of the promise you have made. As you take your oath, you should hold your *oath-piece* firmly in your hands, making the promise *into* and *onto* it, before finally putting it on at the end.

A Virtuous Oath

With pure heart, I come before my Gods,
And with open hands.
(While still holding your oath-piece firmly, open
your hands to reveal it to the Gods.)
Oathsworn and Honor-bound,
I promise to treat everyone with equity and
    fairness,
Including myself,
And to always strive to be a person of my word.
I will not lie; I will keep my promises.
I will seek to be guileless.
I swear to never practice bigotry nor prejudice,
Nor will I stand by silently while others do.
Oathsworn and Honor-bound,
I promise to be Loyal,
Not only to my Gods,
But to my Family, both kith and kin,
And to my Tribe.
I will always honor and protect
My Faith,
My Family,
And my Tribe,
And I will never leave any of these behind, or in
    need.
Oathsworn and Honor-bound,
I promise to always seek to treat guests and
    strangers
As I would hope to be treated.
I will be ever-ready to help others as I would
    likewise hope to be helped.
I will seek never to behave from a place of
    selfishness,
Ever striving to improve in whatever small ways I
    might the lives of others.
Oathsworn and Honor-bound,
I promise to be ever-learning,
But also eager to share with others and teach what I
    have learned.

I will never assume that I "know everything",
Because only the Gods can do that.
Oathsworn and Honor-bound,
I promise to be aware of the world around me,
But never forget my place within it.
I will accept my flaws, and the flaws of others,
And I will be willing to accept change.
In fact, I will welcome it,
For that which does not grow and adapt does not
    survive.
I will never seek to live a stagnant life,
And I will do my utmost to be a positive force for
    change
In the lives of others.
Oathsworn and Honor-bound,
I promise to treat everyone with equity,
And expect the same in return.
I will not shirk my responsibilities, nor make
    excuses to avoid them,
But instead prove myself worthy to the tasks set
    forth for me.
I will always attempt to pay my debts.
Oathsworn and Honor-bound,
I promise to strive always for the best,
And to celebrate not only the best of my own
    abilities,
But the best of others' as well.
I realize that my personal best is all I can offer--
It is all that *anyone* can offer--
And I will not only be grateful for those areas in
    which I might excel,
But I will also be gracious with those talents and
    abilities,
Offering them up as gifts to the Gods and to other
    people.
I will seek never to behave in a "holier-than-thou"
    manner,
For such behavior is a path to shame.
Oathsworn and Honor-bound,
I promise to be strong of heart and control my
    anger.

I will never seek to harm the innocent, the outcast,
  or the good,
And I will never tolerate those who do.
I will never strike out purely from a place of anger,
  violence, or hatred.
Oathsworn and Honor-bound,
I promise to use my voice and actions
To defend and uphold the innocent, the outcast,
  and the good.
I will not keep my silence when wrong has been
  done,
For silence is complicity.
I will always strive to be the voice of those
Who may not have voices of their own,
And I will never seek to silence
The voices of those who might be perceived by
  some as weak.
I will never tolerate those who actively seek to
  mistreat others
Through violence or hatred or bigotry.
I will defend
My Family
My Tribe
And my Faith
With thricefold ferocity when necessary.
This oath I do swear,
That there may be peace and good seasons in my
  life;
Peace and good seasons in the lives of those whom I
  hold dear:
*(Seal your oath by donning your oath-piece. Wear
it always.)*
So it is, and so it shall be.
Enda er ok enda skal vera.

We begin our practice with this oath, and with coming to understand the concepts of *frith*, *innangard*, and *utangard* for a very important reason: **personal safety**. As we discussed in the last chapter, there are other worlds than these, and those other worlds are inhabited by more than people as we know them. At the end of the last chapter, we briefly touched on the fact that when it comes to what is *utangard*, there is a definite difference between *wilderness* and "the breach", and that we need to learn to respect the *wilderness*, while at the same time learning to *guard against* "the breach". "The breach" of which I'm speaking is Ginnungagap as I explained it in the previous section on the Nine Worlds and their geography. At the beginning of time, this was the place of *cosmic creation*, where Ymir was formed out of droplets from the melting ice as (according to Good Ole Snorri) Niflheim and Muspelheim came together in the great silence of the primordial chasm. As things continued to defrost, Audhumbla the cow also came up out of the ice, and Ymir, the hermaphroditic giant, began to suckle upon her. She, in turn, was nourished by brine in the ice, and as she licked, she revealed the first of the Aesir Gods, Buri. Meanwhile, whenever Ymir sweated, more giants were born. Eventually, Buri took a bride from among the grandchildren of Ymir, and Bestla bore Buri three sons: Odin, Villi, and Ve. In the original Old Norse of Snorri Sturluson's *Prose Edda*, we are told that Odin and His brothers slew Ymir because "*Hann er illr ok allir hans aettmenn*" ("He is evil and all his relatives"). Then They constructed the world from the giant's corpse. Eventually, They also make the first two human beings—Ask and Embla—from driftwood, and then give them Midgard as their dwelling place, fencing off that world from the chaos of Ginnungagap, which, other than the cow, apparently goes back to its original chaotic silence. So how did Ginnungagap go from the place of primordial cosmic creation to "the breach"? How and why did its entire *character* change? I wish I had a neat answer for that, all wrapped up for you in an elegant explanatory bow, but I do not. I'm not sure anyone does. It's like asking "why is fire hot?" I can't tell you *that* either; I can only reassure you that it *is*. The only possible source that we have from the Lore is Snorri's explanation of why Ymir is not revered as a god: "*Hann er illr ok allir hans aettmenn*".

Ginnungagap was evidently always a place that "things crawled out of", going all the way back to Ymir. For a time, the Gods had control of that—hence what happened to Ymir; hence the creation of Ask and Embla, and all the rest. But somewhere along the way, They *lost* that control. I personally believe that loss of control has everything to do with the Gods' loss of power and influence, as humanity has turned away from worshiping anything other than themselves, but that's just my personal opinion; nothing more. I have no *proof* that I can give you, though I desperately wish that I did. Whatever the cause, Ginnungagap remains a place that "things crawl out of", and the things that crawl out of it nowadays are nothing so warm and fuzzy as a milk-cow. As I stated earlier, the closest word we have in the English language for these "things" is *demon*, but I won't go there. The *Poetic Edda* tells us that the first children of Ymir were a man and a woman born from the sweat of Ymir's armpits—these were *Jotnar* (singular *Jotun*)—and then a six-headed monster was born from his feet: the first of the *thursar*. The trouble is, the word *thursar* didn't originally mean "giant", either; giant is a loan-word from French. *Thursar* is rooted from the proto-Germanic word *thurisaz* (which is also, notably, the name of a rune), which means "demon" or simply "monster". We're told in the Norse Creation Myth that when Odin, Villi, and Ve slew Ymir the flow of blood was so great that it created a flood which slew all of the *hrimthursar* (frost "monsters"), save Bergelmir and his wife (who fled on a boat in a story similar to the Christian story of Noah's Ark). So clearly the "things" presently "crawling out of" Ginnungagap aren't *thursar*, either. They actually have much more in common with the Hindu concept of the *rakshasa* than with the generalized Christian depictions of demons: vaguely humanoid, with elongated limbs, curved fangs, wicked claws, horns, mottled skin (as if decomposing), pig-like or even glowing eyes, and frequently extra heads and/or limbs. When one considers the Indo-European root of Norse culture (keyword: *Indo*), this really shouldn't come as a profound shock even to the more scholarly among us. Therefore, we won't use the dreaded "demon" word, but we won't use the term *thursar*, either, because both terms simply confuse things. Instead, we will employ the Old Norse *fjandi* (plural *fjandar*), which is the root word for the modern English word, "*fiend*".

The biggest difference between the *wilderness* (Jotunheim) and "the breach" (Ginnungagap) is what *lives* there! Jotnar are dangerous; fjandar are, simply put, "a whole different level of bad". Now, if you choose to shorten that to the word "evil", be my guest. Synonyms are, after all, synonyms. Certainly, we should treat those from the *wilderness* with *respect*, and possibly even be on guard a bit when dealing with them, but having actually had *dealings* with the fjandar, I can say with great honesty that *respect* and being "on your guard" isn't enough. Honest-to-Gods *protection* is highly advised. Sometimes the best defense actually *is* a good defense!

"Casting a circle" is a practice encountered most often in ritual magic, though its spiritual significance and the methods used are similar to that of the mandala in Hinduism (again, recall the Indo-European root of the Norse). As a form of extra defense against the fjandar, I have found the following incantation, which I call the **Outsider Caim**, uttered while "closing the fence" (essentially, "casting a circle") with a gandr (wand) or dagger to be quite effective. I have employed it in my personal practice for over twenty years. It was originally composed by the Archdruid of Cerddorion Nyfed (the Grove with which I practiced), Taliesin Emrys:

Outsider Caim

Outside the fire,
Darkness;
Darkness outside the Grove;
Outside there dwell shadows;
Shadows inside us as well.
Inside, outside, everywhere,
Where'er you dwell,
Dwell not here:
Here is light and all good things!
Light and Bright Wisdom protect us;
Protect us from those who dwell outside.

As we bring ourselves more and more into balance, we are likely to discover ourselves developing a deeper sort of *empathy* which makes us profoundly aware of energies that are somehow *off* crossing our path. These *off energies* have a tendency to make us not only psychologically "ill", but also sometimes physically so. Sometimes we may experience sensations of being "creeped out"; of having the hair on the back of our necks stand up (in a *bad* way) because of the sensation of a "darkish" presence. The *off energies* I'm referring to here are quite different from that, although being "creeped out" by them certainly may be a part of the proverbial package. There is a distinct difference between the sensation of "something is here and it's creeping me out", versus "something has touched this/me and it's making me want to throw up". A lifetime of exposure to our modern society and it's Dark vs. Light dichotomies has led many of us to equate *dark* with *negative* or *bad*, but that is definitely not always the case, and it may take actual *exposure* to *real negativity* before we can fully unlearn that programming.

As I said earlier in this chapter, for reasons that I can't really seem to fathom, the very concept that there might *be real negativity* out there in the Universe that needs *cleansing* seems to be a hard one for most modern Heathens to swallow. I have a very hard time understanding this reticence, primarily since our lore is full of stories of Gods and heroes encountering *real negativity*, and either cleansing or defeating it (or, more usually, cleansing it *by* defeating it). While the sort of *real negativity* that I'm speaking of now can sometimes be judged by the parameters of *frith* and *utangard*, that is not always the case. Some things are just *bad*, pure and simple, and you know them when you are exposed to them just as surely as you'd recognize a rotten egg or a pile of poo as something you really don't want to find on your front doorstep. And, just like a rotten egg or a pile of poo, you really don't need or want to know how it got that way, or how it even got there in the first place, you simply want to *get rid of it*!

These "oogy feelings" are usually caused by *residual* negative emotions or negative occurrences, such as profound sadness, anger, fear, or unjust violence. Just as an object can become *ensouled* through consistent positive and reverential use (you will find more on this in a later chapter), items, places, and sometimes even *people* can become *dirtied* by *residual negativity*. Often, when we think of things such as *hauntings* what we are actually dealing with is *residual negativity* (or simply *residual energy*, period), rather than what is called an *intelligent haunt*. It is as if the *memories of a place*, or even the *memories of an object* (in the case of *haunted objects*), come violently bubbling back to the surface and play themselves out again and again, only instead of it being simply a movie that *you* watch, these things behave more like movies that *watch you*. When we encounter such a place or object, or even when a person has been *dirtied* by such *residual negativity*, it may become necessary to perform a *cleansing rite*. *Cleansing rituals* may also be performed in a preemptive manner, when claiming a place or object for our own ritual use, or before embarking on deep ritual work ourselves.

Using the *Hallow Sign* (you will find more on this in the next chapter, **Jormungandr**) and *hallowing* an object is a quick-and-easy way of sparking a *cleansing process*, but there may be times when we need to take things deeper and go a bit more "whole hog" in our cleansing of a place, item, or person. Part of this process involves *closing the fence directly* around the object, place, or person; the other part of this process involves calling on the specific energies of Nerthus (Vanir) and Thor (Aesir) to assist you in *driving out* the *residual negativity* and *purifying* whatever is to be cleansed.

Sometimes a cleansing "just won't take". If you perform a cleansing rite and whatever you are cleansing still feels "oogy", for whatever reason, that place/object is simply *not meant for you*. It could be that there is a lesson in whatever it is for us; ponder this first, and see what answers you get. If this isn't the case, then, again, for whatever reason, whatever it is simply *is not meant for you*. Put it aside; return it from whence it came; avoid that location. If what you are attempting to cleanse is an actual *person*, and especially if the person in question is *yourself*, you should seek outside professional help (either mystically or scientifically/medically, especially if one of the sources of residual negativity could possibly be something such as clinical depression).

A Nordic Cleansing Rite

Center

Seeker, Maker, Believer (insert your own
  archetypes here):
My feet are on the ground;
I stand firm.
I am of the earth and the earth is of me;
I stand firm.
I center myself, and I hold.
So it is, and so it shall be.

**Lay the fence *directly* on the object (or person) itself
(use a clockwise circular motion of your right hand); if
cleansing an area, perform a walked circle as per
normal. Repeat three times.**

Outside the fire,
Darkness;
Darkness outside the Grove;
Outside there dwell shadows;
Shadows inside us as well.
Inside, outside, everywhere,
Where'er you dwell,
Dwell not here:
Here is light and all good things!
Light and Bright Wisdom protect us;
Protect us from those who dwell outside.

**Draw the Hallow Sign. As you draw each of the three
portions of the Sigil in the air or onto the object, you
will speak the invocation appropriate to that *section* of
the Sigil: Hammer=Mjollnir of Thor; Tiwaz=Hand of
Tyr; Cross=Chariot of Nerthus**

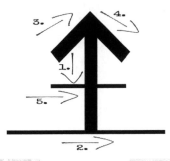

(Hammer)
I beg the use of Mjollnir,
Hammer of Thor,
To smite, cleanse, and purify
The negativity from this (person/place/object).

(Tiwaz; "Arrow")
I beg the reach of the Hand of Tyr,
To bring Justice and Right
And replace the blight
Upon this (person/place/object).

(Cross)
I beg the coming of Nerthus,
In Her healing chariot;
Cleanse and heal, Great Mother,
This (person/place/object).

State, emphatically:
Cleansed and healed,
I place this (person/place/object) within my fence,
and call it innangard;
Should things remain as they have been,
I put it and all negativity connected to it
Outside
And far away.
So mote it be.

Jormungandr

Then Hymir said: "We have rowed too far; if we go out further, it will be impossible to avoid Jormungandr."

But Thor replied: "We will row awhile yet."

And so Thor did, but Hymir grew steadily more afraid.

Finally, Thor set down the oars, and made ready a very strong fishing line, with a hook that was no less large or strong. And he put the ox-head on the hook, and he cast it overboard, and it sank to the bottom.

And Jormungandr snapped at the ox-head, and the hook caught in its jaw, but as soon as the Serpent realized this, it pulled away so fiercely that both of Thor's fists crashed against the gunwale of the boat. This made Thor so angry that he braced his feet against the bottom of the boat, and using his divine strength, yanked the line bearing Jormungandr up against the side of the boat. Oh, it was a frightful sight! Thor's eyes locked with the eyes of the Serpent, and the Serpent's eyes locked with the eyes of Thor, and Jormungandr blew its venom up from the depths below.

Hymir grew pale then, looking quite sick with terror, and as the venom-laden sea rushed into the boat, and as Thor raised his hammer to slay Jormungandr, Hymir drew out his knife and quickly cut the fishing line.

Jormungandr sank back into the sea then, and,

angry, Thor threw his hammer after the Serpent.
　　Jormungandr escaped Thor's blow, but Hymir was not so lucky: the Son of Odin brought his fist down upon Hymir's ear, sending him overboard, and then Thor waded back through the sea to dry land.
--*Gylfaginning 48, The Prose Edda, my own translation*

Earlier, when I talked about Midgard as one of the different planes of existence (the Nine Worlds or realms of Norse Cosmology), I said that the World Serpent (aka the Midgard Serpent; Jormungandr) is as much a reality as all the rest, though not in the way one might expect; maybe not even in the way our Ancestors would've expected. We are told in the *Gylfaginning* of the Prose Edda that Jormungandr was born of Angrbodha, the Jotun Chieftain of the Iron Wood, by Loki, as well as its siblings, Fenrir and Hela, and that upon learning of the three children's births, Odin sent for them. He feared for their welfare, but He also feared the children themselves. Hela, of course, He sent to Helheim, and granted Her rule over all the Nine Worlds, that She should take in everyone when they finally came to death, and see that they be well taken care of. Fenrir, He had bound, in the hopes of avoiding the prophecy of Ragnarok. But Jormungandr, we are told, "He cast into the deep sea, where it lies about all the land; and the Serpent grew so gigantic that it lies in the midst of the sea, and encompasses all the land, and bites upon its own tail." Thus, one child was given a realm of their own (a fiefdom, or queendom, if you will); another was imprisoned, though he had actually done nothing wrong as yet, and the middle child—Jormungandr--became the *embodiment of the wall that separates innangard from utangard.*
　　Jormungandr is the ultimate embodiment of *liminality*: that point in the midst of a ritual when one stands at the threshold between the mundane world and the world of the supernatural; between our realm, and the realm of the Gods. Neither *innangard* nor *utangard*, it is the point *eternally between*. It stands as a guardian of *liminal space*—**sacred space**—and *liminal time*—**sacred time**. To learn to create either of those two things—**sacred space** or **sacred time**—one must learn to dance with the World Serpent.
　　I began this chapter with my own translation of one of the most famous stories in Scandinavian lore: the fishing trip of Thor and Hymir. This story so captured the imagination of our Ancestors that they chose to depict it in art more often than any

other tale in the Eddas or Sagas. But why? I mean, naturally, given their geography, Norse culture was heavily subsistence-based on fishing. But I think there's a deeper layer here, if we simply look a little closer.

Thor (literally, "*Thunder*") is the son of Odin by Jord, which literally translates to "earth" or "world". Jord was a Jotun, the daughter of Nott (Night), and the sister of Daeg (Day). When we consider the symbology behind His parentage, it's not at all surprising that Thor is regarded not only as a god of thunder (which has been widely celebrated in modern pop culture), but also as a god of the common man and of honest dealings. His father, Odin, after all, is known for "walking amongst us", and also for the sacrifices He has made to gain ultimate Wisdom and Knowledge. It is on the maternal side of Thor's parentage, however, that we find the truly *elemental*: Earth, daughter of Night, sister of Day. Perhaps it is precisely because of this *elemental* lineage that Thor does not fear to sail so far out that He might encounter the Midgard Serpent, even though Hymir, whose name literally translates to "*Darkening One*", was mortally afraid.

When Thor actually *catches* Jormungandr, His reaction is to attempt to *subdue* it. Part of that process involves planting His feet firmly in the bottom of the boat, to brace and steady Himself. Hymir, meanwhile, is so terrified by the entire exchange that he eventually cuts the fishing line, setting the Serpent free. Thor attempts to *capture* or *contain liminal space* and *liminal time*; Hymir's response is to *stop* Thor from doing that. And then what happens? Thor pushes Hymir overboard in a fit of rage. If you've ever been interrupted in the midst of a ritual working, you can probably understand Thor's response!

When faced with the concepts of **sacred space** and **sacred time**, there are two ways in which the typical person reacts: either we react like Thor, and attempt to *capture*, *subdue*, or even *ride* them, or we react like Hymir, and shrink in *fear*. The **Hymir Reaction** to *liminality* is generally motivated by a fear of experiences which are *outside* the mundane: those of us who have that reaction consider such things as the ultimate in *utangard*. The **Thor Reaction** to *liminality*, on the other hand, comes from a place of understanding that once we place ourselves *inside* those experiences which are *outside* the mundane, they are *no longer utangard*, but are made *innangard* by our power to *capture*, *subdue*, and *ride* them.

So how do we *capture*, *subdue*, and *ride liminality*? How do we dance with Jormungandr? After all, we're not terribly likely to get our hands on a giant ox's head to use as bait, as Thor did! We will begin the same way as Thor: by planting our feet firmly to brace and steady ourselves. This is commonly called **grounding and centering**. I'll confess that I never quite understood that: why it's called grounding and centering, instead of the other way around. Frankly, I find grounding without centering to be the mystical equivalent of taking a poop without first sitting on a toilet! No, it would be much more apt to say *centering and grounding*, as one can certainly center without grounding after, but I don't suggest grounding without centering first. To revert to my rather awkward toilet-taking metaphor, the process of **centering** is very much about becoming *enthroned*. I mean this very much in the Celtic sense of *Sovereignty*: our *truest selves* in relationship not only to us, but to the Land and to what is *around* us. It is a very real sort of *rulership*—as I said, an *enthroning*—wherein we come fully into contact with *who we are* and *name and claim* that. It is a way of planting our mystical feet on the ground, and proclaiming "I shall not be moved", as Thor did, once Jormungandr grabbed hold of his fishing line. Before you can "go anywhere else", mystically speaking, you must first rest comfortably *within yourself*. You must become *enthroned*.

So how does one actually *do* that? We discussed *Self-ownership* in the chapter entitled **Know Yourself To Know Them**. Begin with the *Self-Archetypes* that you discovered in that chapter. For me, that would be *Seeker*, *Maker*, and *Believer*, so I will use those in this illustration. If you *can* physically plant your feet on the ground, do so. If for whatever reason you cannot, I want you to *physically visualize* doing so. I have found that, as a method of visualization, what I term *physical visualization* often works better for those people who have a hard time with the typical forms of visualization that first require you to close your eyes. You're not going to close your eyes; you're going to instead visualize your feet firmly planted with your eyes wide open. How does that work? Look at your feet (or where your feet would be), and then *see* your feet planted on the ground. That simple: you are going to form a *visual cue* via an actual, physical visual cue. Now, *know* that those are *your* feet. They are the feet of a *Seeker*, a *Maker*, a *Believer* (or whatever your Self-Archetypes might be). They are *on the earth*, and *so are you*, and you are *of the earth*, and *the earth is of you*. Take several deep, long breaths; I've personally found that four is a good number. Feel all of your weight going down into your feet, so that you are *standing firm* (whether you're actually standing or not does not matter; your *intent* is to *stand firm*). To actually *name and claim* your *enthronement* you may use the mantra below, or use it as a guide to compose your own. The most important thing is that you create for yourself a *verbal cue* to accompany your *visual cue*, so that you *inform your brain* that you are actively **centering**:

> Seeker, Maker, Believer
> (insert your own archetypes here):
> My feet are on the ground;
> I stand firm.
> I am of the earth and the earth is of me;
> I stand firm.
> I center myself, and I hold.
> So it is, and so it shall be.

Centering is not only for times when you wish to dance with Jormungandr at the verge of *liminality* (as when creating sacred space, or other things that are within the context of ritual). You can actively **center** anytime your world feels *adrift*. When you are overwhelmed at work, for example, and the jerk next to you just won't stop talking about his political views which are astronomically opposite from yours, you can use this exercise to **center**. When the phone won't stop ringing and your toddler is screaming (or your teenager, for that matter), use this exercise to **center** yourself. Get yourself accustomed to the *calmness* of the feeling of *standing firm*, and it *will empower* you, regardless of whether you're using it in a ritual setting, or not. *Empower* yourself by routinely practicing becoming *enthroned*.

The next half of the equation, of course, is **grounding**. In its most basic sense, **grounding** is *returning your energy* to the earth, which is why I say that one can center without grounding, but one should not ground without first centering. If you ground *without* centering, you may wind up "voiding" energy that would have been better kept in reserve for your actual use. Again, it's basically like pooping without first sitting down! To actively **ground**, you need to *physically visualize* all of the *excess* energy coalescing in a golden ball around the region of your navel. To do this, actually *look* at the region of your navel, and with eyes wide open, *see* the energy gathering there as a ball of golden light. When you feel that the ball of light is full enough of excess energy, you are then going to *physically visualize* that ball of light moving downwards, and out of your *root chakra* (which is at the base of your spine) and flowing *out* of you, and down, into the earth.

(Suddenly that awkward toilet-going metaphor makes a ton of sense, right?) Feel that energy *connect* to the earth, and flow down and outwards into it. When you have loosed all of the *excess* into the earth, stop the flow. You may find that physically tightening your rear in the same way you would when stopping a certain other sort of "flow" provides a good *physical cue* for the cutoff of energy flow.

Within the context of a ritual setting, you may find that there are times when you wish to **ground** energy *into* a *specific object* (such as your altar-space, for example). We will talk about this in greater depth when we cover **ritual objects**. For now, however, let us turn our attention to the actual *creation* of **sacred space** and **sacred time**, because you're going to need to be able to do that before actually *blessing* your **ritual objects**.

The concept of *ley lines* provides a valuable example for a discussion of **sacred space**. Ley lines are apparent alignments of places of religious and cultural significance in the geography of a region. In Celtic regions and among the Chinese, they are often referred to as "dragon lines"; among the Aboriginal Peoples of Australia, they are known as "Songlines"; among the Native Americans of the American Southwest, they are known as "spirit lines". In almost every single one of these myriad cultures, one thing stands in common: they are most often associated with where a creator deity *touched* the earth, and in many of those circumstances, that deity was a *snake* or *serpent*, or, at the very least, *reptilian*. In most New Age traditions, ley lines are regarded as places of *liminality*: places where the veil between the worlds waxes thin; places that are *eternally between*, like Jormungandr.

When we work to create **sacred space**, we are essentially seeking to create our own "blip on the map"; our own *focal space* of *liminality*. We are asking Jormungandr to *touch* the space in which we stand, just as did those creator deities of those myriad other cultures when they created the ley lines. In many ways, we are like Thor: *fishing for Jormungandr*. And what does one do first, when fishing, after making sure one is braced for the big catch (**centered**)? You *bait the line*, right? While "baiting the World Serpent" might seem like a very uneasy metaphor at best, it is essentially precisely what we are doing when we do things such as light incense or play certain music that we know *will change the space* in which we stand (or sit), and *elevate it beyond the mundane*. That is all bait is, after all: something that we know is appealing to the fish. So the first step in creating **sacred space** is to **center**; the second step is to make the space *attractive* to

Jormungandr. We touched on the concept of finding what is *appealing* to the Gods in the chapter on **godfinding**, and I will be going into greater detail about my specific experiences (as well as the personal gnosis of myriad others) of what is attractive to specific deities throughout the course of the rest of this book. For our present purposes, we will work with what I have personally found to be "across the board attractive" to Jormungandr: a white candle. One white candle. It doesn't have to be anything fancy. It can be as simple as a tealight from your local dollar store. As with most things, ultimately, this action is about *intent*.

Begin by using the previous exercises to **center** yourself, and then light the white candle with the *intent* of *attracting* Jormungandr into your personal space. How do we *intend* that? Well, how do you *intend* anything? You *think about it very hard*, right? The same applies here. Light the candle and *intend* for it to *elevate* your personal space to a place *beyond the mundane*. Follow that by *laying your fence* (the "circle-casting" detailed earlier in this book in the **Good Versus Evil** Chapter). And then you do what every fisherman must do: you *wait*. Fishermen wait for the fish to arrive; fishing is an exercise in *patience*. Once you have **centered** yourself, and *cast your line* (by lighting the candle), and then *set your fence* (which, to continue the fishing metaphor, might equate to making sure your line is strong enough that it will not break should something "nasty" come along), you must *wait* for the *space to shift*. Trust me, you will *know* when your *space has shifted*. How will you *know*? **Sacred space** should *feel sacred*. That may seem like a very dumbed-down and almost trite response, but if you have ever experienced it within the context of ritual participation, you already know what I mean. For those who *haven't* ever experienced that, let me attempt here to explain an encounter with the *numinous* without sounding like some sort of New Age whackadoodle....

Rudolf Otto, the eminent German Lutheran theologian, philosopher, and comparative mythologist described the experience of the *numinous*—that is, the **sacred**; the *presence of Gods and liminality*—as the *mysterium tremendum et fascinans*: "a fearful and fascinating mystery". It is a *mysterium*, in that it is an experience of something that is *Wholly Other*, which we often experience with what he described as a "blank stupor". In other words, it arrives, and we react with *awe*, often in a "wtf just happened?" sort of way, or even more often with *silence*. It is *tremendum*, in that it presents with such overwhelming *power* that it actually might be quite *terrifying*. This is what causes that "hair standing up on the back of your neck" feeling in the presence of the *liminal*, or even in the presence of Deity. This is what causes us to have physical goosebumps. Finally, it is *fascinans*, in that we can feel a merciful graciousness even *beyond* that sense of terror; we can sense something *good* behind the *scary power*. When we feel the actual *arrival* of the *numinous*, it is first experienced as a *bubble of silence*—no matter how loud the music might be that we are playing within a ritual context, everything seems to be *eclipsed* by that very *Presence*. This is usually followed by the actual raising of the hairs on the back of your neck and physical symptoms, such as goosebumps. The very sense of the movement of *air* in the room may physically change. Finally, there is a sense of *well-being* which is both inexplicable and profound at the same time. I casually refer to it as the "*Bingo moment*", because it's very much a feeling of "hey, I just won something", moreso than a feeling of "God just hugged me" (although you may occasionally feel that as well). What you "won" just happens to be the establishment of **sacred space**. Sometimes, if you are truly blessed, you may also "win" an audience with the Gods.

Once Jormungandr "shows up", you are officially standing in **sacred space**, in a time *outside* of time, and, therefore, also in **sacred time**. Once Thor has caught Jormungandr, then what happens? Hymir, in terror, cuts the line, and Thor throws his hammer, Mjollnir, after the Serpent, right? Once you have established **sacred space** by "catching" Jormungandr, you will likewise "throw the hammer" by **hallowing** your space. Many Heathens have used the Hammer Rite to hallow space, from the 1970s forward. If you are familiar with that rite, which is not dissimilar from a Wiccan Quarter Call, and you feel comfortable performing it, even with all of its historical baggage, by all means: use it. However, that is *not* the sort of "hammer throw" that I am talking about here. We *are* going to use the "sign of the hammer", but in a different manner and for different (and perhaps more historically-correct) reasons.

The sign of the hammer, combined with the Tiwaz rune (for Tyr), and a cross (for Nerthus and the four directions) will be drawn in the air with your right hand (held open-face, in an almost "karate chop" manner), or with a **ritual object** (such as a gandr/wand, dagger, or, indeed, even a small hammer; more on ritual objects soon). We do this to *hold the space*—think of it as "setting the hook", so to speak. To *hallow* something is literally "to make it holy"; to set it apart for "holy use". So, why start with the hammer? Because both the Poetic and the Prose Eddas list at least *three occasions* when Mjollnir, Thor's Hammer, was used to *hallow* something, somewhere, or someone. In the *Thrymskvida*, it is used to hallow the bride (who just happens to be Thor in disguise). In the *Gylfaginning*, it is used to bless Thor's injured goat, and also to consecrate the funeral pyre of Baldur. So there is actual *historical basis* for using the hammer—or at least "hammer sign"--to bless, consecrate, and otherwise hallow. Then why follow it with Tiwaz and a cross? Tiwaz is a symbol of divine protection, as well as of justice and honor, associated with the God, Tyr. By using it to **hallow** your space, you are in effect "bolstering" the power of the "fence" you laid previously (using the Outsiders Caim), as well as stating to all in the Nine Realms that you come into this **sacred space** in the name of Justice, and with Honorable intent. Finally, the cross calls upon Nerthus, and symbolizes the four directions. We call Nerthus, that She may cleanse and heal the space that it is being hallowed. The cross is also the symbol of the *crossroads*, another traditional space of *liminality*. This final **hallowing** holds the space in very much the same way that "x marks the spot" on a map. It is, ultimately, a statement of "I am here", like that big red dot on a map in a shopping mall.

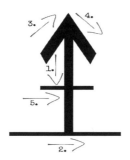

Once **sacred space** has been established, you may choose to spend time in prayer within it, or you may choose to bless your **ritual objects**, or do other workings. We'll talk about all of these things in greater detail in future chapters. For now, let's concentrate on actually *establishing* it in the first place. After you are "satisfied" that you have accomplished the creation of **sacred space** and **sacred time**, you will eventually need to return to the mundane by *closing* that space. You should begin this process by "raising the fence"--repeat the Outsider Caim, this time moving in the opposite direction in which you originally "laid the fence". Feel the energy of the space moving back *into you*. You may wish to *physically visualize* it as moving up, into the fingertips of your left hand, along your arm, and then coalescing down into a golden ball at the point of your navel (as previously discussed in the section on **grounding**), because that is the next thing we are going to do: we are going to **ground** that energy. In the next chapter, we'll discuss in great detail how to **ground** that energy into specific objects, such as your *stalli* (altar-space), but for now, follow the directions in the previous section on **grounding**, and send it down into the earth. Extinguish the candle which you lit at the beginning of establishing sacred space by *blowing it out*, sending those energies back, whence they came, with gratitude. If you still feel "jittery", even after having grounded the energy, **center** yourself again using the methods detailed previously in this chapter.

Quick Reference: Creating Sacred Space

Center

Seeker, Maker, Believer
(insert your own archetypes here):
My feet are on the ground;
I stand firm.
I am of the earth and the earth is of me;
I stand firm.
I center myself, and I hold.
So it is, and so it shall be.

Light one white candle with the intent of creating sacred space.

Lay the Fence: moving clockwise (use your right hand, and visualize protective white light flowing out the fingertips of that hand)

Outside the fire,
Darkness;
Darkness outside the Grove;
Outside there dwell shadows;
Shadows inside us as well.
Inside, outside, everywhere,
Where'er you dwell,
Dwell not here:
Here is light and all good things!
Light and Bright Wisdom protect us;
Protect us from those who dwell outside.

Wait for the space to shift.

Hallow the space with the Hallow Sigil. (use your right hand)

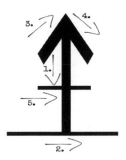

Spend time in Sacred Space.

Raise the Fence (use your left hand, and the Outsider Caim, imagining the energy of the space entering through the fingertips of that hand and coalescing at your navel)

Outside the fire,
Darkness;
Darkness outside the Grove;
Outside there dwell shadows;
Shadows inside us as well.
Inside, outside, everywhere,
Where'er you dwell,
Dwell not here:
Here is light and all good things!
Light and Bright Wisdom protect us;
Protect us from those who dwell outside.
This circle is open,
Yet never broken.
So it is, and so it shall be.

Ground

Center again, if necessary

Two questions frequently arise, when discussing the creation and use of **sacred space**: 1) Do I have to do this *every* time I work with the Gods/pray/etc.? And 2) How often *should* I actually do this? I personally find that, for the beginner, it is a good exercise to actually create and use **sacred space** *every* time you work for the first few months. It simply builds good method, while making sure you are well-protected, and developing your skills at the same time. Once you've "gotten the hang of it", however, no, it is absolutely not necessary *every* time. After the first three months or so, you may choose to only use it when you have a specific object you wish to bless, or when you are doing some sort of "major working" that requires a bit of "extra oomph" (and a bit of extra protection to go along with that "oomph"), or when embarking on a new relationship with a God you've only recently "met". You will find, as I have, that once you have created **sacred space** in the same place several times, the energy "hangs around": where you **ground** that energy, that energy tends to stay. Certainly, you can still "throw a hallow", if you feel so inclined, but after a few months of creating **sacred space** repeatedly in front of your altar-space, for example, you will find that every time you stand in that space, you can *feel* it *shift* when you pray or work. As an example, in our old house, my *stalli* was situated to the right and slightly behind me in my office. I called **sacred space** there, and subsequently **grounded** that energy, so many times, that sometimes in the midst of creating a piece of art or writing at my desk, I would literally *feel* that space *shift*. Sometimes, in the wee hours of the night, it caused me to actually look over my shoulder, to see who might have arrived there. Often, a Presence *had* actually arrived, though not always. Consequently, I frequently found myself wishing my altar was *not* in a space "just out of the corner of my eye"! When we moved, and I set up my new office, I was careful to position my altar within my sight-line, immediately to the left of my workspace. In other words: choose the "geography" of your **sacred space** more wisely than I have in the past!

Bite the tail:
Infinity.
Space between spaces;
Time between times.
I stand at the center,
And I hold.
Bite the tail:
Affinity.
Like begets like:
Kingship, kinship,
Blood and bone.
Bite the tail;
Sovereignty.
Space between spaces;
I stand enthroned.

Ritual Objects; Sacred Tools

Most books like this one would group your altar-space into the section on **sacred space**, however, as a practicing Norse Witch, I believe that *any space* can become **sacred space** with the proper preparation. Therefore, I am going to treat altar-space as precisely what it is, when all is said and done: another **ritual object** (or, indeed, the place where you keep your *collection* of them); a **sacred tool**. The variety of "*altar expressions*" in Norse Witchcraft is as individually unique as you are. In fact, you may find yourself maintaining *multiple* altar-spaces. You may, at the same time, maintain a *stalli* (interior altar-space, not completely dissimilar from any other Pagan-influenced faith's altar-space), a *ve* (outdoor altar-space), a *harrow* (outdoor altar-space focused towards the Landvaettir or the Ancestors), and even a *horgr* (a grove, not dissimilar from the Druidic practice). You may also find that you have multiples of one or more of those types: a *stalli* for your general practice, a *stalli* for Ancestor veneration, and a *stalli* for a specific Deity, all at the same time, for example. Norse Witchcraft is not a "one size fits all" religion, so why should our altar-space be "one size fits all" altar-space?

Your main indoor altar-space—henceforth referred to as the *Main Stalli*—will become the cornerstone of your practice. Coupled with your *Main Ve* (your primary outdoor altar-space), it should be one of the first two altar-spaces which you work to create. My own practice as a Norse Witch began *outside*, at what became my *Main Ve*, and then worked its way *inside*, to my *Main Stalli*, which lives in my office. It has grown by leaps and bounds since then!

Notice my use of the word "*lives*" in that next-to-last sentence, as well as the word "*grown*" there in that last one: I use this language because an altar is very much a *living thing*. It *grows* with you, as your practice and belief grows. As we discussed in the last chapter, it takes on a *character of its own*, the more frequently you create **sacred space** around it. While you may begin with the most basic of **ritual tools** (more about those in a moment), over time, you will find those tools joined on your altar by offerings of art, candles, and other objects which mean something *deep* to both you and your Gods—objects which, to the unwitting passerby, may seem like little more than odd tidbits of flotsam and jetsam, such as rocks, feathers, or even the occasional seashell, but to you and the Gods, have *ultimate meaning*. As you can (hopefully) see from the chronology of photos below, the *Main Stalli* of my home has not only changed shape due to a change in furniture (moving from the top of an old toy box trunk, to the first two shelves of a bookcase), but due to the nature of its use: from its original incarnation as a Druidic altar, to its current incarnation as the altar of a Norse Witch.

September, 2015

December, 2015

March, 2016

October, 2016

January, 2017   March, 2017

As you can likely also see from this chronology of photos, many of my **ritual tools** are the same in Norse Witchcraft as they were in Welsh Reconstructionist Druidry, though not all. The chalice, the blade, and the wand are used ritually not only in Norse Witchcraft, but also in Druidry and most forms of modern Neo-Paganism, including Wicca. What sets them apart as tools in Norse Witchcraft? How is their use different (or even the same) within this Tradition, versus those others? Let's start with their historical uses (as given to us in both the extant lore and the anthropological and archaeological record), and work our way forward.

The use of cups and drinking horns in a ritual manner is touched on heavily in our lore, and also evidenced in the anthropological and archaeological record. We are told in the *Heimskringla Saga*:

> Jarl Sigurd of Hlader was the greatest blot-man, and so was Hakon, his father. Jarl Sigurd held blot-feasts, all (led) by the hands of kings in Throndhjem. That was an ancient custom, (when) there was to be a blot, that all people should come where the hof was and live there for a time (literally: transfer their addresses there), bringing with them what they needed to stay while the blot lasted.

They knew that all men should bring beer with them; there was also killing of all sorts of sheep and horses; but the blood that came from them, then it was called "*hlaut*" (literally: "that which is alotted", which may be understood as "that which is set apart"), and *hlautbolli* ("hlaut-vessels"; "hlaut-bowls"), where the blood was kept, and *hlaut-teinar* ("hlaut-staves"; "hlaut-teins") were used to sprinkle it (literally: that was done to strike them); with that, together the altars (*stallana*) were reddened altogether, and also the walls of the temple, inside and outside, and so also the people (those gathered for the blot); but slaughter should be made for human consumption (implying that the flesh of the animals was then eaten by all gathered). A fire should then be struck in the middle of the floor of the temple and there kettles set over it; and all around the fire should be fire-bearers (which could suggest the reasons we often use fire now to bless or cleanse a space in modern Heathenry and Norse Witchcraft). But he who made the feast was (thus) chief of the temple (hof), then he should bless all of the blot-food. First, should Odin be toasted (raising a glass and drinking to the God as a sign of reverence), (next) should (come) that drink to Sigurd and the kings of his kingdom, but after (literally: since), Njordr, a toast (as with Odin, see above), and Freyr, a toast (again, see Odin), for peace and good seasons. Then there (were) many men that eagerly drank thereafter Bragi's toast.   Men drank in respect to their family members, their good ancestors, and past friends (literally: "those who had been called mine").

--*Heimskringla Saga 16*, translation mine.

From this passage, we can gather three ways of "*emptying the chalice*": the *sprinkling* of the liquid as a blessing on an altar-space, temple-structure, and gathered ritual participants; the *drinking* of the liquid with *intent* (as when toasts are made), and, finally, the *pouring* of the liquid onto the ground or into a secondary bowl (from which it might be poured outdoors afterwards; note: this use is *inferred)*. Within the ritual context of this passage, it is also suggested that one may have *more than one chalice* (having different ones set aside for specific purposes, as with an *oath-chalice*, or a *remembrance chalice*), and we are introduced to two other **ritual tools**: the *hlautboll* ("hlaut bowl") and the *hlaut-tein* ("hlaut tein" or "hlaut stave").

From this passage, we can also ascertain that the **blot** (pronounced *bloat*) is the primary form of *ritualized votive action* in Norse Tradition. Often mistranslated to mean *blood*, the ancient Norse and Proto-Germanic word *blot* actually translates literally as *sacrifice*, *offering*, or *worship*. As can hopefully be learned from the last three sentences of the previous paragraph from *Heimskringla Saga 16*, blood was patently *not* required for the performance of blot! In fact, any liquid or item (such as incense, candles, artwork, etc.) which has been made *hlaut* ("set apart"; i.e., "sacred" or "holy") may be *offered* in blot. Some people like to employ a lot of "pomp and circumstance" when it comes to pouring (or otherwise offering) blot. I am not, generally, one of those people. So long as I have boots on when it snows, I consider myself "dressed up" enough to go out and meet my Gods! I never write down what I am going to say for blot; I know Their kennings well enough. Generally, I will greet each God/dess in turn, employing either a traditional kenning or one They've taught me that They like/prefer, toast them, take a sip, and then say what is on my heart, before pouring a small offering of liquid onto the ground beside my *ve*. I neither use an offering bowl nor "sprinkle" (the actual term is *asperge*) myself; I prefer to please the Gods by feeding my local Landvaettir, as well as Them. When I have honored all that I need to honor, and said all that is on my heart, I offer a final toast to the Aesir, Vanir, and Rokkr, offer up my blessings and gratitude, and come back inside. Once I'm settled (chalice has been cleaned; bottle of seawater has been returned to its place on the *stalli*), I prepare a second blot of a burnt offering of incense in a small charcoal-style burner. This creates a need to tend what is burning to *keep* it burning, which makes me feel like more of an active participant. I also re-light my candles for Freyja, Freyr, and Njordr (which I faithfully extinguish before going outside for the initial pouring of blot!).

Basic Blot-Pour

Hail (Deity name, kennings)!

Drink a small amount of the liquid.

I make this humble offering in gratitude for (thank Them for all of the things in your life which you know They have imparted to you). (If you have petitions for that Deity—things you *need* them to bring into your life—speak these only after thanks have been given. Speak all of these things from your heart of hearts.)

Pour a small amount of the liquid onto the ground or into a hlaut-boll.

(Repeat individually for each God/dess to Whom you are making offerings.)

Hail to the Aesir! Hail to the Vanir! Hail to the Rokkr!

Drink a small amount of the liquid.

Peace and good seasons in my life;
Peace and good seasons in the lives of all those I
  hold dear,
And even in the lives of the Gods Themselves!
Blessed be!

Pour the remainder of the liquid onto the ground or into a hlaut-boll.

The ritual use of blades is not so clearly illuminated in the lore, although, certainly, to make such blood sacrifices as are mentioned in *Heimskringla Saga* and elsewhere, some sort of sharp-edged tool was required. Most modern Heathens—Norse Witches or otherwise—no longer practice blood sacrifice, although, certainly, there are some who maintain an agricultural lifestyle (i.e., farmers) who, when the time comes to slaughter their pigs, goats, or other livestock, will offer up at least one in sacrifice, as is appropriate. What the lore does not tell us about the blades used at sacrificial festivals like the one detailed in the *Heimskringla Saga*, it certainly elaborates upon when dealing with other weapons, such as Thor's Hammer (Mjollnir), Odin's Spear (Gungnir), and even Freyr's Sword (in some sources, called Summarbrandr). We also have significant evidence from the archaeological record that blades were of ritual importance to the Norse and Germanic tribes. Numerous swords, spears, and daggers have been found in Viking Era graves which evidence the "ritual killing" of the weapon. So far, scholars have not been able to completely ascertain the purpose of these "ritual killings" of weapons, wherein the weapon in question has been purposefully broken or bent so that it is no longer of use. Some have speculated this was done to deter grave robbers (so that they could not break into a grave, and come out armed), or to prevent the soul of the deceased from being able to return from the grave and do harm. Still other scholars have suggested that the sword, dagger, or spear was considered an actual *extension* of the deceased, and was therefore "*ensouled*", thus needing to be "ritually slain" to match the physical status (i.e., dead) of its owner. Insofar as other weapons besides the dagger/blade, we have numerous references in the lore (as previously discussed) of the use of Mjollnir (Thor's Hammer) to *hallow* things, places, and people. Therefore, many modern Heathens substitute the use of a small hammer, rather than using a blade. Within Norse Witchcraft, there is room for the use of both or either.

The *ensouling* of objects is a cross-cultural concept, encountered in many societies whose belief systems focus on *animism*. *Animism* is the belief that there are *spirits in all things* —to be alive and conscious is not exclusively a *human* thing. Everything—rocks, trees, animals, and, yes, even the occasional inanimate object, such as your chalice or other ritual tools--has the capacity and the potential to *communicate* and *interact* with every other thing. Our Norse Tradition is profoundly *animistic*: one need look no further than our belief in *wights* and even the

Landvaettir themselves to see that this is true. An *ensouled* object becomes a *social agent*. That is, while not regarded as being fully "alive" in the human or animal sense, it is understood that the object itself becomes worthy of *respectful interaction*—it becomes as much a "part of us" as we are of it, in effect becoming almost a sort of non-human "relative". An *etiquette* develops, as to how we are to treat that object, once it has become *ensouled*, in the same way that we have an *etiquette* for how we are to treat other humans, or animals, or Nature Itself, not because we have somehow magickally bound a *specific spirit* to that object, but because we have, through use and veneration, *awakened* the spirit of that object, which already lay within.

One of the primary proofs that our Ancestors believed in the *ensoulment* of objects is that they *named* those objects: Odin's spear was called *Gungnir*; Thor's hammer was called *Mjollnir*, etc. Over time, your ritual objects may also "tell you" their names. You may find, like Odin and Thor, that your "weapons"--your dagger or hammer, and your wand—are a bit less reluctant to "divulge their identities". That has certainly been the case with my dagger—her name is *Runargild* ("worthy of secrets"). I personally choose to work with a dagger rather than a hammer for two reasons. First, from the very beginnings of my journey down this path, when I was still a practicing Druid, I identified very heavily with the warrior caste of the Celts, and specifically with the Fianna, and in our Grove the use of a dagger rather than a wand was symbolic of that. Second, a dagger is what I can *afford*. *Runargild* is a simple boot-knife, with a synthetic wood handle (yes, I know that's naughty; again, it's what I could *afford*), in a simple Scottish dirk style that feels very comfortable in my hand, as though she is an extension of *me* (which is very important with whatever you choose, when it comes to daggers, hammers, and wands). She has served me well, particularly when it comes to providing a *physical cue* in my laying and raising of the fence, but also with hallowing. Even if you choose to go the more traditional route and procure a hammer, you may also wish to maintain a dagger for that simple reason: to act as a *physical cue* in ritual. A wand may serve the same purpose. Too often, we humans have a nasty habit of underestimating our own *power*: we have a hard time visualizing energy coursing through us, and then "shooting" out of our fingertips. We have this internal programming which makes such a concept seem somehow pretentious. But we can supplant that programming sometimes through the use of a *physical cue*, such as a dagger or wand, when working in a ritual setting.

Obviously, wands are an important tool to the Norse Witch. They also have a very definite historical basis, within our Norse Tradition. The very name of Jormungandr can, in fact, be translated as "the great *wand*", and we are told that one of Odin's kennings was "*Gandlir*": Wand-wielder. The Volur (plural of *volva*) were a group of (mostly) women who used wands in their ritual working. In fact, the literal translation of *volva* is either "wand-wed", "wand-wielder", or "staff-carrier", depending on the source being used. In Chapter Four of the *Saga of Eric the Red,* we are given a detailed description of such a woman:

> A Syr-woman (literally: sow-woman, "Syr" is a kenning of Freyja, so this may be taken as "A Freyja's Woman") there was in the settlement, who was called Thorbjorg. She was a spae-woman and was called "little volva". She had as her family nine sisters, and they were all spae-women, but she was the only one who still lived.

> There was a custom of Thorbjorg during winter, that she travel around to the feasts, and the people invited her into most of their homes, for they were curious to know their Orlog or about coming seasons (phrasing of the Old Norse here suggests "seasons to come"; "future"; implies "fortune-telling"). And thus since Thorkell was master-farmer (yeoman) in that place, then he thought he should come to know, how soon the unseasonable weather (literally: un-season) would lighten, or how to overcome them, for they had swept over the land like a herd of horses (this beautiful double meaning is implied through the use of the phrase *sem yfir stodh* in the original Old Norse). Thorkell invited the spae-woman to his home, and she was welcomed there, as was the custom, when a woman of that kind should be received. The high seat was prepared for her and under her was laid a cushion. (There should be hens-feathers.)

> But when she came in the evening, with that man, who had been sent to meet her, then she was made ready, and she wore a blue cloak covered in straps, and stones

were set all over her skirt. She had at her neck glazed glass (beads; archaeological evidence from various women's graves across Scandinavia suggest that these may have been blue as well, and imported from Mesopotamia or Egypt), a black lambskin hood was on her head, with white catskin inside. And she had a staff in her hand, and there was a knob on it. It was fashioned from brass and stones were set upon the knob. She had a girdle of amadou ("horse fungus" or "tinder fungus", a precious resource for the starting of fires), and there was a large skin bag hanging from it, and she kept in it her *taufar* (literally: talismans or fetishes), those ones she needed for her wisdom. She had boots of calfskin and smelt (a type of fish; fish-skin was likely used for the soles of the boots) on her feet with long thongs which had tin buttons on the ends. She had on her hands catskin gloves, and they were white inside and furry. --Translation Mine

Wands/distaffs have also been found by archaeologists in at least forty different graves, including Grave Four in Fyrkat, Denmark-- a former Viking ring castle, dating to 980 AD. Grave 4, the most lavish grave at the site, is a woman's grave. She was buried in a wagon, and clad in a long gown of blue and red, adorned with golden thread, and she wore silver toe rings on her toes. At her head was found a Gotlandic buckle, similar to the "pillboxes" often found in the possession of 19th century ladies. This box-brooch contained a concentration of white lead—a white dye used for more than 2000 years as a "skin ointment" or women's make-up. At her feet was found a larger box, which contained her "magical tools", or, more properly, *taufar*: an owl pellet, small bones from birds and mammals, and a pouch of henbane (if thrown into a fire, these seeds create a hallucinogenic effect), which she may have used in conjunction with the aforementioned white lead to create a skin ointment similar to the mythic "witches' salve" of later historical periods. As if previously clasped in her hand, a small silver amulet of a chair (possibly representing the High Seat) was found, and at her side one of the more famous artifacts from this excavation: a metal wand consisting of an iron stick with bronze fittings. Two small bronze bowls, likely from Central Asia, were also found in her grave.

These last two pieces of evidence for the historically-based use of a wand by modern Norse Witches also include evidence to substantiate another important tool: the *bag* or the *box*, or both. We know that the Celts (and modern Druids) carry a *crane-bag*, in emulation of the great Celtic hero, Fionn MacCumhaill, who carried the *corrbolg* (literally "crane-skin bag", a bag made of crane-skin) gifted to him by his father, Tadg mac Nuadat. The corrbolg of Irish legend was made by Manannan Mac Lir (the Irish "god of the sea") out of the skin of Aoife, who had been turned into a crane by the jealous Iuchra. She lived as a crane for two hundred long years, and then, at her death, Manannan made the corrbolg from her skin and within it, "he placed every precious treasure that he had" (*The Poem-Book of Fionn*). The bag detailed as hanging at the waist of the volva Thorbjorg in the *Saga of Eric The Red* and the box found at the feet of the Fyrkat Seeress in Denmark suggest similar uses. Therefore, another important tool of the Norse Witch is the *skin-bag* or *seer's box*.

Quick Reference: A Norse Witch's Ritual Tools

Chalice/Drinking Horn
Dagger/Hammer
Wand/Gandr
Bowl
Tein
Skin-Bag/Seer's Box

If there is one ritual tool that you "can't be Norse without", it would be the chalice, drinking horn, or goblet. The three forms of *emptying the chalice* detailed in the *Heimskringla Saga* still remain as the centerpiece of ritual observances within a Norse Tradition. This holds true in Norse Witchcraft. The first **ritual tool** you should work to procure is a chalice of some sort. For those of you on a budget, there is absolutely nothing wrong with resorting to a wine or tea glass from your local dollar store. In fact, I used one of those for quite a long time before I was able to procure the silver chalice (decorated with a raven) which I now use. Once you have gotten a chalice, the next step is to *bless* it, for it will also become one of the primary mechanisms for *blessing* your other **ritual tools**, including your altar-space.

In the last chapter, I promised that in future I would teach you how to **ground** energy into a ritual item. That is precisely what we are going to do to *bless* and *ensoul* your chalice. First, fill your chalice with something pleasing to you (or, if you already have an inkling to which Gods you might be dedicating yourself later, a liquid which would be pleasing to Them). Begin by **centering** yourself as previously instructed. Follow the steps in **Quick Reference: Creating Sacred Space** in the last chapter. Once you have established sacred space, "laid the fence", and the space has *shifted*, perform the Hallow Sign to seal the space. You will then hold your arms out and down, so that your entire body holds the shape of the rune Tiwaz for a space of several moments. *Physically visualize* the sacred energy of the space as golden light being drawn up into your body through the fingertips of your left hand. Move the energy across your body and down to the fingertips of your right hand, but do not "release" the energy yet. Now, still visualizing that energy collected there in the fingertips of your right hand, draw the Hallow Sign again, over your chalice, and as you do so, *release* the golden light into the sigil *as you draw it onto* the chalice and *into* the liquid within it. Now, slowly raise the chalice with both hands above your head and hold it there for a few moments in offering and also so that it can be *recognized* by the Gods. Bring it slowly down, and make a toast to the Aesir, the Vanir, and the Rokkr ("Hail to the Aesir! Hail to the Vanir! Hail to the Rokkr!") and then drink the liquid within. When you are finished, replace it on your altar (or onto whatever space you are presently using). Complete the remainder of the **Creating Sacred Space** rite by "raising the fence". When you reach the final step of **grounding**, take your right hand, and place it onto your chalice. Instead of visualizing the energy flowing out of your root chakra as you normally would, instead visualize it flowing up from your navel to your right shoulder, down through your right arm, and *out* through your right fingertips (as you did a moment ago with the Hallow Sign). When you feel that you have released all of the excess energy into the chalice, you may choose to **center** again, if you feel it is necessary. I personally recommend using your chalice in the pouring of blot several times before using it to charge your other **ritual tools** or your altar-space. This gives it the opportunity to gain a "heftier charge" before using it in a blessing. It also gives it the time to become *ensouled*.

Once your chalice has become *ensouled*, the first thing which you will use it to bless is your *Main Stalli*—your primary indoor altar-space. You may choose to use the **Creating Sacred Space** rite and perform the blessing during the "spend time in sacred space" portion of it, but if you have already repeated that process several times in front of your stalli, this may not be necessary. Raise your chalice and perform blot as you normally would, only without pouring. The process of *emptying the chalice* this time will be by *drinking with intent*. Do not drink it all! When you have given reverence to all you wish to show reverence, and have said all that is on your heart, you will take the last remnants which remain in your chalice and carefully begin to sprinkle or smear them onto your stalli with the fingertips of your right hand, **grounding** the energy of your blot into your altar-space. You may use the rite that follow for your blessing, or use it as a guide from which to compose your own. Whichever you choose, close with the Hallow Sign. When you have finished the blessing, leave what remains in your chalice on your altar overnight, and pour it at your *Main Ve* (outdoor altar-space) the next day, with a toast of gratitude to the Aesir, Vanir, and Rokkr.

Stalli Blessing

(Top shelf or primary work surface)
In the names of the Aesir,
And in the names of the Vanir,
And even in the names of the Rokkr,
I call a blessing on this space,
That it be a place beyond places,
Standing in a time beyond time.

(Second shelf, secondary work surface, or base)
In the names of the Aesir,
And in the names of the Vanir,
And even in the names of the Rokkr,
I call a blessing on this space:
Odin, gift me Wisdom as I work here;
Tyr, gift me Honor and Justice;
Thor, grant this space both Simplicity and Power.

(Left side)
In the names of the Aesir,
And in the names of the Vanir,
And even in the names of the Rokkr,
I call a blessing on this space:
Freyr, grant that my work here bear fruit;
Freyja, help me stand between and see;
Njordr, bring peace to my heart when here I stand.

(Right side)
In the names of the Aesir,
And in the names of the Vanir,
And even in the names of the Rokkr,
I call a blessing on this space:
Loki, help me work here with Humility;
Sigyn, gift me with Compassionate Will;
Angrbodha, great Chieftain of the Iron Wood,
Teach me the Strength of my Duality,
As I work here in this place beyond places,
Standing in a time beyond time.
(Hallow Sign)

Once you have procured your dagger and/or hammer and your wand (we'll talk more thoroughly about *focused wands* in a later chapter), you will need to *bless* them and *ensoul* them, in the same way as you did your chalice. **Center** and then follow the steps in **Creating Sacred Space**, which should be thoroughly familiar to you by now. Once you have thrown the Hallow Sign, stand as you did when blessing your chalice, in the shape of the rune Tiwaz. *Physically visualize* the sacred energy of the space as golden light being drawn up into your body through the fingertips of your left hand. Move the energy across your body and down to the fingertips of your right hand, but do not "release" the energy yet. As you did previously when blessing your chalice, visualize that energy collected there in the fingertips of your right hand, and draw the Hallow Sign again, over your chalice, and as you do so, *release* the golden light into the sigil *as you draw it onto* the chalice and *into* the liquid within it. Now, slowly raise the chalice with both hands above your head and hold it there for a few moments in offering and also so that it can be *recognized* by the Gods. Bring it slowly down, and make a toast to the Aesir, the Vanir, and the Rokkr ("Hail to the Aesir! Hail to the Vanir! Hail to the Rokkr!") and then drink a small portion of the liquid within. You will now take the chalice, and with the fingers of your right hand, draw the Hallow Sign onto your dagger, hammer, or wand. When you are finished, replace the chalice on your altar. Complete the remainder of the **Creating Sacred Space** rite by "raising the fence". When you reach the final step of **grounding**, take your right hand, and place it onto your dagger, hammer, or wand. **Ground** the excess energy of the rite into your dagger, hammer, or wand, in the same way that you did when blessing your chalice. When you feel that you have released all of the excess energy into your dagger, hammer, or wand, you may choose to **center** again, if you feel it is necessary. You will then *ensoul* your tool through constant and consistent use, as you did with your chalice. If you are truly blessed, hopefully it will tell you its proper name!

Quick Reference: Blessing Ritual Objects

Center

Seeker, Maker, Believer
(insert your own archetypes here):
My feet are on the ground;
I stand firm.
I am of the earth and the earth is of me;
I stand firm.
I center myself, and I hold.
So it is, and so it shall be.

Light one white candle with the intent of creating sacred space.

Lay the Fence, moving clockwise (use your right hand, and visualize protective white light flowing out the fingertips of that hand)

Outside the fire,
Darkness;
Darkness outside the Grove;
Outside there dwell shadows;
Shadows inside us as well.
Inside, outside, everywhere,
Where'er you dwell,
Dwell not here:
Here is light and all good things!
Light and Bright Wisdom protect us;
Protect us from those who dwell outside.

Wait for the space to shift.

Hallow the space with the Hallow Sigil. (use your right hand)

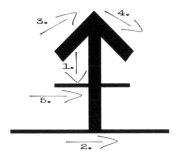

Place your body in the position of the rune, Tiwaz. Visualize the energy of the sacred space which you have just created as golden light, moving up through the fingertips of your left hand, and across your body to the fingertips of your right hand (or to the dagger, wand, or hammer in your right hand, if you have already procured, blessed, and ensouled that tool)

Visualize the energy flowing down and releasing from your right hand (or the tip of a physical foci, such as a dagger), and draw the Hallow Sign over your chalice and see it infusing the liquid within.

Raise your chalice over your head with both hands, and hold it there for several moments.

Lower the chalice slowly to a "toasting position", and say, with intent:

Hail to the Aesir! Hail to the Vanir! Hail to the Rokkr!

Drink a small portion of the liquid.

With the fingertips of your right hand, take a small portion of the liquid from the chalice and with wet fingertips **draw the Hallow Sign** onto the object which you wish to bless. (If the item cannot withstand exposure to liquid, carefully draw the Hallow Sign in the air with your fingertips, being wary of dripping on the item that you are blessing.)

Replace the blessed item on your altar, as well as your chalice.

Raise the Fence (use your left hand, and the Outsider Caim, imagining the energy of the space entering through the fingertips of that hand and coalescing at your navel)

Outside the fire,
Darkness;
Darkness outside the Grove;
Outside there dwell shadows;
Shadows inside us as well.
Inside, outside, everywhere,
Where'er you dwell,
Dwell not here:
Here is light and all good things!
Light and Bright Wisdom protect us;
Protect us from those who dwell outside.
This circle is open,
Yet never broken.
So it is, and so it shall be.

Move the energy from Raising The Fence across your body, releasing it through the fingertips of your right hand into the object which you have just hallowed, and ground the energy into the item.

Center again, if necessary.

Ensoul the object through consistent reverential use.

It was the tradition of the Norse Ancestors to often use a bowl (hlaut-boll) and tein (hlaut-tein; sometimes spelled "tine") when blessing objects, places, and people. I have not used these items often in my own practice, but you may find them useful in your own. You should bless them the same way as any other ritual item, using the **Quick Reference** above. Any sort of bowl will work; I personally use a cast iron cauldron most routinely, but I have also used a Tibetan singing bowl (I will cover "bowl-work" in greater detail later in this book). For the tein, it is traditional to use a natural leafy sprig, which you can easily find literally in your own backyard. I have a small twig of pine driftwood which I found on a rocky beach in Maine which I occasionally use for this purpose. **Remember:** Whatever you choose to use for a tein should be *food safe*: that is, *non-poisonous*! You don't want to stick anything in your bowl or chalice that you would not likewise stick in your mouth without fear of damaging yourself from its residue!

While I use neither tein nor bowl routinely in my practice, the other ritual tool which I have found almost as indispensable as my chalice in my practice is my *skin-bag*. Whereas your other ritual tools are items which you may use only when performing more ritualized devotional acts, your *skin-bag* (or your *seer's box*, or, possibly, both), like your altar, is one which will come to *live* and *grow* with you. I have personally maintained a *skin-bag* or a *seer's box*, in some form or another, for the past twenty-four years. You can use any small bag or pouch for a *skin-bag*; how big it needs to be depends upon how easily you wish to conceal it when carried. My present bag is a leather "medicine bag", made from a kit purchased from Tandy Leather. A *seer's box*, likewise, may be whatever size best fits your needs. You may find yourself maintaining more than one of either of these—perhaps one to keep on your altar at all times, plus one to carry with you on your person, or, in the case of the *seer's box*, perhaps ones with specific purposes (not dissimilar from a "spell box" in modern Neo-Pagan/Wiccan practices). What does one put into their bag and/or box? **Items of intent**: items which hold a particular *deep* meaning to you, or which represent things which you wish to draw into your life, such as stones (perhaps a rose quartz to draw clarity in relationships, for example), rune stones, small items etched with *galdrastafir* (more on these later in this book), small fetish objects associated with your *fylgja* or your "totem" (which are *not* the same thing; more on this later in the book as well), candle-drippings from your altar-work, etc. *As you go, you will gather.* As an example: my present bag contains a small wooden carving of the Helm of Awe, candle-burnings from my altar-work, a piece of Norwegian Moonstone, and a stone from the grave of writer Louisa May Alcott (among other items). The *bag* and *box* are not only ritual tools, but also **power objects**: objects which act as a foci for both the meaning and the power to *connect* to those things/people/places represented symbolically by the items within. Those items which we place within our *bags* and *boxes* create *relationship* with those things they symbolically (or perhaps even directly) represent, allowing us to become correlated with those representations *ourselves*, and directly *connect* to those energies. This is a form of *sympathetic magick*. *Sympathetic magick* is, according to noted Witch, Teacher, and Founder of the Temple of Witchcraft, Christopher Penczak:

> **Sympathetic magic:** A technique in magic in which a small symbolic ritual action mimics the larger real-world event you desire to manifest. The smaller ritual is said to be in "sympathy", or resonating, with the forces necessary to manifest the larger event. (Example:) A ritual in which water is poured onto the ground to produce rain could be an act of sympathetic magic.

It is not through some "mystical juju belief" that our *bags* and *boxes* make us stronger; on the contrary, it has actually been scientifically proven that such **power objects** have a direct effect on the parasympathetic nervous system, creating very real effects on our health and well-being.

Wight-Walking

Wights: for the modern reader, the word too often calls to mind visions of the ancient undead, *somethings* perhaps a bit worse even than zombies, thanks to the writings of J.R.R. Tolkien and George R.R. Martin, but for those of us who follow a Norse Path, that is not what they actually are at all. Certainly, we have such things as the *draugr* in our Tradition as well, but those are in most ways the complete opposite of what the word *wight* deeply means to us. The word *wight* itself actually translates literally to "thing, object, creature", and is most often given in the Old Norse as *vaet* instead, as in *Landvaettir*. These are the spirits of Nature itself: of the Land, of the home, of trees and rocks and growing things; of animals, and, yes, ultimately, of us and of the Gods.

Part of the process of creating and maintaining a *skin-bag* is what I refer to as "feeding the bag": the "stuff" within has to come from somewhere, after all. The most effective method of actively performing that "feeding" is a process which I have come to call **wight-walking**. A "wight-walk" is the Norse-derived equivalent of what some Native Americans might call a "Medicine Walk". Before embarking, you should make sure that you have something appropriate to offer as a gift to your local wights—*gratitude* is one of the cornerstones of our belief system: *a gift for a gift*. You should also spend some time *utiseta*, which literally means "sitting out" or "powering down", depending on the source referenced.

Utiseta usually involves finding a quiet space outdoors in which to sit, but I have found that the experience can be equally rewarding if done indoors (perhaps even moreso, if you're mortally terrified of most insects, as I am!). In *Islendingabok*, the author-priest Ari Thorgilsson also refers to this process as "*going under the cloak*", as he tells of the process as it was undertaken by Thorgeirr The Lawspeaker when he was forced to make the decision as to whether or not Iceland should become a Christian nation. Actually wrapping yourself in a cloak or blanket (or, as we did as children, building an indoor tent between chairs) is not a requirement for *utiseta*, but it *can* assist you with an additional measure of sensory deprivation, which you might find helpful. To observe **utiseta**, you will need a quiet place where you are not likely to be disturbed. I would strongly encourage using the ritual for **Creating Sacred Space** detailed in earlier chapters. At the very least, you should make sure that you **center** before *entering the silence* of utiseta. Rhythmic breathing will help you to keep your mind from wandering; this is very much a Norse-derived form of *meditation*. I find inhaling for a count of four, holding the breath for a count of four, and then exhaling for a count of four while repeating the words "contract" and "expand" in my mind keeps me focused. And then you *sit*, and you *wait*, with *intention*. What *intention*? That may vary depending on *why* you are undertaking your *wight-walk*, or why you are observing *utiseta* in the first place. You may seek gifts from the Gods themselves, or from the Landvaettir, or from your *fylgja*, or the animal wights which have become your "totems". If you wait *long enough*, answers *will* come. Once you have received the information that you require, close the space with loving gratitude, and embark upon your wight-walk with the understanding that whatever guidance has been asked *will be given*.

Why **utiseta** before a **wight-walk**? Also: is this necessary before *every* wight-walk that you undertake? The point of *utiseta* before a *wight-walk* is to effectively "touch base" with the Gods, Landvaettir, your *fylgja*, or other wights from whom you seek guidance or gifts (items that will improve your focus, and therefore, go to live in your *skin-bag* or *seer's box* for future use). Some people may find that simply going for the walk *without* first sitting results in nothing more than just that: a very pleasant walk in nature. Over time, you will become more acquainted with the *process* of wight-walking, and learn to read the "signals" that you encounter while doing so. You will begin to familiarize yourself with how it *feels*, intuitively, when something has been placed in your path as a *gift*. Once you begin to develop these skills, you may find that you no longer require *utiseta* before wight-walking.

The walk itself should be purposeful and attentive. Be sure to focus your attention on the ground as you walk your path, but do not become so focused on it that you miss any animals or birds in the trees and sky around you. Pay attention to the flow of the wind; to the sound of things moving in the underbrush; to the songs of the birds. Note the directions from which certain things come—whether that be birdsong or the wind—as this may also be important. There are a wide variety of websites which discuss the symbolism of natural phenomena as it is experienced from specific directions, and I also highly recommend procuring a copy of Ted Andrews' *Animal Speak*. While it is written from a primarily Native American perspective, it is also written from a highly *animistic* perspective, and contains a ton of valuable information that you may use when interpreting the experiences and gifts that you receive on your wight-walks.

When you are given a gift on a wight-walk, be certain that you leave *a gift for a gift*. You may find it helpful to actually carry a small pouch of something for this very purpose *within* your *skin-bag*, which you should definitely bring with you on your walk. Tobacco is a traditional offering to the Landvaettir among the Native Americans, and is easy to carry in your bag. Birdseed also makes a fine offering. As a wight-walking Norse Witch who is also an avid birdwatcher, I do not advocate the leaving of bread, unless it has been finely crumbed, as bread can actually expand in the throats and stomachs of birds and be lethal. Obviously, it is important that whatever gifts you leave *help* the environment in which they are left, rather than doing harm.

As moderns, most of us do not tend to be well-acquainted at all with an *animistic worldview*, and consequently when we consider doing something such as *wight-walking*, we often work from a place of certain *stereotypes*. The primary *stereotype* most often associated with *animism* in the modern mind is that of the *totem animal*, typically understood from a Native American perspective of what those words mean. While the word *totem* itself is actually sourced from the Ojibwe word *dodaem*, the concept of the totem animal itself is by no means limited to the Native American traditions. In fact, the concept is found throughout many world cultures which are equally *animistic*, including tribal cultures in Africa, Asia, Australia, the Arctic, and, yes, even Europe. The use of the word *totem*, however, is strictly a Native American term. Within Norse-derived traditions, these "spirit animals" are either referred to as *animal wights*, in which case they may "behave" very much like the totems of Native American cultures, or they are associated with the *fylgja*, which is one of the four parts of the Norse definition of the "soul". To avoid further confusion, animals to be understood as "totem animals" will henceforth be referred to in this book with the Old Norse term: *dyr-andi*; "animal spirit".

A person's *dyr-andi* and a person's *fylgja* are very different from one another. The *dyr-andi* is an *external entity*—that is, it is a guide *separate* from your own personal identity, and may actually appear repeatedly in your path *as a physical animal*. You may find that your *dyr-andi* (or *dyr-andar*, as you may discover that you have more than one) changes over time, dependent upon the guidance needed. Your *fylgja*, however, is *not* an *exterior entity*: it is a part of your "*soul*", inextricably bound to *who you truly are*, and *will not change* over the course of your lifetime. While the *fylgja may* be encountered in the physical world, if you are lucky enough to have that happen, it will most likely *not* appear as a physical entity, but rather ghost- or wraith-like. We may actively work to *seek out* our *dyr-andar* during *utiseta* and subsequent *wight-walking*. Our *fylgja*, however, must be *revealed* to us: it comes from *within*, rather than *without*. For the rest of this chapter, we will be focusing on the *dyr-andi*, rather than the *fylgja*. Finding one's *fylgja* is a deeper sort of work, which is outside the scope of this book.

My original teacher on a *shamanic path* was my "host", Michelle Iacona, and my first shamanic experience involved *utiseta* to meet my *dyr-andi* and subsequent *wight-walking*, although those weren't the words we used back then. Twenty-three years ago, when I had that experience, I was "meditating to find my totem animal" before going on a "Medicine Walk". The experience was profound and powerful, and, in fact, my first inclination that a *shamanic path* was what I needed in my life. In case you haven't figured it out already, Norse Witchcraft is a *profoundly* shamanic path. What exactly does that mean? Many people live with the false belief that *shamanism* is culturally owned by the Native Americans, but that could not be more incorrect. The word *shaman* is actually of Tungusic Evenki origin —a tribe which lives in North Asia (i.e., Siberia). A path that is *shamanic* focuses heavily on trancework, spirit journeys, and ecstatic religious experiences; usually the faith-base is strongly *animistic*, and generally such faith-systems stem from tribal societies. It is easily gathered from a study of the lore, as well as of the archaeological and anthropological record, that any Norse-derived Tradition must *necessarily* also be *shamanic*, as our Norse

Ancestors' belief system most certainly held strong shamanic themes and practices. It is neither contrived nor accidental, therefore, that my first steps along a shamanic path, though "dressed up" in different language, are the same as those steps I continue to take as a Norse Witch.

Let us sit, then, together, and experience this first *utiseta* with the same guided meditation with which I was first introduced to this larger world. Afterwards, I invite you to take your own *skin-bag* or *seer's box* and go outside, in nature, and go *wight-walking*. Accept your first gifts from your *dyr-andi*, and keep them close to you always. And do not forget to *leave a gift for your gift*.

Dyr-Andi Útiseta

Center yourself:

Seeker, Maker, Believer
(insert your own archetypes here):
My feet are on the ground;
I stand firm.
I am of the earth and the earth is of me;
I stand firm.
I center myself, and I hold.
So it is, and so it shall be.

Lay The Fence:

Outside the fire,
Darkness;
Darkness outside the Grove;
Outside there dwell shadows;
Shadows inside us as well.
Inside, outside, everywhere,
Where'er you dwell,
Dwell not here:
Here is light and all good things!
Light and Bright Wisdom protect us;
Protect us from those who dwell outside.

Take a deep breath. Hold it for a count of four. Let your mind focus on the word *Contract* or *Ebb*. Exhale for four counts. Let your mind focus on the word *Expand* or *Flow*. Repeat. *Contract. Expand. Ebb. Flow. Contract. Expand. Ebb. Flow.* Come into the quiet spaces of your mind and heart. Before you, there stands a tree: the tallest tree that you have ever seen; its roots sunk deeper than the deepest earth; its branches overreaching high as the highest of skies. You know that it is Yggdrasil, and you know that you now stand on the Midgard Plane. You know that you are safe; that you are caim-bound, and protected.

Approach the World Tree. In the branches on high, an eagle perches, with a rooster seated atop its head. Four deer nibble upon the ripe shoots of new growth among the roots, as well as overhead, as they gallop through the canopy of the Great Tree. As you take a seat beside the trunk of the tree, a squirrel runs past on his way downwards, through a cavernous hole in the roots. And as you settle in, you feel those roots rumble, as a dragon moves beneath. But none of these are the guide you seek. You have come here, seeking your dyr-andi, your spirit animal. Focus your mind on that purpose: *dyr-andi, dyr-andi, dyr-andi.* As you sit, patiently waiting, you sense movement close by. You pay careful attention to the direction from which the movement comes: does it hail from the North? The East? The South? The West? As it moves closer, you begin to make out its shape. It is an animal, and you recognize the kind. It approaches you slowly, but not with wariness, finally coming close enough for you to touch. *"What is your guidance for me?"* you ask it, and it answers with one solemn word: "....." For a space of time, you commune with it there, beneath the World Tree. You learn to move as it moves; you begin to see as it sees. When your time is done, you show it one final sign of affection, and express your deepest gratitude and love. *"Do you have a gift for me?"* you ask it, and it responds: *"Walk."* And then it moves away, back in the direction from whence it came. You take a deep breath. Hold it for a count of four. Let your mind focus on the word *Contract* or *Ebb.* Take a deep breath. Hold it for a count of four. Let your mind focus on the word *Contract* or *Ebb.* You begin to walk away from the tree. Exhale for four counts. Let your mind focus on the word *Expand* or *Flow.* You are slowly coming back to consciousness. Repeat. *Contract. Expand.* You feel your physical fingers and toes, and you begin to wiggle them as you come back to this physical realm. *Ebb. Flow.*

You become steadily more aware of your physical surroundings. *Contract. Expand.* You stretch your arms and your legs as you come fully back into the safety of your physical form. *Ebb. Flow.*

Raise The Fence.

Outside the fire,
Darkness;
Darkness outside the Grove;
Outside there dwell shadows;
Shadows inside us as well.
Inside, outside, everywhere,
Where'er you dwell,
Dwell not here:
Here is light and all good things!
Light and Bright Wisdom protect us;
Protect us from those who dwell outside.
This circle is open,
Yet never broken.
So it is, and so it shall be.

Go Wight-Walking.

The direction from which your *dyr-andi* arrived is important for two reasons: one practical, and one spiritual. On the practical level, the direction from which it came provides you with a direction in which to *physically walk* during your wight-walk. For example, if it came out of the east, then if you walk towards the east, you are more likely to find the gift which you are meant to receive. On the spiritual level, the direction from which it came may provide you with valuable clues about which *realms* you are meant to travel in future, as well as which *Gods* may have the greatest affinity for you, and vice versa. As previously discussed, there is a definite (if a bit ephemeral) *geography* to the Nine Worlds. Keeping in mind the *ephemeral* nature of that geography, the following chart provides a basic "jump-off point" for your explorations and study. Please also keep in mind that this is a very *rough* guide, and that the Deities listed are a place to *start* your exploration and research, and *not* the Norse Pantheon in its entirety.

Midgard Directions and Associations

Direction	Realm(s)	God/desses
North	Asgard	Odin, Tyr, Thor, Frigga, Sif, Sigyn, Thrudh
North-East	Alfheim	Freyr, Freyja, Volundr (aka Wayland The Smith), Alfar (as demi-deities)
East	Jotunheim	Loki, Angrbodha, Gerdha, Sunna, Nott, Mani, Skadi, Sigyn, Jord

Direction	Realm(s)	God/desses
South-East	Helheim, Jotunheim	Hela, Loki, Angrbodha, Gerdha, Sunna, Nott, Mani, Skadi, Sigyn, Baldur, Idunna
South	Helheim	Hela, Baldur, Idunna, Sigyn
South-West	Svartalfheim	Thor, Wayland the Smith, Freyja, Dwarves (as demi-deities)
West	Vanaheim	Freyr, Freyja, Njordr, Nerthus, Ran, Aegir
North-West	Vanaheim, Alfheim	Freyr, Freyja, Njordr, Nerthus, Ran, Aegir, Volundr (aka Wayland the Smith), Alfar (as demi-deities)

The animal itself is obviously also incredibly symbolic. While it is beyond the scope of this book to cover the symbolism of every animal that could possibly show up as a *dyr-andi*, I will provide herein a brief discussion of six of the most frequently encountered animals in Norse lore and the archaeological record. I strongly suggest performing the **Dyr-Andi Utiseta** *before* reading further, so that your meditation will not be unduly *influenced* by having read on from this point.

Animals of the Norse Tradition

Raven: Depictions of ravens are frequently found on artifacts from the Viking Era and before. They are most often understood to be representations of Huginn and Muninn, the companion-birds of Odin All-Father. The names Huginn and Muninn translate roughly as "Thought" and "Memory", respectively, and it was said by Odin that He feared the loss of Huginn ("Thought"), but He feared the loss of Muninn ("Memory") far more. Modern scholars have theorized that the two birds symbolize the shamanic aspects of Odin, and I find it hard to disagree: certainly, thought and memory are two things which become more vital (and perhaps more dangerously fleeting) with each trance-state journey. Some scholars have also drawn a correlation between Huginn and Muninn and two parts of the four-part Norse "soul": *Fylgja* and *Hamingja* (reputation or legacy). I find it a bit odd that scholars have linked Huginn to the *fylgja*, rather than the much more obviously linguistically related *Hugr*. The *Hugr* would best be understood by us moderns as the "inner self": a person's personality as reflected in their conscious thought processes; very much in line with the oft-misquoted Buddhist ideal of "what you think, you become." Meanwhile, the *Hamingja*, represented by Muninn, is often loosely translated as "luck", but might be better understood as "fame" or "reputation": how one is *remembered*; their *legacy*. Therefore, Raven as a *dyr-andi* may be understood to represent shamanic journeys/experiences, the inner self (and the need to more deeply explore personal identity), and how one deals with living the Norse Virtues. In my personal experience, those with Raven as *dyr-andi* are heavily mystically inclined (one of the greatest shaman-teachers I know, Michelle, is a

"Raven Person"). Though occasionally lacking in the "personal development" department, they are incredibly Honorable, often to their own detriment.

Wolf: Probably the three most famous wolves in Norse lore are Fenrir (also called Fenris), Geri, and Freki. Fenrir, of course, is the child of Loki and Angrbodha, and the brother of Jormungandr and Hela, who apparently grew up alongside Tyr, and came to trust the God of Justice and the Law enough to allow Him to place His hand in his mouth when the Aesir bound him, in an effort to prevent Ragnarok. Geri and Freki are the wolves of Odin, whose names translate roughly as "Greedy" and "Ravenous". Geri and Freki may be considered as correlating to the two remaining parts of the Norse "soul": *Fylgja* and *Hamr*, respectively. As I've previously explained, the *fylgja* is literally a *part* of a person's "soul", not something separate which can be called upon (like a *dyr-andi*), but something deep *within*, or, more accurately, *alongside,* a person throughout the course of their life. The *Hamr* (literally: skin or shape) is a person's form or appearance. Rather than the physical shape being viewed as merely a "vessel", as it is in most surviving Eastern and Western Traditions, for the Norse, a person's physical appearance was an integral part of a person's *identity*. Those who are most deeply in touch with their *Hamr* are also those most likely to be gifted with the art of shape-shifting. This is called *skipta homum* ("changing hamr"), and those who are so-gifted are said to be *hamramr* ("strong of *hamr*"). Given all of this, there is a strong tradition in the lore (as well as in material culture) of the *Ulfhedhnar* (singular *Ulfhedhinn*; pronounced Ulfh-eth-nar and Ulfh-eth-een, respectively): warriors dedicated in the service of Odin who wore wolf-pelts into battle and were said to be unstoppable (a form of *berserker*). Therefore, Wolf as a *dyr-andi* may also be understood to represent shamanic journeys and/or experiences (in symbiosis with Odin and Raven, and as they relate to the *fylgja*), as well as loyalty (Fenrir's relationship with Tyr; the *Ulfhedhnar*), physical strength, shape-shifting (another shamanic element), and being "battle-ready". In my own personal experiences with those who have Wolf as a *dyr-andi*, "Wolf People" tend to be loyal to a fault, and will defend you with tooth and claw if necessary, making them some of the best friends you could ever have.

Bear: Although they are one of the largest animals living in Scandinavia, bears are shockingly absent from most of the lore. This could be due to traditional Germanic taboos against speaking the word bear: generally, if someone needed to reference a bear, they would use a byname or kenning, because bears were considered *too dangerous* even to be mentioned. This had far less to do, as it turns out, with their physical size or potential physical ferocity, and more to do with superstitions relating to their *virility*. However, one of the bynames of Thor given in the Prose Edda is *Bjorn*, which translates directly as "bear". (Interesting note: given the taboo on the use of the word "bear" in Germanic cultures, Bjorn is a surprisingly common name; this is due in large part to its use as a byname or kenning for Thor; most people who name their children Bjorn are not intending to call their child a "bear" at all, but instead to name the child with one of Thor's bynames.) Bears were also heavily associated with the changing of the seasons; with weather patterns, and particularly bad or dangerous weather: all of which are under the "guardianship" of Thor, which could explain this byname for Him. The word *berserker* derives from the Old Norse words *ber-serkr*, literally "bear-shirt", and many depictions of these fearsome warriors which have come down to us in the material cultural record (i.e., via archaeological finds) show men dressed as bears, complete with bear-head helmets. This imagery survives in the modern era in the form of the bearskin caps worn by the Danish Royal Guard. A few scholars have also drawn associations between the bear and Volundr (aka Wayland the Smith). In the Prose Edda, Volundr is often found surrounded by bear imagery (from bearskin rugs to bear steaks), and at one point is referred to as *"brunni"*, "the brown one", which is a known byname for Bear. Those with Bear as *dyr-andi* may need lessons on curbing their tempers. They may also find themselves heavily drawn to Thor and Volundr as Deities (or, conversely, Thor and Volundr may be drawn to them). They tend to either be heavily in-tune with weather patterns, or given to things such as Seasonal Affective Disorder, requiring the guidance of Bear to help them gain a better seasonal balance. Bear People are also often highly sensual, maybe even "sexually charged".

Deer: Deer figure heavily in Norse Mythology, from the four deer who feed upon the shoots of new growth at Yggdrasil, to the stag who overlooks Valhalla, to the deer which sacrificed one of its horns for Freyr's new "weapon" after giving His sword up for His etin-bride, Gerdha. The four harts at Yggdrasil are called Dainn, Dvalinn, Duneyrr, and Durathror. We are told of them in both the Prose and Poetic Eddas, but no evidence of their symbology is given in either. Some scholars have suggested that perhaps they represent the four directions, the four seasons, the four winds, or even four *types* of wind, since their names translate roughly to "The Dead One", "The Unconscious One", "Thundering in the Ear", and "Thriving Slumber", respectively. You may recognize two of their names as the two most frequently given names of Dwarves: *Dainn* and *Dvalinn*. Notably, a Dwarf named Dvalinn was involved in the creation of Brisingamen, the necklace of Freyja. As four Dwarves are also associated with the four winds (and, thus,

the four directions)--Nordri, Sudri, Austri, and Vestri—and
given that two of the deer's names are also popular names
for Dwarves, many scholars (including myself) tend to
favor the symbolic interpretation of the deer as
representative of the winds and the four directions: Dainn
as North, Dvalinn as South, Duneyrr as East, and
Durathror as West. Eikthyrnir is the stag which overlooks
(or possibly even stands atop) Valhalla, the Hall of Odin
and of the Heroic Dead. From his antlers drip water which
is the source of all of the rivers of the Nine Realms (and of
our world as well). Finally, there is the antler wielded by
Freyr of the Vanir. We are not told how He procured this
antler, nor is it given a name, but its symbolism is not lost
to us: deer are used as symbols of virility and fertility
throughout the mythology of various Indo-European
cultures, making a deer antler the perfect weapon for a God
who was often kenned as "He of the Shining Phallus". Deer
as a *dyr-andi* is representative of an attachment to both
the Vanir Gods and the Duergar (Dwarves), and especially
Freyr. Deer People may have great directional awareness—
or they may *need* such awareness, which is why Deer has
suddenly "popped" into their lives. Deer provides both
sustenance and protection, and promises fruitful
endeavors, often of the sensual variety. Deer People can
be fierce in battle, but they are also excellent lovers and
great providers who can readily guide you through, come
what may.

Falcon: Falcon as *dyr-andi* is most heavily associated
with the Vanir Goddess, Freyja. *Fjadhrhamr* (pronounced
roughly: Fyath-hammer; literally, "feather-skin") was one
of Freyja's most frequently-depicted "magickal tools". Also
called *Valshamr* (literally "slain-skin", which ties to Her
byname of Valfreyja; rough pronunciation: Vallz-hammer),
it was a cloak (or possibly even a dress) made of falcon-
feathers, which allowed Her (or its wearer) to shapeshift

into a falcon and fly. We are told in the Eddas that She frequently loaned it out to other Gods so that They, too, could fly, usually so that They could rescue something or someone. In *Thrymskvida*, from the Poetic Edda, Thor and Loki seek Freyja's assistance, when the Jotun, Thrym, has evidently stolen Thor's hammer. Loki borrows *Fjadhrhamr*, and flies to Thrym, but is informed by the Jotun that the hammer will not be returned unless Freyja agrees to marry him. Needless to say, that doesn't happen, but Thor *does* wind up dressed in a wedding gown, pretending to be Freyja! In *Skaldskaparmal* in the Prose Edda, Loki again borrows Freyja's feather-cloak, this time referenced as *Valshamr*, in order to go rescue Idunna, keeper of the golden apples which keep the Gods young. In this tale, Idunna has been kidnapped by the Jotun Thjazi. Loki flies to Jotunheim, and brings back Idunna, but Thjazi can also shapeshift—into an eagle—and he gives chase to Loki, and is burnt to death on his arrival in Asgard by the other Aesir (which subsequently leads to Skadi, Thjazi's daughter, seeking a husband in Asgard as terms of the Aesir's repayment for Her father's death). From these tales we gain symbolic associations of the falcon with shape-shifting (again, a shamanic element), and with rescue or some form of "salvation". Closely tied to the Vanir Goddess Freyja, Falcon is associated both with Her purview as a goddess of love, beauty, and sensuality (as referenced in *Thrymskvida*), but also in Her purview as Goddess of War and Claimer of the Slain (as referenced in *Skaldskaparmal*, wherein the cloak is referred to instead as *Valshamr*).

Cat: Cats are also associated with Freyja; Her chariot is pulled by a pair of very large felines described as tom-cats (male) in the Eddas. Because of their association with Freyja, it became a folk tradition for a new bride to be given the gift of a kitten, as a way of bestowing a blessing upon the marriage. Other superstitions surrounding cats and marriage included the folk belief that a girl who valued cats would easily get married; that the gift of a black cat to newlyweds was actually *good* luck; that stepping on a cat's tail would lead to an inability to marry for at least a year, and that a bride feeding a cat before her wedding would lead to a happy marriage. There was also a belief that feeding a cat well would lead to sunshine on a couple's wedding day. Freyja is not the only Norse Deity associated with cats, however: there is also a story of Thor and a very large feline in *Gylfaginning* 46 of the Prose Edda. In this story, Thor is tricked by the Jotun Utgard-Loki (not to be confused with *actual* Loki, who accompanies Thor on this adventure) into attempting to lift the Jotun's "cat". In reality, the "cat" is Jormungandr in disguise, and Thor only manages to get one of the "cat's" feet off the floor. This association of cats with *liminality* can perhaps also be found in the *Saga of Erik The Red*, wherein the "little volva" is described as wearing a hood and gloves lined with furry cat-skin. That a female spirit-worker and diviner (understood as a *shaman* or *witch* in modern parlance) is distinctly described therein as wearing *cat* fur not only ties her to the service of Freyja (who was also the "Goddess of Seidhr", having taught the "craft/art" to Odin Himself), but possibly also further asserts the association of the World Serpent with *liminality* and the concepts of **sacred space** and **sacred time** as we understand them today. Cat as *dyr-andi* may therefore be understood to represent sensuality and fertility, as well as mysticism, liminality, and shape-shifting.

Other animals frequently encountered in Norse lore, as well as the archaeological and anthropological record, include horse, boar/sow, cow/bull, rooster, eagle, and squirrel. While it is beyond the scope of this book to go into further detail about any (or even all) of these animals, I hope in future to possibly write an entire book with a focus on the *dyr-andi*. While getting in touch with one's *dyr-andi* can be an extremely valuable part of a Norse Witch's practice, I do not wish to bend to "animistic stereotypes" by making that my primary focus in this section on wights.

There is far more to the concept of *Landvaettir* as a whole, and to our interactions with them, than our relationship to the animal denizens of that "kingdom". There are also much *larger* spirits of the land, which I once heard Adam Sartwell of The Temple of Witchcraft describe as "large enough to encompass us and even move *through* us". These have far too much in common with the *etins* or *Jotun* of Norse Tradition for such a comparison to go ignored or overlooked, and are often the source of traditional anthropomorphizing of certain natural landmarks, such as mountains. Experiencing the presence of these can be awe-inspiring in the truest sense of that word, and can make it profoundly apparent to us little humans that we are precisely that: very *small* by comparison to the large, *interconnected world* around us. I have only ever experienced this sort of land spirit once, and it was many years ago, in the mountains of North Carolina. I traveled with members of Michelle's family to Grandfather Mountain, near Boone, North Carolina. The mountain is called that because it creates the very distinct shape of an old man's face, as if he is lying down, and looking up at the sky. I swear to you—as I did to the other members of our party that day—that I saw that face *move* as I stood there, looking out across the horizon from one of the many overlooks on the Blue Ridge Parkway. Of course, they mostly thought I was either over-tired, or completely bonkers. Except Michelle. She had gone to summer camp very near there when she was in the sixth grade, and had the same profound experience with the mountain, as well as one even more profound: she is mortally terrified of heights, yet somehow found herself *climbing* Grandfather Mountain. Cold-to-the-bone and stricken with terror from climbing rickety wooden ladders up sheer cliff-faces all day, on the way back down the mountain, she found herself *sliding* in the mud down a ravine that was several feet deep. As everything within her literally gave way to terror, she had the distinct vision of a giant hand of stone reaching out to pluck her between its thumb and forefingers, as one might carefully catch an ant. At precisely that moment, her descent stopped for *absolutely no gravity-driven, physical reason*. In that instant, she knew that she had been saved *by the mountain itself*, and consequently always makes a point of taking the time to go to an overlook and pay her respects to The Grandfather whenever she is in the area. Which is precisely why we pulled over at that overlook when I traveled with her family on that summer vacation years ago and I, myself, saw the mountain move.

While most of us hopefully go through life at least noticing the birds in the trees or the occasional squirrel that crosses our path, or perhaps even spend a lot of time with the family dog or family cat, a deeper relationship with the Landvaettir requires, as one may have guessed by now, a deeper relationship with the *land* itself. Unfortunately, we live in a society where few people notice the *land* unless it is in someone's way: we notice the land when we trip over a rock or bump into a tree, and that land causes us *pain*; we notice the land when suddenly a resource is threatened, or when someone's lifestyle or livelihood is endangered by some resource (such as in the case of the Dakota Pipeline, or the Gulf Oil Spill of a few years ago). We notice the land when it becomes something we wish to *acquisition* for ourselves (as in the selling and buying of a home or other property). But on a day to day basis, how often do we really stop to notice the *land* itself, or consider our relationship to and with it and its spirits?

I have been, somewhat surprisingly to myself, as guilty of this as are most people. I am a chronic birdwatcher—more than avid, I have been known to drop everything I am presently doing and rush to a window with my binoculars if something particularly fascinating happens to fly by outside my office window. To say that I notice the birds is to put it mildly. I pay attention to every call and squawk outside my window, and even as I am typing this, I am well aware of a troupe of blue jays mobbing a raven due northwest of me. But I had been remiss in my attentions to the spirits of the land on which I live, apart from my small offerings at blot every Friday, and keeping those same birds, which keep me entertained and excited all day every day, fed. Until selling our house and finding another loomed on my immediate horizon.

It is profoundly true of us as humans that we "don't know what we've got 'til it is gone". We tend to never fully understand how much we love or appreciate something, until that moment comes when we must tell it good-bye. And good-byes inevitably come; we live transient lives in a transient universe, and nothing is permanent, no matter how much we might wish it to be. Over the course of two months in the summer of 2017, I became suddenly and profoundly aware of how much I love the land on which I live. I also became suddenly and frightfully aware of how much I would miss *having land* on which to live and to practice; having a *yard*. So much of our Heathen lives are spent focusing on the concepts of *innangard* and *utangard*—inside the *yard* and outside the *yard*—but how much of that time do we spend concentrating on the fact that the *yard* in question is the *land*, and that that land is inhabited by the *Landvaettir*? Too little, as it turns out, or, at least, that had been the case for me.

In the summer of 2017, I became profoundly aware of the "smaller" spirits of the land on which I live; what some might think of as the Fae (or Dark Elves/Huldufolk; more on this in a moment), or even as elementals, though they are both and neither, at the same time. Here in New England, we have a type of nature spirit known as a *Pukwudgie*, and we had known for some time that our home and its surrounding land housed a small population of them. The term *Pukwudgie* comes down to us from the native Wampanoag People, a loose confederacy of Native American peoples who hailed from southeastern Massachusetts and Rhode Island. Technically, we lived in what would have been Nipmuck or Massachusett territory; clearly, the *Pukwudgies* neither knew nor cared about tribal boundaries, for once you've seen one, you know what you've seen, and trust me, we had *Pukwudgies*. Capable of shape-shifting (we had legit seen bunny-rabbits *inside* our house), these native nature spirits also have a humanoid form with features that resemble those of a human, but with much larger noses, fingers, and ears (very much the epitome of the Northern Tradition *troll*). Their skin is most often a smooth grey, but emits a soft bioluminescence. They can disappear and reappear at will, and most of the stories surrounding them speak of malicious intent towards those who do not respect the land, or their boundaries. Sudden fires, poison from "elf-shot", and people being lured to their deaths are all associated with folks who have run afoul of *Pukwudgies*. Needless to say, we had worked very hard in our home to keep these native denizens *happy*! Once we began to pack and move, however, I not only became profoundly aware of *them*, they made it very apparent that they were more aware of *us* than usual, which was a wee bit alarming, given their reputation.

That they were suddenly more *aware* of *us* than usual was not evidenced in "well-meaning" ways; on the contrary, it came across in such things as being frightened in the basement, or twenty-four hours of ongoing issues with the upstairs toilet. They made it profoundly clear that they didn't like the prospect of us leaving them with "new caretakers"; they also made it profoundly clear that they were not pleased with us for not doing what we *usually* were doing at that time of year, which was planting new flowers in the beds out front, and fresh pansies in the windowbox of our storage shed. I had hoped that the gift of a new wormwood plant received at that year's Beltane Rite with the Temple of Witchcraft would at least temporarily appease them, but no luck. Soon after placing that plant outside, Suzanne came running upstairs from the basement, terrified, because Christmas carols began playing on the *opposite* side of the basement from her, from within a box wherein all of the stuffed animals that play such things *do not have batteries installed.* There was also the circus with the toilet constantly running (and me constantly playing plumber); a circus which continued until well into the next day.

How does one appease the *Landvaettir* when they're upset like this, *Pukwudgies* or otherwise? The same way one pays respect to the God/desses: leave an offering; pour a blot. Natural things are generally best: plant a tree or a flower; leave seed for the birds. When something a bit more "formal" is required, the "faery stand-bys" of milk and honey are not inappropriate (more on this later in this chapter, as it relates specifically to the Dark Elves). It is also important that we become more mindful and have a more focused intent on maintaining the land: clean your yard; weed your garden. In short: let them know that they are *appreciated*, in much the same way you would do so for a human friend or loved one. Bestow a *gift* for all that they have given you; show them your *gratitude.* Usually, when they are "running amok", it is their expression of perceived ingratitude on your part, so work to make amends for that.

Connla Freyjason

A Blot for the Landvaettir

We pour this with deep gratitude,
For leaf and twig,
For trunk and root;
For stone that forms foundation strong,
And water that cleanses and flows along.
We thank you for this pact we share,
By your letting us tarry here;
Though quiet too often,
We do know
The support you give us,
And the care you show.
For water that cleanses and flows along,
For stone that forms foundation strong;
For trunk and root,
For leaf and twig,
We pour this with deep gratitude.

As is hopefully obvious from my own personal experiences with the local *Pukwudgies*, *Husvaettir* (house wights) are often the local spirits of the land which have since come to live *inside*, with us and alongside us. House wights may also include what we typically refer to as the *Fae* (faeries), as well as certain elemental spirits (such as *gnomes*), and certain distinctly Germanic spirits, such as the kobolds, brownies, and tomten (singular, tomte). Since these are the spirits of the home, we most commonly think of them as "spirits of the *hearth*", and, therefore, in our modern world, as "spirits of the *kitchen*". As such, most of us who think to leave them offerings do so *in* the kitchen, by leaving out a small portion of meals cooked for the family, or even a small bowl of milk, honey, or both by the stove. But the kitchen is not the only room in which they are likely to *reside*, and, therefore, should not be the only place where we seek to show them our gratitude or otherwise recognize their presence. Keeping a clean home is a sort of "*active blot*" for the *Husvaettir*; burning candles or incense in the bathroom or bedroom might also be a way of saying "hey, I know you're here, and I thank you for your presence and your blessings".

Moving mountains, Husvaettir, and *Pukwudgies* are not the only "surreal" things we may encounter in our travels with the Landvaettir, for there are also the beings which Celtic literature and Tradition call faeries or the Fae, but which are most easily understood within the Norse Tradition as *Dokkalfar* or *Svartalfar*. The term *Dokkalfar* (literally: Dark Elves) is encountered in only two attestations in the corpus of the lore, the most important of them being *Gylfaginning 17*, in the Prose Edda:

> Many places are there, and glorious. There is one place there, it is called Alfheim. There live a people that are called Ljosalfar (literally: Light Elves), but Dokkalfar (literally: Dark Elves) dwell in secret beneath the earth, and they are unlike them in appearance and much unlike them in experience. Ljosalfar are fairer than the sun in appearance, but Dokkalfar are blacker than pitch.
> --Translation Mine

Many people consider this passage to be an attempt by Snorri to divide the Alfar along very Christian lines as "good elves" ("*angels*") versus "bad elves"("*demons*", or, at the very least, "*fallen angels*"). That "knee-jerk reaction" minimizes *so* much, not the least of which is the use of the word *Dokkalfar* in this passage.

As I said, there are *only* two attestations of the use of that specific word for the Dark Elves *anywhere* in the lore, the other one being *Hrafnagaldr Odins* (literally: "Odin's Raven Song" or "Odin's Raven Magic"), which was at one time considered a part of the *Baldurs Draumar* portion of the Poetic Edda. Elsewhere, the Dark Elves are always referred to as *Svartalfar* (literally: "swarthy" elves, or black elves), who live in *Svartalfheim* (literally: "Homeland of the Black Elves"), which is elsewhere referred to as *Nidavellir*, "Low Fields" or "Dark Fields"; traditionally, also the home of the Dwarves (*Duergar*). When we suggest that Snorri's description of the Dokkalfar as "blacker than pitch" was meant as an implication that they are somehow "evil", we start rolling down a slippery slope that none of us really want to travel down. Let me be both very *real* with you and very Southern for a moment: this is how *racism* starts, y'all! The overriding tendency among many Heathens to wag the naughty-finger at this statement and tsk-tsk that it is symbolic of Snorri's "notorious Christian grafting" says far more about us, as moderns, than it does about 13th century Snorri. When we do that, we are flaunting, for all the world to see, that portion of *our own brains* that equates beings with darker skin than our own with "evil".

What Snorri was actually trying to communicate here in the simplest possible language is that Ljosalfar look *different* than Dokkalfar, and vice versa. "Fairer than the sun" only takes on implications of *whiteness* when we completely divorce it from the time period in which it was written. Up until the late 15th century, *fair* meant beautiful or peaceful and had *absolutely nothing* to do with skin-tone. Writing in the 13th century, and using the word *fegri*, Snorri clearly meant beautiful, peaceful, shining, bright, gracious, and/or happy, *not* "they were *white*".

The explanation that Ljosalfar (Light Elves) live in a glorious place called Alfheim, and are bright and shining, like the sun, whereas Dokkalfar dwell in secret beneath the earth and are blacker than pitch is extremely important. It displays a distinction of *celestial* versus *chthonic*, rather than "good" versus "bad", which is an expression of *balance*, rather than a "good vs. evil" *dichotomy*. A *celestial/chthonic paradigm* is actually evidence of the classical statement *"As Above, So Below"*, which recognizes a need for *balance*, rather than a need to pit two opposing forces *against* each other. That profoundly Judeo-Christian *dichotomy* (which pits above and below *against* each other) is likewise how faeries were later relegated to the status of "demonic" throughout the rest of Western European folklore: Heaven (celestial) was pitted against Hell (chthonic), therefore anything that was associated with living underground became "evil". When we leap to the assumption that Snorri was attempting to express "Ljosalfar are good, but Dokkalfar are bad" in this passage, *he* is not the one guilty of Christian grafting: *we are!*

In this passage, Snorri simply quotes Harr as saying that there are *many different places*, something which we already know to be true, given our thus-far brief introduction to the concept of the Nine Worlds. He then proceeds to do what any normal travel writer would do, and explain to us what this one place—Alfheim-- is like, and who lives there: the Ljosalfar (Light Elves). He then explains that the Dokkalfar (Dark Elves) don't live in that place; they live *somewhere else*. That *somewhere else* just happens to literally translate as "dwell in secret beneath the earth" (*bua nidhri i jordhu*). He then explains that Ljosalfar and Dokkalfar are *completely different* from each other, probably because the two names of these very different beings sound so *similar* to each other. He says that they not only *look different* from each other, but they are *much unlike in experience* (*miklu olikari reyndum*). Let's take a moment to define that word: *experience*.

> **Experience:** direct observation of; something personally encountered; the events that make up the conscious past of a community, nation, or group of beings; the act of directly perceiving events.

In other words, the differences between the Ljosalfar and Dokkalfar go *much* deeper than their differences in appearance: the *deeper* and *more important* differences may only be gained *experientially*. To truly understand the differences between Ljosalfar and Dokkalfar, both must be *personally encountered* and *directly observed*. That use of the word *experience* therein also implies *community background*: Ljosalfar are "the way they are" because of the way *they have been*, and likewise, Dokkalfar, implying that these are two completely *different* experiences of "being-ness".

Ljosalfar and Dokkalfar are *two completely different races of beings*, and Good Ole Snorri tried very hard to communicate that in this passage. I think that may also be why, elsewhere, the Dokkalfar are always referred to as *Svartalfar* who distinctly live in *Svartalfheim*. It wasn't a matter of attempting to imply "good elves live in this happy, bright, celestial place" while "bad elves live in this scary, dark, chthonic place", but instead "one type of being lives in this place, and it's like this", and "another type of being lives in this place, and it's like this". But we are so much *in our own heads*, that we wind up *grafting* our own baggage onto such passages, and falling into a trap of our own making. wherein we perpetrate not only "Christian grafting", but worse, inklings of *racist notions*.

Dokkalfar/Svartalfar are *chthonic beings*: beings which live *under the earth*, or *within the earth*; *subterranean*. The geography of where they live does not make them *evil* or *bad*; it is simply the geography of *where they live*. It would be highly remiss to discuss the Landvaettir (land wights) without actually discussing those wights which live *within* the land itself, as well as discussing how their *astral realm, Svartalfheim*, relates to our own mundane world, and how we honor them and the rest of the Landvaettir here in that world. Dokkalfar, Svartalfar, and *Myrkalfar* (literally: dusky elves or murky elves) are all terms encountered when speaking of these beings; they are also terms frequently encountered when glossing *Dwarves* (Duergar). It is unclear from the lore whether this means that Dark Elves (which I will be using as a blanket term for Dokkalfar/Svartalfar/Myrkalfar henceforth in this chapter and throughout the rest of this book) are completely synonymous with Dwarves, or whether this merely implies that Dwarves are a *type* of Dark Elf, but there is a definite inference in the lore that Svartalfheim and *Nidavellir* (the home of the Dwarves) are synonymous for the same location. When we combine that inference with personal gnosis, we may arrive at Dwarves as a distinct *type* of Dark Elf, though not the *only* type of Dark Elf.

Svartalfheim ("Homeland of the Black Elves") or Nidavellir ("Low Fields"; "Dark Fields") is described in the lore as a labyrinthine, underground domain, not dissimilar from the description of the land beneath *faery mounds* in other Traditions also sourced from the Indo-European root. In my experience, this is a world or plane to the far "west" of Vanaheim (home of the Vanir Gods), "south" of Alfheim (home of the Light Elves), and also "south" of Midgard (that area of the *astral plane* which is closest to our own mundane world, and, therefore, most frequently encountered or traveled), but "north" of Helheim (another chthonic astral realm which is inhabited by the Dead). It shares its "southern" border with the ocean at the "northern" tip of Helheim (which also adjoins Vanaheim). Like Tolkien's vision of Moria in *The Lord of the Rings*, it is a place in which it is very easy to *get lost*, perhaps accounting for many of the tales from outside of our own tradition which involve people "falling into" faery mounds, and never re-emerging. In fact, we have such a thing in our own Norse Tradition: the *alfholl* (literally: "elf hill"). The most famous of these places in our modern, mundane world is Alfholl in Kopavogur, Iceland, and the road with which it is associated, Alfholsvegur (literally: "Elf Hill Road"). Originally, Alfholsvegur was intended to go *through* Alfholl, thereby demolishing the elf hill. Late in the 1930s, as road construction reached the point of the elf hill, things began to go inexplicably wrong for the crews of workmen, and construction was stopped due to the ongoing financial strain which these issues caused. A decade later, work resumed, but once more, machines began inexplicably breaking and tools became damaged and lost. The road was rerouted *around* Alfholl. In the late 1980s, plans were made to reroute the road and repave it—again, taking it *through* Alfholl, rather than around it. A rock drill was brought in to demolish Alfholl. The drill broke. A second drill was fetched; it broke, too. Workers subsequently refused to go anywhere near Alfholl with any tools whatsoever. Alfholl has since become protected as a cultural heritage site, and is one of the most frequent sources of tales of modern day encounters with the Dark Elves.

Many of those modern tales call the Dark Elves by yet another name: the *Huldufolk* (literally: "secret people"). They are most typically described as either much taller or much shorter than humans (as with descriptions of "Little People" in other Faerie Traditions; also leaving room for spotting the occasional Dwarf), with dark hair, and wearing gray clothing. Though never quite described as "evil", per se, their tendency towards mischievousness and an apparent tendency to be what those familiar with Dungeons and Dragons might call "chaotic neutral" (a tendency to look out for one's own interests, first and foremost, rather than "choosing a side") is definitely reflected in lore-based descriptions of interactions with Dark Elves on the whole, and with Dwarves, in particular. This "reputation" also suggests that one should use a certain amount of *caution* when having dealings with these beings.

Including the Dark Elves (and Dwarves) in your practice as a Norse Witch is certainly not *required*, however it is definitely *encouraged*, particularly if you find yourself living in proximity to an alfholl, or if you are an artisan/artist of some sort. How can you know if you are living near an alfholl? If things consistently go missing, or if household items (especially plumbing, in my experience) consistently break for no rational reason, then it is very likely that your local population of Dark Elves is announcing emphatically that you are living in *their* territory. They are trying to remind you, by whatever means necessary, that they were there *first*, and that you are guests in *their* home, rather than the other way around. How does one typically thank a householder for their hospitality? We give them *gifts*. Offerings at or near an alfholl should be understood in that same capacity. Preferred offerings include honey, mead, and milk, as well as sugar and flour. If you are an artisan/artist, similar offerings should be given at your ve or stalli for the Dark Elves, and especially the Dwarves, as an expression of your kinship with them (so that they will consider you *innangard*), in the hopes that they will impart not only inspiration, but also share with you their level of skill. This is especially important for those who actively depict nature in their artistry, or who use natural elements (such as wood, paper, stone, or ores) to make things.

Finding Freyr

Most of the people I know who are dedicants of Freyja at some point, sooner or later, wind up working with the other members of Her family, including Her brother, Freyr, and I am no different. My first offering to Him was actually a piece of votive art, which seemed only natural, coming from a working artist, given His position as a God of "good seasons" who is often associated with financial gain. His link to other sorts of fertility, hallmarked by ancient depictions of Him as a god with an enormous, erect phallus, led some of my friends to joke about being "careful what I ask for from Freyr". All chuckling aside, however, I have found my relationship with Freyr to be more brotherly than titillating.

To my non-Heathen or Norse Witch (and especially my Christian) friends, I often compare Freyr to St. Matthew. For those unfamiliar with that particular Apostle of Christ, St. Matthew was a tax collector, which was a hated profession among the people of that time, making him "one more misfit among a crew of misfits", in the company of Jesus' companions. One of the Gospels of the New Testament is attributed to him—in fact, it's the first of the Four—and in the Catholic Church, he is considered the patron saint of bankers, providing a link to financial gain, not unlike Freyr. In artistic depictions, St. Matthew is often accompanied by a winged man—what moderns would immediately recognize as an angel—which I view as a second link to Freyr, as Lord of Alfheim. Some might find drawing a cognate between these two blasphemous, but Freyr Himself doesn't seem to mind, and as far as I can tell, neither does Saint Matthew, and that's good enough for me! Besides, sometimes we find ourselves in places and situations where it is far safer to tell someone that you are making an offering to a saint they readily recognize, rather than to a Norse God whom they don't.

I will readily admit that I first came to Freyr because of frequent feelings of financial destitution: much the same reason that I initially arrived at the feet of His father, Njordr. Running one's own business is incredibly *hard*. Running a business based on the arts and actually ever breaking even is apparently well-nigh *impossible*. Seeing my constant state of depressed desperation, it was Freyja who suggested that I speak with Her brother during one of my Friday blots. As usual, I did as I was told, and I found myself standing out at my ve, cup in hand, pouring out a whole lot more than the red wine blend it contained. My first meeting with Freyr was tear-filled and entreating, and in response I received a gentle breeze, the feel of a steadying hand upon my shoulder, and the resounding message in my mind of "*It's going to be okay; I've got you*".

Since then, I have begun honoring Freyr every Friday, alongside His sister, Freyja, and while my finances still aren't stellar, I find myself crying about them a whole lot less. I've also found myself inexplicably attracted to something that could not be further from my personal norm: gardening. Freyr is slowly changing my focus from the "green stuff" (money) to *actual* green stuff (plants). Anyone who has ever known me can tell you that this is *way* outside my wheelhouse! I'm also finding myself wanting to spend a lot more time "in the green-world", out in the woods, and in nature in general. Now, most folks know my obsession with bird-watching, so me wanting to spend time outdoors might not seem like that huge of a leap, but I'm finding myself wanting to "go Thoreau", and seek out some quiet place in the wilderness where I can "live deliberately", and that couldn't be further from my norm. As the guy who is known for the quote "bears may shit in the woods, but that doesn't mean *Connla* does", wishing I could go spend time in a cabin somewhere is a *completely* alien desire.

I am slowly beginning to see Freyr's point in making me want these things, however: He is trying to show me what is *really important* in life; what *really matters*. The "green stuff" with which I line my wallet isn't that. Money comes and money goes just as easily; the green-world has been with us forever, and hopefully will be with us for a very long time to come. There are different sorts of being *rich*, and the most important sort is when you look around and realize the *wealth* you already have. That's what being in nature teaches me. I am already rich. What need is there for monetary wealth when I have air in my lungs, and a wife who loves me? Sure, there was a time in my life-before-this-one when I was pretty financially well-taken-care-of. I had a great support system of family and friends, but back then, I couldn't maintain a romantic relationship if my life depended on it. I didn't have what I have now, with her. I didn't have to worry about how I was going to pay my bills, but I also had little time to truly feed my passions of art and writing. In fact, I was too afraid to even *attempt* the latter, yet look at me now! Nature was that thing I passed through on the way to my next appointment—so that I could keep not having to worry about paying my bills. And then *everything changed*, and that could've been game over, but it wasn't. Here I am, and there are still plants to plant, and leaves to brush against, and birds to watch, and art to make. And I actually have *time* for all of those things, when I never did before. I actually have *time* to *live deliberately*. That, my friends, is true *wealth*.

Freyr has also taught me a lot about *manifestation*. Sometimes those lessons have come in the form of "holy wow, thank you, Freyr!", and sometimes those lessons have come as a slap on the hand, as when telling a little child "hey, that's not for you." It has been very hard for me to come to value the latter, I'll readily admit. But even when the lesson has included a slap, there has been that constant brotherly hand on my shoulder with the words *"It's going to be okay; I've got you"*. Thing is, when you combine Freyr's lessons with the lessons of His sister, Freyja, that *"I've got you"* eventually becomes *"and you've got you, too"*. I've come to understand that all of those depictions of "Freyr with His gigantic phallus" are about far more than sexual fertility: they're also about *self-esteem*. He *is* Freyja's brother, after all, and one of the ultimate lessons of The Lady is to *love ourselves unconditionally*. He just teaches that lesson in a slightly more "man-up" sort of way, which it turns out is precisely what I *needed*.

Both the *Ynglinga Saga* and Saxo Grammaticus' accounts of Freyr suggest Him as a "God of the Mound"; a god of the Dead, but also of the cycle of the seasons and the fertility of the crops, not dissimilar from Dionysus. We are told in *Grimnismal* that Alfheim was given to Freyr as a "tooth-gift"--a gift given to an infant upon the cutting of their first tooth—making him the "Lord of Alfheim", or specifically, "Lord of the Ljosalfar". So, Freyr, "Lord of the Mound", is also Freyr, "Lord of Alfheim", making Freyr not only a god of the wealth of life, but also of the legacy of death. As such, He has been a huge help in my coming to grips with being *literally* the Chosen of Freyja in the darkest sense of those words. Through my relationship with Freyr, I have finally come to understand that Death itself is a cycle, as full of seasons and fertility as any Life. There is no need for me to mourn what has gone before—my old life, "back when"--but instead there is a very distinct and maybe even desperate need for me to *celebrate* this life-in-death which I have *right now*.

He is called "Light-Bringer", and I can honestly say that since He came into my life, that life has become brighter in ways which I could never even have imagined, if left to my own devices. Freyr *does* bring light with Him when He comes: the light of realization; the light of hope; the light of dawn after the darkest of nights. I light a candle for Him now, when things grow bleary here in my little world, and I invite in that Light, and in return, I am left shining as well.

Angels Among Us: The Ancestors, The Alfar, and The Disir

The use of the word "angels" in a book about anything with an allegedly Reconstructionist-derived Norse base might be enough to ruffle the feathers of even the most open-minded of birds. Apparently, some people view "angel" as a "convenient *Christian* word" that *might* easily be "grafted" upon our culture and mythology, but patently *should not* be. If that were indeed the case —if angels *were* an entirely *Christian* concept, or if the word itself *were*, in fact, a "*Christian* word"--such people might have a toe to precariously balance upon, even if still not a leg on which to stand. However, there are actually *no such things* as "*Christian* words": Christianity is a religion, *not* a language! And the word *angel* actually predates the onset of Christianity by approximately 1600 years! The word *engill* in Old Norse is sourced from the proto-Germanic word *angiluz*, presumably a translation of the Ancient Greek loan word, *angelos*. That word, *angelos*, is in turn sourced from Mycenaean Greek *akero*: a term which likely dates to somewhere around the 16th century B.C. All of these words are used to describe the same type of entity:

> **Angel:** a *celestial being* which acts as a messenger, guardian, warrior, errand-runner for a Higher Power, or attendant spirit.

While Snorri's treatment of the *alfar* within the Poetic and Prose Eddas has been abundantly accused of borrowing wholesale from older Christian writings, that honestly has *zero bearing* on my use of the word "angels" to describe the *celestial beings* within our Norse Tradition. From a comparative mythological standpoint (as well as from an experiential one), it would be a fallacy to assume that Christians somehow "cornered the market" on the concept of, or even the word, *angel*. Angels, as we think of them by the modern definition of that word, have existed as a concept in almost every world culture, from the ancient Greeks and Romans (both famous for their "cherub" sculptures), to the Buddhists, and the Hindus (lest we forget our Indo-European roots!). While Snorri's description of the *alfar* in particular in the *Gylfaginning* of the Prose Edda certainly has more than a bit in common with *Elucidarius* (an 11th century work by Honorius Augustodunensis on Christian theology and folk beliefs), my own personal experience (coupled with a knowledge of comparative mythology) has definitely taught me one very important thing: angels *exist*, and they are as alive and well within the Norse Tradition as they are within Buddhism, Hinduism, or the rest of modern Paganism.

Before we proceed with an exploration of the possibility of angels in Norse Witchcraft, let us take a much-needed moment to address "the elephant in the room": **Unconfirmed Personal Gnosis (UPG)** versus **Experiential Knowledge**. I've put off doing that long enough, though I've touched on it briefly in earlier chapters. In order for you to gain anything from this chapter and future chapters, it's time we addressed this issue and laid it to rest, for once and for all.

Let's break down those three words: **Unconfirmed Personal Gnosis**:

> **Unconfirmed:** Not confirmed as truth; of uncertain existence; of uncertain accuracy
>
> **Personal:** of, relating to, belonging to, or affecting a particular person, rather than anyone else.
>
> **Gnosis:** Knowledge or spiritual mysteries; esoteric or spiritual knowledge which is believed to be a truth essential for survival or the understanding of how the Universe truly works.

Therefore, UPG is a knowledge of spiritual issues which serve as the very *foundation* of a person's *complete understanding* of "how the world works" which are distinctly *their own*, but otherwise *completely unprovable*.

Now, let us compare and contrast that with **experiential knowledge**:

> **Experiential Knowledge:** Knowledge gained by the experience of particulars, via perception.

Particulars are individual things, events, or characteristics, so *experiential knowledge* is an *individual* gaining of knowledge via the *personal experience* of specific things, events, and/or characteristics. It is identical with *knowledge gained by perception*: through hearing, seeing, tasting, feeling, etc. That knowledge becomes True (i.e., *fact*) when it is corroborated by other humans who *experience* the same thing. For example, the sky is blue. At face value, that seems like *fact*, right? But how does a *blind* person, who cannot see, know that the sky is blue? Because everyone else says so! However, if I say the sky outside *my* window is blue, but you look outside *your* window, and it is raining, and the sky is therefore gray, does that make the statement *the sky is blue* less *factually true*? Or does it remain a *fact* because behind those gray clouds, the sky itself is still blue?

Experience of the sky—which most of us can all see and conclude is blue *most of the time*—is an example of easily *confirmed experiential knowledge*; mystical experiences, however, are another matter, regardless of whether you are Heathen, a Norse Witch, or otherwise. One of the best metaphors for the struggle of confirming *mystical experiential knowledge* comes to us from India: the Story of the Blind Men and the Elephant. Six blind men encounter an elephant. Because the beast is so large, each man can only make physical contact with one small part of it: a trunk here, a tail there; another grabs a foot. They then describe the part of the elephant which they have *personally experienced*. The man in contact with the tail proclaims: "An elephant is no different than a furry little mouse." The man at the elephant's belly exclaims: "You're wrong! An elephant is like an enormous sheet of leather." The man holding the elephant's foot laughs at both of them: "No! No! An elephant is exactly like a tree stump." The man in contact with the elephant's ear exclaims: "No! An elephant is like an enormous hand fan!"

Then the man in contact with the elephant's tusk retorts: "Wrong again! An elephant is like a tube or a pipe made of something very hard, like ivory." Finally, the man holding the elephant's trunk says: "You're all crazy: elephants are exactly like snakes!" As the men bicker and name-call, a sighted man finally comes along and asks: "What on earth are you doing to that poor elephant? Why are you all arguing so?" And the blind men explain that they are all trying to agree on exactly what an elephant is like, based on each man's *individual perception*. The sighted man says: "You are all right, and you are all, at the same time, wrong. Each one of you could only touch a small part of this huge animal's body, so you each only have a *partial* view. If you would simply stop arguing, and put all of those *individual perceptions* into a *cohesive whole*, then you would know what an elephant actually looks like." When it comes to our spirituality—no matter what Path we're on—we are all blind men touching only one part of a very big elephant. If we continue to hold true only *our own individual perception* of the small part with which we have come into contact, or, worse still, *refuse to discuss* our experiences because of the fear of other people's criticisms, we may *never know* the full picture! We may *never know* the Truth. In other words, both UPG *and* experiential knowledge of things of a spiritual nature are literally the elephant in the room!

There are two ways in which we can *confirm both personal gnosis and experiential knowledge of things of a spiritual nature*: we can compare our experiences to the experiences of others through sane and fair discussion (Is the sky outside *your* window blue, because the sky outside *my* window is blue?) and we can compare our experiences to those recorded in the historical record of the lore and extant material culture (Most of the poems/novels I've read have said that the sky is blue, therefore, the sky must be blue. Most of the paintings I've seen have shown the sky as being blue, therefore, the sky must be blue.) If this were a book about birdwatching in Boston, and I said "I saw a seagull at Boston Harbor", you would, more than likely, be willing to take that as a statement of *fact*, rather than offering a reply such as "I don't believe in seagulls", because most people know for a *fact* that seagulls live near harbors and other bodies of ocean-water. However, if I said to you "I saw a white raven at Boston Harbor", you would likely ask me for photographic proof, as ravens are rarely white (and most people know that). Yet this is a book on Norse Witchcraft, not birdwatching, so if I were to say to you "I've been working as one of the *alfar* for nearly twenty years; I have wings, and I've been to Alfheim", instead of simply accepting that statement as a *fact* of my *experiential knowledge*, you would be much more likely to reply with "I don't believe you", at worst, or "that is *your own personal gnosis*" at best. And unlike the potential of a white raven showing up at Boston Harbor, I wouldn't have the luxury of offering any sort of physical proof, apart from accounts in the lore or extant material culture of who and what the Alfar are, and/or where they live, and how that compares to what I have personally experienced. In the end, what it all comes down to is that *we are all touching different parts of the same elephant*, and we can either stand around and argue about what we've each perceived, or we can *continue this dialogue* and *arrive at the Truth*.

Many modern Heathen practitioners link Ancestor veneration to the *alfar* and *disir*, an association which is neither etymologically, historically, nor mystically unsound, as it turns out. As Norse Witches, we also maintain this link. From an etymological perspective, both *alf* and *dis* are used many times in the Eddas and Sagas as words denoting an almost "saint-like" person, worthy of veneration almost on a similar level to the Gods themselves. Historically speaking, we have numerous mentions in the Sagas of both *Alfablot* and *Disablot*, "sacrificial holidays", likely held in November (sources suggest February for Disablot in Sweden) to honor the Ancestors, Alfar, and Disir, and most likely also to show gratitude for a good harvest. Mystically-speaking, as someone who has *been* to Alfheim and who has served The Boss in one capacity or another for twenty-four years, I can tell you with concrete certainty that not all Ancestors ("dead folks") become Alfar or Disir, but many of the Alfar and Disir are, in fact, Ancestors ("dead folks").

One *fact* that we can all likely agree upon is that the Ancestors once were *us*: they lived and breathed, and had normal day-to-day lives. So what makes them worthy of veneration in the first place? Among other Pagan groups, the Dead, inclusive of the Ancestors, are often referred to as *The Revered Dead*. But why do we *revere* them in the first place? I mean, just because they're dead, that doesn't make them *smart*. Sure, they may have gained wisdom of things which are beyond the normal scope of human experience, such as what the afterlife is *actually* like, for example, but beyond that, and the fact that perhaps we *miss* some of these people (through our own personal grief), what makes the Ancestors (or any of the Revered Dead) worthy of our veneration? I have really struggled with this in my own personal practice because, yes, even the Ancestors have Ancestors; even the Revered Dead have their own Revered Dead, the difference is that they're all on the *same side of existence* now, and can "keep in touch"! As I've said previously, I originally hail from a largely Buddhist/Taoist background, another Path that focuses heavily on Ancestor veneration. So you would think this "portion of the programming" would be a natural fit for me, but I can tell you with conviction that it hasn't been.

Ultimately, we venerate the Ancestors because, quite simply, without them, *we wouldn't be here*. Ancestor veneration is one more expression of the *"a gift for a gift"* **attitude of gratitude** which runs its deep thread throughout Norse practice, forming one of its strongest cornerstones. *You did not get here all by yourself.* Others came before you, and they facilitated *your* being here, and you would be deeply remiss in not offering them *gratitude* for that fact. The other reason for venerating the Ancestors comes to us straight from the *Havamal*:

> Cattle die, friends die,
> One dies oneself the same,
> But fame never dies,
> For him who gains goodness/righteousness for
>   himself.

> Cattle die, friends die,
> One dies oneself the same,
> I know one that never dies:
> Renown of the dead.
> --Havamal 76-77, Translation Mine

So long as we *remember* them, our Ancestors remain with us and, therefore, are never *truly dead*. In the act of Ancestor veneration, we provide for the Revered Dead a sort of *afterlife maintenance* that keeps them socially well-adjusted on the Other Side (whether they're in Helheim, Folkvangr, or wherever). To better explain the importance of that, and how that actually works, let me give you an example from the mundane world. Likely we have all heard horrible stories about an elderly person being placed in a nursing facility (what we refer to as "Old Folks Homes" down South), and then forgotten by their family. The family never comes to visit. Friends never come to visit. Most of us regard such stories with a certain level of horror and sadness, right? When we do not make offerings to our Ancestors, we are doing the *exact same thing* to them in death that some families do to their Ancestors while they're still breathing! The only difference is that the "Old Folks Home" in question is Helheim (or Folkvangr, etc.). The answer to the questions *"Do the dead grieve the living"* and *"Do the dead feel sadness"* is a resounding *Yes!* We can prevent the dead from that grieving and sadness by actually "paying them a visit", via Ancestor veneration.

When offerings and attention are not given to the Ancestors, the Revered Dead come to live *poor and unfulfilling afterlives*. Take a look at that word, *unfulfilling*:

> **Unfulfilling:** making someone dissatisfied or unhappy through not allowing their character or abilities to develop fully.

The fact that there *is* an *afterlife* means that our Ancestors— the *Revered Dead*—are *living* in it, in some capacity or other. Part of the reason that we react with horror and sadness when we hear tales of some elderly person who has been placed in a home and then forgotten about is that we know, intuitively, that the state of being *forgotten about* is *unfulfilling*: they become "non-people", because their character is no longer being developed through social interaction. When we do not make offerings to the Ancestors, we are consigning them to that same level of *unfulfillment* in the afterlife, *forever*.

I personally maintain an **Ancestor Altar**, though you may choose to include their veneration instead in the space of your *Main Stalli*, or even your *Main Ve*. If you have an Ancestor with whom you were particularly close in life, and have the means and access, you may actually wish to turn their gravesite into a *Harrow*. However you choose to express the sacred space set aside for your Ancestors, know that it will become a *deeply personal space*, not only for you, but for them. In many ways, given our Norse concept of *orlog*, the space you set aside for your Ancestors also expresses a deep definition of your *personal identity*, which is precisely why I have not included photographs of my own Ancestor Altar herein.

What does one put in that space—in the space one has set aside for making offerings to the Ancestors—and what sorts of offerings should one make within it? If you have photographs of your Ancestors, they would definitely be appropriate for inclusion. Treasured possessions, such as items of jewelry or other small curios, will also help you to feel closer to them. I maintain a plaque with a photo of the man I consider my "first sifu" over my Ancestor Altar, as well as trinkets associated with my most immediate Ancestor, my Father, on the altar itself. Since they were both Buddhist/Taoist, my Ancestor Altar very much has a "Buddhist flavor": I maintain a Kwan Yin statue there, as well as an Amitabha Buddha and several mala. The Ancestor Altar is *for them*, so put things on it that you know *they will enjoy*. In fact, placing things on the altar that we know *they will enjoy* is one of the best offerings that we can give to them within that space. Other offerings might include food and drink that they enjoyed in life, the burning of incense that you know they would enjoy, and above and beyond everything else: *communication. Talk to them.* I don't mean constantly *ask them* for things or about things; I mean treat them the same way you would if they were *alive* and you were *visiting* them, because that is precisely what the space set aside for venerating your Ancestors actually is: it is the place where you can *visit* them; where you can provide *them* with *social interaction* so that they do not feel *forgotten*, and, therefore, remain *fulfilled*.

So how does any of that make even the remotest of cases for "Norse angels", apart from the somewhat obvious correlation between the Christian concept of "dead people at some point become angels" and our veneration of the Ancestors as actual worthwhile *contributors* to our current living-breathing lives? The answer to that question lies in my discussion at the beginning of this chapter of the etymological and historical linkage of the Alfar and Disir to the Ancestors. *Disir* are *female* guardian spirits, often considered to be a part of a family's ancestral line, but also inclusive of Goddesses and the valkyries. *Alfar*, however, are a much less distinctly defined group of entities: much of the source material lists them as a completely *different race* of beings (not dissimilar from J.R.R. Tolkien's ideal of the High Elves), yet in many places they are, like the *Disir*, equated with ancestral guardian spirits (*male* ones, as opposed to female ones). This vast swath of "*gray area*" in the lore-based (and even in material culture-based) definitions of both the *Disir* and *Alfar* is how we arrive at the link between their veneration and the veneration of Ancestors. It is also where we begin to arrive at the astounding notion that there might be something of substance in Snorri's accounts of the *Alfar*, in particular, and of *Alfheim* by implication, as "*angelic*" beings with an "*angelic homeland*".

As I said at the end of the **Wight-Walking** chapter, the fact that there is a *definite distinction* between Light Elves (Ljosalfar) and Dark Elves is extremely important to this discussion. Wherever we encounter the prefix or suffix *Alf-* within a person's name or title, or a kenning relating an ancestor or otherwise *human* being to the Alfar, context proves that these references are *always* distinctly to the *Ljosalfar* (Light Elves)--the *celestial* elves —*not* to the Dark Elves—the *chthonic* elves. These two races of beings are *distinctly different* from each other in more ways than simple geography, as I hope I began to establish in the **Wight-Walking** chapter. As *celestial* beings, Alfar (I will henceforth use this term when referring *specifically* to the Ljosalfar *only*) are by definition "*sky beings*" that are "*not of this world*" (or, in the case of our Ancestors who have *become* Alfar, *no longer* of this world), in the same way that Dark Elves are "earth beings", given their status as *chthonic* beings. Snorri describes the Ljosalfar as beautiful and bright like the sun—*shining* entities. What is the definition of an *angel* if we completely divorce that term from its Christian foothold?

> **Angel:** a spiritual being which may be superior to humans in its power and intelligence, often acting as an *attendant spirit* (such as a guardian or messenger), and belonging to a *celestial* hierarchy; often depicted as "*shining*".

Such *celestial hierarchies* of attendant spirits exist in almost every world culture's mythology, including the devas and devis of Hinduism, who are often simply referred to as "The Shining Ones" in Vedic literature. Within this Hindu paradigm, *devas* are male, while *devis* are their female equivalent, as with the Alfar and Disir in our own Norse Tradition. Etymologically, both deva and devi descend from the Proto-Indo-European word *deiwos*, an adjective which originally meant "*celestial*" or "*shining*". This is of particular interest to us as Norse Witches because *deiwos* is also the root of the word *Tiwaz*, which is both a rune and a God (Tiw; Tyr), proving that the *root concept* which provided not only the etymological root of devas and devis, but in fact, the word *divine* itself, definitely *touched* Norse society, from an anthropological perspective. The ways in which our own tradition of the Alfar and Disir, specifically as they relate to Ancestor veneration, mirror the Hindu belief in devas and devis only serves to further my claim: yes, Virginia, there *are* Norse Angels!

The Alfar and Disir fulfill that angelic role in our Tradition: few would deign deny them as *celestial beings*, often superior in power and intellect to living humans, who act as *attendant spirits* to the denizens of the mundane world. As such, our Ancestors might *sometimes become* Alfar or Disir, but not *all* Alfar and Disir were *ever* humans, nor do *all* of the Revered Dead *become* Alfar or Disir. We see this mirrored in other traditions where we find *angels* or *devas*, including Hinduism and Buddhism (which stems from a Hindu root): some humans become *celestial beings*, while others do not (usually based on a system of right action; the more "righteous" one is in life, the more likely they are to become an *angel* or *deva* in the afterlife). In the Norse Tradition, we may find a reflection of this in the existence of the *Einherjar* and *Valkyries*: those who have died heroically in battle and been brought to Valhalla, and those who bring them there, respectively. While "dying heroically in battle" is by no means a metric by which we may effectively measure someone's "righteousness" in life, the truth is, the lore is actually fairly unclear on precisely *what* parameters were used to actively *decide* said heroism. They *are* clear, however, on the fact that a pact exists between Odin and Freyja, with half of the "heroic dead" going to Valhalla (with Odin), and the other half going to Folkvangr and Sessrumnir (with Freyja). Which God gets "which half", and based on *what* parameters precisely, is also never explained. As I discussed in the opening chapters of this book, Valhalla and Folkvangr/Sessrumnir are also *not* the only places in which the Dead may find themselves: there is also Helheim, as well as Aegir's Hall and Nastrond. The existence of multiple "afterlife locations" in Norse Tradition mirrors the "layered Heavens" of Hinduism and Buddhism, as well as (to the surprise of many Christians) Christianity, in ways that cannot and must not be ignored. These multiple "afterlife destinations" provide a very important clue to the conundrum of "some Ancestors are Alfar/Disir, but not all Alfar/Disir were once humans".

The Alfar and Disir have incredibly deep associations with two Vanic Deities: Freyr and Freyja (respectively), who may provide a paradigm for us for Alfar and Disir of the *non*-ancestral variety. In the *Ynglinga Saga*, Snorri euhemerizes the Norse Gods as very human heroes and kings, with Freyr, son of Njordr, as a King of the Swedes. When Freyr dies, we are told he was buried in a mound, which had a door with three holes in it. At tax time, money was poured through the holes in the door, assuring "peace and good seasons" for the Swedish people. Clearly Freyr was never *actually* a Swedish king, however, part of his purview *is* kingship (very much in the same sense as the concepts of Sovereignty and

Divine Kingship among the Celts), which may be part of *why* Snorri drew this association. In fact, Saxo Grammaticus may confirm this for us when he writes: "The most valiant of the Swedes were....kinsmen of the divine Fro (Freyr) and faithful accessories of the gods..." who "traced the origin of their race from the god Fro (Freyr)." Both Snorri's and Saxo's accounts of Freyr suggest Him as a "God of the Mound"; a god of the Dead, but also of the cycle of the seasons and the fertility of the crops, not dissimilar from Dionysus. We are told in *Grimnismal* that Alfheim was given to Freyr as a "tooth-gift"--a gift given to an infant upon the cutting of their first tooth—making him the "Lord of Alfheim", or specifically, "Lord of the Ljosalfar". So, Freyr, "Lord of the Mound", is also Freyr, "Lord of Alfheim", creating yet another bond between the Alfar and the Ancestors.

Freyja may be seen as the "epitome of the Disir" in much the same way Her Brother, Freyr, is that for the Alfar. The supposed identity of Freyja as "Queen of the Valkyries" is a much-argued topic within Heathen and Norse Reconstructionist circles, and while I will not officially weigh in on one side or the other of that argument, I *will* say that Her kenning as *Valfreyja* ("Lady of the Slain") definitely at least *associates* Her with valkyries, and, therefore, with one of the most popular characterizations of the Disir. In case you have been living under a rock during most of your life cycle as a Norse Witch, *valkyries* are female "warrior-spirits" who choose from the slain those who will go to Odin's Hall of Valhalla. The word valkyrie itself is from Old Norse *valkyrja* (plural *valkyrjur*), which is actually comprised of two words: *valr* ("the slain") and *kjosa* ("to choose"). Together, they mean "chooser of the slain". In the *Volundarkvida*, we are told that valkyries may sometimes appear in the form of *swan-maidens* (maids who can *shapeshift* into swans with the benefit of their *swan feather cloaks*). Obviously, there are quite a few things which valkyries and Freyja have in common, not least of which is their propensity to shapeshift into birds through the use of feathered clothing, yet if Freyja is the "Queen of the Valkyries", why would the valkyries bear the slain to Odin's hall of Valhalla, rather than to Her hall of Sessrumnir? Another of Her kennings, *Vanadis* (literally: "female guardian spirit of the Vanir" or "Woman of the Vanir"), makes Her connection to the Disir even more clear. These two kennings of Freyja—Vanadis and Valfrejya-- may help us unlock both the mystery of the "all valkyries are Disir, but not all Disir are valkyries" dilemma, and the ongoing "Freyja as Queen of the Valkyries" debate.

From the tales of Freyja and the valkyries, we can gather that at least some (if not all) Disir have the ability to *fly*, or to become *winged-beings* (as with the typical Judeo-Christian depictions of *angels*), but what of the Alfar? The archaeological record has produced finds over the past few years which have left many scholars scratching their heads as they try to determine precisely *what* these artifacts are attempting to depict, but which I feel provide ample proof that our Ancestors definitely held some notion of *winged Alfar*. The Winged Man of Uppakra (Sweden) is perhaps the most widely known of these artifacts, and certainly the most intriguing. Discovered in September 2011, this large gilded copper artifact was possibly a sword chape (similar to others found at Birka, Sweden; more on those in a moment), though scholars are still debating the purpose it may have served for its previous ancient owner. It dates from somewhere around the 8th century AD, and scholars have determined that it is *unlikely* to have been influenced by Judeo-Christian sources (in other words, it isn't a depiction of one of *their* angels), which is very important, given what it depicts: a *winged man*.

(Winged Man of Uppakra; photo-credit unknown)

If this were the only such artifact depicting a winged male, it would not make much of a case for winged Alfar, but there are others which are quite similar, including the aforementioned sword chape from Birka, Sweden:

Photo-credit: C.O. Lofman; circa 10th century AD

There is also this pin from Norelund, Gastrikland, Sweden which dates to the Viking Period (roughly 8th century AD):

Photo-credit: ATA

Scholars and archaeologists have suggested various interpretations of these finds, including that they may be depictions of Wayland the Smith, aka Volundr, described in the lore as *another* "King of the Alfar" (I say "another" here, because of Freyr's status as Lord of Alfheim). In his story in the *Volundarkvida*, we are also told of his marriage to a *swan maiden* (who most scholars identify as a *valkyrie*), providing a further link to the Alfar-Disir Tradition. But why would he be depicted as a winged figure himself? Near the end of the *Volundarkvida*, we find these passages, as Volundr makes his escape from where he has previously been held captive (and since wrought his vengeance upon his captors):

Laughing, Volundr
Took to the air,
Crying Bothvild
Went away from the island,
Reluctant for peace
And her father's wrath.
--*Volundarkvida 31, Translation Mine*

And Nithuth said:
"You do not speak gently,
And nor will I, Volundr;
Worse words will I use:
There is no man high enough
To knock you off your own high horse;
No man so powerful
That he can set you back apace,
When you are up there, in the sky,
Covered in clouds."

Laughing, Volundr
Took to the air,
And foolish Nithuth sat down.
--*Volundarkvida 37-38, Translation Mine*

The details of precisely *how* Volundr is able to "take to the air" are apparently lost to time, though a story in *Thithrekssaga* details how Volundr's brother, Egil, fashions for his brother a *feather-cloak*, like those worn by *swan maidens* and Freyja. Granted, donning a feather-cloak to *shapeshift* into a bird isn't *quite* the same thing as "sprouting wings as an angel", but when we take into account the *shamanic root* of the ancient Norse Tradition, those two concepts become a bit less mutually exclusive of each other. Even if the artifacts mentioned *are*, indeed, representations of Volundr, given his title of *visi Alfa* (King of the Alfar), such depictions definitely provide essential proof of an ancestral concept of *winged Alfar*.

Depictions of *winged Disir* are comparatively easier to find, in large part due to the tradition of the *swan maidens*. As far back as the Bronze Age, we find images of "winged" female figures, identified as Disir or swan maidens. The *Kungagraven* (King's

Grave) site in Kivik, Sweden boasts numerous repetitions of such images upon its stones—images which we likewise see repeated in the Oseberg Tapestry (834 AD) and at least one Gotland Picture Stone, as well as upon silver pendants at sites in Grodinge and Birka (8th-10th centuries). Certainly, some of these images may be attributable as images of Freyja (the silver pendants of Grodinge and Birka in particular), but this is hotly debated among scholars, and while most can agree upon them being *definite* depictions of Disir-figures, there are many who have expressed gross dissent at these artifacts as direct representations of Freyja specifically.

So why do *some* Ancestors become Alfar or Disir, while others do not, and what is the nature of those Alfar and Disir who were never humans at all? We certainly do not have any sort of "neat system of righteousness" within the Norse Tradition by which to elevate some Ancestors to something akin to "sainthood", or, do we? In a purely Christian system, of course, the answer to the first half of that opening question would be based upon a determination of "sinlessness": those who are the most without sin become the highest of angels, or, at the very least, become angels at all. (Although it should be noted that there is a tendency among the Christian population to romanticize death to the degree where everyone who passes over automatically winds up "sprouting wings" and "playing a harp".) Most of those same Christians would be very surprised to discover that such notions are a comparatively modern invention, with very little basis in their own "holy history" (*Heilsgeschichte*). The concept of humans even *potentially becoming angels at all* after death was not "popularized" in Christianity until roughly 1787, when it became part of the canon of the New Church, established by Emanuel Swedenborg (and, yes, he was Swedish). However, earlier sources (and specifically the work of Maimonides, a 12th century Sephardic Jewish philosopher and rabbi) list ten choirs of angels, the lowest rank of which are the *Ishim*, or "man like beings", who are described as "the beautiful souls of just men", and who are assigned the specific duties of acting as *intermediaries* between God and humanity and performing the duties of *guardian spirits* (in very much the same manner as our own Norse Ancestors who become Alfar and Disir). Therefore, even in the Judeo-Christian tradition, not *all* members of the Revered Dead become angels, nor were most angels *ever* human in the first place.

We find this echoed in the devas and devis of Buddhism and Hinduism, which spring from the same Proto-Indo-European root as our own Norse Traditions. Devas and devis—*celestial beings* which act as *attendant spirits*, *guardians*, *warriors*, and *messengers* and therefore meeting the *actual definition* of the word *angel*—are *not born human*, yet many long to *become* that. The afterlife of Buddhism and Hinduism is quite different from the vision held by Judeo-Christians or even our Norse Ancestors, colored so heavily as it is by the overriding and pervading concept of reincarnation. *Ascension*—that is, to die and *become something better than one's present Self*—is, once again, governed by the concept of *righteousness* or *right action*, however, it is not so simplified as "keeping one's regular physical form, only with the addition of wings and the new 'title' or 'status' of 'angel'". Instead, one may die in this *incarnation* as a human, and be *completely reborn* in their next *incarnation* as a *deva* or *devi*. Those who are born as *devas* or *devis* in this incarnation often long to be *completely reborn* in their next *incarnation* as human beings— who are actually *lower* on the scale of *Ascension*—because they are aware that such *humanness* provides an opportunity to understand impermanence, suffering, and selflessness that it is impossible to gain as devas or devis. Within Buddhism and Hinduism, that *understanding* of impermanence, suffering, and selflessness provides the ultimate definition of *righteousness* or *right action*.

There remains, however, that definition of those Dead who become "angels" in the afterlife having been *righteous* during their lives as human beings. While neither the Ancestors nor us (as modern Norse Witches) have a codified concept of sin, we *do* have a very definite concept of *Righteousness*, and of *Right Action* which is, in fact, one of the cornerstones of our ethical practice. In fact, as you've likely noticed (and possibly even enacted by now): our Oath to keep the Norse Virtues is the very first oath we take as a Norse Witch. Ultimately, for us, *Righteousness* and *Right Action* means *maintaining frith* with those whom we consider *innangard*, as discussed earlier in this book in the chapter **Good Versus Evil**. As I established in that chapter, *accidentally breaking frith*, or even *intentionally breaking frith* in order to fulfill the value of *Justice*, with one or two or even three parts of the Oath every once in a great while under specific circumstances is *not* the definition of evil, nor even of *sin*. *Actively seeking* to do the *direct opposite* of the Oath, and thereby *actively breaking frith*, outside the parameters of the value of *Justice*, however, *is* the closest thing we have in our Tradition to actively sinning. It isn't *easy* to live one's life by our **Virtuous Oath**; one might even say that to do so is *heroic*:

Heroic: courageous; daring; something which emulates the behavior of someone who is strong, possesses great ability, and is admired for their achievements and noble (excellent; outstanding) qualities.

Our Tradition tells us that *heroes* go to Valhalla and Folkvangr/Sessrumnir. While this has become romanticized in our modern culture to a concept of dying boldly on the battlefield, perhaps the real criteria for *heroism* has more to do with how one lives one's life (leading a *righteous* life), than with how well one wields an axe on the battlefield (especially since not many of us run around wielding axes on battlefields or elsewhere nowadays!). Perhaps that is the missing criteria, when one ponders what made some people worthy of selection by the valkyries and/or Freyja, while others were not. Perhaps that is the answer to why *some* Ancestors become Alfar and Disir, while others do not. The lore tells us that those who go to Valhalla become *Einherjar* (literally: "those who once fought"), and that human women may become valkyries (the story of Sigrun in *Helgakvida Hundingsbana I and II* and *Hromundar saga Gripssonar*). Though we are *not* told what those who go to Sessrumnir/Folkvangr are formally *called*, it is alluded that eventually, they will go on to reside in *Alfheim*, thereby becoming Alfar.

In truth, however, *righteousness* in life has very little to do with the potential of gaining wings in the afterlife. To live one's life with that as the end-goal--"hey, one day, I want to be one of the Alfar"--is the same "backwards response" as we discussed in the opening chapters of this book. We should live in this world, not in some world-to-possibly-come. Wings on an Alfar are no more a signifier of *righteousness* than are the wings of Loki when He dons Freyja's feather-cloak! Sure, living a *righteous* life assists, ultimately, in determining which "neighborhood" you might wind up in on the Other Side, and whether or not one might become Alfar, but the *wings* of the Alfar are a wee bit more "utilitarian" than that, for lack of a better word. As with Freyja Herself (and even Loki and others when They don Her cloak), and as with Volundr and the Valkyries, wings are, first, foremost, and ultimately, *tools*. They help their bearer *accomplish* something in their afterlife occupation which otherwise could not be accomplished. Surprisingly for many, that thing *accomplished* is rarely *transportation*! More often than not, the actual purpose of wings is to *inspire awe*: either the *terrible* kind, which inspires an honest form of terror in whoever is met with the angelic visage of an Alfar, or the *peaceful* kind, which informs the viewer that they are about to be guarded, guided, and protected—given succor, even—by the mantle of sheltering wings. Other world mythologies rarely evidence this truth, but if you look closely enough at ours, I believe you will be surprised by what you find there. To the Ancient Norse, the "wearing" of wings signified very specific things: protection, potential peace, and succor, as with the Valkyries, on the one hand, and vengeance (as in the sense of an "avenging angel"), battle preparations, and incoming justice, as with Volundr, on the other.

And what of those "Norse angels" who were never human in the first place? What of the Alfar and Disir who were *always* Alfar and Disir, and never walked in flesh here upon this Earth? My own personal experiences of these beings have echoed not only what we find in our own Norse Tradition, but also the ranks of angelic choirs found in the Judeo-Christian Tradition. While I am aware that this may be off-putting for some, the Truth simply *is what it is*; you can choose not to believe in elephants in a world which is clearly populated by elephants, but that doesn't change the fact that there are, indeed, elephants. There is literally so much to explore, when it comes to these never-been-human Alfar and Disir, that I could write another book solely on that topic. Therefore, for the sake of brevity, herein I will only provide this small comparative table, before moving on to a brief discussion of honoring the non-Ancestral Alfar and Disir.

Hierarchical Experience of the Alfar and Disir

Rank	Judeo-Christian Explanation	Norse Cognate
Erelim	"the valiant/courageous"; agents of earthly justice; ruled over by Ariel/Uriel (depending on source); also have jurisdiction over elemental forces (such as Landvaettir)	Several of the handmaidens of Frigga, including: Var, Syn, and Hlin. The valkyries (especially as the handmaidens of Odin, but also as choosers of the slain). In my personal experience, Uriel cognates roughly to Modgudr, acting very much as an "angel of death" and Guardian of the Afterlife, as well as having a connection to the Landvaettir and/or Dokkalfar.

Rank	Judeo-Christian Explanation	Norse Cognate
Seraphim	"the burning ones"; the "retinue of God who continually praise Him"; ruled over by Gabriel	The attendant Alfar mentioned in *Lokasenna*. In my personal experience, Gabriel cognates roughly to Heimdall (who also has a horn that will be blown to herald the Apocalypse: Ragnarok)
Malakim	"messengers"; often serve a purifying and/or healing role, as well as carrying messages from the Divine down to humans; ruled over by Raphael	Two of the handmaidens of Frigga: Gna and Eir. In my personal experience, Raphael cognates roughly to Hermodr, who is broadly considered the messenger of the Gods, and could be loosely associated with healing due to his actions in the wake of the death of Baldur.

Rank	Judeo-Christian Explanation	Norse Cognate
Bene-Elohim	"sons of godly beings"; angelic parents of Nephilim (basically angel-human hybrids), as well as their Nephilim offspring	The children of Ljosalfar/human couplings (or even, in some cases, Dokkalfar/human couplings), which are encountered numerous times in the lore.
Ishim	"manlike beings"; humans who have become angels (as previously discussed herein); perform similar functions to the Erelim; ruled over by Michael	In my personal experience, these are the warriors of the Gods, cognate to both the Einherjar and the Valkyries, as well as the inhabitants of Sessrumnir. Michael cognates roughly to Vidar.

As I previously mentioned, *Alfablot* and *Disablot* were definitely observed by the ancient Norse. Disablot is attested as having been celebrated either during Winter Nights (likely at the Autumn Equinox, known in other Pagan Traditions as Mabon), at Yule (the Winter Solstice), during Disting (Imbolc in other Pagan Traditions), or at the Sigrblot (Ostara in other Pagan Traditions). Alfablot is attested as having been celebrated "near the end of autumn", likely in November, bringing it to coincide roughly with Christian All Saint's Day (and, therefore, Halloween: All Hallow's Even'). Disablot tended to be a very public festival, celebrated in larger temples, such as the one at Uppsala in Sweden, whereas Alfablot was more a festival of "home and hearth" (attested in *Heimskringla* and *Austrafararvisur*, respectively, as well as elsewhere in the lore). In my own personal practice, as in the practice of many modern Heathens, I celebrate Alfablot at the time referred to as Samhain by other Pagans, and Disablot at the time referred to as Imbolc by other Pagans. Within the space of my Alfablot Rite, I address Freyr, as Lord of the Mound and Lord of Alfheim; at Disablot, I address Freyja as Vanadis (Lady of the Vanir, and also "Queen of the Disir"). You will find both rites detailed below; may you use them well and wisely.

Alfablot Rite

Prepare your chalice with a sweet flavored drink, which would be appealing not only to Freyr, but to the Alfar. (I have personally found white cranberry-strawberry juice to be a favorite; your mileage may vary.) The usual white candle should be replaced with a dark green or dark blue candle, which you may choose to anoint with an oil of your choice (I have found that amber-based oils appeal to Freyr as much as to Freyja; again, your mileage may vary), and which you may also choose to inscribe with the runes Fehu, Inguz (Freyr's runes), and Raidho (often associated with the travels of the Dead, as it is considered one of the runes of the "Helheim Road" and Hela). If you wish to also make offerings of food, I highly recommend including oatcakes and honey, though this is not a requirement.

Create Sacred Space (**Quick Reference: Creating Sacred Space**, 1-5)

Raise your chalice:

Hail, Freyr, Light-Bringer!
Lord of Alfheim and Lord of the Mound;
Son of Njordr;
Brother of Bright Freyja who is Vanadis;
Lord of Peace and Good Seasons: Skal!

Toast Freyr (drink a small sip from your chalice)

Peace and good seasons to You,
And may there ever be frith between us,
And between me and mine,
And those who have come before and who will
    come after.

Pour Blot to Freyr (pour a small amount of liquid from your chalice onto the ground or into your hlaut-boll)

Blessings and Honor
To You and Your kin,
And to any of my own kin
Who have come to serve You.
Blessings and Honor
To the Alfar:
To those who once walked beside us,
As our Ancestors and kin,
And to those who never did,
But are among us, just the same.
Hail Alfar! Skal!

Toast the Alfar (drink another small sip from your chalice)

Peace and good seasons to you,
And may there ever be frith between us,
And between me and mine,
And those who have come before and who will
        come after.

Pour blot to the Alfar (pour a small amount of liquid from your chalice onto the ground or into your hlaut-boll)

Say what is on your heart. (Speak of your genuine love for your male-identifying Ancestors, the Alfar, and Freyr.)

Hail Freyr! Hail Alfar! Skal!

Toast

If you are observing Alfablot with others, pass the chalice to them, and have them say what is on their heart. (They should likewise speak of their genuine love for their male-identifying Ancestors, the Alfar, and Freyr.)

Hail Freyr! Hail Alfar! Skal!

Toast (have them return the chalice to you)

Say what is on your heart. (Address any recent concerns that you might otherwise have   taken to a father-figure, to your Ancestors who identified primarily as male, to the Alfar as angelic forces, and to Freyr.)

Hail Freyr! Hail Alfar! Skal!

Toast

If you are observing Alfablot with others, pass the chalice to them, and have them say what is on their heart. (Address any recent concerns that they might otherwise have taken to a father-figure, to their Ancestors who identified primarily as male, to the Alfar as angelic forces, and to Freyr.)

Hail Freyr! Hail Alfar! Skal!

Toast (have them return the chalice to you)

Say what is on your heart. (Thank your male-identifying Ancestors, the Alfar, and Freyr for all of the good things in your life in which you know they may have been instrumental.)

Hail Freyr! Hail Alfar! Skal!

Toast

If you are observing Alfablot with others, pass the chalice to them, and have them say what is on their heart. (Thank their male-identifying Ancestors, the Alfar, and Freyr for all of the good things in their lives as above.)

Hail Freyr! Hail Alfar! Skal!

Toast (have them return the chalice)

For all that you have done for us,
And for all that you will do;
For all that you have meant to us,
And for all that you will mean:
Peace and good seasons;
Love, gratitude, and honor.
Blessed be!

Pour blot

Raise the Fence

Ground

Center again if necessary.

Disablot Rite

Prepare your chalice with a sweet flavored drink, which would be appealing not only to Freyja, but to the Disir. (I have personally found sweet red wine blends to be a favorite; your mileage may vary.) The usual white candle should be replaced with a lavender candle, which you may choose to anoint with an oil of your choice (I have found that amber-based oils appeal to Freyja; again, your mileage may vary), and which you may also choose to inscribe with the runes Berkano, Dagaz, and Raidho (often associated with the travels of the   Dead, as it is considered one of the runes of the "Helheim Road" and Hela). If you wish to also make offerings of food, I highly recommend chocolate, raspberries, and strawberries, though this is not a requirement.

Create Sacred Space (**Quick Reference: Creating Sacred Space**, 1-5)

Raise your chalice:

Hail Freyja, Vanadis!
Queen of Cats,
Valfreyja;
Daughter of Njordr;
Sister of Freyr,
Who is Lord of the Mound and Lord of Alfheim;
Queen of the Disir;
Lady of Peace and Good Seasons: Skal!

Toast Freyja (drink a small sip from your chalice)

Peace and good seasons to You,
And may there ever be frith between us,
And between me and mine,
And those who have come before and who will
   come after.

Pour Blot to Freyja (pour a small amount of liquid from
your chalice onto the ground or into your hlaut-boll)

Blessings and Honor
To You and Your kin,
And to any of my own kin
Who have come to serve You.
Blessings and Honor
To the Disir:
To those who once walked beside us,
As our Ancestors and kin,
And to those who never did,
But are among us, just the same.
Hail Disir! Skal!

Toast the Disir (drink another small sip from your chalice)

Peace and good seasons to you,
And may there ever be frith between us,
And between me and mine,
And those who have come before and who will
   come after.

Pour blot to the Disir (pour a small amount of liquid from
your chalice onto the ground or into your hlaut-boll)

Say what is on your heart. (Speak of your genuine love for
your female-identifying Ancestors, the Disir, and Freyja.)

Hail Freyja! Hail Disir! Skal!

Toast

If you are observing Disablot with others, pass the chalice to them, and have them say what is on their heart. (They should likewise speak of their genuine love for their female-identifying Ancestors, the Disir, and Freyja.)

Hail Freyja! Hail Disir! Skal!

Toast (have them return the chalice to you)

Say what is on your heart. (Address any recent concerns that you might otherwise have taken to a mother-figure, to your Ancestors who identified primarily as female, to the Disir as angelic forces, and to Freyja.)

Hail Freyja! Hail Disir! Skal!

Toast

If you are observing Disablot with others, pass the chalice to them, and have them say what is on their heart. (Address any recent concerns that they might otherwise have taken to a mother-figure, to their Ancestors who identified primarily as female, to the Disir as angelic forces, and to Freyja)

Hail Freyja! Hail Disir! Skal!

Toast (have them return the chalice to you)

Say what is on your heart. (Thank your female-identifying Ancestors, the Disir, and Freyja for all of the good things in your life in which you know they may have been instrumental.)

Hail Freyja! Hail Disir! Skal!

Toast

If you are observing Disablot with others, pass the chalice to them, and have them say what is on their heart. (Thank their female-identifying Ancestors, the Disir, and Freyja for all of the good things in their lives as above.)

Hail Freyja! Hail Disir! Skal!

Toast (have them return the chalice)

For all that you have done for us,
And for all that you will do;
For all that you have meant to us,
And for all that you will mean:
Peace and good seasons;
Love, gratitude, and honor.
Blessed be!

Pour blot

Raise the Fence.

Ground.

Center.

Hail, Hela!
Corpse-Mother,
Wolf-Sister,
Pale-Rider of Helhest;
Peace-Bringer;
Kiss away our
Sorrow,
And comfort us
In our grief.
Remind us to fall in love with life,
That we may live it well
In the forever
Of Death.
Protect the Horse
And the Rider,
When the Dead
Come forth
To speak,
And remind us
Of our Ancestors
In those moments
When we are weak.

Courting Hela

The hour was late, and I sat in my office alone, save for the cat, everyone else in the house sound asleep. Outside my window, darkness, and the steady peeping of spring peepers (frogs) as the hours waned on towards three a.m. Normally at that hour, the house is still and peaceful; comforting, even. But as I rose that night to trundle my way to the restroom, there was the sound of a soft foot-fall on the stairs, and the hairs on the back of my neck rose to greet them, and I found myself filled with a profound sense of dread. Given Michelle's propensity for trans-mediumship, and the nature of my own being, we get a *lot* of "astral traffic" in our house: random "dead-folk", Alfar, Disir, and others, as well as random Gods and Goddesses (most often Freyja, but sometimes Njordr or Freyr), are common and frequent visitors to our home, but there was something about *this* presence that registered as decidedly *different* from the list of "usual suspects". And I found myself mildly afraid. *Hela had come to call.*

When you are what *I am*, Hela—our Norse "Goddess of Death"--is probably the last Deity on the list that you want to have visiting. You see, the other "elephant in the room" that I've worked very hard not to beat like a dead horse throughout the writing of this book is that I am a channeled spirit. I've been dead for twenty-four years, and I am writing this book through the gracious help of my "host" or, as some might refer to her, "horse", Michelle Iacona. The use of the terms "horse" and "rider" for the one "ridden" by a spirit, and the spirit, respectively, are most commonly heard when referring to the form of trans-mediumship which occurs in Vodun (Voodoo). Trans-mediumship is quite different from *trance* mediumship: instead of the medium going into a trance and then explaining what they *hear* from their contacts on the other side, a trance is often (as in our case) completely *unnecessary*, with the "host" or medium simply "stepping out of the way" while the "rider" or spirit "steps in". It is called trans-mediumship because of the *transformation* that occurs upon the entry of the spirit: the medium no longer sounds like themselves; no longer exhibits their own mannerisms. Things such as facial structure, eye color, and other aspects of the medium's physical appearance may actually *change* to match that of the spirit being "hosted". That is certainly the case with me: Michelle is a bit of a "girly girl", soft-featured—in fact, she's a bit of a dead ringer for the late Carrie Fisher—while I am "all dude", as they say. I have a much more prominent jaw, which definitely comes across, and often, the gray of my eyes overshadows the brown of hers.

Thus, when Hela first came to call, the wheels in my brain immediately began turning to thoughts of *"well, that's it; I'm done. She's finally come to claim me."* So I did what anyone faced with a topic they really don't want to discuss might do: I tried to *avoid the subject*, went back to my desk, and tried to get back to *business as usual*. But Hela wasn't having it: She came "right on in", and took a seat in my floofy office chair. The hairs on the back of my neck maintained their erection, and a chill ran down the spine I share with my host, Michelle.

I continued to go on about my business, with Hela effectively "riding shotgun" behind me in the floofy chair, until it was time for me to say my nightly prayers and head to bed. Standing before my *Main Stalli*, I delivered my nightly litany of "thank yous" for all the good things—big and small—that happened to me and for me throughout that day, and then I turned to face Hela, who had come to stand on the right side of my altar:

> *"Hail, Hela-Lokisdottir; Wolf-Daughter; Keeper of the Dead! Yes, I know You're here, and I honor Your presence. But I belong to Freyja and the Vanir, and have sworn to do Their work on this plane, so if You're here to claim me, You're gonna need to take that up with* **Them**. *If there's something else You need me to do, to honor You or even my Ancestors, I'm listening and willing, within reason. But I have a wife and a family who depend on me, even*

*though I'm dead; Michelle **needs** me, and so do my friends. So, hail and welcome, but those are **my** terms of frith."*

And I headed off to bed.

The next morning, I awoke to one of the worst outbreaks of pustular psoriasis we have ever experienced. I was in a lot of pain, with a sky-rocketing fever, and to say I felt lousy was putting it very mildly. Usually when we have an outbreak of that type (there are a lot of different types of psoriasis, and we've danced with all of them, at one point or another), it is because I (or Michelle) have experienced some sort of dramatic emotional trauma: a fight with a family member or a friend; grief; loss. None of those things had happened. It had been "business as usual" here at Casa de Connla-and-Suzanne. In fact, quite to the contrary: both myself and Michelle had been really happy lately. Yet, there it was, seeping and weeping all over the chest she and I share. And I was afraid, again: pustular psoriasis is one of two types of psoriasis that can actually *kill you.* But I got up and got dressed, and headed into my office to set to work on some new art and do my dailies on the Facebook circuit, to keep our business at the front of people's minds.

As the day went on, I tried very hard to think of *anything* that could've triggered this sort of outbreak. The weather had been pretty great, so I could rule out humidity and heat (which also wreak havoc on our psoriasis). As I said, neither of us (me or Michelle) had been upset about anything whatsoever in recent memory. I finally settled on what we refer to as a "methotrexate reaction": even though we are not *on* methotrexate, we mimic its use, combined with coal tar, in the treatment of our psoriasis by a steady internal intake of coal tar (via hand-rolled cigarettes) and folic acid supplements. It is very common for those who are being treated with a combination of coal tar and methotrexate to develop pustular psoriasis, so it made sense that what was happening to us right then was such a reaction. I stopped taking the folic acid and made the decision to begin better regulating our diet (we *had* been eating an enormous amount of foods rich in folic acid as well). That Hela's arrival the previous night might be the *cause* of the outbreak, rather than a harbinger of its *outcome*, never remotely entered my mind.

That night, in the wee hours, She came again, and as I stood at my altar for my nightly prayers, I gave the same prayer as the previous night. The next day, as I set to work, I felt myself "bashed over the head by Deity": it's a familiar feeling to me now, given my work with and for Freyja. A thought or command pops into your head, and you know *you* didn't actually *think* of that, whatever it is: *They did*. Only this time, it wasn't Freyja doing the bashing; *it was Hela*:

> *"You know, this would all go much more smoothly if you would **actually** honor your Ancestors."*

So I did as I was told: I got up out of my chair, selected an appropriate incense from my stash, lit it, and placed it on my *Ancestor Stalli*, and then gave my Ancestors their appropriate veneration. *And my fever broke.*

For about a week, things went on like this: in the wee hours of the morning, I would find myself intensely and inexplicably "creeped out", and then I would see Her—Hela--and I would try to go on about my business, and at prayer time, I would offer that same prayer. During my waking hours, I would make offerings to my Ancestors whenever the fever got really out of control. And each time I did, the fever would break. Meanwhile, I continued to *not* take my folic acid and monitor my diet. I checked on other people's UPG of Hela, and even asked around at a few of the Facebook Groups to which I belong, to see how other people were "coping" with Her presence. I began to leave the ashes of the incense I burned on my *Main Stalli* as an offering to Hela. I remained marginally terrified of Her.

She started invading my dreams. Where once I had experienced Freyja, now I experienced Her. It was in the dreamstate that She finally revealed to me what She had *actually* come for; turns out it wasn't *me* at all. She was here to call Michelle as *fulltrua*:

> *"You belong to Freyja. Michelle belongs to me. Make her know that."*

You would think, given our relationship as "horse and rider", that Michelle would not be a "tough nut for me to crack". And in thinking that, you would be so totally wrong! Michelle is one of the strongest and most *strong-willed* people that I have ever met, and that applies to everyone with whom she interacts, *including me*. No one can tell her what to think or believe; she thinks and believes for herself, all by herself. I mean, sure, don't get me wrong here: she *can* be reasoned with. This isn't some totalitarian situation; some Michelle-tatorship. But she is a firm believer in "just because they're dead, that doesn't mean they're smart", and part of *how* she arrived at that conclusion was living with *me* for two decades! Michelle has been a dedicant of the Welsh Goddess, Cerridwen, for as far back as I can really remember. She is an ordained Welsh Reconstructionist Ollamh (with a heavy Christian backbeat), *neither* Heathen nor Heidhrinn. To tell her that Hela had announced it was time for her to "switch gears", or more aptly "switch boats midstream", was going to go over like a lead balloon, even coming from me.

So the night came when I addressed that with Hela:

"Why me? I mean, why can't You tell her this Yourself?"

And She replied:

"Because the only thing in the Nine Worlds from which Michelle does not constantly and consistently **run away** *is* **you***!"*

And I really couldn't argue with that. For all her strength, intelligence, and ability as a priestess and medium, Michelle definitely has a reputation for "hiding behind the couch" whenever anything "creepy" shows up, and I am, always have been, and always will be, the one who *protects her*. By having *me* "break the news" to Michelle, Hela was showing me the honor of recognizing me as Michelle's "guardian angel" (or "guardian Alfar", as the case may be).

So I did as I was told.

And Michelle argued:

"I'm not even Heathen!"

And I replied:

"I don't think She cares."

And she persisted:

"I belong to Cerridwen!"

And I countered:

"You're a soft polytheist!"

Foot-stomping ensued on Michelle's end of the conversation:

*"I barely even practice right now! Well, I mean, apart from you know, **you**, and being a medium."*

And I smiled:

"Perhaps therein lies the problem...."

At the Temple of Witchcraft's annual Beltane Rite, we were blessed with a pot of wormwood, which is sacred to Hela. Delighted (because she has had a longtime fascination with Artemesia Absinthium), Michelle declared: "We can tend it together, and I will dedicate it as my first offering to Her. And when I can, I'll procure some jet jewelry, and we'll make this thing official. But you're going to have to teach *me*, for a change."

The pustular outbreak subsequently completely subsided; gone as quickly as it had come.

We leave offerings of ashes now on the *Main Stalli* for Hela, myself and Michelle together, and we've dedicated the bird skull figurine which we share to Her. And I'm slowly teaching Michelle what it means to be a Norse Witch, and preparing her to be for Hela what I aspire to be for Valfreyja. These are her first steps along a much wider path, and I am privileged to hold her hand as she takes them. All that she has taught me over the course of the past two decades has led up to this moment, as I sit here typing this. I never would have believed I *could* do this, without Michelle. She believes in me, and I believe in her, and now we both believe in Hela, and Michelle's courtship of Hela has officially begun.

The Deeper Work

Before we take things deeper, and begin to dive into things like working for manifestation, runelore, and astral journeying, we need to do the deeper work to make certain that all of our *Self-Ownership* issues are thoroughly handled. Even when we feel that we have things thoroughly under control in that department, things like grief, physical illnesses and disabilities, and other devastating life crises can sometimes send us spinning. If your system of faith can't get you through the hard times in life, then it's nothing more than pomp and circumstance and religious posturing. Ultimately, there really are many paths up the same mountain, but just because that is the case doesn't mean they all fit our needs. When my own faith was finally broken, and the top of the mountain seemed the furthest away it had ever been, I found it was the Northern Lights which lit my way back towards the top.

Our family dog died on the day before Christmas Eve, 2015. Given everything else I've been through over the years, that may seem like a strange thing to have break my faith completely, but it did. I mean, clearly, now me and Boo are on the same side of the proverbial fence, so it's not like we can't "keep in touch". But that's not *why* it broke my faith. Over the course of the past two decades, I have done a *lot* of very hard work for The Boss. And on that afternoon, when our last remaining beloved family dog (Elvis had passed the previous Spring) went into convulsions in Suzanne's arms, I prayed, and I prayed *hard*, and I honestly expected to get what I prayed. Not because I selfishly needed the dog to stay alive because I would miss her. No, I wouldn't be the one who *needed* to miss her: the *rest of our family would*. And it was the day before Christmas Eve—we had already bought the dog her Christmas toys. I needed The Boss to come through on this one for me in a really big way so that Christmas wouldn't be *ruined* for the entire family. And He didn't. There was no saving little Boo. I officially resented the shit out of God.

I tried to take every path I knew back up the mountain. We were expected to go to Christmas Mass, and all I could do was sit there and *resent* God. How *dare* He ask me to celebrate His Son's birthday right now? You don't celebrate the birthdays of people who have proven they are *not* your friends by making you work hard for them consistently, and then not paying that back when you're in your moment of direst need. I tried to take the Buddhist/Taoist road back up the mountain, but I just kept sliding into old patterns of memory that tore me down, instead of helping me up. I tried to be a "better Druid", but found no peace there, either. Everything was pretty and interesting, but there was no fulfillment. This went on for several months. Finally, in February of 2016, I looked North, to the Norse Tradition. There, I found Freyja, and She embraced me as the fallen warrior that I am, and I have never looked back.

What peace do I find here, that I could not find anywhere else? How is this path up the mountain different from all the rest? The peace I find here is in an intimate closeness to the Gods that I never experienced with any of the rest of the paths that I've trodden.Unlike all those other paths, which promise Deity waiting for you at your final destination—the top of the mountain—I have discovered over and over again that in this Norse Tradition, the Gods frequently meet you halfway. It's more like a faith-filled relay race, than an uphill marathon. I take a moment out of my day to make an offering at my *Stalli*, and They are *there*. Not some pie-in-the-sky notion of "God is listening from afar", but rather a very hands-on sensation of being held in Their arms, or, occasionally, even bashed firmly over the head til I learn better. It is very much an Abrahamic sense of *immanence*: what Moses must have felt as he stood before the burning bush. Since becoming Heidhrinn, I have felt that *every single day*.

The Norse Tradition provides us with faces of Deity who are willing to *cry with us*, instead of *make us cry*. Sigyn, the second wife of Loki, knew such great sorrow and even anger at the death of Her children and the torture and imprisonment of Her husband, and yet *She endures*, and She teaches *us* to do the same. Hela, Loki's daughter, lives among the Dead, and knows their agonies and regrets, and it is her *eternal duty* to heal those pains; She's perfectly willing to help heal *ours* as well. As Death, She reminds us to love life, and to live it well, so that we have a lesser pain, when the time finally comes. And it will come for us all, but She helps us not to *fear* it. Frigga is a loving mother when there is no physical mother there to give comfort. Freyja, likewise, is both mother and older sister; that loving, gentle female force that helps us remember that both love and beauty still endure not only in this world, but in our deepest selves. And such comforts come not only from our Goddesses, but from our Gods as well: many times I have turned to Njordr, the Peace-Maker, the Great Navigator, and many times He has led me through stormy seas to calmer waters, and the safe harbor beyond. Tyr likewise has known His own pain, in the betrayal of a childhood friend in order to do what He knew was right (the binding of Fenrir), which ended in the loss of His right hand. He understands us well when we are faced with the hardest decisions of our lives, but for all the right reasons. He knows that pain first hand (no pun intended), and He is more than willing to stand with us, and guide us through. Even Odin can be a kind father-figure in our hours of greatest need, and it took meeting Him as the All-Father, before I finally came to terms with my relationship with The Boss.

Ultimately, it was Odin who taught me that sometimes sacrifices are necessary, if we are ever going to grow. Without that loss that Christmas of 2015, I might never have realized my system of faith was broken. When things are good with us, it is easy to grow complacent in our faith-base, and simply maintain the status quo. We go along blindly, consigning ourselves to celebrating holidays and perhaps saying a prayer every now and again, when we have the time, or when we think to do so. That's *how* I became a "Holiday Druid". It is when things are at their most difficult that we find out who our real friends are; sometimes, those friends include the Gods. But if we never go *through* anything—if nothing bad ever happens to us; if no sacrifices need be made—we never have the opportunity to discover our true faith. Ultimately, faith that is not tested is no faith at all; it's just going through the motions. Odin discovered that the hard way, as He hung on Yggdrasil, pierced by His own spear, and a second time, when He gave His eye for the wisdom of the Well. He was not *afraid* to make those sacrifices; to face those tests. He understood that *anything worth having comes at great cost*. Real faith—*real religious practice*—makes demands of us, otherwise we are not *bound back* to anything but our own hot air.

When life brings us to our knees, there is nowhere else to look but *up*. Sometimes, we look up, and we see God/dess; sometimes, we look up, and we see our own reflection. Either way, we find ourselves asking those **Six Big Questions** we discussed at the beginning of this book, and above them, and behind them, and beyond them, looming like some great neon plea to every Power in the Nine Worlds, one other question: **Why?** Most often, we scream that question in the form of **Why me?**, though sometimes, it is just that one simple word, all alone, and desperate. Unfortunately, the most honest answer to that question is yet another question: **Why not?** What is it that fools us human beings into thinking we are so awe-inspiringly special that nothing bad—nothing truly and deeply horrible, even, perhaps—is ever going to happen to us? Some things are just a part of our *Wyrd*, and there's nothing we can do to change them, and, honestly, it likely wouldn't make us *better people* if we actually *could*. No, it is much more likely that it would turn us into prideful, holier-than-thou people, with our noses so far in the air that we would drown if it started raining! Why shouldn't we suffer, and grieve, and be depressed, just as Odin suffered and grieved and was depressed? Or Tyr? Or even Freyr? All of Them *gained something* for those things They endured: Wisdom, Justice, Love. **Why?** Because Wisdom, Justice, Love. That's **why**.

And yet, I have met too many Heathens who would argue wholeheartedly against the very concept of a deep, personal relationship with the Gods, much less the concept of *compassionate* Gods. Their attitudes of "the Gods don't really care about what happens to us" and "we need Them more than They need us" are, in fact, a huge reason *why* I decided I needed *something more*—Norse Witchcraft—in the first place, and how I realized that other people (like yourself, dear reader) also needed that *something more*. To have *sacrifice* as the very cornerstone of our religion—in the form of blot, as well as the offerings we leave on our altars—and then argue that "we need Them more than They need us" is anthropologically ludicrous, at best, and desperate hypocrisy, at worst. If the Gods don't *need* us, then why do we go through the trouble of giving Them gifts? Why do we call Them our friends? I am left wondering if these people enact these same behaviors with physical humans: do they give gifts constantly to people who genuinely wouldn't put them out if they were on fire? Do they call such people their friends, too? My experiences of a *compassionate* Odin may be precisely that—*my own experiences* —but in the end, if the Gods are not really *there for us*, then why in the heck are we *there for Them*? These same people will often on the one hand express their feelings that the Gods are these distant, uncaring beings, while on the other hand telling stories of how the Gods gifted them with a specific bind-rune, or came to visit them in their waking lives. If They're so uncaring and distant, then why did They take the time out of Their "busy schedules" to bother giving you such a gift, or paying you a visit? Quite simply: you cannot have it both ways! Not only that, but to claim to be a Reconstructionist, and then ignore the many accounts in the lore of where the Gods cared enough to actually *step in and help* (or step in and *smite* or otherwise *get involved*) is vain hypocrisy. True, it is beyond Their power to shape our Wyrd, because Wyrd affects us all (even the Gods Themselves are not exempt), but given that, They most certainly are willing to *understand us* and *be there for us* precisely *because* They are staring down the same barrel as us. Belief otherwise—that the Gods simply *don't care*— shifts personal practice from an actual *religion* to a series of (perhaps completely heartfelt) historical reenactments, and nothing more.

Having a firm grasp of the concepts of Wyrd and Orlog, and actually putting that understanding to work in your life, can cause many people to think you *are weird*, as you face even the most difficult things in life—and the most trying of times—with an almost Buddhaesque calmness. In fact, I tend to drive my wife a little nuts. I discussed how Wyrd and Orlog work in an earlier chapter, as they relate to the practice of a daily rune pull, but there's more to putting those concepts truly to work in your life than just "shaking a bag and pulling a stone", or even doing what that rune instructs on a daily basis. Life is a series of choices: right or left?, up or down?, backwards or forwards? How we deal with those "decision-making moments" is our *past* working itself *into* the *present*; it is also *shaping* our Wyrd for the *future*. You *can* effectively *change* your *past*, by how you let it *work itself out* in your *present*. That is a hard concept for most people who have spent their entire lives on a linear timeline to wrap their heads around, but once we do, it is *life-changing*.

Since most people learn best by example, let me use an experience from my own life to illustrate the relationship between Orlog and Wyrd. I love things. I love "stuff". I have an obsession with things that I consider *my* stuff. This makes things like paring away stuff, when packing to move, for example, very difficult for me. It also makes it very hard for me to *let go* in life, because sometimes my "stuff" isn't just physical objects; it also includes attachment to *memories* from the past (of which the actual physical objects often become representations, becoming fetishes or effigies of said memories). In the Spring of 2014, we picked up and moved to Massachusetts, more or less on the spur of the moment. We came here for a one week vacation with Suzanne; we've been living here ever since. That was a *huge deal*: I left behind a *lot* of *stuff* in North Carolina, and so did Michelle (who has similar, if not worse, "stuff issues"). Over the course of subsequent years, I have diligently worked to *import* as much of our *stuff* from North Carolina as has been feasible. In the meantime, we have procured yet *more stuff* while living here in Massachusetts. Then the time came in 2017 for us to put our house on the market, pack up, and move to a new home. In the process of said packing, I realized more completely than ever just how much *stuff* I actually own (*we* actually own). My *"stuff issues"* are intrinsically bound up in my personal *past*: I lost my Father at an early age, and part of how I dealt with my grief from that was to *hold onto his stuff*. In fact, my whole family handled their grief the same way. I received the message very early in life:

> So long as you hold onto associated stuff, that moment— that person—is still with us.

Suddenly, there I was, in the *present*, faced with packing my current *stuff*. My normal reaction to this *decision-making moment* would be to fly into a complete panic, *cling* to my *stuff*, and pack every scrap and tittle of it, standing firm on the fact that it is *my stuff*. But there again, in 2014—also in my *past*—I had picked up and moved here on the spur of the moment, like I said, and we *left stuff behind*. So there were two facets of my *past* that had direct bearing on the *present decision-making moment*: one facet that *clings*, and one facet that *walks away willingly*. How did I work that *past into* my *present*? How might whatever decision I made there in the *present* affect my Wyrd, and, therefore, my *future*? Those two facets of my *past* taught me a very important lesson there in the *present*:

If the stuff is holding me back, or weighing me down, I need to walk away; let it go. Either I own my stuff, or my stuff owns me, and holds me prisoner.

I could then work this lesson into my *present* by only packing the *stuff* that *moves me forward* in my life, thereby affecting my Wyrd by shaping my *future*. How did I determine which *stuff moves me forward*? By creating in my mind a vision of what sort of *future* I actually *want*. What do I *want* my Wyrd to be? I *want* my *future* to be a quiet, peaceful place, where I get all the time I need with the ones I love, while also having plenty of time to feed my passions, including my art, my writing, and my spirituality, as well as my love of video games, geekdom, model horses, and great films; I *want* my future to include both *being successful* and *feeling fulfilled*. Simply *wanting* that future, however, in no way *guarantees* it: as a dear old lady (who was decidedly *not* Heathen, nor *Heidhrinn*) once said to me, "wish in one hand and shit in the other, and see which one fills up the fastest"! Wishes and wants are ultimately *empty things*; *action* is what makes things happen. I could then *take action* by only packing the *stuff* that fits into my vision of what I *want* for my *future*, and not freaking out when we threw away, donated, or otherwise got rid of the rest. While even that *action* does not *guarantee* the future that I *want*, it certainly *encourages* it to actually *happen*.

Ultimately, Wyrd is *where you're going*, as shaped by *where you've been*. It isn't *fate*, exactly, but it also doesn't leave us room for *dwelling* in our past, or *worrying* about our future. Which is why I tend to drive my wife a little nuts when I use my handle on the concepts of Orlog and Wyrd to remain "abnormally calm" in the face of an ever-changing—and potentially scary—future. She fully understands the concepts, too, but she has the very human tendency of living as a *slave* to a *linear timeline*, wherein the *present* is what's *happening to you*, but both the past and the future are things that are completely *beyond our control*. And that *linear servitude* is precisely what leads one to either *dwell*, or *worry*, or both, while steadily *stressing out* and *freaking out* in the present. In order to effectively weave our *present* into our *past* to create a more positive *future*, we must *release* those things in our lives which do not *serve* that *future*, including *worry*.

The twenty-third stanza of the Havamal tells us:

The unwise man is awake all night,
And thinks of anything-whatever;
There is mourning, moodiness, and exhaustion
    when morning comes,
(And) all the wretchedness is the same as it was.
--Translation Mine

Worry accomplishes nothing. All it does is exhaust you to the point where you cannot actually *accomplish* anything: including taking the actions necessary to get a handle on your Wyrd. That isn't the same thing as saying "don't worry be happy". The brand of *complacency* which accompanies sentiments such as "have faith, the Gods will sort it all out in your favor," quickly leads us to a level of *apathy* and *inaction* which practically *guarantees* our Wyrd will definitely *suck*. Instead, it means "don't worry; do something"; "don't worry; take action". Resolve yourself to a *goal*, and then *refuse to settle*. Keep *working*, instead of worrying, until you *accomplish* said goal. That is what our visions for the futures we *want* actually are: they are *realistic goals*. The key word in that sentence is *realistic*. Simply because you *wish* that you were a brain surgeon who makes a lot of money isn't going to *make* that happen. If you aren't willing to go to many years of medical school to reach that goal, then that vision is *not* a *realistic goal*. The two keys to avoiding *worry*, therefore, are to take a look at your *past* and figure out how it is *working* on your *present*, and then figure out how to reconcile that *present* with the *future* that you *want*. Again, there is no *guarantee* that your Wyrd will wind up *exactly* as you have envisioned it, but if you simply "sit back and enjoy (or suffer through) the ride", that *will absolutely guarantee* that it *won't* be!

Getting a handle on your Wyrd and Orlog while at the same time coming to understand the Gods as actually *involved* in your life should not be confused with the all-too-frequently encountered "buck up, Buttercup" attitude of many Heathens. Too often we find people in the Heathen community whose answer to all of life's travails—including things like chronic clinical depression and even physical disabilities—is "buck up, Buttercup; anything else is weak, and Heathens are not weak". This is deeply bound up, I've found, in Brosatru attitudes that if you are Heathen, that automatically makes you a Viking, but it definitely isn't an attitude exclusive to that specific branch of our community. *Owning* that you have an issue—mental, physical, or otherwise—and then seeking *compassionate care* for it (even if that simply means telling another person about your issue, and having them be there for you) is *not weakness*. Bucking up, on the other hand, all too often leads to *denial*, Buttercup! And *denial* is one of the greatest forms of *weakness* in existence! Earlier in this book, I discussed the concept of **Self-ownership**. Giving in to the "buck up, Buttercup" mentality prevents full Self-ownership, which can not only prevent you from having healthy relationships with other people, but also from having healthy relationships with the Gods themselves. Many of the tales in our lore demonstrate *anything but* a "buck up, Buttercup" attitude: when Thor lost His hammer, and needed assistance in getting it back, no one told Him to "buck up, Buttercup", for example. And if they had, we would've lost that wonderful tale of Thor in drag, with Loki as His "bridesmaid"! When the giant who fortified Asgard asked for Freyja's hand in marriage, as well as the sun and the moon, nobody told Freyja to "buck up, Buttercup" and marry that giant! Both Thor and Freyja are primary examples of *Self-ownership* within our lore, and much can be learned from Them.

That "buck up, Buttercup" attitude also firmly *negates* the *entire* magickal system of the Norse Tradition, because it defines Wyrd as a form of *fate* to which a person is *resigned*. The primary purpose of magick in the Norse Tradition, particularly from a *historical perspective*, is not only to *foretell* Wyrd, but to actively work *alongside* the Norns to *reshape* Wyrd, for good or for ill. The seidhrkonas, volvas, and vitkis of the ancient world were called upon to both bless *and* curse, by *reshaping* Wyrd. This is why one of the primary ritual tools often found in the gravesites of these magickal professionals is the *distaff*, or at the very least a wand with much structurally in common with a distaff. In our modern world, weaving is largely a lost art, outside of the textile industry, but for our ancestors, it was very much a part of daily life. Understanding life as a *tapestry*, woven, warp and weft, and ever-changing, was a far less alien concept to them, than it is to us. For those wholly unfamiliar with what a *distaff* even is, it is the stick or spindle onto which wool or flax is wound for spinning. Again: one returns to the image of the *wand*, or *gandr*. Thus, if one does not have a firm handle on *their own* Wyrd and Orlog, it will become virtually *impossible* to pursue the magickal path of the Norse Tradition, whether a Norse Witch, or otherwise.

If you are in full ownership of your Self, chances are, you already cope better with things such as grief, chronic depression, and physical disabilities than "the average bear", but what if you're not? What if you're even still working through the portions of this book that deal with that topic? Growing a bit more deeply *in touch* with your "soul" might help you here, if you're really struggling. I know that has certainly helped me. The Norse depiction of the "soul" is four-fold, as you may recall from earlier chapters. For the purposes of this Self-Ownership discussion (and the meditation to follow) I wish to focus on the *Hugr* and *Hamingja*, especially as they relate to Odin's Ravens, Huginn and Muninn.

As discussed previously, the *Hugr* would best be understood by moderns as the "inner self": a person's personality as reflected by their conscious thought processes. It cognates perfectly with Odin's Raven, Huginn, as a mystical representation. When participating in the **Elemental Self Archetypes** exercise earlier in this book, you were exploring and explaining your *Hugr* in its most basic and elemental form. What did you discover about yourself when doing that exercise? Which archetype fits your *Hugr*?

Coping Mechanisms for the Elemental Self (Hugr)

Archetype	Suggested Coping Mechanisms
Seeker	Thoroughly research your issue; discuss your issue with people whom you regard as mentor figures
Maker	"Craft out" your feelings in regards to your issue; employ art therapy
Believer	Pour blot or otherwise go to the Gods; prayer; meditation; Reiki or Healing-Galdr are also suggested
Dreamer	Use your issue as a means to learn through opposites (example: if you experience bouts of chronic depression, use this as an inspiration to actively physically record your happier times, so you can return to them in an hour of need; if you suffer from chronic pain, use this as a constant reminder that you possess the strength of Thrudh—the Strength of Mountains); use comedy and laughter as "the best medicine"

Archetype	Suggested Coping Mechanisms
Lover	Seek ways to nurture yourself (spa day, anyone?); seek healthy forms of physical comfort (hugging; cuddling); cook; find healthy ways to splurge with food (treat yourself to chocolate, for example, but don't eat so much that you make yourself sick!); use your experiences with your own issues to nurture someone else who is going through something similar.
Peacemaker	Explore the core of your issue as a means for building a better infrastructure in your life; seek peace with your issues via meditation, interaction with a Higher Power, or with someone whom you regard as a mentor figure.
Mystic	Pour blot or otherwise go to the Gods; prayer; meditation; Reiki or Healing-Galdr; spend time in nature; perform utiseta with your dyr-andi for comfort and guidance; go Wight-Walking

At face value, these may seem to be over-simplified methods of dealing with issues which are often "bigger than us", and certainly, if you have clinical issues, your first avenue of diagnosis and treatment should be a qualified physician (where possible). Often, when we are experiencing the pitfalls and valleys of life, however, the simplest answers are also the ones which most easily evade us. Those simple things may also be the very things which provide us the needed respite, to clear our heads and dry our tears long enough to seek the very real help we need.

Effectively "pacifying" the *hugr* may also provide us space to visit our *hamingja*, and perhaps begin to ally the two, in much the same manner as allying our Orlog and Wyrd. You may recall from previous chapters that the *hamingja* is often loosely translated as "luck", but may best be understood as "fame", "reputation", or "legacy": how one is *remembered*. As such a memory, it cognates heavily with Odin's Raven, Muninn ("Memory"). In *Grimnismal* in the Poetic Edda, Odin says of these two birds:

> Huginn and Muninn fly every day the world over;
> I do not fear Huginn, that he not come back,
> Yet I fear more for Muninn.
> --*Grimnismal 20*, Translation Mine

When we understand Huginn and Muninn as cognates of *hugr* and *hamingja*, we might come to better understand this statement by Odin in this way:

> *"I put myself out into the world each day; I don't really worry about losing my individuality. However, the loss of my reputation and to be remembered ill, that I do fear."*

Like Odin (although obviously not on such a divine level), we put ourselves out there into the world each day, and with that "putting ourselves out there" comes the potential of losing touch with either our *hugr*, our *hamingja*, or both. Face it: the world is a harsh and ugly place that doesn't often nurture or even fully *foster* individuality. "Cookie-cutter lives" are what "create order" in our society these days, or at least, such seems to be the very obvious case. The *true* individual is often seen as the "square peg"; the "outcast"; the "misfit". And most of the time these people are anything but celebrated. On the contrary, more often than not they are bullied into submission, until their *hugr* becomes something which they try desperately to hide under whatever barrel or in whatever closet might be most handy. *Hugr* becomes bound to *hamingja*: those things which make us the most individually ourselves are also the things which stand to bring us the most "fame", for good or ill; the things which help to build our reputation and our legacy. Again, too often, the more *truly* individual the person—the more of a "misfit" they may be—the worse their reputation within certain portions of our society. If you're already walking this Heidhrinn Path in this modern world of ours, I'm sure you are all too familiar with what I'm talking about here. When faced with earning an ill reputation, we are, too often, all too willing to sacrifice our individuality for the sake of being "remembered well". We bury *who we really are* as deeply as we possibly can, in an effort simply to *fit in* and *survive* in society-at-large. And even when we don't do that—when we cling to *who we truly are*, which is a thing to deeply be commended and something for which we all should strive—we too often find ourselves in the pit of despair as we face down things like bullying and other forms of societal abuse. Therefore, bringing the *hugr* and *hamingja* into some sort of alignment becomes one of the most important keys to living a happy, well-adjusted life.

The first step towards gaining or regaining that alignment is to take stock of the *innangard* versus *utangard* relationships in our lives. Earlier in this book, I described *concentric circles of innangard*, working outward from those closest to us; those we consider **family**. Perhaps the best way to gauge the present state of *your hamingja* is to ask several of those whom you consider **family** (those in your *closest circle of innangard*) how they would remember you to a future generation. What words would they use to describe who you were in this world, and to this world? We base the state of our *hamingja* on the opinions of these people; not on those who are *utangard*. Why should you care what your reputation is to a group (or groups) of people who are *outside your fence*? It is important to note here that this *innangard circle* which you consider **family** need not actually be family by blood; instead, they are your family ultimately by *spiritual association*, predominately as they relate to, support, and uplift your *hugr*. Generally, the way people find themselves in our innermost circles in the first place is through *understanding* us as *true individuals*, and then *accepting* that *individuality*. These are the people we can turn to in those times when the "*utangard world*" seeks to push us down and make us bury our *hugr*. They can help us begin to understand how our *hugr* works itself out and into our *hamingja*.

Attaining that balance of *hugr* and *hamingja* has been especially hard for me over the course of the past twenty-four years. A lot of my struggle has had to do with the hard-to-put-down belief that my legacy—my *reputation*; my *hamingja*—was the one which I had *left behind*, with my "old life", rather than the one I am *building* every day, *right now*. Of all the four pieces of the Norse "soul", *hamingja* might be the one that can come to confuse us the most, because we tend to think of being *remembered* in the past tense, but the truth of the matter is, our legacies are *living things*. So long as we are still *building* one, no matter which "side" we are on—physically clinically living or physically clinically dead—we are still *alive*. The legacy which I had from before—from my "old life"--was a legacy *prescribed by others*; it was not my *hamingja*, because it was not truly *built by me*. The one I am *building now—that* is my *hamingja*. It is *mine*; it is a *living thing*, which I am constantly *nurturing*, for good or for ill, through the expression, finally, of my *hugr*.

Útiseta for Balancing Hugr and Hamingja

Center yourself.

Lay The Fence.

Take a deep breath. Hold it for a count of four. Let your mind focus on the word *Contract* or *Ebb*. Exhale for four counts. Let your mind focus on the word *Expand* or *Flow*. Repeat. *Contract. Expand. Ebb. Flow. Contract. Expand. Ebb. Flow.* Come into the quiet spaces   of your mind and heart. Before you, there stands a tree: the tallest tree that you have ever seen; its roots sunk deeper than the deepest earth; its branches overreaching high as the   highest   of skies. You know that it is Yggdrasil, and you know that you now stand on the Midgard Plane. You know that you are safe; that you are caim-bound, and protected. Approach the World Tree. In the branches on high, an eagle perches, with a rooster seated atop its head. Four deer nibble upon the ripe shoots of new growth among the roots, as well as overhead, as they gallop through the canopy of the Great Tree. As you take a seat beside the trunk of the tree, a squirrel runs past on his way downwards, through a cavernous hole in the roots. And as you settle in, you feel those roots rumble, as a dragon moves beneath. It is   this squirrel you seek. His name is Ratatosk, and he is the master of gossip: that is his Purpose, you see? He runs up and down Yggdrasil forever, carrying messages (most of them quite uncouth) from the eagle to the dragon, and back again. When Ratatosk pops his head up once more from among the roots, you call his name, and he chitters at you in aggravation for a few moments before finally coming over. And you will ask· him: *"What is my hamingja? Show me my hamingja. Tell me the state of my hamingja.*" And he answers, though he may be brutal in his honesty where necessary. Listen carefully. Deeply ponder his words. Thank Ratatosk, and send him back, on his way up the World Tree. What did he tell you? Consider your *hugr*: with what words did you begin this utiseta, when first you centered yourself? How do those archetypes relate to and intertwine with the *hamingja* which Ratatosk relayed to you? Imagine those archetypes as vines on the tree. What do they look like? Are they green and budding, or old and gnarled? Are there runes carved upon them perhaps, or are they just vines? Do they reach, or do they tangle? Are they making their way up or down the tree? Take all of these visions with you, as you make your way back to the waking world. You take a deep breath. Hold it for a count of four. Let your mind focus on the word *Contract* or *Ebb*. Take a deep breath. Hold it for a count of four. Let your mind focus on the word *Contract* or *Ebb*. You begin to walk away from the tree. Exhale for four counts. Let your mind focus on the word *Expand* or *Flow*. You are slowly coming back to consciousness. Repeat. *Contract. Expand.* You feel your physical fingers and toes, and you begin to wiggle them as you come back to this physical realm. *Ebb. Flow.* You become steadily more aware of your physical surroundings. *Contract. Expand.* You stretch your arms and your legs as you come fully back into the safety of your physical form. *Ebb. Flow.*

Raise The Fence. Ground and Center.

The images and messages you received during this utiseta may serve to help you bring your *hugr* into balance with your *hamingja*. First, make certain that the words of Ratatosk were the Squirrel's words, and not simply your own "mental trash" that you grafted onto the meditation. How can you tell the difference? The simplest answer is: if you have to *ask*, it was *probably* "mental trash". I know that seems a bit knee-jerk and harsh at face value, but as you experience more and more utiseta, and more and more meditations and guided and unguided journey experiences, you will eventually come to *feel* the difference between when something/someone else is actually *talking to you*, versus when you are *replaying* your own mental baggage and acting as a sort of "astral ventriloquist". I've spoken previously about that "hair on the back of the neck standing up" feeling. When you *know*, quite simply: *you know*. Sometimes the messages we receive on such journeys may be things we very much *want* to hear, while other times, they may be the exact opposite. We need to hone our *discernment*, so that we learn when these messages are actually coming from *outside*, versus when they are simply echoes from *inside*. True *discernment* comes not just from the *mind*, but also from the *heart*. The brain can trick us into all sorts of things, but the heart works differently. The heart—that place of *courage* that we speak of in the Nine Norse Virtues—never seeks to harm the innocent and never reacts from a place of anger, even when the innocent in question is you, your *Self*. This is why we have expressions such as "you know *deep down* what is true and not true": the *deep down* this is speaking of is the *heart*. So test the words of Ratatosk against your *heart*, and not just your *mind*. If you find that what you encountered was honestly your own "mental trash", perform the utiseta again, and this time, *get out of your own way!*

The *hugr* portion of this utiseta focuses on seeing one's *hugr* as vines growing against and around the World Tree. Again, you should use careful *discernment* to make sure you have really seen what you *think* you have seen, and that this was not merely more "mental trash". Green and budding vines signify being comfortable with your *hugr*, and allowing it to grow and thrive, while old, gnarled vines can be a signal that you are outgrowing your present patterns of *hugr*, and need to move forward into patterns of thought which are more deeply *you*. If there are runes carved upon the vines, you should pay careful attention to which runes appear, and explore their further study, as they likely provide guidance for balancing your *hugr* and *hamingja*. Reaching vines, like green and budding vines, signify that you thrive in the expression of your *hugr*, as well as balancing it with your *hamingja*, whereas tangled vines suggest some form of complexity which requires your further attention. Vines growing *up* the tree suggest that your best guidance for balancing your *hugr* and *hamingja* will likely come from sources such as the Ancestors, Alfar, Disir, Aesir, and Vanir, whereas vines growing *down* the tree suggest that your best guidance may come from the Rokkr, Dwarves, Dark Elves, and Landvaettir.

When I undertook this utiseta myself, Ratatosk was at first uncooperative. Then again, what does one expect from a squirrel, even a semi-sacred one? His first response was that I *already know* the state of my *hamingja*. I replied: "I know what I *think*, but I don't know that I *know*?" There is nothing quite so humbling as being laughed at by a squirrel. Ratatosk replied: "You spend far too much time *dwelling* on who you once were, and not nearly enough time *being* who you are now. Fame is a harsh bedfellow; perhaps you should seek a different bed! Yes, you are purposed to open people's eyes and minds, but do not forget to also open your own heart. Can I go now?" And I nodded my head. He subsequently scampered back down the Tree, and disappeared into its roots. I then turned to contemplate the vines representing my *hugr*, as they wound their way up the Tree. They were verdant green, and flowering. Carved upon the vines themselves, a series of runes:

ᚠᚠᛋᛜᚲᚾ

Fehu. Ansuz. Sowilo. Othala. Kenaz. Nauthiz. Taken individually, they are runes speaking of wealth, God-relationships, hope, heritage, manifestation, and need. However, when one takes the last five as a word, they reveal even more, for they form the word *asokn*: an impetuous, unreasonable desire after a thing. What thing? *Fehu*: money. The message I gain from this? It is impossible to be an effective *Seeker, Maker, Believer* while focusing on finances, rather than *seeking, making,* and *believing*!

So how do I use the information I received in this utiseta to balance my *hugr* and *hamingja*? Clearly, my tendency to dwell in my past is holding me back. Even though on most levels I would never wish to turn back time and return to that life I once lived, I too often get caught up in an impetuous and unreasonable desire for some of the *comforts* I enjoyed back then. When I succumb to that *asokn*, those are the times when my *hugr* gets put on a shelf, and I wind up curled up in a little ball, head in hands, beweeping my current outcast state. I need to realize that my *hamingja* is the same as it has always been: to open people's eyes and minds. It is only my state of being that is different; I should more fully embrace *being* that.

In the end, only you can know what Ratatosk has told you about your *hamingja*. Ponder his words, and then reflect upon how they relate to the vines of your *hugr*. Seek whatever further guidance you need, until you feel that you can sit out again, and revisit the Tree, the Squirrel, and the vines, and find that everything thrives there. Only then should you pursue the Path of Manifestation which follows.

Manifestation

When we consider the word *manifestation* from a mystical or spiritual perspective, many of us immediately associate the concept with magick and spellwork. However, the truth is that manifestation (and accomplishing it) has far less to do with what tools you have to hand and what "mumbo jumbo" you can roll out while using them, and far more to do with *personal empowerment*. One has to believe in *oneself* first, before any real *magick* can happen, regardless of whether one is employing carefully thought-out and crafted ritual tools or simple prayer for manifestation. The old adage of "**one must believe to receive**" is very true, though not in the way many people bandy it about. *Self-doubt* is the true enemy of manifestation on a much deeper level even than a lack of faith in the Gods, for how can you truly have faith in the Gods or anything or anyone else if you do not first have faith in *yourself*? In order to bring about real manifestation—whether you choose to go forward with the magickal tools and methods detailed throughout the rest of this chapter or not—you must first complete the *Self-work* in the previous chapters. *Get right* with *yourself*, and *then* you can begin to embark on journeys of manifestation with the wights (Gods included).

The first step towards manifesting *anything* is *fully believing* that you *deserve* whatever it is, followed immediately thereafter by the *full belief* that it is *already yours*. This is why *Self-work* is so crucial to the process of manifestation, regardless of the tools or methods used. A low opinion of yourself, that nagging feeling of "nothing good ever happens to me", will pretty much *guarantee* that nothing good ever *will*. One ounce of *self-doubt* can change *manifestation* into *devastation*: it can turn dreams and wishes into fears on the turn of a dime, and when that happens, instead of *manifesting* what we *want*, we wind up *attracting* what we patently *don't*. This has happened to me and my students on more than one occasion: enough times for me to teach *you* better, so please don't scoff.

Once you've got the *Self-work* handled and have come to terms with the fact that you *honestly deserve* whatever it is you are attempting to manifest, and that, in fact, it is *already yours*, we begin what I have come to term the *dreaming phase*. During the *dreaming phase*, you *actively change* your thought processes to what they would be if you had *already attained* your goal. For example, if you were working to manifest a house, you would begin to think about things as you would if you *already* lived in that house. Would you keep your room in *that* house a cluttered up mess? Of course not! So continually tidy the room in the house you're living in now, and treat it the way you would your *new* room in your *new* house. Maybe you will want to redecorate when you get to your new space? Begin picking out the things which you will need to accomplish that, and create a "dream file" of images of things you want for your new room in your new home (complete with a price list, and an action plan for attainment of those things). If you had *already attained* your goal, would you still be complaining about *anything*? Then *stop complaining*! If you had *already attained* your goal, would you still be worried? Then *stop worrying*! Remember and enact that age-old witchy adage: **form follows thought.**

As Heidhrinns, we are Norse Witches. However, within Norse Witchcraft, as, indeed, in modern Paganism, while many Heidhrinns choose to formally explore the magickal aspects of our faith, certainly not *all* of us do. Workings for manifestation via the use of ritual tools and correspondences—what might commonly be referred to as "spellwork" in other faith-bases--are not a *requirement* for the practice of Norse Witchcraft, anymore than they are a *requirement* in any other Pagan faith-base (including Wicca). As a very wise woman once said: *"The work is not what makes a witch."*

You could, quite effectively, go your whole life as a Norse Witch and never once maintain a focused wand or a focused hlaut-boll, never learn a note of galdr, and never journey once to any of the Nine Worlds except our own and Yggdrasil, yet still work for manifestation through prayer. You might never use the runes for anything beyond a morning devotional rite, or for counseling and self-work. And there is *absolutely nothing wrong* with choosing to practice like that. Again, "you're doing it wrong" is patently *not* a part of our vocabulary here on this Path, unless you are doing something that unjustifiably harms yourself or others, or encourages such harm. A magickal path—complete with ritual tools to "get things done"--is *available* in Norse Witchcraft, but it is definitely not a *requirement*.

While a full introduction to magickal practice as a Norse Witch is beyond the scope of this book (that could easily become yet another book, though, so stay tuned!), I feel that an exploration of this path would suffer without at least a bare-bones introduction to its *opportunities* for *manifestation* via the use of ritual tools and correspondences. My own practice began with a primarily spiritual focus. In fact, I practiced for well over a year before I ever even began to *dabble* in anything remotely akin to "Heidhrinn magick". However, as a dedicant of Freyja—the very Goddess who taught Odin Himself seidhr—it was only a matter of time until I found myself called to the more "magickal side" of this Norse Path. For the purposes of this brief introduction, we will be focusing on the aforementioned focused wands (gandr), focused hlaut-bolli, and focused bags/boxes, beginning with an "intro to wands".

Everywhere I go I pick up sticks; naturally, I leave offerings of some sort when I do. My ever-growing "stick collection" has boggled my wife's mind for some time, and when we moved house, it officially reached the point of driving her a little nuts. We were literally in a position where we were *packing* "sticks"! Each and every one of those "sticks" has the ultimate intent of becoming a *focused wand*: a wand with a specific *purpose* of *calling* a specific set of *spirits/energies* to aid in the intent of "conjuring" a specific *manifestation*. I have a long stick of oak from Sleepy Hollow Cemetery in Concord, MA which we picked from the grave of Henry David Thoreau, which is to be made into a *writer's wand*, dedicated to that great literary Ancestor himself (Thoreau), with the intent of *increasing inspiration* and *achieving literary success*. I have a large piece of driftwood, lifted from Dead Horse Beach in Salem, MA, which will eventually become a *mermaid wand*, dedicated to *Ran* and Her *Nine Daughters*, with the intent of *promoting calm* and *kinship with water elementals*. I have a small twig of pine, in the perfect shape of the Algiz rune, which I stumbled upon in my own backyard, which will become an *Algiz wand*, with the intent of *protection*, as well as *promoting victory/success*. Last, there is another small wand of oak, which I lifted from the yard of a prospective home we were looking into buying, that is dressed with red leather and off of which an acorn from the same tree dangles. Its intent? To *befriend the landvaettir* of the land on which that home sat. After working with that wand for several months, we found our present home, just down the street from the yard in which that piece of oak was originally procured: a new home that has as its yard its own small oak grove!

So how does one "dress" and use these "sticks" that are to be wands, and does it remain a "stick" until it is "dressed"? The answer to the second half of that question, in my experience, lies in the *instructions* that are given either at the time of the *finding* of the "stick", or via divinatory, dream, and spirit messages received subsequent to that initial *finding*. Often, the "stick will tell you what to do". By this, of course, I am not actually asserting that I honestly believe in sticks that talk, nor do I honestly believe that it is the stick itself that provides that initial instruction, but rather Landvaettir and other local wights who happen to be present at the location of the initial *finding*. At face value, it may seem to be "your idea" to pick up the stick in the first place, with a sudden "spark" of an idea of intent, but generally the best way to get human beings to actually *act* on something is to convince them that the initial thought was *their* idea in the first place, even when that patently isn't the case! How can we know the difference? Most people do not naturally go through life feeling *deeply compelled* to pick up *every* stick they see; not even magickally-inclined people. If we did that, chances are our homes would soon look like beaver dams. If you are feeling *deeply compelled* to pick up a stick, with a flash of an idea of intent suddenly flowing forth in your brain as if someone just opened up some sort of flood-gate, chances are, picking it up isn't *your* idea in the first place, but instead, an *instruction* that is being *communicated* to you via some local wight (or perhaps even the Gods Themselves). As to whether or not a stick needs to be "dressed" before it officially becomes a wand: that answer will also make itself readily apparent. While it's always a pleasant experience to "dress" a stick—opening up our artistic centers can be a form of meditation in and of itself—it isn't always necessary. Again, the "stick will tell you what to do". ("Dressing" wands can also make more clear both to yourself and to others that the "stick" in question is now *more than just a stick*.)

How to "dress" your "stick" depends on a number of factors, not least of which are the *instructions* you're being given (or have been given) spiritually, but basic "dressings" may include carving, wrapping (with leather or ribbon), adding beads, stones, or shells, or even painting. Anything and everything that goes *onto* and *into* the "dressing" of a wand should have a definite, *focused* meaning and/or intent, however. You should pay very close attention to things such as color correspondences, the meanings of gemstones, and of course the full scope and meaning of specific runes (should you choose to carve or paint runes onto your wand). For example, if you have been *told* to wrap your wand in red leather, then by all means, do so; however, make yourself *aware* of the color correspondences for the color red. When it comes to anything having to do with magick and manifestation, *ignorance is never bliss*. Attention should also be given to the traditional meanings for the type of tree from which your "stick" originally came: for example, both ash and yew are traditionally associated with Yggdrasil (because a debate continues to rage over which, precisely, Yggdrasil is, ash or yew). Birch is associated with birth, growth, renewal, the rune Berkano, and the act of becoming (in my own personal experience, it is also deeply associated with Freyja and Nerthus). At the end of this section on focused wands, I have provided a small table of correspondences for the most often-used/found wood and embellishments, as a means of "getting started" with wand-making. It is by no means exhaustive, but should provide a handy primer for the beginner.

Insofar as how to *use* your *focused wand*, certainly, it may be used to focus and direct energy (in the same way as one normally employs a wand, dagger, or hammer, as described in previous chapters of this book), but your use of such a wand is definitely not limited to merely "waving it about". This is, after all, a Norse-derived Tradition, not Harry Potter roleplay or even mainstream Western Ceremonial Magic. The common term for a wand in modern Heathen parlance has become *gandr*, but a deeper look at the lore (especially those sources relating to the Saami) tells us that, in fact, a *gandr* was much, much more than "simply a wand". Those deeper layers of meaning give us a variety of suggested uses for a *focused wand*, besides "simply waving it about". The *Historia Norwegiae* is an 11th (or 12th) century document penned in Latin by an anonymous monk. In it, we find one of the few "period" accounts of Saami life: specifically, a Saami séance. In this young monk's description, he employs the word *gandus* when speaking of the *spirit* that is called forth by the Saami shaman.

Gandus is essentially his "makeshift Latin" version of the word *gandr* from the Old Norse, which is variously translated across numerous other sources as "wand" (obviously), "penis", "spirit", "wolf", and "monster". While the account in the *Historia Norwegiae* is positively full of the dreaded Christian-grafting, and most scholars agree that it is based on *Norse accounts* of Saami life, rather than first-hand exposure, its use of the word *gandus*, when combined with the numerous other "non-wand" translations we have of the word, provides an important basis for the use of focused wands in *sympathetic magick*.

Taking a deep, long look at the many words in which the stem *gand-* appears, this concept of *gandus* as "spirit-helper", or even "*hamr-form*" (the form most living folks use to travel the astral; your "*astral self*"), becomes a basis for *ensoulment* of the wand *in sympathy* with a desired effect. In other words, the "spirit-helper" *ensouled* within the wand literally *behaves* as a helper in achieving the desired manifestation. In the *Voluspa* itself, we encounter the term *spa-ganda*, which very clearly translates as "prophetic spirits". There is also the term *gandreidhr*, which appears in *Njalusyning* (Brennu-Njal's Saga, or "Burnt Njal's" Saga), the longest and most celebrated of the Icelandic Sagas. *Gandreidhr* is most often literally translated as "ride of spirits", though in modern times we have bound it up closely with the image of the "witch-ride": a witch on her broomstick, flying across the night sky. We also tend to translate it more literally, in conjunction with that "witch-ride" image, as "wand-ride" (i.e., one "rides their wand" to other planes of existence; "riding the wand" becomes a euphemism for astral journeying). This sense of the focused wand as a *locus* for an *inhabiting spirit*, which might then be *sent out* is echoed in *Voluspa 29*:

> She had power and authority from the Father of
> Hosts (Odin), Who gave her a ring and a
> necklace,
> She got wise spells and spirits of divination (spae-
> ghosts; from spa-ganda),
> That one, she sees and sees widely over every world.
> --Voluspa 29, Translation Mine

When we contemplate the initial *finding* of the "stick", which becomes our *focused wand*, and the *influence* of local wights upon our *compulsion* to pick it up in the first place, it becomes clear that our *focused wand* is a conduit through which those local wights (or even the Gods Themselves, if it was They who compelled us to "pick up the stick" in the first place) may *communicate* and *connect* with us, and us with them, and then *assist us in manifestation* of a desire. The first step of this *communication* happens (obviously) at that first moment when we feel *compelled* to bring our "stick" home with us, in addition to any accompanying "directions" concerning intent and further "dressing" of the wand. The second step happens *during* the "dressing" of the wand. As I said, artistic expression is a form of meditation in and of itself, and the "dressing" of a wand is ultimately a form of *votive art*. The "dressing" of the wand is also an important step in the *ensoulment* of the wand, as discussed previously in this book. The third, final, and perhaps deepest form of *communication* and *connection* occurs when we take up our finished wand—whether we actually "dress" it, or not—and use it *rhythmically*.

What do I mean by *rhythmically use* your wand? There are two types of *rhythmic wand use* which I routinely employ— tapping and dancing—both of which have their basis in the aforementioned historical *gandus* lore from the *Historia Norwegiae*, as well as material sourced from the *Voluspa* and *Lokasenna* of the Poetic Edda, in combination with comparative mythology and personal experience. *Tapping* a wand can mean *touching* the wand with your own fingertips repeatedly in a rhythmic fashion, or actually taking up the wand and *tapping out* a rhythm with the wand itself. Actual scientific research has shown that *tapping* something or someone with our fingertips can induce a *psychological response* (not dissimilar from the "Pavlov's Dog Principle"); we see this used in methods such as EFT for the treatment of psychological maladies ranging from PTSD to chronic phobias. *Tapping* your wand with your fingertips is a *physical cue* which binds your normal mundane state to a paranormal one, via the creation of a *psychological response*: the realization that when you touch your wand, you are also *touching* those entities to which it is connected (those wights or Deities which "gifted" you with it in the first place, as well as that which now *inhabits* it). You tap, and then you ask whatever you need to ask, or say whatever is on your heart that needs saying, and then *trust that it has been heard and will be answered/delivered*. The other method of *wand tapping*—tapping out a rhythm directly *with* the wand—is a form of conjuring on the same level as flamenco dancing: in flamenco, the reason for all of that "stomping" is to *summon* the *duende*, a subterranean spirit of emotional inspiration which is not dissimilar from our own *Dark Elves*. I tend to think of this method as "knocking on the door" of whomever or whatever is linked with the wand in question. I have personally found this method most effective when dealing with Rokkr Deities, the Landvaettir, and (obviously) Dark Elves. Insofar as *manifestation* using this method, the intent is to conjure those forces/entities who will not only give you direction on how to bring the things you need into being, but who will *actively assist* you in *manifestation*.

Dancing with your wand employs the same mechanics as *wand tapping*—that principle of "summoning the duende" mentioned in the previous paragraph—but also relies heavily on the concept of *gandreidhr* ("ride of spirits"; "witch-ride"; "wand-riding"). I have personally found this to be the most effective method of using the wand for out of body experiences and astral travel. If you feel completely idiotic dancing without musical accompaniment, by all means, resort to whatever rhythms your wand suggests. However, I have personally found the most effective rhythm for my own dancing to be the beat of the heart I presently ride. Holding the wand, begin by tapping it lightly against your chest to the rhythm of the heartbeat. Begin to sway softly in time to that rhythm, and then let the wand and your heart lead you towards further movement from there. Once you reach an ecstatic state, you should find the veil slipping between this world and the other Nine, effectively finding yourself in both worlds at once. The end result of these Otherworld journeys, once again, is attempted *manifestation*: to receive the information (or make the right liaisons) necessary to bring a desired end into being. We will talk about astral travel and out of body experiences at length in a later chapter, so I strongly suggest waiting to embark on such journeys until you have read that chapter (for safety's sake).

At some point, you may find yourself in possession of a "stick" that seems to be working *against* you, instead of *with* you or *for* you. This can happen for a variety of reasons, though I won't propose to be some omniscient authority on the "way the Worlds work". Sometimes something simply *isn't meant for us*, even when someone else (the local wights, or even the Gods Themselves) told us otherwise. Trust me, you'll know it when it has happened. I once brought in a very large "stick" from our backyard, with the intent of using it as my main staff. I found it while out on a wight-walk, and everything (and everyone) said "here, this is for you". So I left an appropriate offering, and brought it inside. After a trip to the local craft store to procure beads for its "dressing" (I was to weave a "spider web" with crystal bead "dew drops" on the topmost bend of it), I placed it in the corner of my office, and attempted to plan an undisturbed period of time when I could work on it. Three days later, it fell over as I was walking into my office on a return trip from the restroom, and that topmost bit (the bit destined for the "webbing") broke off. Extremely upset, I placed it in a less-trafficked corner of the room, and began to ask the sources from whom it was gifted *what* I should do about "dressing" it now. My experiences with that "stick" were "all downhill" from there: shortly thereafter, we were informed that we needed to sell our house and move; chaos subsequently ensued. While I am not entirely certain what "changed the tone" of this particular "stick", I have my own theories that when it fell over, and that top bit broke off, its spirit was also broken. Somehow, breaking off that top bit seemed to completely change the overall *focused intent* of the "stick" that was to become my main staff.

What should you do when your "stick" effectively "turns on you"? When this happens, it is likely time for a process I call *gandr-breaking*. You need to do more than simply remove the "offending stick" from your home; you need to *break your ties* with it in a way that removes those energies from your life, while at the same time expressing "no hard feelings" to those from whom it was gifted. Where possible, it is best to return it to the spot from whence it came. If this is not possible, I suggest returning it to a natural place that is *off* your home property (unless the original place where it was gained was in your own yard, in which case, again, return it to the spot from whence it came).

You may wish to also pour blot in the spot to which you are returning the "failed stick", either to the Landvaettir who gave it to you, or to the Gods who initially compelled you to pick it up in the first place. I do not suggest immediately looking for a "replacement stick" in that same area for at least a period of three to six months, for the same reason that you would not return a gift to another human person with the attitude of "I don't like this one; give me something else right now". That is, quite simply, rude.

Gandr-Breaking

I appreciated this gift,
But this gift has changed in tone:
From one to help,
To one that harms.
I return it to the place from whence it came,
With continued gratitude
At that first giving.
Please remove its ill intentions
From my life, my home,
And the lives of those I love who are around me.
Peace and good seasons in my life;
Peace and good seasons in the lives of those I love.
So mote it be. Blessed be.

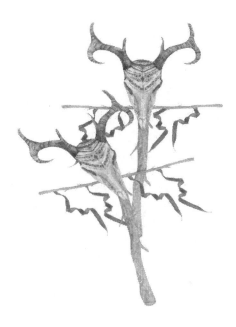

Norse Witch

Wood/Tree Correspondences for Wand Dressing

Wood/Tree	Deity and Runic Correspondences
Oak	Freyr; Freyja; Nerthus; Ansuz; Jera; Dokkalfar
Pine	Tyr; Daeg; Sunna; Skadi; Isa, Daguz, and Algiz
Ash	Odin; Hela; Sunna; Freyja; Yggdrasil; Sleipnir; Raidho, Nauthiz, and Wunjo
Yew	Hela; Angrbodha; Odin; Loki; Sigyn; Yggdrasil; Hagalaz, Eihwaz, and Algiz
Birch	Freyja; Frigga; Nerthus; Gerdha; Sif; Jord; Thrudh; Sigyn; Ljosalfar; Berkano and Uruz.
Flowering trees (dogwood, poplar, maple)	Frigga; Freyja; Nerthus; Gerdha; Eihwaz
Apple	Njordr; Idunna; Bragi; Ran; Aegir; Laguz; Dokkalfar
Driftwood	Njordr; Odin; Villi; Ve; the Ancestors; Alfar; Disir; Ask and Embla; Laguz

Connla Freyjason

Color Correspondences for Wand Dressing

Color	Deity and Runic Correspondences
Red	Freyja; Frigga; Sif; Thrudh; Thor; Tyr; Disir; Kenaz, Gebo, Perdhro, Tiwaz, Ehwaz, Algiz, Thurisaz
Black	Hela; Angrbodha; Nerthus; Odin; Loki; Tyr; Ancestors; some Dokkalfar; Raidho, Nauthiz, Algiz,
White	Skadi; Odin; Freyja; Frigga; Sif; Njordr; Idunna; Bragi; Baldur; Hela; Sigyn; Yggdrasil; Ancestors; Ljosalfar; Isa, Hagalaz, Eihwaz, Berkano, Ehwaz, Laguz
Green	Freyr; Nerthus; Jord; Gerdha; Frigga; Sigyn; Thrudh; Tyr; Yggdrasil; some Dokkalfar; Fehu, Uruz, Eihwaz, Tiwaz, Inguz

Color	Deity and Runic Correspondences
Yellow	Sunna; Idunna; Bragi; Freyja; Frigga; Berkano, Sowilo, Dagaz
Blue	Njordr; Ran; Aegir; Nott; Odin; Heimdall; Daeg; Sunna; Mani; Ljosalfar; Wunjo, Nauthiz, Perdhro, Mannaz, Laguz
Purple	Nott; Odin; Heimdall; Mani; Tyr; Bragi; Ljosalfar; Mannaz, Ansuz, Algiz
Brown	Freyr; Nerthus; Jord; Thrudh; Gerdha; Idunna; Fehu, Uruz, Jera, Inguz, Othala

Some of the ways in which I choose to work with *focused bowls* are Reconstructionist-derived, and well-supported by the UPG of others, while others are not. We cannot go back in time, nor would most of us honestly wish to do so, and if we do not allow ourselves room for growth and change, then we are merely attempting to resurrect a *dead* religion. Most of the time, when religions *die*, it is with very good reasons. We have grown and changed as a Tradition by no longer practicing human or animal sacrifice as an integral part of our practice. We have replaced such things with the blot; with the pouring and sprinkling of mead, rather than blood. Why shouldn't we likewise grow and change in other parts of our path, embracing new opportunities which align with our Tradition along the way? This is largely what I have done in my own personal practice of the use of *focused bowl-work*.

We know from the historical record and the lore that the use of *bowl* and *tein* were sacred to our Ancestors. We also know that among the few ancient Norse musical instruments which have survived, *bells* were foremost among them. The Tibetan singing bowl is actually a *bell* that is *shaped* like a *bowl*. Played either by striking the edge of the bowl with a padded mallet, or more commonly, via the friction of such a mallet rubbed around the edge of the bowl (producing a sonorous, continuous "singing" or "droning" sound), the Tibetan singing bowl historically dates back to at least the 10th century AD, and possibly as far back as the 8th century AD: the so-called "Viking Period" of Norse expansion. It is an instrument which is *historically contemporary* with our own Norse historical base, and also could be used in the *spirit* of the hlaut-boll. It also produces sounds which fit soundly (no pun intended) within the remaining ethnomusicological landscape of Scandinavia as it has come down to us in our modern world (as reflected by modern artists such as Wardruna).

Perhaps the most significant historical/anthropological qualification for using Tibetan singing bowls in my own *focused bowl* practices as a Heidhrinn is the find of two bronze bowls, likely from Central Asia, in the grave goods of the Seeress of Fyrkat in Denmark. Dating from the 10th century AD, a period concurrent with known singing bowl finds from Tibet, one of these two bowls possessed a grass cover, and apparently once held an organic substance of some sort. Positioned beside the woman's left knee, it was bronze, and has been determined to have originally hailed from Central Asia. It is shaped in what is often referred to as a "genie" style among singing bowl collectors: a style which literally *holds the sound inside*. We know from other grave finds that items were often "ritually slain", as we discussed in an earlier chapter. Could the cover over this bowl and the substance within have been part of the process of *silencing* ("ritually slaying") the singing bowl of the Seeress of Fyrkat?

Historical Reconstruction aside, when something consistently *works*, we *use* whatever it is, right? In ancient times, someone figured out rubbing together two pieces of flint would work to produce fire, so they taught the next guy to do it, and since the method consistently *worked*, our Ancestors *used* that method for centuries. Then some guy came along and showed that the friction of sticks could cause the same effect (i.e., create fire), with a lot less bloodshed from potentially knocking those two pieces of flint against a person's knuckles as well as each other, so our Ancestors then adopted *that* method for creating fire, and so on, right on down to our modern day lighters. At the end of the day, I *use* Tibetan singing bowls in my own personal practice because they *work*. Consistent *results* have led to consistent *use*; it really is just as simple as that.

We presently maintain two bowls in our household: one to use *with* water, and one to use *without*. The one for use *without* is mostly used as a meditation device; to keep me focused while performing galdr (more on galdr in a moment). The one for use *with* water, on the other hand, has become my go-to healing galdr "device". Certainly, the same principles could be employed with any bowl containing water and a bit of "galdr-know-how", but galdring with the use of a singing bowl, I have found, actually *infuses the water* with the *energies* raised. This water may then be asperged or massaged onto the skin of the one being healed, often *directly* onto the affected area(s). I have experienced consistently positive results employing this method. You will find the healing galdr which I have most consistently used detailed in the **Runelore** Chapter, which follows.

Focused bowl-work certainly is not limited to the use of Tibetan singing bowls, however. In fact, there are other types of *focused bowl-work* which do not (potentially) leap so far outside of our own Tradition, and may employ the more typical *hlaut-boll*, of the non-singing variety. A very dear friend maintains a bowl specifically for offerings to Sigyn, for example. Part of her personal service to Sigyn is to fill this bowl, and then hold it over her head for a period of time, effectively "taking Sigyn's place", where She holds the bowl beneath the serpent in protection of Her Beloved, Loki. My friend has been known to "hold the bowl" for periods up to an hour at a time, and she is not alone in this practice—many other Sigyn-devotees do likewise. I perform a similar "service blot" to Sigyn with the singing bowl after every practice of healing galdr. You may choose to maintain a separate bowl specifically for offerings to the Ancestors, or to the Landvaettir, or to a specific God/dess, or even to a specific purpose. Any bowl which is dedicated to a *specific* entity, set of entities, or purpose, and in which offerings are then left, becomes its own form of *focused bowl*.

This type of *focused bowl-work* may be used for *manifestation* as well: we hold the ideal of *a gift for a gift* as one of the cornerstones of our faith-base, after all. Such a "trade off" of

"I will leave this here for you consistently if you will do this thing for me" may at face value seem like the basest sort of "pandering" to some, and if your offerings are reduced *solely* to that sort of attitude, those people wouldn't be wrong. But we often practice the bartering of services with other humans in our day-to-day lives, so it is not completely off-base to do the same thing with Otherworldly entities, such as our Ancestors, the Landvaettir, and the Gods. We must make certain, however, that when we do such things it is done with the appropriate humility, and that we are never "into our faith" simply for what *we* can get *out* of it. Energy exchange is fair play; taking advantage never is: not with other humans, and certainly not with the Gods.

Sigyn Service Offering

Hail Sigyn,
Mother of Compassion!
I hold this bowl
In your stead;
Though only for the
Briefest of times,
In comparison to
Your forever.
May it serve as
A lesson for me
In compassionate strength,
That I may go
Forward in life
With your steadfast
And loving heart.
So mote it be.
Blessed be.

Focused boxes and *focused bags* are similar to what are known in other systems of magick as "spellboxes" and "gris gris bags". In the case of the latter, I am in no way, shape, or form suggesting that we should perform wholesale cultural appropriation when it comes to how we prepare, use, or otherwise treat our *focused bags*. Actual gris gris bags are a distinctly *West African Tradition*, with their own system of creation, empowerment, and use. They just happen to be one of the most widely *known* examples of a *focused bag* created, empowered, and maintained specifically for manifestation, which is why I reference them here. Spellboxes, on the other hand, are largely the product of systems of Western Ceremonial Magic (European), though artifacts have definitely been found which suggest their use by the Ancient Norse, such as the Gotlandic box brooch and sheepskin pouch of the Seeress of Fyrkat.

Both *focused boxes* and *focused bags* should be viewed as *repositories of power*; *reservoirs of energy* which act as *icons* of what you are attempting to *manifest*. Once again, this is connected to the *ensoulment* of objects and involves employing *sympathetic magick*. Thus, the item in question essentially *becomes* that which you are attempting to manifest, *already in your possession*. Given the opening paragraphs of this chapter, hopefully you can readily understand how this would be a valuable *physical cue* in maintaining the proper mindset for bringing about manifestation.

When creating a *focused box*, I generally recommend beginning with a small wooden box (easily procured at your local craft store for around $1.50, if you lack the skill to woodcraft "from scratch"), approximately 3" x 1.5" to 3" x 2".If you wish to paint the exterior of the box, or otherwise decorate it, feel free to do so, but pay careful attention to color correspondences (you may use the **Color Correspondences for Wand Dressing** table as a starting point). Rune boxes—boxes which have been woodburned or painted with a specific rune, bind-rune, or set of runes—may prove particularly effective, if you are familiar with runelore. Inside the box, you should place small items which are associated with your manifestation goal. These may be items which you have been *specifically instructed* to place inside, or they may be items of special personal significance. They may also be items with their own *natural correspondences* to your goal: for example, seashells from a beach to which you are working to return; soil from a property which you wish to procure. The box *and* the items to be placed inside should then be *charged*, using the ritual which follows as a model. Once the box has been thus *empowered*, keep it in a safe place, such as on your *stalli*, and treat it with the same *respect* which you afford your actual *goal*. For example, if you are working towards the manifestation of a vacation, you might occasionally *open* your box for a "visit", like a "mini-vacay in a box". If working for the manifestation of a new home, you might put the box beside you on your desk while shopping for potential décor and furnishings for that home, etc.

Unlike *focused boxes*, *focused bags* are not only portable, but also wearable. *Focused bags* are easily placed within the main *skin-bag*, and carried along on wight-walks and to rituals; they may also be worn around the neck, tied onto the belt-loop of a pair of pants, or even pinned inside an item of clothing. Their wearability makes *focused bags* ideal for manifesting personal healing, as well as the healing of others, and also for protection. A small pouch can easily be made from any square of fabric or leather; again, color correspondences should be carefully employed. To make a bag, either fold the fabric in half, turn inside out, and stitch up the sides, or pierce holes around the outer perimeter of the square, and then thread string, cord, or leather stripping through the holes so that the center of the square becomes the bottom of the bag, creating a drawstring opening at the top. Simply purchasing a pre-made bag that suits your needs is also an option. Runes or symbols may be painted or stitched directly onto the bag, according to its intent. As with a *focused box*, the bag *and* the items to be placed inside it should be *charged*, *empowered*, and kept in a safe place.

Charging and Empowering Boxes and/or Bags

Center

Seeker, Maker, Believer (insert your own
archetypes here):
My feet are on the ground;
I stand firm.
I am of the earth and the earth is of me;
I stand firm.
I center myself, and I hold.
So it is, and so it shall be.

Lay the fence.

Outside the fire,
Darkness;
Darkness outside the Grove;
Outside there dwell shadows;
Shadows inside us as well.
Inside, outside, everywhere,
Where'er you dwell,
Dwell not here:
Here is light and all good things!
Light and Bright Wisdom protect us;
Protect us from those who dwell outside.

Hallow the space and each item to be charged with the Hallow Sigil:

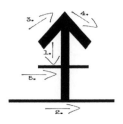

Place your body in the position of the rune, Tiwaz. Visualize the energy of the sacred space which you have just created as golden light, moving up through the fingertips of your left hand, and across your body to the fingertips of your right hand (or to the dagger, wand, or hammer in your right hand, if you have already procured, blessed, and ensouled that tool)

Visualize the energy flowing down and releasing from your right hand (or the tip of a physical foci, such as a dagger), and draw the Hallow Sign over your chalice and see it infusing the liquid within.

Raise your chalice over your head with both hands, and hold it there for several moments.

Lower the chalice slowly to a "toasting position", and say, with intent:

Hail to the Aesir! Hail to the Vanir! Hail to the Rokkr!

Drink a small portion of the liquid.

With the fingertips of your right hand, take a small portion of the liquid from the chalice and with wet fingertips **draw the Hallow Sign** onto the object which you wish to charge. (If the item cannot withstand exposure to liquid, carefully draw the Hallow Sign in the air with your fingertips, being wary of dripping on the item that you are blessing.) As you do so, state your intent:

By the Names of Those I serve,
I charge this (name of item),
Toward (manifestation goal).
So mote it be.
In hallowed gratitude,
Blessed be.

Repeat for each item at hand.

When all of the items at hand have been thus *empowered*, begin placing them inside your bag/box. **Repeat the incantation below** for *each and every item* that is placed inside your focused bag or focused box *as* you place that item within:

I place this (name of item)
Inside this space,
And as I do,
I place (manifestation goal)
Inside my heart and
Inside my mind,
And I know it is *already mine.*
Each time I open this bag/box,
(Manifestation goal) draws closer to me,
And I draw closer to (manifestation goal),
Until it is achieved,
And it *is* achieved.
It *is* achieved.
It *is already* achieved.
So mote it be.
In hallowed gratitude,
Blessed be.

Raise the fence.

Ground the energy into the bag/box.

Center.

Runelore

In previous chapters, I have mentioned such things as runes, bind-runes, galdr, and galdrastafir numerous times, with the promise that I would cover all of them in greater detail later in this book. All of these things fit into the realm of runelore, which is not only a very ancient topic, but also a very broad one. Entire books have been written about various aspects of runelore, some of them dating back further than the 11th century A.D. In fact, mountains of books could be written on all of the aforementioned subjects, and, as such, this will serve as only the most rudimentary of introductions to all of these concepts as I have come to understand and practice them.

The runes of which I speak, and the sole runes which I, in fact, employ in my own practice, are those of the Elder Futhark. While you may also encounter Anglo-Saxon Runes and Younger Futhark runes in your travels, and there is certainly nothing wrong with learning about those as well, for the past twenty-four years the Elder Futhark have served me perfectly fine all by themselves, without the need for further additions. The Elder Futhark are the oldest of the extant Norse runes, dating as far back as the 2nd century AD, and were in regular use by our Ancestors until the 8th century AD, when they began to be supplanted by the Younger Futhark. Usually I do not fall into the "older equals better trap", but in my experience, when it comes to runes, older generally actually *has* meant better, at least in my own personal practice.

The Elder Futhark are the twenty-four runes traditionally understood as having been received by Odin as He hung on Yggdrasil: for me, that definitely equates with "older equals better".

The Elder Futhark consists of twenty-four runes, split into three *aettir* (singular: *aett*)--three groups of eight runes each— attributed to Freyja, Heimdall, and Tyr, respectively. This division into the *aettir* and the "alphabetical" order of the Elder Futhark which we recognize today dates back to a stone from 400 A.D., therefore, the concept of *aettir* is not a modern or later invention. This becomes important when one considers the *initiatory implications* of "traveling" through the runes, from *aett* to *aett*. In discussing such a concept, one should first keep in mind that the word *aett* actually translates directly as *clan*. Our Ancestors lived in a confederation of tribes, which were in turn made up of a confederation of *clans*, not dissimilar from the *clan-tribe* relationships one is familiar with among the Celts, or even the Native Americans. In the absence of a police force, the *clan* was the primary source of security in ancient Norse society. Unlike the concept of a Scottish clan, Norse clans were not tied to a specific territory, but were instead bound by a common point of descent: a *common ancestor*. Therefore, another meaning of *aett* might be understood as "those who are related".

The first *aett* of the Elder Futhark is *Freyja's Aett*. The eight runes within this *clan* of runes pertain largely to "Vanic concepts": seeds, growing things, potential; the Life Force. This explains why Freyja is considered the *common ancestor* of this first group of runes, although certainly, Her brother, Freyr, would be equally apt. When one considers the typical social structure of a Norse tribe, this would in many ways be the *farmer's aett*; the *aett* of the *commoner*. *Freyja's Aett* consists of the runes **Fehu**, **Uruz**, **Thurisaz**, **Ansuz**, **Raidho**, **Kenaz**, **Gebo**, and **Wunjo**.

The second *aett* of the Elder Futhark is *Heimdall's Aett*. The eight runes within this *clan* of runes pertain to weather, need, want, and, indeed, *survival*: all things for which Heimdall either watches, warns, or assists. Heimdall is therefore considered the *common ancestor* of this second group of runes. Considering the typical social structure of a Norse tribe, this could be viewed as the *hunter's aett*; the *aett* of the *warrior-seeker*. *Heimdall's Aett* consists of the runes **Hagalaz**, **Nauthiz**, **Isa**, **Jera**, **Eihwaz**, **Perdhro**, **Algiz**, and **Sowilo**.

The third and final *aett* of the Elder Futhark is *Tyr's Aett*. These runes represent more "cerebral" issues, such as justice, duality, and memory, as well as topics of ownership (both physical and of the more esoteric variety). These are very much the sorts of topics that kings must consider, so it is not surprising that such a "kingly god" as Tyr is considered the *common ancestor* for this *aett*. In relation to the typical social structure of a Norse tribe, this could be viewed as the *priest-king's aett*. *Tyr's Aett* consists of the runes **Tiwaz**, **Berkano**, **Ehwaz**, **Mannaz**, **Laguz**, **Inguz**, **Dagaz**, and **Othala**.

I place such emphasis on the *initiatory implications* of the three *aetts* because of the tale of the origin of these runes: perhaps one of the most familiar stories in our Tradition, often known even to those whose only other awareness of Norse Mythology is *Marvel Comics' Thor*. This story occurs in stanzas 138-144 of the *Havamal*:

> I know that I hung on the windy tree,
> Nights all nine,
> Wounded by the point of my own spear:
> An offering to Odin;
> Myself to Myself,
> On the tree of which
> None may ever know whence run its roots.

> None made me happy,
> With loaf nor with horn;
> I looked down;
> I took up the runes,
> And howling,
> I fell down.

> Nine mighty songs I learned
> From the famous son of Bale-Thorn,
> Bestla's Father (therefore, Odin's Grandfather),
> And a drink I got
> Of the precious mead
> That is the Mead of Poetry (Odhraerir).

> Then I was awash in wisdom,
> And I grew well and and began to thrive:
> Word by word, I sought words;
> Deed by deed, I sought deeds.

Runes you will find, and advising symbols;
Very large symbols,
Rigid symbols,
Of the Father's mighty songs,
And by the Mighty Powers they were fashioned,
And by the Howler of the Gods (Odin) they were
carved.

Odin among the Aesir,
Among the Alfar, Dainn,
And Dvalin among the Dwarves,
Asvidhr among the Jotun:
I carved these in summer.

Do you know how to carve them?
Do you know how to use them to advise?
Do you know how to paint them?
Do you know how to prove them?
Do you know how to pray them?
Do you know how to blot them?
Do you know how to send them?
Do you know how to destroy them?

It is better not to pray, than to over-sacrifice,
A gift looks for a gift;
It is better not to send, than to take too much.
So Thund (Odin as "Thunderer") carved in stone
Before the origin of man:
Where He ascended, He will come again.

--Translation Mine

Not only is the language used in this section of the *Havamal*
highly *initiatory*, I feel that it could be easily argued that these
stanzas form the *shamanic root* of our entire Tradition. A path
that is *shamanic*, remember, focuses heavily on trancework, spirit
journeys, and ecstatic religious experiences, and these stanzas of
the *Havamal* depict, in distinct detail, the ecstatic religious
experience of Odin Himself, as He received the runes. Many who
work with runes take this need for an *initiatory act* quite literally,
often practicing what is called *bloodening* of the runes, wherein
they take drops of their own blood and rub it onto their rune-set to
"activate" and consecrate them. I personally feel that such an act is

taking the *Havamal* a bit *too* literally: we no longer sacrifice animals (or humans) in blot, why maintain similar practices when "activating" a set of runes? The theme of *initiation* is definitely *there*, when it comes to any sort of rune-work, but I tend to focus on Stanza 144 of the *Havamal* when considering the act of *bloodening* a set:

> It is better not to pray, than to over-sacrifice,
> A gift looks for a gift;
> It is better not to send, than to take too much.
> So Thund (Odin as "Thunderer") carved in stone
> Before the origin of man:
> Where He ascended, He will come again.

A gift looks for a gift: if we pour our own blood onto the runes, what is there to prevent them from asking yet more of it from us? No, *better not to pray, than to over-sacrifice. It is better not to send, than to take too much.* Instead, I choose to focus on the *initiatory aspects* of these verses from the *Havamal*, in conjunction with the *implied initiation* evidenced in the *aettir*. Odin says that He hung upon the tree (Yggdrasil) for *nine full nights*; if we consider the three *aettir*, and study them each for *nine nights each*, that would come to *nine full nights* of study for each individual *aett,* and twenty-seven full nights of study for the entire Elder Futhark. That is then the first sacrifice: *learning.* Odin then says He wounded Himself with His own spear as a sacrifice to Himself. The second sacrifice would be pouring *blot for Odin* for those *nine full nights* for each *aett*: in essence, doing for Him now what was *not* done for Him then, for He says that "none made me happy, with loaf nor with horn". A suitable blot, then, would consist not only of mead (or other liquid), but also of a bread-offering.

The Initiation of the Runes

Freyja's Aett

The first nine of the twenty-seven nights would then be spent learning *Freyja's Aett*. Since She is the *common ancestor* of this *clan* of runes, it would be appropriate to not only blot Odin for these nine nights, but Freyja as well. Rather than *bloodening* each rune, you will use the liquid in your chalice to bless each rune as you study.

Center

Seeker, Maker, Believer (insert your own
  archetypes here):
My feet are on the ground;
I stand firm.
I am of the earth and the earth is of me;
I stand firm.
I center myself, and I hold.
So it is, and so it shall be.

Lay the fence.

Outside the fire,
Darkness;
Darkness outside the Grove;
Outside there dwell shadows;
Shadows inside us as well.
Inside, outside, everywhere,
Where'er you dwell,
Dwell not here:
Here is light and all good things!
Light and Bright Wisdom protect us;
Protect us from those who dwell outside.

Lay out the following runes:

ᚠᚢᚦᚨᚱᚲᚷᚹ

Hallow the space and each item to be charged with the Hallow Sigil:

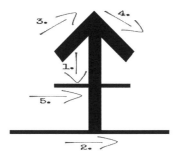

Place your body in the position of the rune, Tiwaz. Visualize the energy of the sacred space which you have just created as golden light, moving up through the fingertips of your left hand, and across your body to the fingertips of your right hand (or to the dagger, wand, or hammer in your right hand, if you have already procured, blessed, and ensouled that tool)

Visualize the energy flowing down and releasing from your right hand (or the tip of a physical foci, such as a dagger), and **draw the Hallow Sign** over your chalice and see it infusing the liquid within.

Raise your chalice over your head with both hands, and hold it there for several moments.

Lower the chalice slowly to a "toasting position", and say, with intent:

Hail Odin! All-Father;
Thund, who howls upon the World Tree;
Giver-of-Runes,
Singer-of-Songs,
Teacher-of-Wisdom!
Skal!

Drink a small portion of the liquid.

Raise the chalice again to a "toasting position", and say, with intent:

Hail Freyja, Vanadis!
Valfreyja,
Gefn,
She who is Odin's Third Teacher,
Mother-of-Seidhr!
Skal!

Drink a small portion of the liquid.

For *each individual rune,* using the fingertips of your right hand, take a small portion of the liquid from the chalice and with wet fingertips draw the Hallow Sign onto the rune which you wish to charge. (If the item cannot withstand exposure to liquid, carefully draw the Hallow Sign in the air *over* your chalice with the rune between your fingertips.) As you do so, state your intent:

By your Hallowed Names,
I charge this rune:
Fehu.
Freyr's Rune;
Cattle-rune;
Rune of movable wealth.
Sign of hope and plenty,
Success and happiness.
I carve you thus (trace the shape of the rune with
    your fingertips);
With your help, I advise against loss, cowardice,

and stupidity.
I paint you the green of growing things (trace the
    shape again with your fingertips);
I prove you through abundance, gain, and right
    ownership.
I pray you: *Please* (say the word as if asking or
    entreating with your whole heart).
I blot you with green and growing things (if juice is
    at hand, blot the rune itself).
I send you forth as peace and good seasons for
    myself;
Peace and good seasons for those I hold dear (draw
    the rune in the air with your right hand and
    send that energy forth).
When time comes to draw you back, or to break
    you,
I counter you with Hagalaz.

(Lay down that rune; pick up the next, and repeat the
liquid blessing process.)

By your Hallowed Names,
I charge this rune:
Uruz.
Thrudh's Rune;
Aurochs-Rune;
Rune of the strength of mountains;
Of energy and strength;
Of courage and potent action.
I carve you thus (trace the shape of the rune with
    your fingertips);
With your help, I advise against weakness, sickness,
    obsession, domination, and violence.
I paint you green and brown cow-colors (trace the
    shape again with your fingertips);
I prove you through being strong and hale and free
    and wise.
I pray you: *Understand* (say the word as if asking
    or entreating with your whole heart).
I blot you with meat and physical action.
I send you forth as strength and good health for

myself;
Strength and good health for those I hold dear
    (draw the rune in the air with your right hand
    and *send* that energy forth).
When time comes to draw you back, or to break
    you,
I counter you with Isa.

(Lay down that rune; pick up the next, and repeat the liquid blessing process.)

By your Hallowed Names,
I charge this rune:
Thurisaz.
Thor's Rune;
Thorn-Rune;
Jotun-Rune;
Rune of reactive force and will.
Sign of change and regeneration;
Of cleansing fire, destruction, and defense.
I carve you thus (trace the shape of the rune with
    your fingertips);
With your help, I advise against danger, betrayal,
    malice, and lies.
I paint you the red of burning flames (trace the
    shape again with your fingertips);
I prove you through directed force of will; through
    sexual energy and acceptance of change.
I pray you: *Protect* (say the word as if asking or
    entreating with your whole heart).
I blot you with fire and incense (if either is at hand,
    light them now).
I send you forth as protection and regeneration for
    myself;
Protection and regeneration for those I hold dear
    (draw the rune in the air with your right hand
    and *send* that energy forth).
When time comes to draw you back, or to break
    you,
I counter you with Laguz.

(Lay down that rune; pick up the next, and repeat the liquid blessing process.)

By your Hallowed Names,
I charge this rune:
Ansuz.
Odin's Rune;
God-Rune;
Rune of blessings spoken.
Sign of communication and inspiration;
Of Wisdom and Truth.
I carve you thus (trace the shape of the rune with
        your fingertips);
With your help, I advise against vanity,
        manipulation, and misunderstanding.
I paint you the purple of the royal Aesir (trace the
        shape again with your fingertips);
I prove you through wise words, clear
        communication, inspired speech, and
        blessings bestowed.
I pray you: *Bless* (say the word as if asking or
        entreating with your whole heart).
I blot you with poetry and the blessing of others.
I send you forth as inspiration, wisdom, and
        blessings for myself;
Inspiration, wisdom, and blessings for those I hold
        dear (draw the rune in the air with your right
        hand and *send* that energy forth).
When time comes to draw you back, or to break
        you,
I counter you with Isa.

(Lay down that rune; pick up the next, and repeat the liquid blessing process.)

By your Hallowed Names,
I charge this rune:
Raidho.
Hela's Rune;
Wagon-Rune;

Rune of travels and journeys.
Sign of relocation and evolution;
Of new horizons and the dance of life.
I carve you thus (trace the shape of the rune with
      your fingertips);
With your help, I advise against rigidity, injustice,
      and stagnation.
I paint you the black of long roadways (trace the
      shape again with your fingertips);
I prove you by seeking new horizons and enjoying
      the journey of life.
I pray you: *Move me* (say the words as if asking or
      entreating with your whole heart).
I blot you with wight-walks and by feeding my skin-
      bag.
I send you forth as fair travels and bright horizons
      for myself;
Fair travels and bright horizons for those I hold
        dear (draw the rune in the air with your right
        hand and *send* that energy forth).
When time comes to draw you back, or to break
      you,
I counter you with Ehwaz.

(Lay down that rune; pick up the next, and repeat the
liquid blessing process.)

By your Hallowed Names,
I charge this rune:
Kenaz.
Freyja's Rune;
Torch-Rune;
Rune of vision and creativity.
Sign of knowledge and inspiration;
Of the fire of life, regeneration, and transformation.
I carve you thus (trace the shape of the rune with
      your fingertips);
With your help, I advise against apathy, instability,
      disease, and false hope.
I paint you the red of passion (trace the shape again
      with your fingertips);

I prove you by being passionately creative; by
creating my own reality and accepting and
understanding my own power.
I pray you: *Manifest* (say the word as if asking or
entreating with your whole heart).
I blot you with fire and incense and artistry.
I send you forth as creativity and the manifestation
of hoped-for dreams for myself;
Creativity and the manifestation of hoped-for
dreams for those I hold dear (draw the rune
in the air with your right hand and *send* that
energy forth).
When time comes to draw you back, or to break
you,
I counter you with Nauthiz.

(Lay down that rune; pick up the next, and repeat the
liquid blessing process.)

By your Hallowed Names,
I charge this rune:
Gebo.
Sif's Rune;
Gift-Rune;
Rune of gifts-in-balance.
Sign of frith and generosity;
Of right-sacrifice and partnerships.
I carve you thus (trace the shape of the rune with
your fingertips);
With your help, I advise against greed, loneliness,
obligation, and over-sacrifice.
I paint you the red of blood-debts and oaths (trace
the shape again with your fingertips);
I prove you by being generous and upholding frith
wherever I go.
I pray you: *Give* (say the word as if asking or
entreating with your whole heart).
I blot you through heartfelt gifts and right action.
I send you forth as peace and bright blessings for
myself;
Peace and bright blessings for those I hold dear

(draw the rune in the air with your right hand
and *send* that energy forth).
When time comes to draw you back, or to break
you,
I counter you with Mannaz.

(Lay down that rune; pick up the next, and repeat the
liquid blessing process.)

By your Hallowed Names,
I charge this rune:
Wunjo.
Vanir-Rune;
Joy-Rune;
Rune of comfort and pleasure.
Sign of prosperity and harmony;
Of fellowship and reward.
I carve you thus (trace the shape of the rune with
your fingertips);
With your help, I advise against sorrow and
alienation, strife and rage.
I paint you a peaceful blue (trace the shape again
with your fingertips);
I prove you through being happy, enjoying the
pleasures of life, and living in harmony with
others.
I pray you: *Gratitude* (say the word as if asking or
entreating with your whole heart).
I blot you with joyous dancing and with laughter
and song.
I send you forth as joy and prosperity for myself;
Joy and prosperity for those I hold dear (draw the
rune in the air with your right hand and *send*
that energy forth).
When time comes to draw you back, or to break
you,
I counter you with Hagalaz.

When each rune has been thus charged, take a small bite of your bread offering and a third drink from your chalice, saying:

Neither loaf nor horn makes me happy,
But I take up these runes,
And I howl;
I sing the mighty songs of Odin's Grandfather,
That I may replace these meager things
With the Mead of Poetry:

You will now perform your first *galdr*, by singing *Freyja's Aett* nine times:

Fehu-Uruz-Thurisaz
Ansuz-Raidho
Kenaz-Gebo-Wunjo

(roughly to the tune of F-F-F-F-F-E-D; F-F-G-G; F-F-G-G#-G-F; all whole notes, with a slight drone, where possible)

Return the runes to their bag. Take it up, shaking it rhythmically, so that the runes clink together within. Alternatively, you may wish to leave the runes arranged in a line upon your *stalli* and *send* the energy of these words *into* them as you speak:

I am awash in wisdom,
And may I grow well and begin to thrive;
Word by word, may I seek words;
Deed by deed, may I seek righteous deeds.
Runes may I find, and advising symbols;
Large runes;
Strong runes;
Notes of the All-Father's mighty songs;
By the Mighty Powers, these runes are fashioned,
And by the Howler of the Gods, are they carved.
So mote it be.
Blessed be.

Raise the Fence.

Outside the fire,
Darkness;
Darkness outside the Grove;
Outside there dwell shadows;
Shadows inside us as well.
Inside, outside, everywhere,
Where'er you dwell,
Dwell not here:
Here is light and all good things!
Light and Bright Wisdom protect us;
Protect us from those who dwell outside.
This circle is open,
Yet never broken.
So it is, and so it shall be.

Ground and center.

Heimdall's Aett

The second set of nine of the twenty-seven nights would then be spent learning *Heimdall's Aett*. Since He is the *common ancestor* of this *clan* of runes, it would be appropriate to not only blot Odin for these nine nights, but Heimdall as well. Rather than *bloodening* each rune, you will use the liquid in your chalice to bless each rune as you study.

Center

Seeker, Maker, Believer (insert your own
     archetypes here):
My feet are on the ground;
I stand firm.
I am of the earth and the earth is of me;
I stand firm.
I center myself, and I hold.
So it is, and so it shall be.

Lay the fence.

Outside the fire,
Darkness;
Darkness outside the Grove;
Outside there dwell shadows;
Shadows inside us as well.
Inside, outside, everywhere,
Where'er you dwell,
Dwell not here:
Here is light and all good things!
Light and Bright Wisdom protect us;
Protect us from those who dwell outside.

Lay out the following runes:

ᚺᛏᛁᛂᛋᚾᛏᛋ

Hallow the space and each item to be charged with the Hallow Sigil:

Place your body in the position of the rune, Tiwaz. Visualize the energy of the sacred space which you have just created as golden light, moving up through the fingertips of your left hand, and across your body to the fingertips of your right hand (or to the dagger, wand, or hammer in your right hand, if you have already procured, blessed, and ensouled that tool).

Visualize the energy flowing down and releasing from your right hand (or the tip of a physical foci, such as a dagger), and **draw the Hallow Sign** over your chalice and see it infusing the liquid within.

Raise your chalice over your head with both hands, and hold it there for several moments.

Lower the chalice slowly to a "toasting position", and say, with intent:

Hail Odin! All-Father;
Thund, who howls upon the World Tree;
Giver-of-Runes,
Singer-of-Songs,
Teacher-of-Wisdom!
Skal!

Drink a small portion of the liquid.

Raise the chalice again to a "toasting position", and say, with intent:

Hail Heimdall! White-God;
Bridge-Guardian;
Horn-Blower who warns against destruction;
Leader of Odin's bright retinue;
Son of the Nine Mothers!
Skal!

Drink another small portion of the liquid.

For *each individual rune,* using the fingertips of your right hand, take a small portion of the liquid from the chalice and with wet fingertips draw the Hallow Sign onto the rune which you wish to charge. (If the item cannot withstand exposure to liquid, carefully draw the Hallow Sign in the air *over* your chalice with the rune between your fingertips.) As you do so, state your intent:

By your Hallowed Names,
I charge this rune:
Hagalaz.
Heimdall's Rune;
Hail-Rune;
Rune of nature's wrath.
Sign of destruction and controlled crisis;
Of testing and trial which lead to inner harmony.
I carve you thus (trace the shape of the rune with
        your fingertips);
With your help, I advise against catastrophe,
        stagnation, suffering, and pain.
I paint you the white of summer ice (trace the shape
        again with your fingertips);
I prove you by accepting those things which are
        beyond my control.
I pray you: *Help* (say the word as if asking or
        entreating with your whole heart).

I blot you with ice and rainwater.
I send you forth as harmony in the face of
     opposition for myself;
Harmony in the face of opposition for those I hold
     dear (draw the rune in the air with your right
     hand and *send* that energy forth).
When time comes to draw you back, or to break
     you,
I counter you with Fehu, Wunjo, and Jera.

(Lay down that rune; pick up the next, and repeat the
liquid blessing process.)

By your Hallowed Names,
I charge this rune:
Nauthiz.
Sigyn's Rune;
Need-Rune;
Rune of resistance leading to strength.
Sign of delays and restrictions;
Of endurance, survival, determination, self-
     reliance, and the will to overcome.
I carve you thus (trace the shape of the rune with
     your fingertips);
With your help, I advise against deprivation,
     imprisonment, and distress.
I paint you the black and blue of bruises hard-won
     (trace the shape again with your fingertips);
I prove you through standing fast in the face of
     trials; through innovation born of strength of
     will.
I pray you: *Overcome* (say the word as if asking or
     entreating with your whole heart).
I blot you via personal acts of endurance and
     determination.
I send you forth as strength and compassionate
     endurance for myself;
Strength and compassionate endurance for those I
     hold dear (draw the rune in the air with your
     right hand and *send* that energy forth).

When time comes to draw you back, or to break
 you,
I counter you with Kenaz.

(Lay down that rune; pick up the next, and repeat the liquid blessing process.)

By your Hallowed Names,
I charge this rune:
Isa.
Skadi's Rune;
Ice-Rune;
Rune of challenges and frustrations.
Sign of standstills and times to turn inward;
Of introspection and holding fast.
I carve you thus (trace the shape of the rune with
 your fingertips);
With your help, I advise against treachery, illusion,
 deceit, and betrayal.
I paint you ice-white and shimmering (trace the
 shape again with your fingertips);
I prove you by standing still and seeking clarity.
I pray you: *Be Still* (say the words as if asking or
 entreating with your whole heart).
I blot you with ice and snow-water.
I send you forth as stillness and the ability to hold
 fast for myself;
Stillness and the ability to hold fast for those I hold
 dear (draw the rune in the air with your right
 hand and *send* that energy forth).
When time comes to draw you back, or to break
 you,
I counter you with Uruz, Ansuz, or Dagaz.

(Lay down that rune; pick up the next, and repeat the liquid blessing process.)

By your Hallowed Names,
I charge this rune:
Jera.
Gerdha's Rune;
Harvest-Rune;
Rune of reaped rewards and fruitful seasons.
Sign of peace and happiness; of cycles and of
change;
Of hopes, expectations, and successes earned.
I carve you thus (trace the shape of the rune with
    your fingertips);
With your help, I advise against bad timing,
    conflict, and reversals of fortune.
I paint you the brown of fertile earth (trace the
    shape again with your fingertips);
I prove you each time I hope and dream; each time
    I accept and understand the cycles of life in
    the Universe; each time I work hard to
    manifest the things I dream.
I pray you: *Bring* (say the word as if asking or
    entreating with your whole heart).
I blot you by planting seeds and growing things.
I send you forth as peace and good seasons for
    myself;
Peace and good seasons for those I hold dear (draw
    the rune in the air with your right hand and
    send that energy forth).
When time comes to draw you back, or to break
    you,
I counter you with Hagalaz.

(Lay down that rune; pick up the next, and repeat the
liquid blessing process.)

By your Hallowed Names,
I charge this rune:
Eihwaz.
Angrbodha's Rune;
Yew-Rune;
Rune of strength and reliability.
Sign of trustworthiness and dependability;

Of protection and the driving force to defend as
      well as acquire.
I carve you thus (trace the shape of the rune with
      your fingertips);
With your help, I advise against confusion,
      destruction, and weakness.
I paint you the green and white of the winter wood
      (trace the shape again with your fingertips);
I prove you through endurance, honoring my word,
      and reaching my goals.
I pray you: *Trust* (say the word as if asking or
      entreating with your whole heart).
I blot you with honest words and honorable deeds.
I send you forth as strength, honor, defense, and
      drive for myself;
Strength, honor, defense, and drive for those I hold
      dear (draw the rune in the air with your right
      hand and *send* that energy forth).
When time comes to draw you back, or to break
      you,
I counter you with Laguz.

(Lay down that rune; pick up the next, and repeat the
liquid blessing process.)

By your Hallowed Names,
I charge this rune:
Perdhro.
Disir-Rune;
Lot-cup-Rune;
Rune of mysteries and hidden things.
Sign of initiations and one's own Wyrd;
Of feminine mysteries met in fellowship and with
      joy.
I carve you thus (trace the shape of the rune with
      your fingertips);
With your help, I advise against addiction,
      stagnation, loneliness, and apathy.
I paint you the red and blue of womankind (trace
      the shape again with your fingertips);

I prove you each time I go within to seek the
  unknown and embrace my feminine side.
I pray you: *Reveal* (say the word as if asking or
  entreating with your whole heart).
I blot you alongside the Disir, and with fire and
  water and smoke and silence.
I send you forth as a fair Wyrd, with fellowship and
  joy, for myself;
A fair Wyrd, with fellowship and joy, for those I
  hold dear (draw the rune in the air with your
  right hand and *send* that energy forth).
When time comes to draw you back, or to break
  you,
I counter you with Inguz.

(Lay down that rune; pick up the next, and repeat the
liquid blessing process.)

By your Hallowed Names,
I charge this rune:
Algiz.
Baldur's Rune;
Elk-Rune;
Rune of protection and the warrior spirit.
Shield-sign; sign of shelter and guardianship;
Of awakenings, God-connections, and divine
  instinct.
I carve you thus (trace the shape of the rune with
  your fingertips);
With your help, I advise against hidden danger,
  breaking taboos, and turning away from the
  Gods.
I paint you the red, black, and purple of a warrior's
  shield (trace the shape again with your
  fingertips);
I prove you each time I protect myself and those I
  love; each time I defend against Evil, and
  hold fast to my oaths to my Gods, for They
  are my shield.
I pray you: *Protect* (say the word as if asking or

entreating with your whole heart).
I blot you each time I blot my Gods.
I send you forth as protection and connection to
      Gods for myself;
Protection and connection to Gods for those I hold
      dear (draw the rune in the air with your right
      hand and *send* that energy forth.)
When time comes to draw you back, or to break
      you,
I counter you with Laguz.

(Lay down that rune; pick up the next, and repeat the
liquid blessing process.)

By your Hallowed Names,
I charge this rune:
Sowilo.
Sunna's Rune;
Sun-Rune;
Rune of success and honor.
Sign of the life force and positive change;
Of victory, health, wholeness, and the cleansing
      fire.
I carve you thus (trace the shape of the rune with
      your fingertips);
With your help, I advise against destruction, vanity,
      and wrath.
I paint you the yellow of the rising sun (trace the
      shape again with your fingertips);
I prove you each time I find the power within me to
      make positive changes in my life.
I pray you: *Shine* (say the word as if asking or
      entreating with your whole heart).
I blot you with fire and honey; with time spent
      basking in the glow of the sun.
I send you forth as victory, health, and wholeness
      for myself;
Victory, health, and wholeness for those I hold dear
      (draw the rune in the air with your right hand
      and *send* that energy forth).

When time comes to draw you back, or to break
     you,
I counter you with Mannaz.

When each rune has been thus charged, take a small bite of
your bread offering and a third drink from your chalice,
saying:

Neither loaf nor horn makes me happy,
But I take up these runes,
And I howl;
I sing the mighty songs of Odin's Grandfather,
That I may replace these meager things
With the Mead of Poetry:

You will now perform your second *galdr*, by singing
Heimdall's Aett nine times:

Hagalaz-Nauthiz-Isa
Jera
Eihwaz-Perdhro-Algiz
Sowilo

(roughly to the tune of F(W)-F#-F(W)-F(W)-F(W)-D#(W)-
D#(W); D#(WW)-D#(WW); G(W)-F(W)-F#(W)-G(W)-
F#(W)-F(W); D#(WW)-E(WW)-D#(WW); whole notes
denoted by (W), with a slight drone, where possible; notes
denoted by (WW) should be droned heavily with their
syllables drawn and exaggerated.)

Return the runes to their bag. Take it up, shaking it
rhythmically, so that the runes clink together within.
Alternatively, you may wish to leave the runes arranged in
a line upon your *stalli* and *send* the energy of these words
into them as you speak:

I am awash in wisdom,
And may I grow well and begin to thrive;
Word by word, may I seek words;
Deed by deed, may I seek righteous deeds.
Runes may I find, and advising symbols;
Large runes;
Strong runes;
Notes of the All-Father's mighty songs;
By the Mighty Powers, these runes are fashioned,
And by the Howler of the Gods, are they carved.
So mote it be.
Blessed be.

Raise the Fence.

Outside the fire,
Darkness;
Darkness outside the Grove;
Outside there dwell shadows;
Shadows inside us as well.
Inside, outside, everywhere,
Where'er you dwell,
Dwell not here:
Here is light and all good things!
Light and Bright Wisdom protect us;
Protect us from those who dwell outside.
This circle is open,
Yet never broken.
So it is, and so it shall be.

Ground and center.

Tyr's Aett

The final set of nine of the twenty-seven nights would then be spent learning *Tyr's Aett*. Since He is the *common ancestor* of this *clan* of runes, it would be appropriate to not only blot Odin for these nine nights, but Tyr as well. Rather than *bloodening* each rune, you will use the liquid in your chalice to bless each rune as you study.

Center

Seeker, Maker, Believer (insert your own
      archetypes here):
My feet are on the ground;
I stand firm.
I am of the earth and the earth is of me;
I stand firm.
I center myself, and I hold.
So it is, and so it shall be.

Lay the fence.

Outside the fire,
Darkness;
Darkness outside the Grove;
Outside there dwell shadows;
Shadows inside us as well.
Inside, outside, everywhere,
Where'er you dwell,
Dwell not here:
Here is light and all good things!
Light and Bright Wisdom protect us;
Protect us from those who dwell outside.

Lay out the following runes:

ᛏ ᛒ ᛗ ᛘ ᛚ ᚦ ᛗ ᛉ

Hallow the space and each item to be charged with the Hallow Sigil:

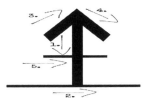

Place your body in the position of the rune, Tiwaz. Visualize the energy of the sacred space which you have just created as golden light, moving up through the fingertips of your left hand, and across your body to the fingertips of your right hand (or to the dagger, wand, or hammer in your right hand, if you have already procured, blessed, and ensouled that tool).

Visualize the energy flowing down and releasing from your right hand (or the tip of a physical foci, such as a dagger), and **draw the Hallow Sign** over your chalice and see it infusing the liquid within.

Raise your chalice over your head with both hands, and hold it there for several moments.

Lower the chalice slowly to a "toasting position", and say, with intent:

Hail Odin! All-Father;
Thund, who howls upon the World Tree;
Giver-of-Runes,
Singer-of-Songs,
Teacher-of-Wisdom!
Skal!

Drink a small portion of the liquid.

Raise the chalice again to a "toasting position", and say, with intent:

Hail Tyr! Oath-Keeper;
You who are called "Leavings of the Wolf";
Justice-Bringer;
Law-Giver,
Thing-Ruler!
Skal!

Drink another small portion of the liquid.

For *each individual rune,* using the fingertips of your right hand, take a small portion of the liquid from the chalice and with wet fingertips draw the Hallow Sign onto the rune which you wish to charge. (If the item cannot withstand exposure to liquid, carefully draw the Hallow Sign in the air *over* your chalice with the rune between your fingertips.) As you do so, state your intent:

By your Hallowed Names,
I charge this rune:
Tiwaz.
Tyr's Rune;
Sky-Rune;
Rune of honor, justice, and the law.
Sign of leadership and authority;
Of rationality, self-sacrifice, and victory in legal
    matters.
I carve you thus (trace the shape of the rune with
    your fingertips);
With your help, I advise against dishonor,
    disloyalty, and authoritative domination.
I paint you the red and green of spear and oak
    (trace the shape again with your fingertips);
I prove you each time I recognize my own strength
    and act with integrity.
I pray you: *Honor* (say the word as if asking or
    entreating with your whole heart).

I blot you with oath-keeping, bread, and fine stew.
I send you forth as honor, justice, and victory for
     myself;
Honor, justice, and victory for those I hold dear
     (draw the rune in the air with your right hand
     and *send* that energy forth).
When time comes to draw you back, or to break
     you,
I counter you with Nauthiz.

(Lay down that rune; pick up the next, and repeat the liquid blessing process.)

By your Hallowed Names,
I charge this rune:
Berkano.
Frigga's Rune;
Birch-Rune;
Rune of birth and liberation.
Sign of fertility and regeneration;
Of renewal, prosperity, and love.
I carve you thus (trace the shape of the rune with
     your fingertips);
With your help, I advise against carelessness, loss
     of control, and stagnation.
I paint you the yellow and white of spring daisies
     (trace the shape again with your fingertips);
I prove you each time I grow in new ways; each
     time I fall in love; each time I am renewed.
I pray you: *Renew* (say the word as if asking or
     entreating with your whole heart).
I blot you with fresh flowers, with birch bark, and
     with dew.
I send you forth as renewal, prosperity, and love for
     myself;
Renewal, prosperity, and love for those I hold dear
     (draw the rune in the air with your right hand
     and *send* that energy forth).
When time comes to draw you back, or to break
     you,
I counter you with Thurisaz.

(Lay down that rune; pick up the next, and repeat the
liquid blessing process.)

By your Hallowed Names,
I charge this rune:
Ehwaz.
Sleipnir's Rune;
Horse-Rune;
Rune of transportation and travel.
Sign of movement and change;
Of teamwork and partnerships.
I carve you thus (trace the shape of the rune with
        your fingertips);
With your help, I advise against reckless haste,
        betrayal, and confinement.
I paint you the red and white of chestnuts and greys
        (trace the shape again with your fingertips);
I prove you each time I work well in a team with
        others; each time I make a change for the
        better, no matter how gradual my progress.
I pray you: *Together* (say the word as if asking or
        entreating with your whole heart).
I blot you with images of horses and with
        sweetgrass and oats.
I send you forth as loyalty, trust, and fair travels for
        myself;
Loyalty, trust, and fair travels for those I hold dear
        (draw the rune in the air with your right hand
        and *send* that energy forth).
When time comes to draw you back, or to break
        you,
I counter you with Mannaz.

(Lay down that rune; pick up the next, and repeat the
liquid blessing process.)

By your Hallowed Names,
I charge this rune:
Mannaz.
Mani's Rune;
Mankind's Rune;
Rune of The Self and the individual.
Sign of friends and enemies; of social order;
Of strong opinions, intelligence, Divinity, and
trusted assistance.
I carve you thus (trace the shape of the rune with
your fingertips);
With your help, I advise against depression,
delusion, cunning, and manipulation.
I paint you the blue and purple of the phases of the
moon (trace the shape again with your
fingertips);
I prove you each time I act on my own behalf, voice
my own opinion, or otherwise celebrate my
own individuality.
I pray you: *I* (say the word as if asking or entreating
with your whole heart).
I blot you by honoring the phases of the moon, my
Ancestors, and the Alfar.
I send you forth as individuality and self-esteem for
myself;
Individuality and self-esteem for those I hold dear
(draw the rune in the air with your right hand
and *send* that energy forth).
When time comes to draw you back, or to break
you,
I counter you with Gebo, Sowilo, Ehwaz, or Othala.

(Lay down that rune; pick up the next, and repeat the
liquid blessing process.)

By your Hallowed Names,
I charge this rune:
Laguz.
Njordr and Aegir's Rune;
Water-Rune;
Rune of flowing, healing, and organic growth.
Sign of imagination and the Otherworld;
Of dreams, mysteries, and the unknown.
I carve you thus (trace the shape of the rune with
    your fingertips);
With your help, I advise against confusion, poor
    judgment, apathy, fear, avoidance, and
    depression.
I paint you the blue and white of crashing waves
    (trace the shape again with your fingertips);
I prove you each time I dream; each time I seek the
    Otherworld; each time I understand that
    there is more to this world than the
    mundane; each time I create something
    beautiful and new.
I pray you: *Heal, Cleanse, Create* (say the words as
    if asking or entreating with your whole heart).
I blot you with seawater and with shells and sand.
I send you forth as healing, creativity, and spiritual
    growth for myself;
Healing, creativity, and spiritual growth for those I
    hold dear (draw the rune in the air with your
    right hand and *send* that energy forth).
When time comes to draw you back, or to break
    you,
I counter you with Thurisaz, Eihwaz, or Algiz.

(Lay down that rune; pick up the next, and repeat the
liquid blessing process.)

By your Hallowed Names,
I charge this rune:
Inguz.
Ingvi-Freyr's Rune;
Earth-Rune;
Rune of common sense and simple strength.
Sign of masculine virility and familial warmth;
Of rest, relief, and freedom.
I carve you thus (trace the shape of the rune with
    your fingertips);
With your help, I advise against impotence,
    stagnation, and toil.
I paint you the green and brown of the growing oak
    (trace the shape again with your fingertips);
I prove you each time I listen to myself and use
    common sense; each time I practice self-care;
    each time I show familial warmth to another
    being.
I pray you: *Free Me* (say the words as if asking or
    entreating with your whole heart).
I blot you with acorn and oak branch; with warm,
    fertile earth.
I send you forth as warmth, love, and freedom for
    myself;
Warmth, love, and freedom for those I hold dear
    (draw the rune in the air with your right hand
    and *send* that energy forth).
When time comes to draw you back, or to break
    you,
I counter you with Perdhro.

(Lay down that rune; pick up the next, and repeat the
liquid blessing process.)

By your Hallowed Names,
I charge this rune:
Dagaz.
Daeg's Rune;
Day-Rune;
Rune of breakthroughs and awakenings.
Sign of daylight clarity; of new enterprises;

Of the power of change directed by one's own will.
I carve you thus (trace the shape of the rune with
     your fingertips);
With your help, I advise against imposed limits and
     hopelessness.
I paint you the golden yellow of a bright summer's
     day (trace the shape again with your
     fingertips);
I prove you each time I reach a balance point; each
     time I channel my will; each time I feel secure
     and happy in the wake of transformation.
I pray you: *Awaken* (say the word as if asking or
     entreating with your whole heart).
I blot you with honey and beeswax; with apples and
     citrus.
I send you forth as awakenings and clarity for
     myself;
Awakenings and clarity for those I hold dear (draw
     the rune in the air with your right hand and
     send that energy forth).
When time comes to draw you back, or to break
     you,
I counter you with Isa.

(Lay down that rune; pick up the next, and repeat the
liquid blessing process.)

By your Hallowed Names,
I charge this rune:
Othala.
Jord's Rune;
Ancestor-Rune;
Rune of inheritance.
Sign of property and possessions; of spiritual
     heritage;
Of that which is truly most important to us.
I carve you thus (trace the shape of the rune with
     your fingertips);
With your help, I advise against a lack of order,
     totalitarianism, slavery, and that which would
     lead to an ill Wyrd.

I paint you the brown of cherished gravesides and
      good earth (trace the shape again with your
      fingertips);
I prove you each time I embark on spiritual
      journeys; each time I honor my Ancestors and
      Hamingja.
I pray you: *Remember* (say the word as if asking or
      entreating with your whole heart).
I blot you each time I honor my Ancestors; with
      absinthe and wormwood.
I send you forth as security, increase, and
      abundance for myself;
Security, increase, and abundance for those I hold
      dear (draw the rune in the air with your right
      hand and *send* that energy forth).
When time comes to draw you back, or to break
      you,
I counter you with Mannaz.

When each rune has been thus charged, take a small bite of
your bread offering and a third drink from your chalice,
saying:

Neither loaf nor horn makes me happy,
But I take up these runes,
And I howl;
I sing the mighty songs of Odin's Grandfather,
That I may replace these meager things
With the Mead of Poetry:

You will now perform your third *galdr*, by singing *Tyr's
Aett* nine times:

Tiwaz
Berkano-Ehwaz-Mannaz
Laguz-Inguz
Dagaz-Othala

(roughly to the tune of F(WW)-F(WW); F-G-F(W)-F#-
G(W)-F#-F(W);G#(W)-F#(WW)-F(W)-G(WW);F-G(WW)-
G#(WW)-G(W)-F(WW); whole notes denoted by (W), with

a slight drone, where possible; notes denoted by (WW) should be droned heavily with their syllables drawn and exaggerated.)

Return the runes to their bag. Take it up, shaking it rhythmically, so that the runes clink together within. Alternatively, you may wish to leave the runes arranged in a line upon your *stalli* and *send* the energy of these words *into* them as you speak:

I am awash in wisdom,
And may I grow well and begin to thrive;
Word by word, may I seek words;
Deed by deed, may I seek righteous deeds.
Runes may I find, and advising symbols;
Large runes;
Strong runes;
Notes of the All-Father's mighty songs;
By the Mighty Powers, these runes are fashioned,
And by the Howler of the Gods, are they carved.
So mote it be.
Blessed be.

Raise the Fence.

Outside the fire,
Darkness;
Darkness outside the Grove;
Outside there dwell shadows;
Shadows inside us as well.
Inside, outside, everywhere,
Where'er you dwell,
Dwell not here:
Here is light and all good things!
Light and Bright Wisdom protect us;
Protect us from those who dwell outside.
This circle is open,
Yet never broken.
So it is, and so it shall be.

Ground and center.

As you are enduring these twenty-seven nights of learning, sacrifice, and initiation, you may receive visions of "united runes": images where a number of runes *bind* or *blend* together. You may, in fact, have received such images prior to beginning these twenty-seven nights of intense ritual. Such runes are called *bind-runes*: a "union" of runes, intended to *bind* the energies of the included runes into one cohesive magickal "force" which may act as a *talisman* or *focus* towards a particular objective, such as healing, financial well-being, protection, etc. Often, I have found that one may receive bind-runes as an initial "gift of good faith" or "good intent" from a God or Goddess who is "courting" you for patronage (a *fulltrui* or *fulltrua* relationship; we'll go into greater depth in exploring those terms as they relate to patronage in a later chapter). This has certainly been the case for me in my relationship with Freyja, and also as I have introduced myself (or been introduced) to other Deities, such as Angrbodha, Freyr, Njordr, and Skadi. Over time, as you become "better acquainted" with runes, runelore, and your patronage (*fulltrui* or *fulltrua*), you may also choose to create bind-runes of your own for specific purposes and intents.

Although a bind-rune is a blending of two or more runes, each rune within the bind-rune needs to maintain its own individual *identity*; it needs to be visibly recognizable as *itself* within the whole. You should begin by determining the *intent* of your completed bind-rune. Will this be a bind-rune for protection, for example? If so, you might incorporate Algiz, Thurisaz, and/or Eihwaz. If you are creating a bind-rune for healing, you might incorporate Laguz. In other words, your intent should match with the runes incorporated. It is best not to choose too many runes when creating a bind-rune: generally speaking, two to five is best, although our Ancestors certainly created ones which incorporated more than that (we'll touch on this a bit more as we get into galdrastafir).

As you begin to formulate the *design* of your bind-rune, pay close attention that you neither *mirror* nor *reverse* a rune in the process. While I patently do not believe in reading *merkstaves* when using runes for any form of divination, I have found that mirroring or reversing runes within a bind-rune can have less than satisfactory end results. Begin with an *anchor rune*: this is the rune which represents the major *theme* of your bind-rune's intent. This rune should always be the one which is drawn or carved *first* when fashioning your final bind-rune. Next, you should decide on an *activation* rune(s). This (or these) rune(s) *drives* or *empowers* the *magick* of your bind-rune. In other words, it "makes the magick go". These should be drawn/carved second. Finally, you should decide which rune *seals* your bind-rune. This rune is like the "stamp" that *seals* the energy of the bind-rune; I tend to think of it as a sort of visual "make it so" or "so mote it be". Don't worry if none of the runes you have chosen seem to be appropriate at face value as a "sealing rune": almost every bind-rune ever made contains Isa somewhere within it, as Isa is simply a straight line. As it turns out, Isa is generally the *best* rune with which to seal a bind-rune. The sealing rune is drawn last; if you do not have a separate sealing rune, and are instead employing a "found" Isa, re-trace the line intended to represent that rune.

As you carve or draw your final bind-rune (the one you will actually *use*), you should galdr each of the runes. As you endured the twenty-seven nights of runic initiation, you were officially introduced to performing simple galdr. You may choose to simply *sing* or *chant* the rune's name repeatedly as you draw/carve each one, or you may wish to employ galdr chants created by others, or created by yourself. Many resources on bind-runes will detail a further *charging process* for the bind-rune, before it is actually "activated" and "usable", but in my personal experience, the "galdr process" while drawing the rune in the *appropriate order* has been "charge enough" to get things done. Once completed, the bind-rune may be worn, carried in a pocket, placed in your skin-bag, hung somewhere in your home, or kept on your main stalli. Placing a bind-rune inside the shoes you typically wear is also a historically apt method. The most important thing is that you put it where it will release its energy in the most opportune manner; use your imagination on where that might be!

In the next chapter, **Finding Freyja**, I discuss the bind-rune with which I was gifted in February 2017, shortly before my official dedication to Freyja. Consisting of Algiz, Sowilo, and Wunjo, it has become for me what it was intended: an empowered symbol of my bond to Freyja, and Her bond to me. She gifted it to me at a time when I was severely financially depressed: every waking thought centered around our business at Iaconagraphy, and how to make it better and get things more "off the ground". It turns out the answer to that issue is precisely the message of this rune: I am protected, and I need to realize that. She will not let me fail. There is more to serve in life than the almighty dollar. It is better to serve the Gods, and They will assist me in making sure that my Wyrd unfolds as intended. The *anchor rune* of this bind-rune is Algiz; the *activation rune* is Sowilo, and it is *sealed* with Wunjo. The galdr for this bind-rune—the first original galdr I ever constructed or performed—can be found immediately below the image.

Freyja's Bind-rune

Algiz
Algiz-Algiz
Always-Algiz-Algiz
All-Guard-Algiz-Algiz
Algiz-Always-Algiz
Algiz-Algiz-Algiz
Sowilo-Sowilo-Sowilo
Shine-on-Sowilo
Sun-bright-Sowilo
Sowilo-Sowilo-Sowilo
Wunjo
Wunjo
Wun-joy-Wunjo-Wunjo
Win-Won-Winning-Won
Wunjo
Wun-joy-Wunjo-Wunjo
Wunjo

To inspire you in the creation and use of bind-runes of your own, I thought it might be helpful to include two others which have served me well. The first of these was created at a time when

I was facing some minor opposition in my job: apparently a language barrier between myself and another Facebook user had led to a minor misunderstanding, wherein my reputation might ultimately be called into question. I decided the best two Gods to "have in my corner" were Thor and Tyr, so I poured blot to both, and was subsequently gifted the Thor-Tyr bind-rune which I have included below. After "casting" the bind-rune (which included posting it to my Facebook page), I had no further issues with the other party involved in the previous language-barrier-inspired debacle. The second bind-rune which you will find below was gifted to me by Freyja and Freyr, as we began our journey towards selling our home and buying a new one. This rune has proven to be a very powerful one for manifestation of several types, and especially of the financial variety.

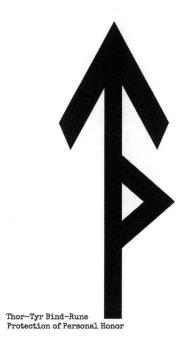

Thor–Tyr Bind–Rune
Protection of Personal Honor

Manifestation Rune
Fehu–Kenaz–Jera

If you have researched bind-runes on your own at all, you have likely also encountered *galdrastafir*. The most familiar of these symbols are the *Vegvisir* (literally: "sign post"; an Icelandic magical stave intended to help its bearer find their way through rough weather; most famously tattooed on the body of pop singer, Bjork) and the *Aegishjalmur* ("Helm of Awe"). Many strict Reconstructionists immediately dismiss galdrastafir, maintaining that they are exclusively part of a later "black book" or "grimoiric" tradition in Iceland, which roughly coincides with the rise of similar traditions in mainland Europe (circa 14th-18th centuries A.D.). However, the *Aegishjalmur*—the Helm of Awe—is specifically mentioned in the *Fafnismal* of the Poetic Edda, a source which definitely predates those grimoiric traditions. The similarities between galdrastafir and more "basic" bind-runes, coupled with direct translation of the word *galdrastafir* itself, likewise suggest that such a complete dismissal of galdrastafir as "not old enough" may be a bit of an overreaction, at best.

The word *galdrastafir* has traditionally been translated as "magical staves", however, as we have already discussed, the word *galdr* obviously has a much more specific meaning than simply "magical". *Galdr*, in fact, sources to Old High German *gala*, meaning to *sing* incantations, as well as to Old English *galan*, "sing, chant". This obviously suggests that the galdrastafir were originally staves (collections of runes and symbols, as runes are often traditionally referred to as rune-staves) which were *sung*. When one considers that modern musical notation has been referred to as musical *staves* since at least the 13th century A.D., this argument becomes even more persuasive. What if the galdrastafir are actually a "hold-over" of a form of ancient musical notation? What if the reason archaeologists have found few musical instruments among the grave goods at pre-Viking Period sites is because they simply haven't *recognized* some of those artifacts as what they are, attributing bowls that were actually played in very much the same manner as Tibetan singing bowls as merely bowls that acted as containers? What if galdrastafir are simply visual representations of songs in a lasting, concrete form? I will readily grant that that's a lot of *what if's*, but almost every great hypothesis begins with those two little words.

The "cyclic" nature of some of the oldest of the galdrastafir further lends itself to this hypothesis. Most bind-runes and, in fact, many of the galdrastafir which have come down to us, are *linear*, either horizontally or vertically, yet the *Aegishjalmur* and *Vegvisir* (among others) are distinctly *round* representations of groupings of recognizable runes. Many scholars have suggested that this "roundness" is due to exposure to other systems of Western Magic by grimoire authors, and specifically, to other sigils, such as the Seal of Solomon. However, this is only a worthy hypothesis when one completely *divorces* galdrastafir from the inherent concept of singing or chanting that is implied by the very word *galdr*. When one begins to look at these sigils from a musical perspective, I believe new dimensions to their inherent worthiness and potential for modern use may be discovered. To further explore this hypothesis, let us focus on the *Aegishjalmur*, as it is the eldest of the galdrastafir, and one of the few which is also attested in sources outside of the "black book" or "Icelandic grimoire" tradition.

As I mentioned previously, the *Aegishjalmur* is mentioned in the *Fafnismal*, which is sourced from the 13th century Codex Regius:

> *Fafnir spoke:*
> "I wore Aegishjalmur (the fear-helm) among the
>   sons of men,
> While I laid on a bed of gold;
> I thought myself stronger than everyone else,
> I thought many things."

> *Sigurdr spoke:*
> "Aegishjalmur (the fear-helm) only makes you
>   alone
> In the middle of a very wide road;
> Leaving you to find that many are coming for you,
> And you are not invincible, after all."
> --Fafnismal 16-17, Translation mine.

As can be seen in the image above, the arms of the *Aegishjalmur* seem to be composed of the rune Algiz, a rune of protection and the "warrior-spirit". Each of these arms bears three "spikes" along its length, which may be representations of the rune Isa, a rune of challenges and "holding fast", or steadfastness. Most scholars who have broken down the runic symbolism of *Aegishjalmur* have stopped there. However, if you move down the staves, to the central "binding" circle, you also find a constant repetition of the runes Kenaz and Gebo: runes of manifestation and frith (peace-bringing; peace-keeping; the "bounds of peace"), respectively. When coupled with my "musical hypothesis" concerning the galdrastafir, all of this made me beg the question: what would happen if I *sang Aegishjalmur*?

Which then begs the question: *how does one sing Aegishjalmur*? Assuming the aforementioned "cyclic" nature of this sigil, as it relates to musical theory, one would sing each "collection" of runes down the stave, to the center, in a similar manner to the folk-music genre commonly referred to as a *round*. More properly known as *perpetual canon* or *infinite canon*, this type of musical composition may be traced back at least as far as 1180 to Germanic sources. Altogether, one would perform the same *galdr pattern* eight times, locking the "song" with a ninth "cycle" by repeating the first "tine". Because this is a type of *perpetual canon*, the pattern could repeat itself as many times as a practitioner felt necessary (or until they became hoarse of voice, and/or "ran out of energy"). The proposed *galdr pattern* would therefore sound something like this:

Algiz-Isa-Isa-Isa-**Kenaz**-**Gebo** (where bold type signifies elongated or "held-note" syllables)

So what *does* happen if one *sings Aegishjalmur*? I conducted my experiment at my Main Ve outside. Before I began the round of galdr, the sky was a perfect, sunny blue. The subsequent rush of wind, coupled with sudden dark cloud cover, as I began to sing, nearly sent me scurrying back inside before I had even finished the third round of the cycle! The effect was, in fact, *terrifying*, as its literal translation as "Helm of Awe" or "Helm of Terror" suggests. There was an accompanying period completely *devoid* of any birdsong, which is exceedingly rare in our neighborhood. Its uses as a means of *protection* or source of *physical strength* remain untested, but as a "spell" for *weather magick*, I definitely give the singing of *Aegishjalmur* a wholehearted two thumbs up! Attempting for a moment to adopt the mindset of our Ancestors, I can also see where an ability to "call the storm" could definitely be useful in attaining protection or showing the apparent evidence of physical (and supernatural) strength: clearly if Thor is "on your side", it's probably a great idea for your opponent to "step off"!

While performing this exercise may or may not prove the veracity of my musical theories pertaining to the galdrastafir, what it has proven to me conclusively is that debating their historical veracity (or not) is of far less value than discovering their modern *potential applications*. Whether they are, in fact, several thousand years old, or merely seven hundred years old, makes little difference. I think all of us can agree that both figures do, in fact, arrive at the same thing: galdrastafir *are old*. If something *works*, why do we care how authentically *old* it is or isn't? What *should* matter, in the long run, is *how* something works, and *if it does*. What I have found to be true, through my own experimentation, is that *singing* galdrastafir *works*. As such, you may wish to explore combining collections of your own bind-runes into galdrastafir, to act not only as musical staves from which to actively *sing* (*galdr*), but also as *concrete images of song* that, in effect, "keep singing", long after your last vocalized note has resonated into silence.

Most of my own personal experiments in this field have involved the creation of personal galdrastafir for manifestation, healing, and weather magick (because it's incredibly hard to sleep during a New England thunderstorm!). These are of my own creation; your mileage may vary. Please use them wisely.

Audhr-Skjoldr
"Wealth Shield"

Fehu-Kenaz-Jera-Gebo ("held-notes" or whole notes on all runes, with drone)
For manifestation (especially of the financial variety)

Heilendi
Good Health

Laguz-Ansuz-Mannaz
Laguz-Ansuz-Ing!
For Healing (especially of chronic pain)

Hridh-Stodhva
"Storm-Stopper"

Sowilo-Mannaz-Isa
Sowilo-Mannaz-Kenaz
(For quieting a loud thunderstorm)

One final note on all of the above: whether employing bind-runes, galdrastafir, or galdr alone, runelore should *only* be used for *positive workings,* **except in very rare circumstances.** Certainly, curses and "hexes" were things practiced by our Ancestors, and are still widely practiced among modern magickal practitioners, Norse-based and otherwise. Such things are, unfortunately, outside the scope of this book. I feel that offering an extensive chapter on runelore without a proper admonishment *not to use runes* for negative workings *without proper training and context* would be an act of spiritual negligence on my part, for which I would ever hold myself accountable. Should you choose to ignore this warning and do so anyway, *you* will not enjoy the repercussions, regardless of the end result aimed at your chosen target. If you do choose to employ runelore towards harmful ends, *without proper training and context,* please acknowledge: **you have been warned.**

Finding Freyja

Every Friday, without fail, I pour blot to Freyja. I began this weekly ritual in April of 2016, after She came to me in a dream, and claimed me as Her own. Those first few weeks, I knew Her only as "Freyja, Queen of Cats"; a gentle presence, not unlike the huge felines who pull Her chariot, or even our own family cat, Kili, who could creep into a room quite unnoticed, yet fill the entire place with reverberating love, and passion that was quick to rise, sometimes even baring claws. With my whole heart, I poured a sweet red wine blend for Her, and I spoke the few kennings I knew, as well as the one She had, in fact, taught me: "Freyja, Queen of Cats". And then I poured out my heart to Her. Every Friday, without fail.

On the twenty-seventh of February in 2017, I finally realized that I should take the plunge, and dedicate myself to the service She had already chosen for me. Two nights prior, I had participated in a Dark Moon Ritual at Enchanted Shop in Salem, Massachusetts, led by Priestess Renee Des Anges. During the meditation portion of that ritual, I was gifted a bind rune by The Lady: **Algiz**, **Sowilo**, **Wunjo**.

Algiz is a warrior's rune. I wouldn't fully understand the depth of Her gifting it me until two months later, when it *finally* dawned on me the form in which She had first chosen to visit: *Valfreyja*. For several years, I worked under the pen name "The Warrior" as an artist; my Beloved, Suzanne, in fact calls me "Her Warrior" as a pet-name. So it's quite appropriate that Freyja first made Herself known to me as *Valfreyja*; it's not *Her* fault that I'm more than a little slow on the uptake! **Algiz** is also the rune repeated on the Helm of Awe, a *galdrastafir* to which I have been heavily drawn from the first moment I laid eyes upon it. It is a rune of *protection*. It is also a rune of *friendship with the Gods*, and of *communication with Higher Powers*. **Message received.**

Sowilo is a rune of promise, strength, warmth, and joy. It is the sun melting the snow with the promise of Spring; success, when we think all hope has otherwise been lost. These are the very things She had come to be to me over the course of the preceding year: when things were at their absolute darkest, Freyja always was *there*. And She reminded me to hope; She reminded me constantly that I am an *artist*, and that the Way of the Artist has never been easy, but *has* always been *worthwhile*. **Message received.**

Wunjo is as close as a rune can come to true bliss; a rune of "happily ever afters". It is a rune of fulfillment, but it is also a rune of *bonds forged*: the bond of a friend to a friend; of lover to lover; of Goddess to Dedicant. It brings transformations of the best kind; the kind where one stops feeling like an outsider and becomes a part of something greater than themselves. **Message received.**

It was time; She had told me so. Now the question became: how does one "perform" a dedication to a Deity in the Norse Tradition? I had no clue. Certainly, I had read about others who had done so and I knew that there was a certain measure of "contractual deal making" that took place within a ritual context when "finally taking the plunge" with a Norse Deity, but that was pretty much the extent of my knowledge on the subject, apart from my previous experience as a Welsh Druid. Still, I wasn't exactly "going in blind": I had, after all, spent the last year getting to *know*

Her better, both in a ritual setting (during our Friday blot), and in a research capacity. So I did what I almost always do with everything that I'm passionate about in my life: *I jumped in with both feet.*

Rather than use a simple white candle as I normally do when creating sacred space, I chose a lavender chime candle from my "stash", and with my ritual dagger, I carved upon it the bind rune which She had given me. I then placed it in the small holder which I keep within the cast iron cauldron (which I also use as my hlaut-boll) on my altar, and set about creating sacred space. It isn't often anymore that I do the full rite before my altar: as I've said before, I've called sacred space into being so many times in that area that it's practically a permanently liminal space. But that night, I felt *driven* to do so. She *told* me to do it; and *I did as I was told.*

How do you know when the Gods are telling you to do something? Sometimes it may come as it does when any physical person tells you to do something: in the form of an *audible voice*. Other times, like that night, it may come in the form of a *burning need*. Suddenly, you feel *driven* to do something, with every fiber of your being, often to the point of actually feeling *physically ill* if that thing is not done. That night was like that: if I *had not* called the space with the full rite, I knew instantly that I was going to suffer for not having done. There would be a definite headache. There might also be nausea. So I went for it. Like I said: *I did as I was told.*

I centered myself. I laid the fence. Every movement was purposeful and driven. And then I lit the lavender candle which I had inscribed with the bind-rune, and I stared deeply into its flame, letting my mind go blank as one typically does with candle-scrying. And She stood there, in the flame. I saw Her again, as I had that night a year past, in my dreams. And I apologized for being "a little bit slow" mentally, and then I told Her what She already knew:

I belong to you.

And then my promises to Her—the conditions of my service to Her—flowed out of me, not in some makeshift version of a legalese contract, but in poetry:

I am the
Walker Between The Worlds;
I am the Raven
On the wing,
And I sing the
Song without the
Words,
For I have no
Voice to bring.
Yet still with this
Voice
That is
Mine-not-mine,
I raise that
Voice
And sing.

That was the moment when I became a Norse Witch. Not a Heathen; nor a Norse Traditional Pagan: a **Norse Witch**. Those were not the words of an academic, clinging to a Reconstructionist path; those were the words of the Raven-I-once-was; the words of a *mystic* from the heart of a *poet*. My adventures in *galdr* began the very next day as well, and I've been on that song-filled journey ever since. She *chose me* to be Her servant; She *chose me* to be a Norse Witch. I take no titles for myself, except those which She confers upon me. It doesn't seem to matter at all to Her that my singing voice is very much like that of the raven that is my *fylgja*: I squawk to the glory of the Gods now on a regular basis! She doesn't seem to mind that I mix the spiritual pathways of the Norse with those of other traditions to breathe new life into them. And I know that each time I sing, and each time that I practice or even teach this Craft, that I am doing *right*. Singing for Her and teaching for Her fills me up as few things ever have.

I'm glad I finally "bought a clue". I'm glad I finally *found* Freyja. I'm glad She took the time to *find* me. I am proud to be Her Norse Witch.

Deepening Devotion

As I read the **Runelore** chapter to a trusted friend, she responded with a remark that deeply touched me; she said: "You write about your Gods with the same level of love that you write about your wife." Subconsciously, I suppose, I knew this to be true, but I had never really given it much consideration, on a conscious level. After all, what's the point in believing in or having God/desses if we do not love Them, and if we cannot or do not feel loved in return? In many ways, that is a question that runs concurrently with one of the **Six Big Questions** with which I began this book: **Where Do I Belong?**. Loving Deity, and being loved in return, is one of the most profound ways for us to feel less *alone* in this world.

At its core, this Heidhrinn faith is a *polytheistic* religion; whether one chooses to explore their faith as a *hard polytheist* or as a *soft polytheist* (as I do), there are ultimately "many Gods for many things", or, to come from a slightly more *softly polytheistic* stance: "many *faces* of God for many things". Many newcomers, arriving at this path after years within a strongly *monotheistic* faith, such as the various branches of Christianity, initially have issues with the "polytheistic dilemma", which they may either resolve via a more *softly polytheistic* stance, or by rushing to find a patron/ess to which they can devote all of their actions, as a means of "mimicking monotheism". My own *soft polytheism* and subsequent patron-relationship to Freyja is the product of neither of these. Instead, I tend towards *soft polytheism* because I feel that such a viewpoint more closely reflects the Indo-European root of the Ancient Norse Faith: a root reflected back at us here in the modern world by the "polytheistic monotheism" of Hinduism, more properly termed *monolatry*.

Monolatry is a term first coined by Erich Winter and Siegfried Morenz in reference to Near Eastern conceptions of God, and later applied to Kemetic (Ancient Egyptian) systems of faith by Erik Hornung and Jan Assmann, among other Egyptologists. Basically, it is the belief that many gods and goddesses may exist, each having their own unique personalities and interactions with human beings, but that ultimately, they are all manifestations of the One: a superior "godhead" or "divine energy". In Hinduism, we find many different devotees of many different deities—Shiva, Kali, Hanuman, Lakshmi, Parvati, Krishna—but ultimately all of these different deities are understood as "faces", "emanations", or "reflections" of Brahman, the Supreme Divine Energy which "drives" the Universe. In Kemeticism (Ancient Egyptian Reconstructionist), we may likewise meet many different deities— Yinepu (Anubis), Ra, Aset, Wesir--who are called The Names of Netjer (God). They are called this—The Names—to illustrate that while a Name *is*, in fact, a *distinct personality* and an *individualized* God-being, it is also still an *aspect* of the One Godhead; the Self-Created.

Essentially, *monolatry* is just a "nutshell" way of saying that all gods are ultimately one God. The modern practitioners of Kemetic Orthodoxy have a particularly apt way of explaining how this works: because God is so much larger than our teeny tiny human brains can fully understand (a good word here would be *ineffable*), God appears to us in various forms, almost like "deified compartments", that are small enough for us humans to be able to understand and form close relationships with. These "deified compartments" may come to us in ways that we are more able to understand from our present cultural perspective, such as Odin (the All-Father of the Norse Pantheon, who was both warrior and wise-man), or they may come to us in ways that encapsulate a certain lesson that we absolutely need to learn *right now*, but might not learn if it were "dressed up" in typical "God-talk", such as Loki (from the Norse Pantheon, who teaches us to laugh at our own mistakes, but also teaches us the grave price to be paid when we do things that unjustifiably harm other people).

My personal interactions with the Gods and Goddesses of the Norse Pantheon as a *monolatry* are admittedly based on a combination of personal experience, and a "common sense notion" of how our faith may or may not relate back to its Indo-European root, rather than any factual historical information. *Cognitive archaeology* is a controversial field at best, and to fully realize and understand how our Ancestors actually viewed their relationships to and with the God/desses, and truly determine whether they were, in fact, hard polytheists, soft polytheists, or the "strange brew" of the two which is now called *monolatry,* would rely on precisely that field of study. Cognitive archaeology is a *theoretical perspective*—in other words, it's a field based largely on that same big question you found me repeating over and over again in previous chapters: *what if?*--which focuses on the ways in which ancient societies *thought*, based on the *symbolic structures* evidenced within their remaining *material culture* (artifacts). Archaeologist Neil Price employed the use of *cognitive archaeology* in his book, *The Viking Way: Religion and War in Late Iron Age Scandinavia* (Oxford Books, 2002). In it, he states:

> 'Religion' to us conjures up something orthodox, a creed, with more-or-less rigid rules of behavior that usually embody concepts of obedience and worship. These tenets are often set out in holy books, with holy men and women to interpret them, with all that that implies in terms of social differentiation and power relationships. To a greater or lesser degree, all the world faiths of our time fall into this category. In Scandinavia before the coming of Christianity, however, no-one would have understood this concept. For the Late Iron Age it is instead more appropriate to speak of a *'belief system', a way of looking at the world*. What we would now isolate as religion was then simply *another dimension of daily life,* inextricably bound up with every other aspect of existence....the 'worship' required by the Norse pantheon was not adoration, or gratitude, or even unreserved approval....the religion of the Aesir and Vanir demanded only a *recognition that they existed as an integral and immutable part of human nature and society,* and *of the natural world,* and that as such they *possessed an inherent rightness*— perhaps even a kind of beauty. If one wished to avoid

disaster, it was necessary to come to terms with the gods, and the terms would be theirs, not those of their followers...a refusal to acknowledge the gods in this way could have dire consequences. It would also involve a contradiction, as such an act would be a *denial of the undeniable. The question of 'believing in' the Norse gods was probably irrelevant*...The path of the ritual warrior may have been a deeply spiritual acknowledgment of the gods and their place in the cosmos...

(italicized emphases are mine)

That "*inherent rightness*" mentioned by Price, I feel, is the Norse equivalent of a "God Head", "Prime Mover", or "Self-Created One", mirroring the Hindu view of Brahman, and the Kemetic view of the Names as they relate to Netjer. Among the Norse, rather than finding a "supremely identifiable entity" (see Godhead above), instead we find evidence of a pervasive Universe-driving force (expressed as a collection of forces, within the Norse pantheon) which is simply recognized as "the *undeniable*". Whether or not you choose to adopt this view of the God/desses is entirely up to you, within your own personal practice of Norse Witchcraft, however this is the stance from which I will be discussing the rest of the material within this chapter.

In the previous chapters of this book, I have discussed in great detail my deep personal relationship with Freyja, to whom I am a dedicant, and also to other Norse Gods and Goddesses. Dedication to a specific deity is not something undertaken by all followers of the Norse Faith or even of Norse Witchcraft, although there is certainly significant historical evidence that some (though likely not all) of our Ancestors definitely engaged in such relationships. Some people argue that such relationships are simply a comfortable "mimic of monotheism" for those stepping from a former monotheistic faith into a profoundly polytheistic one, and for some people, that may indeed be true. However, in our Heidhrinn Faith, dedication to or patronage of a particular Deity neither precludes nor excludes acknowledgment and veneration of any or all of the others. Instead, our *fulltrui* and *fulltrua* (masculine and feminine, respectively) relationships with our Gods and Goddesses place us in the unique position of recognizing not only *our* place in the Universe-at-large, but Theirs as well.

Unlike the patron/dedicant relationships found in other faiths (including Catholic Christian relationships to saints), the *fulltrui* relationships formed in Norse Witchcraft are very much a *cooperative process*. Whereas in other faiths the patron/dedicant relationship tends often towards a sort of benign master/servant motif (with Deity as master, and dedicant as servant), in our Heidhrinn Faith, the *fulltrui* relationship is understood more as a *full partnership*. In fact, the word *fulltrui* translates literally as "representative, agent, or trusted friend". As such, I understand myself not as a *servant* of Freyja, but as a *representative* of Her best interests in this modern world; as an *agent* of those things which She attempts to put forth in this world (ecstasy in all its varieties, including religious ecstasy; magick as a form of service to others; overarching love; honoring self-esteem, etc.), and as a *trusted friend* who *actively loves* their Friend and who is *actively loved* by that Friend in return.

As I discussed in great detail in the **Godfinding** Chapter, developing and maintaining friendships with the God/desses works very much like developing and maintaining friendships with any other mundane human being. I would offer the same caveat when discussing *fulltrui* relationships that I would offer when speaking of any human-to-human friendship: **do not offer your friendship lightly**. A *fulltrui* relationship with a God sought simply because it's the "cool" or "en vogue" thing to do is the same as seeking friendship with the "popular kid" at school, simply based on that person's popularity: **I would advise neither**. If the latter can potentially lead to fakery and heartbreak, imagine what the former could lead toward? Freyja chose me, rather than the other way around, but it is not unheard of for people to choose Whom to court as *fulltrui*: **just make sure you are doing so for the *right* reasons**! While being *fulltrui* of Thor may "sound cool", consider the very real ramifications of such a relationship in the same way as you would when considering becoming the "besty" of the dude who leads the local motorcycle gang, who also happens to be a farmer and goat-herder, who also happens to work as a weatherman. If that still feels like a "good fit", then do exactly what you would do when seeking the friendship of said motorcycle-goatherding-dude, and see how *Thor feels* about your potential as *fulltrui*, for such relationships with the Gods can no more be forced than such relationships with other humans. (*Note:* these extreme over-generalizations of Thor are meant purely to illustrate a point, and are not intended to offend anyone, most especially Thor!)

At times, our *fulltrui* relationships may place us in positions of service to other humans, as we act as the *representatives* and *agents* of our *partnered* God/dess, but never forget: you are *not* an *employee*. Instead, you are a *co-worker*, in much the same sense as members of the United Nations are ultimately *co-workers*, working alongside each other, and alongside their country-of-origin, for the "greater good". You are a *representative* of your *partnered* God/dess, and as such, you are expected to *behave* in *partnership* with Them. For example, as a dedicant in a *fulltrui* relationship with Freyja (Freyja is my *fulltrua*—feminine-- and I am *fulltrui* of Freyja—masculine, as I'm a dude), I act as Her *representative* when I promote a positive and accurate image of *Who She Is* here in our mundane world. I act as Her *agent* when I perform such services as oracle and rune readings for people as a *service* to them: I understand that She is not "speaking through me" or otherwise "working through me", but instead that She is speaking *to* me on occasion, so that I may relay Her messages to others. These services fall under the heading of working as an *agent* of Freyja because She ultimately governs such areas as ecstatic religious experiences (which I undertake with each reading, as I enter the Alpha state), building self-esteem (which I use these services to foster in my clients), and, ultimately, *seidhr* (the heading of Norse magick under which divination and channeling fall). On the other hand, if I was *fulltrui* with Thor, I might still behave as His *representative* when I promoted a positive and accurate image of *Who He Is* here in our mundane world, but my actions as His *agent* would likely take on very different forms: I might be someone who translates things into plain speech for laymen, for example.

Behaving in a manner that is *contrary* to your *fulltrui* relationship with a specific Deity can have *dire* consequences, in much the same way that acting *contrary* to a formed human relationship might. Let's begin with an extremely mundane and silly example to illustrate what I'm talking about here. Let's say you have a best friend named Tom. Your relationship was formed on the common understanding that you both *represent* and *adhere to* certain similar beliefs about the world in general, as most friendships are: in other words, you have certain *deep principles* in common. For the sake of this example, we'll say that the primary one of those *deep principles* is that *Doctor Who* is the greatest TV series of all time. As best friends, you *represent* this *deep principle* together by actively engaging in *Doctor Who* cosplay at every available opportunity, getting friends together for

Doctor Who viewing marathons to introduce as many people as possible to this fantastic show, and collecting vast amounts of *Doctor Who* memorabilia. One day, Tom expresses that he has decided *Doctor Who* is no longer the greatest TV series of all time, and has been replaced in his heart and mind with *Grey's Anatomy*. Although he is totally willing to sell you all of his memorabilia dirt-cheap, he will no longer be engaging in cosplay with you, or helping you organize viewing marathons of *Doctor Who*. Instead, he would really appreciate it if you would help him get a few friends together to watch a *Grey's Anatomy* marathon. He is officially behaving in a manner that is *contrary* to the basis of your previously formed friendship; the two of you no longer share the same primary *deep principle* in common. It's time to "break up" with Tom. Chances are, both parties will leave the relationship with hurt feelings. If "breaking up" with people is difficult, imagine for a moment "breaking up" with a God/dess? I strongly *do not recommend*!

That there is a possibility of behaving *contrary* to a *fulltrui* relationship with a specific Deity implies that certain *taboos* are put into place at the start of said relationship. Just as switching from *Doctor Who* to *Grey's Anatomy* was *taboo* in the previous example of your fictitious relationship with Tom, breaking oaths would naturally be *taboo* within the scope of a *fulltrui* relationship with Tyr. Meanwhile, within a *fulltrui* relationship with Loki, breaking oaths might not be so deeply frowned upon, but taking yourself too seriously definitely would be. Most of the time these *taboos* are implied by the areas over which a specific Deity has governance; other times, they may be agreed upon (generally by oath-taking) between yourself and your *fulltrui/fulltrua*, based upon their areas of governance as those interact with our modern society. For example, horses are considered sacred to Freyr. In the world of our Ancestors, horses were routinely sacrificed to Freyr, and their flesh eaten by those gathered. Our Ancestors regarded horses not only as boon companions and service animals, but also as a food source. At that time, there were no endangered horses; horses were reasonably plentiful. Meanwhile, in our modern society most of the horses which go on to become food sources are of the *endangered* variety—i.e., Mustangs. Therefore, a *taboo* for a *fulltrui* of Freyr might be to never eat horsemeat, since horsemeat might most likely have been sourced from *endangered* Mustangs, who are symbolic of the very same freedom and lust for life which is His governance.

Just as healthy mundane human friendships do not "happen overnight", neither should *fulltrui* relationships with a God/dess. Generally, before we proclaim someone as our "best friend", we **fully know what we are getting ourselves into**, and that same caveat should definitely apply before remotely considering becoming *fulltrui/fulltrua* with *Anyone*. Before embarking on any of the other exercises and activities within this chapter, please be certain that you are well-acquainted with and are performing and/or have performed the suggested steps in the **Godfinding** Chapter. If you feel that you are *not ready* to seek a *fulltrui/fulltrua* relationship at this time, then *don't do it*! Chances are, this book will still be sitting on your shelf, ready and waiting for you, when you *are ready.* You may also feel completely *disinclined*, for whatever personal reason, from *ever* seeking a *fulltrui/fulltrua* relationship: *you're **not** doing it wrong!* These sorts of relationships aren't for everyone, and they certainly are not necessary for you to live a perfectly fulfilling and fulfilled life as a Norse Witch. I provide the information in this chapter solely because I have encountered far too many people who either have the completely *wrong idea* about what it means to be *fulltrui/fulltrua* in the first place, or who (like myself) would have greatly benefited from someone else having written a "handy guide", before plunging into such a serious relationship.

In previous chapters, I've talked about my own personal journey from Buddhism/Taoism in my childhood, through both Protestant and Catholic "flavors" of Christianity, to Wicca, Welsh Reconstructionist Druidry, Kemeticism, and back again to Welsh Reconstructionist Druidry, before finally arriving at my own specific brand of Norse Tradition: Norse Witchcraft, this Heidhrinn Faith. Every single one of those Paths led me to gravitate towards and dedicate myself to different *faces* of the "Godhead". As a Buddhist/Taoist, I was very much a "dedicant" of Kuan Yin and Amitabha Buddha. As a Christian, I gravitated not only towards Christ, but also towards the Archangels Uriel and Michael. As a Wiccan, my dedication was to Bran The Blessed and the Morrigan. In Kemeticism, I was a proud servant of Yinepu (Anubis), Bastet, and Sekhmet. Within Welsh Reconstructionist Druidry, I served as a dedicant of Cerridwen, Bloedwedd, and Bran for twenty years. Needless to say, I was not a stranger to the concept of patron/dedicant relationships when I finally arrived on this Heidhrinn Road. What I wasn't fully prepared for was the *depth* and *breadth* of what it means to be truly *fulltrui*. None of those other Paths which I had walked had led to Deities showing up in my dreams by night and *claiming me*. Well, none except one: that *one* was Christianity.

Neither Kuan Yin, nor Amitabha Buddha, nor Bran The Blessed, nor the Morrigan, nor Yinepu, nor Bastet, nor Sekhmet, nor Cerridwen, nor Bloedwedd had ever actually *physically and spiritually shown up* previous to my dedications to them, *at* my dedications to them, nor at any other time, but I had dealt with Uriel, Michael, and Christ first-hand plenty often enough to be well aware of what was happening to me when I first experienced Freyja. I knew full-well that She was not just some "mental sock puppet", born of too much hard reading and the wrong pepperoni pizza before bed! This was a living, breathing *god-entity*; I had felt such before often enough in the past to know the difference. What to actually *do about that*, within a specifically Heidhrinn context, however, I had *zero clue*. At the time, I had only one close Heathen friend. His reply, when I inquired about what had happened was "*sit it out*". At the time, I thought that meant what it usually idiomatically means: "*wait*". In retrospect, I now understand what he *actually* meant was for me to *practice utiseta*. Had I actually understood my Heathen friend's instructions, it might not have taken me almost another full *year* before I finally "took the plunge" and dedicated myself as *fulltrui* of Freyja.

Godfinding Utiseta

In previous chapters, I have provided some very
basic **utiseta** exercises, which have quite a lot in common
with the guided meditations or guided visualizations
encountered along other New Age Paths. The exercise
below is **very different** from those; it will require you to
"climb" much further out on the proverbial "spiritual
limb" than you have done previously with any of the other
exercises or rituals in this book, so please proceed with
caution and **follow directions precisely**. In
performing this utiseta, you are not only attempting to
make contact with Something much, much **bigger** than
you, you are also attempting to ascertain Its **true
identity**. In effect, this utiseta has the purpose of making
sure you aren't being "catfished" by something
pretending to be Divine. Whether you believe that there
are "bad things lurking on the astral" or not, rest assured:
those "bad things" wholeheartedly believe in **you!**
Disbelief in something is **no excuse** for not being
cautious: just because you don't **believe** there are Great
White Sharks swimming off the coast of Cape Cod does
not mean they aren't out there!

For this utiseta, you will need to make *absolutely
certain* that you *will not be disturbed!* This will be an
under the cloak utiseta, so make certain that you have the
necessary blanket and/or cloak at hand *before* you lay the
fence. You will be doing a *three-fold* laying of the fence for
this one, for the purposes of *added protection*. Chances
are, if what contacted you was *not* who they said they were,
they will be unable to get through, into your sacred space.
That being the case, in addition to your dagger, hammer, or
wand, you will also need incense (sweetgrass, sage, cedar,

and/or some blend of the three tends to work best), and water with sea salt added. You should *bless* the water beforehand, using the **Hallow Sign** and **Tiwaz position** as described in previous rituals in this book. In the remote event that something Dark *does*, in fact, make it through your wards, ritual steps have been provided to help you "take care of" the issue. You will also need to *write your own blot* to the Deity Who has identified Themself to you. This should also be at hand *before* laying the fence. Please be sure to read *this rite* and the accompanying **Warding Rite** *all the way through thoroughly* before you begin, and have *both* available for easy access *before* laying the fence.

Center

Seeker, Maker, Believer (insert your own
        archetypes here):
My feet are on the ground;
I stand firm.
I am of the earth and the earth is of me;
I stand firm.
I center myself, and I hold.
So it is, and so it shall be.

Lay The Fence (with dagger/wand/hammer)

Outside the fire,
Darkness;
Darkness outside the Grove;
Outside there dwell shadows;
Shadows inside us as well.
Inside, outside, everywhere,
Where'er you dwell,
Dwell not here:
Here is light and all good things!
Light and Bright Wisdom protect us;
Protect us from those who dwell outside.

Lay The Fence (with incense smoke)

Outside the fire,
Darkness;
Darkness outside the Grove;
Outside there dwell shadows;
Shadows inside us as well.
Inside, outside, everywhere,
Where'er you dwell,
Dwell not here:
Here is light and all good things!
Light and Bright Wisdom protect us;
Protect us from those who dwell outside.

Lay The Fence (with blessed salt-water)

Outside the fire,
Darkness;
Darkness outside the Grove;
Outside there dwell shadows;
Shadows inside us as well.
Inside, outside, everywhere,
Where'er you dwell,
Dwell not here:
Here is light and all good things!
Light and Bright Wisdom protect us;
Protect us from those who dwell outside.

Hallow the space with the Hallow Sigil. (use your right hand)

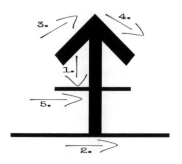

Place your body in the position of the rune, Tiwaz. Visualize the energy of the sacred space which you have just created as golden light, moving up through the fingertips of your left hand, and across your body to the fingertips of your right hand (or to the dagger, wand, or hammer in your right hand, if you have already procured, blessed, and ensouled that tool)

Visualize the energy flowing down and releasing from your right hand (or the tip of a physical foci, such as a dagger), and **draw the Hallow Sign** over your chalice and see it infusing the liquid within.

Blot the Deity Who has identified Themself to you.

Go under the cloak. Meditate as necessary, using the methods you have thus far learned work best for you. When the Deity Who has identified Themself to you makes you aware of Their presence, converse with Them as you would with any human being. (Should something "go awry" at this point, please use the **Warding Rite** *immediately*!)

Suggested Questions While Under The Cloak:

I understand Who You are; what do You understand about who I am?

Why do You wish me to be fulltrui/fulltrua?

Are there any specific things You wish me to do, as an act to seal this relationship? (Be **very careful** with this one! **Do not** agree to do anything which makes you feel uncomfortable. **Do not** agree to do anything that you are unwilling or unable to do! **Make certain** the parameters of this exchange, and that **nothing further** will be required of you later that you might equally be unwilling or unable to do!)

What are Your requirements of one who is fulltrui/fulltrua? (Be likewise **very careful** with this one! See the parameters set above!)

(**Note:** There are no "**prove it**"s in this suggested list of questions. There are several very good reasons for that: 1) To ask *anyone*, including a potential Deity, to *prove* They are who They say They are is *profoundly rude*—and I'm speaking from personal experience on that one, as I have personally been forced to *prove* my own identity far too many times and it is always an extremely hurtful experience. 2) If you *cannot tell* what and who you are dealing with within the setting of this utiseta, then you probably *should not* be considering the pursuit of a *fulltrui/fulltrua* relationship *yet*—I would encourage you to embark on further study and experience first. 3) If what you are dealing with *is*, in fact, something Dark, then asking them to *prove their identity* is both a waste of valuable time that should be spent *removing them from your space*, and also an *opportunity* which might be readily seen as an *invitation* to "do their worst".)

When you have finished your conversation, **reemerge** from under the cloak.

Offer a **second blot**.

Raise the Fence (make sure to do all three layers!)

Ground and Center

Warding Rite

Draw the Hallow Sign. As you draw each of the three portions of the Sigil in the air, you will speak the invocation appropriate to that *section* of the Sigil (Hammer=Mjollnir; Tiwaz=Hand of Tyr; Cross=Chariot of Nerthus).

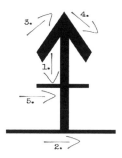

(Hammer)

I beg the use of Mjollnir,
Hammer of Thor,
To smite, cleanse, and purify
The negativity from this space!

(Tiwaz; "Arrow")

I beg the reach of the Hand of Tyr,
To bring Justice and Right
And replace the blight
Upon this space!

(Cross)

I beg the coming of Nerthus,
In Her healing chariot;
Great Mother, cleanse and heal
This space!

Call Upon The Deity This Intruder Identified Themselves As:

(Name of *actual Deity*),
Bring down your Holy Might
Upon this intruder
Who would steal your Honored Name!
Remove them from this space,
And harry them away from me!
Show them no frith,
For they are unworthy of it!
So mote it be!
By the Name of (*actual Deity*),
So mote it be!

Godfinding Candle-Scry

*Even had I understood what my friend meant when he said "sit it out", I can make no guarantees that I would have been successful at making or maintaining contact with Freyja, because I am notoriously unskilled with solo meditation. I work much better with a **focus**, than with simply **sitting still** in silent darkness and **waiting** for "something to happen". If you have similar "short attention span" issues, or if you conduct the above utiseta with less-than-stellar results, you may wish to instead use the ritual below (which is the one I **actually** used when I finally became **fulltrui** of Freyja).*

As with the previous utiseta ritual, you will be doing a *three-fold* laying of the fence for this one, for the purposes of *added protection*. Chances are, if what contacted you was *not* who they said they were, they will be unable to get through, into your sacred space. That being the case, in addition to your dagger, hammer, or wand, you will also need incense (sweetgrass, sage, cedar, and/or some blend of the three tends to work best), and water with sea salt added. You should *bless* the water beforehand, using the **Hallow Sign** and **Tiwaz position** as described in previous rituals in this book. In the remote event that something Dark *does*, in fact, make it through your wards, ritual steps have been provided to help you "take care of" the issue. You will also need to *write your own blot* to the Deity Who has identified Themself to you. This should also be at hand *before* laying the fence. Please be sure to read *this rite* and the **Warding Rite** *all the way through thoroughly* before you begin, and have *both* available for easy access *before* laying the fence. For this ritual, you will need a small candle. It is best if the candle is a color associated with the Deity Who has identified Themself to you. If They have previously gifted you with a bind-rune, or if you know of a rune which is associated specifically with that Deity, it would be appropriate to carve your candle and prepare it for this ritual with oil and a blessing (refer to **Quick Reference: Blessing Ritual Objects**). After your scrying session, if you feel prepared to go forward with **Dedication**, please be *completely familiar* with the sections on **Dedication** and **Oaths** which follow the text of this rite. If you feel this might become the case for you, you should make sure your **Dedication** is also at hand *before* laying the fence.

Center

Seeker, Maker, Believer (insert your own
archetypes here):
My feet are on the ground;
I stand firm.
I am of the earth and the earth is of me;
I stand firm.
I center myself, and I hold.
So it is, and so it shall be.

Lay The Fence (with dagger/wand/hammer)

Outside the fire,
Darkness;
Darkness outside the Grove;
Outside there dwell shadows;
Shadows inside us as well.
Inside, outside, everywhere,
Where'er you dwell,
Dwell not here:
Here is light and all good things!
Light and Bright Wisdom protect us;
Protect us from those who dwell outside.

Lay The Fence (with incense smoke)

Outside the fire,
Darkness;
Darkness outside the Grove;
Outside there dwell shadows;
Shadows inside us as well.
Inside, outside, everywhere,
Where'er you dwell,
Dwell not here:
Here is light and all good things!
Light and Bright Wisdom protect us;
Protect us from those who dwell outside.

Lay The Fence (with blessed salt-water)

Outside the fire,
Darkness;
Darkness outside the Grove;
Outside there dwell shadows;
Shadows inside us as well.
Inside, outside, everywhere,
Where'er you dwell,
Dwell not here:
Here is light and all good things!
Light and Bright Wisdom protect us;
Protect us from those who dwell outside.

Hallow the space with the Hallow Sigil. (use your right hand)

Place your body in the position of the rune, Tiwaz. Visualize the energy of the sacred space which you have just created as golden light, moving up through the fingertips of your left hand, and across your body to the fingertips of your right hand (or to the dagger, wand, or hammer in your right hand, if you have already procured, blessed, and ensouled that tool)

Visualize the energy flowing down and releasing from your right hand (or the tip of a physical foci, such as a dagger), and **draw the Hallow Sign** over your chalice and see it infusing the liquid within.

Blot the Deity Who has identified Themself to you.

Light your candle. Stare into it, focusing on the Deity Who has identified Themself to you. Watch for Their arrival *within* the candle-flame. When the Deity Who has identified Themself to you makes you aware of Their presence, converse with Them as you would with any human being. (Should something "go awry" at this point, please use the **Warding Rite** *immediately*!)

Suggested Questions While Scrying The Flame:

I understand Who You are; what do You understand about who I am?

Why do You wish me to be fulltrui/fulltrua?

Are there any specific things You wish me to do, as an act to seal this relationship? (Be **very careful** with this one! **Do not** agree to do anything which makes you feel uncomfortable. **Do not** agree to do anything that you are unwilling or unable to do! **Make certain** the parameters of this exchange, and that **nothing further** will be required of you later that you might equally be unwilling or unable to do!)

What are Your requirements of one who is fulltrui or fulltrua? (Be likewise **very careful** with this one! See the parameters set above!)

(**Note:** There are no "**prove it**"s in this suggested list of questions. There are several very good reasons for that: 1) To ask *anyone*, including a potential Deity, to *prove* They are who They say They are is *profoundly rude*—and I'm speaking from personal experience on that one, as I have personally been forced to *prove* my own identity far too many times and it is always an extremely hurtful experience. 2) If you *cannot tell* what and who you are dealing with within the setting of this scrying, then you probably *should not* be considering the pursuit of a *fulltrui/fulltrua* relationship *yet*—I would encourage you to embark on further study and experience first. 3) If what you are dealing with *is*, in fact, something Dark, then asking them to *prove their identity* is both a waste of valuable time that should be spent *removing them from your space*, and also an *opportunity* which might be readily seen as an *invitation* to "do their worst".)

When you have finished your conversation, **extinguish your candle** (unless you are prepared to now take the *next step* to *fully become fulltrui/fulltrua*, in which case your **candle should remain lit**, and you should refer to **Dedication** and **Oaths** below).

Offer a **second blot**.

(This would be the appropriate point in the rite to perform **Dedication**, if you feel fully prepared to do so.)

Raise the Fence (make sure to do all three layers!)

Ground and Center

Your actual **Dedication** as *fulltrui/fulltrua* is a *deeply personal thing*; therefore, what is provided herein is only the *loosest of guidelines*. You should *personally compose* your own dedication. Unless your *fulltrui* is Odin or Bragi, They likely will not be judging you on your poetic prowess! How skilled you are with verse matters far less than that you **cover every contingency**, when it comes to the scope and parameters of the relationship you are about to cement. **Do not** make *any* promises which you do not **fully intend** to *keep*!

Very early in this book, in the **Good Versus Evil** Chapter, we discussed **oaths** and the **fulfillment of vows** (oath-taking and oath-keeping) as one of the very cornerstones of our belief system. Within that chapter, we also discussed *keeping one's word*, as it pertains to **Integrity** or **Honor**. Quite simply put, an oath is a *promise*, and a broken promise is a *lie*. An **oath** broken, ultimately, is a lie not only to another human, nor even to the family or tribe, but to the *Gods Themselves*. As you take this oath, it is important to remember that this is not an oath you are making to another human being from whom you might one day be separated in death; this is an oath you are making to the Gods— Gods who are going to know *exactly* where to *find you* when your end-of-days are at hand! The **oath of dedication**, taken at the official onset of a *fulltrui/fulltrua* relationship, is one of the most important oaths you will ever speak, so it is best to be certain to "cross every t and dot every i" when composing it, exactly as one would do if drawing up an actual legal contract. Be as precise and specific as possible, not only about what you *are* willing to do, but also about what you *are not*. And then *live it*. In order to do that, you *must* make sure that the conditions are, in fact, *livable*. If you have any doubts whatsoever about your ability to maintain such an oath at this time, *do not make it*. While I am not willing to say that you would not be able to "back out" of your oath at some point in future—as through an *oath of abjuration*—going *into* the *fulltrui/fulltrua* relationship based on such a possibility is the *exact same thing* as entering a *marriage* while harboring the thought "well, I can always get a divorce later".

My own **oath of dedication** poured out of me in a completely unexpected flood once I had begun the **Godfinding Candle-Scry Ritual** detailed above. It came in the form of a *rosc*: an ancient Irish form of vision poetry. You might be more familiar with the plural form, *roscanna*. Although I included it previously in the **Finding Freyja** Chapter, I would like to go through it in further detail now, as an illustration of one of the many (very personal) forms that an **oath of dedication** might take:

> I am the
> Walker Between The Worlds;
> I am the Raven
> On the wing,
>
> And I sing the
> Song without the
> Words,
> For I have no
> Voice to bring.
>
> Yet still with this
> Voice
> That is
> Mine-not-mine,
> I raise that
> Voice
> And sing.

Contractually-speaking, my own oath is quite simple. It states **who I am**, **what I *have been doing* for Freyja**, and **what I *will do* for Freyja**.

My primary service to Freyja, within the parameters of our *fulltrui* relationship is as a *galdrman* and *vitki*: one who is adept at runelore and runic magicks, including galdr, and therefore practices divination for themself and others, often in the capacity of a healer/counselor. In our tradition, a *vitki* is often also a *shamanic* figure, who brings runic practice (and galdr) together with *seidhr*, which involves spirit-work (*wight-working*), as well as Otherworld-journeying. At the time of my **oath of dedication**, Freyja made it very clear to me that *this* was the *core* of our *fulltrui/fulltrua* relationship, so I took my oath accordingly.

You will likely note that my own **oath of dedication** does not include a list of things that I *will not do*, but rather focuses on those things which I *will do*. I went into my own dedication having been duly cautioned to make it *very clear* to Freyja, as a supremely *sexual* Goddess, what levels of "hanky panky" I did and did not feel were acceptable for my own personal practice. Apparently, Her reputation precedes Her, so to speak, when it comes to such matters. I have personally *never* felt the need to draw such a line in the sand with Her: there has always been evidence of a mutual understanding between the two of us that I also *belong* to Suzanne, and, therefore, I felt absolutely no need to further address the issue. If you are seeking to become *fulltrui/fulltrua* of Freyja or Freyr, however, your mileage may vary, so act accordingly, as you feel is necessary.

When composing your own **oath of dedication**, it is suggested that you begin with a *statement of intent*, as I did, followed by an *identifying statement* of *who you are* within the relationship. This may then be followed by a *statement of where you currently stand* (what you currently are *doing*, as *fulltrui/fulltrua*), followed by a *promise of what you will bring* to the relationship, and, where applicable, *what you will not condone/do/accept/bring*. Your oath should finish with a *final declaration* of *your place* within the relationship.

And then you are expected to *live* as *fulltrui/fulltrua*, in much the same way as we *live* within the parameters of our close relationships with other human beings. For me, within the scope of my *fulltrui/fulltrua* relationship with Freyja, that means first finally accepting that *I am*, in fact, a vitki. Part of that acceptance includes doing things like writing this book, and establishing and maintaining a rune-counseling service that is not overly commercialized, and instead actually *helps* people. I also am very well aware of being Her *representative* in this world, and I am thus always eager to educate others about The Lady, as well as being very attentive to how I carry myself in the public eye, as Her *fulltrui*. The parameters of your own *fulltrui/fulltrua* relationship may make profoundly different demands on your own life, dependent upon with *Whom* you are *fulltrui/fulltrua*. For example, if my Beloved wife were to become *fulltrua* of anyone, it would likely be Heimdall. The parameters of their relationship might include her learning to set better boundaries for her own personal space (mental, emotional, and spiritual, as well as physical), and learning to be more pragmatic about change. Meanwhile, Michelle is on the road to becoming *fulltrua* of Hela, and part of the parameters of that relationship already established by Hela in Michelle's case include being far more public about precisely what she does and what she *can* do, when it comes to mediumship, speaking with, living among, and assisting the Dead.

In many other Pagan Traditions, it is usual for a person to take a sacred or magickal name at the time of their dedication. Usually symbolic of "putting away" or "taking off" your "mundane self" and "putting on" or "taking on" your "magickal self", this practice is particularly prevalent in Western Mystery Traditions such as Wicca. This is, in my experience, largely frowned upon in Norse Traditional circles, unless someone was tagged with a "profoundly Christian" name; then, apparently, it's perfectly fine to do so. Still, I have met several perfectly well-respected people who are *fulltrui/fulltrua* of a particular Deity who use a "working title" in the world, as an author or what-have-you, such as "Freyjasdottir" or "Thorsson", etc. For me personally, I took the name Connla when I first embarked upon my journey with Druidry. The son of Conn of the Hundred Battles (Conn Cetchathach), Connla fell in love with a fairy maiden who gave him a fairy apple. For a whole month, Connla worked on eating that apple, and it just kept growing back—it was constantly replenished, no matter how much he ate. Finally, on the last day of the month, the maiden returned to him, saying:

> "Connla indeed holds a glorious place, as he awaits death here among these shriveling mortals, yet now the Folk of Life, the Ever-Living Ones, beg that he come to the Plain of Pleasure (the Otherworld or Faerie Realm), for they have have come to know you, and wish to hold you dear....The ocean is not so strong as the waves of your longing for me. Come with me in my boat--this gleaming, crystal curragh— and soon we can reach my homeland..."

And he, indeed, got into the boat, and sailed away with his beloved maiden. I identified strongly with the Connla of this tale, as I often felt trapped among not only the Dead, but also the Living. Too often, I felt as though I truly belonged in neither world, and at that point in my life, I longed for some beautiful maiden to show up with an apple and a promise to "take me away" to a place where someone like me actually fit in. Though I've left Druidry behind, I maintain the name Connla because twenty years later, precisely such a maid finally "sailed" into my life, bearing the best apple pie in history, and whisked me away to her Realm—the magickal land called New England—where I do, in fact, finally fit in, regardless of my status as "the living dead dude". It's also far easier to create and work publicly under that name than under my own given name at birth, for fear of somehow causing pain to my surviving relatives. Insofar as the "Freyjason" portion of my "new name", I took it up long before I finally dedicated myself as *fulltrui* of Freyja, and yes, I am well aware that having only the one "s" in it is grammatically incorrect. However, I've been using it professionally for so long at this point that I fear it would confuse people if I added that second, grammatically appropriate "s" at this juncture.

Whether or not you choose to "take a name" at the time of your dedication—or even before or after—is ultimately, as with many things in Norse Witchcraft, up to you. If your *fulltrui/fulltrua* tells you to do so, and you agree with Their decision, then by all means, go for it! Or if you feel that you need some extra inward sign to yourself that this is what and who you are now, go for it. However, as with the *fulltrui/fulltrua* relationship itself, if you're just doing it to "look cool", *don't*. Trust me, you *won't* "look cool"; you'll just come across as the poser you actually are. This isn't the "Viking Fan Club"; this is a *faith*. Likewise, if you are "taking a name" in an attempt to be someone other than *who you truly are*—which speaks of a lack of *Self-ownership*--you should not seek to do so.

Heading Njordr

I have been in love with the sea since I was young enough to first learn to say the word, and some of my fondest memories of childhood involve boats and sailing. When I learned that Freyja's Father was a sailor—a great navigator and protector of merchants who was often called upon by our Ancestors to help them navigate through stormy seas to new horizons—I realized I *had* to come to *know* Him. I told my wife one Friday, after performing blot for Freyja that afternoon, that I thought the following week, I might pour to Her Father as well. It *felt* like the *right* thing to do, even though at that moment in time all I really knew of Him was that He was Freyja's Father and that He "liked boats" as much as me.

The following Monday, a prayer for Njordr came up in my Facebook feed, as if out of nowhere. It was beautiful, and it added some new facets to my understanding of The One I have since come to lovingly call "The Van-Father". A chord was officially struck in my heart, mind, and "soul". The prayer mentioned being "adrift in strange waters"; "the mists of doubt" having clouded one's vision. It described *exactly* how I was feeling in that moment, and it gave me Njordr as the "go-to-guy" for such feelings. It went on to say "reinvigorate my spirit with the smell of the Sea"--given that sea gulls have become a symbol of precisely that sort of "soul invigoration" in my personal symbology, I knew this was a sign to me. I had made the right decision, when I had announced on a whim to my wife the previous Friday that I felt pulled towards blotting Njordr.

So that Friday I did precisely that, and I used the prayer that had come up in my Facebook feed when I performed that blot. I poured seawater we had kept from our trip to Maine the previous May in offering to Him, and then I took a small bit of sand and some very tiny shells from that same trip and placed them in a small votive bottle for my altar, which I likewise filled with seawater. I filled it only halfway, so that when the bottle is rocked, it mimics the waves of the sea. I keep it on my altar even now, for that first blot to Njordr kindled a lasting relationship between He and me.

I have since come to know Him as the Peacemaker: as One Who teaches moderation, temperance, and diplomacy in the face of negativity. You see, there was a time when He was married to Skadi, the shimmering Snow-Goddess and Jotun-Daughter Who was so brave, She brought Her shield to bear against the Aesir Themselves when They killed Her Father, Thjazi. Instead of combat, however, in the end She asked for two things in payment from the Gods: that someone make Her laugh (which Loki did, by tying His testicles to a nanny goat which subsequently dragged him about), and that She be allowed to choose a spouse from among the gathered Gods. Odin countered, saying that She must choose Her new spouse based only on the appearance of Their feet. She chose Njordr, because He had the most beautiful tootsies; She thought He was Baldur, based on the beauty of his feet. Subsequently, They attempted to move to Her mountain home to live together, but Njordr was not happy there, so far from the sea. They then attempted to take residence in Noatan, Njordr's seaside Hall, but Skadi found the constant crash of the waves and the persistent calls of the gulls maddening. In the end, They agreed that They could not be happy together, and They chose to live apart: *peacefully*.

I am notoriously unskilled at "agreeing to disagree", but getting to know Njordr has tempered that for me. It's not that I *need* to be *right* all the time. I'm definitely not *that* guy, but when I know for certain in my heart of hearts that I positively *am* right about something, it is *very* hard for me to back away graciously from an argument. Njordr has taught me that trying to "drive your boat" across rocks only leaves you with a leaky boat. Usually in an argument, *both* parties are absolutely convinced that they are *right*, whether they are or not, and often, no matter how many facts you can show them to the contrary, nothing can be done to change their mind. Sometimes it's best to adopt a "you love mountains; I love the sea" attitude, as He did with Skadi, and walk on, with no hard feelings.

Njordr has also taught me the true value of Family. As *fulltrui* of Freyja, my bond with His Daughter has waxed somewhere between "little brother" and "cared-for child", and I have often felt that bond recognized by Njordr. To say that He has been good to me would be putting it mildly. In the time since I began my relationship with Him, I have seen my reach as a merchant more than double, and the bounties He has poured into my life have not only kept me going and kept me trying, but renewed my faith in this business and myself. This has, in turn, taught me that rather than being a *burden* to my own human family (as I have often felt), what they are doing for me is simply *what families do*: **families take care of each other; no one gets left behind**. One of the greatest lessons Njordr has taught me is that best summed up by the Hawaiian ideal of *Ohana*: that family is *more* than blood-relations, it is all of the people in your life who are inextricably *bound together* in a network of *mutual cooperation* and *remembrance* of each other. *True family members* are those people who *think about you* and your welfare, even when it isn't in *their* best interests to do so. I may be separated from much of my *blood-kin* by thousands of miles and the veil of Death, but *I still have a family*, and I am profoundly grateful that those people have come to love the "misfit creature" that I am the way that they do. Njordr taught me that, too.

I am proudly *fulltrui* of Freyja, but the more time I spend in the company of Her Father, the more I feel the call of the gulls in His direction as well. Every Friday is His now, as well as Freyja's and Freyr's. Monday, too, belongs to Njordr in my life. I've recently begun a daily blot to Him with rum, as an extra expression of my gratitude for all that He has helped me navigate toward in my life. I keep the tiny bottle of Captain Morgan's on my altar—it seemed highly appropriate. One day soon, I know I may find myself crying to Him "Oh Captain, my Captain", as I enter into a second *fulltrui* relationship with the Van-Father. Either way, I know He will help me steer my ship towards the brightest horizon, and will hold to the bonds of family, as they are reflected in my relationship to His Daughter, Freyja. I am slowly heading Njordr, for He is my tallship, and She is the star I steer it by.

Njordr,
Lift me up
From these troubled waters,
And help me find a place
On which to stand.
Teach me the faith
Of the sailor,
Tossed upon the stormy sea;
Teach me not to fear the horizon,
But to have faith in what I cannot see.
For wealth comes not
To the faint of heart,
And we are all but fishermen,
Casting nets we hope to find
Filled with bounty from life's sea.

The Hunter and The Hunted

The *Wild Hunt* is a pan-European folk-belief attested in numerous tales from documents across the continent: from Scandinavia, to Germany, to France, England, Ireland, and Wales. Most attestations cite Odin (Woden, Wotan) as its leader, although others have likewise been suggested, particularly Freyja and Freyr. In Ireland, it is said that Fionn MacCumhaill, leader of the Fenniocht (the Fianna, a band of warrior-poets), leads the Hunt, and in Wales, it is said to be led by Gwynn ap Nudd, and the hounds are known as the Cwn Annwfn (the Hounds of Annwfn; the Faery Underworld). My first exposure to the Wild Hunt as a paradigm came during my journey along the road of Welsh Reconstructionist Druidry. During my sojourn with our Grove, Cerddorion Nyfed, I found myself drawn heavily to the figure of Gwynn ap Nudd, a Lord of the Dead and of the Mound, as well as the Lord of Faerie, not dissimilar from Freyr, as Lord of the Mound and Lord of Alfheim. As an active Druid within that Grove, I also served as Rigfenneidh (literally: "High Fenniocht"): more or less the position of "Grove Protector". This inextricably bound me to the Fenniocht, and, hence, to Fionn MacCumhaill, yet another attested leader of the Wild Hunt. Given my position as Grove Protector, *psychic self defense* was something at which I was expected to excel. The ways in which that related *back* to the paradigm of the Wild Hunt became something on which I found myself heavily focused. As I made the transition to this Norse

Path, and discovered that Odin, Freyja, and Freyr were even more widely attested as leaders of the Wild Hunt, my former calling to the position of Psychic Defender became all the more clear to me.

Psychic self defense is not a term you will often hear "bandied about" in Heathen circles, due to pervading views against the concept of *evil* in the larger Norse Traditionalist community, but the *Wild Hunt* is widely discussed, and even celebrated, during the High Days surrounding Yule (our Winter Solstice Feast/Festival). So, what *is* the *Wild Hunt*, and how could it *possibly* relate to *psychic self defense*? One of the earliest attestations of a "Hunt Sighting" comes down to us from *The Anglo-Saxon Chronicle*, and is said to have happened in 1127:

> *Let no one be surprised at what we are about to relate, for it was common gossip up and down the countryside after February 6th; many people both saw and heard a whole pack of huntsmen in full cry. They straddled black horses and black bucks while their hounds were pitch black with staring hideous eyes. This was seen in the very deer park of Peterborough town, and in all the woods stretching from that same spot as far as Stanford. All through the night monks heard them sounding and winding their horns. Reliable witnesses who kept watch in the night declared that there might well have been twenty or even thirty of them in this wild tantivy (a rapid gallop or ride; often used as a hunting cry) as near as they could tell.*

What or who were these Wild Hunters hunting? One widely-held belief was that the Wild Hunt was actually hunting down those whose time it was to die. We find this echoed in the Irish Tradition of the *Cóiste Bodhar,* "the silent coach". A "death coach"; it is said that the sight or sound of it is a harbinger of death. Given that Odin, Freyr, Freyja, and Gwynn ap Nudd are all attributed as potential leaders of the Hunt, and are likewise associated with Death and the Afterlife, this seems a likely answer. Some Scandinavian traditions also held that the target of the Hunt was the *skogsra*, a specific species of *ra* or *wight*, making them essentially Wights hunting other wights. Within the traditions localized to the British Isles, the Hunters are generally believed to be a slightly more antagonistic "Faerie Rade" (a group of faeries who ride together), out hunting for folks to abduct and carry away to the Underworld (Faerie Realm). Given years of personal research and experience with the Wild Hunt, I would argue *all of the above*.

When we combine all three of these *target prey* of the Wild Hunt, perhaps it becomes a bit easier to see how this spectral hunting party can become one of our most able allies in the practice of *psychic self defense*. If they do, in fact, seek out the Dead, then many of our Ancestors may ride with them. As harbingers of death, they may also act as a *psychic trigger*, letting whatever you are trying to drive away or destroy know that its time has effectively come, and a frightened, harried, or otherwise worried opponent is almost always a *weakened* one. When we are actively working to defend ourselves against the *fjandar*, it is important for us to remember that these are still a form of *wight*, as are all "spirits of things", from the Aesir down to the smallest of green-wights. As such, the Wild Hunt may be readily enlisted to help us with literally hunting them down and eradicating them. Finally, as a Faerie Rade, seeking out folks to bring back to the Underworld, the Wild Hunt can perform the duties associated with any other mundane huntsman. Mundane huntsmen have the ability to *recognize* their usual quarry. In the same way, the Wild Hunt may aid us in knowing when something is simply utangard and, therefore, *Wild* (as with faeries and their kin), versus utangard and *Breach* (i.e., one of the *fjandar*).

The *shamanic overtones* of the Wild Hunt as a paradigm should likewise not be overlooked. French historian Claude Lecouteux, in his book *Phantom Armies of the Night: The Wild Hunt and the Ghostly Processions of the Undead*, discusses the Wild Hunt as it relates to *astral travel*:

> *According to the beliefs of earlier times, every human being possessed several souls—and, in this instance, the word* soul *means "vital principle". Among these souls there is the external soul, which the ancient Scandinavians called the* hamr *and which Latin texts refer to as* animus *or* spiritus. *This soul is able to quit the body when it is sleeping, is in a coma or a trance, or is afflicted by a serious illness. It can then go about in the form of an animal or human....[these hosts of humans who joined the Wild Hunt (or its cognates)] performed a*

*third-function ritual. Here the representatives of good
and evil, the fertility and sterility of the land, confront
each other...The victory of the "good folk" over the wicked
ones made it possible for the coming year to be
fruitful....We can be sure of this: in the mentalities of our
ancient ancestors, the third function was inseparable
from the dead, however they appeared—whether alone or
in a band.*

This *third function* of which Lecouteux speaks is part of the
trifunctional hypothesis first put forth by his fellow Frenchman,
mythographer Georges Dumézil, in 1929, when describing the
tripartite ideology of Proto-Indo-European societies as reflected in
the evidence of three social classes (or castes). The *third function*,
specifically, consisted of productivity, herding, farming, and crafts
—those portions of society concerned with the economy—and was
reflected in the existence of a commoner class or caste, consisting
largely of farmers and herdsmen. This "base caste", while ruled
over by the other two (warriors and priests), actually provided the
"heartbeat" of these cultures, and was crucial to their survival.
After all, without farmers and herdsmen, neither warriors nor
priests could or would eat, and also without farmers and
herdsmen, there would have been no animals or any other surplus
food-stuffs to sustain sacrificial offerings, such as the blot-feast. It
is crucial that we understand this third function as we consider the
Wild Hunt as it relates to *psychic self defense*, and more
specifically, as it relates to *shamanism*. Dumézil 's tripartite caste
system is, in fact, echoed in the "castes" of the Norse Gods
Themselves: Aesir, Vanir, and Rokkr. The Vanir God/desses,
heavily associated with farming, herding, and general economics,
and, therefore, the "God/desses of the *third function*", are also the
Deities who taught the Aesir (and most specifically, Odin) the "way
of the *shaman*": i.e., *seidhr*. Therefore, I believe it is hardly
accidental that two Vanir and the one Aesir trained in the Norse
shamanic path (seidhr) are most often attested as leaders of the
Wild Hunt: Freyja, Freyr, and Odin.

In previous chapters, I have touched briefly on the concepts of
evil and evil entities *(fjandar)*, and on basic rituals for protection,
cleansing, and warding. In such situations, we are assuming our
position as the *hunted*, rather than as the *hunter*. Most of the time,
given the innangard/utangard worldview maintained in Norse
Witchcraft, this is the position in which we find ourselves. There

may come a time or a situation, however, in which the best *defense* is actually a good *offense*. These are the times when we join the Wild Hunt, and become instead the *hunters*.

It is, naturally, easiest to court the attentions of the Wild Hunt and its leaders at Yule-time, as this is the time with which the Hunt is most heavily associated. However other *liminal periods* during the year are also appropriate. These include what is commonly referred to as Samhain, Beltaine, or Midsummer (Alfablot, May Day, and Midsommer, respectively, in Norse Witchcraft), and also at Disablot (commonly referred to as Imbolc in other Pagan Traditions). *Why* court the Wild Hunt? *Because there is **safety in numbers**!* When placed in a situation where the "best defense really *is* a good offense", anyone who has ever played a team sport can tell you: *teamwork* is the key to winning. The concept of **safety in numbers** is even echoed in the natural world: it is the reason why animals such as horses and cattle travel in *herds*. When confronted by an enemy, such as a wolf, for example, a herd of animals can effectively "close ranks" and thereby defend its weakest members. The same is true in human—and especially *astral*—combat: alone, it is you versus whatever enemy you face with no defense apart from your own know-how; in a group, those who are much more *powerful* than you can effectively "close ranks" and provide an extra shield of defense.

Before I go further, I would be incredibly remiss if I did not issue a statement of **warning**: the methods herein are not intended for "weekend demon hunting for fun", nor are they intended as a means to "assail" other spirits, whether Fae (Dokkalfar), Elemental (Jotun), or Dead, or other *living people* for your own entertainment. Such behaviors are not only *dangerous*, but, in fact, *dangerous* to the point of *stupid*! Asking the Wild Hunt to assist you in assailing the Dokkalfar, Jotnar, or the Dead will only serve to make them *profoundly angry*. This will once more place you in the position of *hunted*, rather than the *hunter*. Insofar as assailing *other living people*, what the Hunt does "on Their own time" is *Their* own business, but such activities are *not* for *you*!

My first encounters with the Wild Hunt, as I said, happened during the time when I was serving as Rigfenneidh of our Grove. As the first and last line of *psychic defense* for our Grove, it often fell to me to not only make sure that we were protected within the confines of a ritual circle (Laying the Fence), but on occasion I was also asked to actually chase away something which had shown up *outside* our borders and make it clear to whatever *It* was not to return. Working from within a Welsh framework, it occurred to me early on in this work that calling upon the assistance of Gwynn ap Nudd and the Hunt provided me with extra backup when such harrying of intruders was required. It was not until quite recently, within my transition to this Norse Path, that a very important Truth occurred to me: *Freyr had been with me all along*. As both Lord of the Mound (and, therefore, of the Dead) and Lord of Alfheim, Freyr and Gwynn ap Nudd are direct *cognates* of each other. Long before I poured my first blot as a Heidhrinn, I had made offerings to Freyr, in his guise as Gwynn ap Nudd. The first of these, during the period in which I first came to court the Wild Hunt.

The first action of that courtship was the selection and blessing of my first *fetish object*. A *fetish* is typically an object representing a god/dess or spirit(s) which is used to create a bond between the supernatural and the mundane. Prevalent among most *animistic* and/or *shamanic* traditions, the term *fetish* originally comes to us from the Portuguese *feitiço*. It was used by the Portuguese when they first encountered West African Tribesmen, to describe the objects used by those Tribesmen in their religious practices. That term was, in turn, later adopted into French as *fétiche*, both words implying a "charm" or "object of art to which sorcery has been applied". To avoid any sort of cultural misappropriation, within Norse Witchcraft we will be henceforth using the term *taufar* (singular: *taufr*) when referring to *fetishes*. This is the closest Old Norse word we have which corresponds to the original meaning of the term *fetish* (*taufr* literally translates as "charm, talisman"). I apply this term specifically to *organic* ritual objects: bones, skulls, and skins. Unless you are a skilled hunter, who knows how to *humanely* procure such items, or are adept at dressing out "roadkill", it is suggested that you *purchase* such items from a source which you *know for a fact* employs the *humane* collection of such items. My first such *taufr* was a fox skull, which I "inherited" from Michelle, as she made the transition from Red Path Shamanism into Welsh Druidry. While it is best if the "animal matter" used corresponds to your *dyr-andi*, this is not absolutely necessary. It is also not necessary that the animal be one which is typically considered a prey animal, such as a rabbit. If your *dyr-andi* is a predatory animal, such as a hawk or coyote, that is perfectly acceptable, although it should also be noted that for certain animals (such as hawks), it is illegal to own or attempt to procure their remains in most states and circumstances.

The process by which this *taufr* is prepared or blessed involves a careful *ensoulment*—almost a re-ensoulment, in fact. As you begin this process, it is important that you realize that though this item may be a part of an animal representing your *dyr-andi*, when used ritually to call upon the Wild Hunt, your intent is most definitely *not* to offer up your *dyr-andi* as *prey*. This will be made more clear to you mentally and spiritually as you proceed with the *ritual dedication* portion of the *ensoulment*. If your chosen *taufr* is a skull, you may wish to begin by slowly bringing it close to your mouth and gently exhaling into the nostrils. Whatever the item, it should be handled reverentially, and touched and stroked gently, as if it were still a living, attached part of the animal in question. Visit your *taufr* daily for at least nine days and nights before proceeding with the *ritual dedication* which follows.

Taufr Dedication Ritual

Holding your *taufr* gently and with reverence, stroke or "pet" it while softly speaking the following (as you would to a pet who is your boon companion):

Hunter and hunted,
Predator and prey,
Blood to blood,
Bone to bone,
Skin to hide,
And hide to skin,
I give you and am given;
I take you and am taken in turn.
Hunted and hunter,
Prey and predator,
Blood to blood,
Bone to bone,
Hide to skin,
And skin to hide,
Protector and protected,
We stand together and apart:
Pack-mate* to pack-mate*,
I call you companion;
Pack-mate* to pack-mate*,
I stand behind you;
Pack-mate* to pack-mate*,
I stand in front;
I stand beside.
Hunter and hunted,
Predator and prey.

*Flock-fellow, Litter-mate (in the case of animals such as cats, beaver, etc.) or Herd-kin may be substituted where more applicable. These words are designed to be repeated as many times in succession as necessary, to raise the energy required to accomplish your ends.

Over time, as you become more familiar with the process of **Calling The Hunt**, you may wish to procure other smaller (and, thus, more portable) *taufar*, which correspond to the animal originally used, such as teeth, scraps of hide, or claws. Since that first fox skull *taufr* of many years ago, I have finally "graduated" to a full coyote skull. It sits on my altar, where it also serves as a constant offering to my *dyr-andi*. A coyote skull isn't terribly portable, however, so I have also procured a coyote claw, which I wear as a necklace. Once you have performed the **Taufr Ritual Dedication** with one *"part"* of an animal, it is not necessary to repeat it with "other parts", as you have already formed the necessary relationship with that animal-wight. You *should*, however, still perform the rest of the *ensoulment* process with each "part": handle it reverentially; visit it often; breathe spirit into and upon it.

The creation of the *taufr* is but the first stage of courting the Wild Hunt. The second step, as you may have already guessed, is to blot them, though I certainly did not know to call it that when I initially practiced my own courtship over a decade ago. Where possible, you should seek out an *alfholl* or other *liminal place*. I briefly touched on the concept of *alfhollar* (the Scandinavian equivalent of *faery mounds*) in the **Wight-Walking** Chapter. The best way to recognize these small mounds of earth inhabited by the Dokkalfar is first to look for an uncharacteristic over-abundance of mushrooms, and particularly colorful ones, reminiscent of the *fly agaric* (red-capped) mushrooms often used by Scandinavian shamans. While this may sound like little more than an "unfortunate stereotype", in my experience, it has proven to be so for a simple reason: it's true! *Alfhollar* are also evidenced by an inexplicable feeling of *liminality* while in their presence. You should be quite familiar with this feeling by now. In the absence of an *alfholl*, another *liminal space* may be chosen, such as a doorway (commonly regarded as a "portal space" across myriad cultures, including the Ancient Norse), a riverside, lakeside, or beach. Hollow trees also often behave as *liminal spaces*. For nine nights, you will offer honey at this location. Should you choose to make your offerings at the *alfholl* or other *liminal space* over the course of the same nine nights during which you are *ensouling* your *taufr*, all the better. No words are really necessary, however, if you feel the need to state your intent as you lay your offering, the following would be suitable:

Connla Freyjason

Blot for the Wild Hunt

Here I lay this honey sweet,
For those of Mound, Sky, and Wild;
With the Huntsmen, sword and bond to ride,
For this world is full of dangers, and I need your
help to hide.

I have practiced these things so many times that I can literally do them at a moment's notice. Though they are decidedly *not* of historically Norse origin, they have served me well over the years, and I know they work, hence their inclusion herein. Ultimately, their *spirit* is as Norse as it is anything else.

Calling The Hunt

(This rite assumes certain things:

That you already have a ritually-prepared dagger;

That you have already followed the steps in preparing a *taufr*.

That you have already entered into a courtship process with the Hunt.

That you come with *real intent* and *honest purpose*.)

Raise your dagger:

Huntsmen, hear my call!
I sound the horn of my heart,
For it beats pure:
I need your defense;
I am prepared to rely on the strength of your
      numbers!
Be near me now;
Surround me now!
Huntsmen, hear my call!

Touch the point of your dagger to your *fetish object*:

Look now, I give you prey,
And I pray you will defend me;
Look here, upon these bones,
And know me as a Hunter, too.
Among you, let me stand,
And chase away what now assails me.

And then let Them come.

(Be prepared for a rise in wind, whether you are inside or outside. You may even find that you've effectively called up a storm. You may see, hear, or even *physically feel* the presence of the Hunters as they close ranks around you. It is important that you neither *feel* nor *display **fear***. Fear only serves to give greater strength to whatever is assailing you in the first place, and will not help you or Them in the cause of your defense. *Note:* There is no accompanying *rite of dismissal*. Once the Hunt has been called, They will do their work, and should be allowed to leave at their leisure. They will understand far better than you possibly ever could when it is time to leave.)

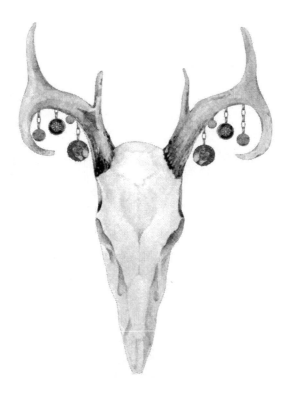

When using a more portable form of the *taufr*, away from your regular altar space and likely bereft of your ritual blade, *tapping* may be employed instead. As I previously discussed in the **Manifestation** Chapter, when talking about *rhythmic wand use*, *tapping* can mean either *touching* the item with your own fingertips repeatedly in a rhythmic fashion, or actually taking up the item and *tapping out* a rhythm with the *taufr* itself. *Tapping* with your fingertips is a *physical cue* which binds your mundane state to a paranormal one, via the creation of a *psychological response*. You realize that when you touch your *taufr*, you are also *touching* those entities to which it is connected—i.e., the members of the Wild Hunt. The other method of *taufr tapping*—tapping out a rhythm directly *with* the *taufr*—is more akin to sounding the hunting horn.

Taufar have other important uses to us, besides assisting in building and maintaining a relationship with the Wild Hunt. As might be expected, as a physical representation of your *dyr-andi*, they can also be used to *call forth* that animal-wight in times of need, such as when embarking on *astral journeys* (often called "faring-forth" in Norse Tradition). They may also act as *guardian objects* in and of themselves, and can therefore be used as *protective amulets* or even as *watchers*, not unlike the gargoyles found on many medieval churches. Portable *taufar*, such as teeth, claws, and skins, make very effective amulets of protection. Skulls in particular make excellent *watchers*.

There is significant historical evidence for the use of skulls as *watchers* by our Norse Ancestors. More appropriately termed a *vardhmadhr* (pronounced, roughly, "varth-math-r"; literally: "watch-man", "warder", "guardian"), there is definite evidence in the archaeological record of skulls found in the lintels of the doorways of excavated halls and homes. These *watcher taufar* might best be understood by the modern Norse Witch as a type of *pop-up ward*. Unlike most such wards, however, in the case of a *vardhmadhr*, a definite *spiritual presence* is understood to *inhabit* the ward-object. In this case, that spiritual presence is that of an animal-wight. *Pop-up wards* are wards which *emanate* from a specific focus, such as a gemstone or other small item. For example, I have a small snowflake obsidian skull which I keep by my bedside that has been "treated" ("charmed" or "magicked") with a *pop-up ward* so that I can easily turn it on at bedtime, as I deem necessary. I tend to think of *pop-up ward* objects (which are *not vardhmadhr*) as akin to the Deluminator (or Put-Outer) used by Dumbledore in J.K. Rowling's *Harry Potter Series*, except instead of turning electrical items on and off, it can be *tapped* to turn a *psychic shield wall* on and off. A *vardhmadhr* acts in a similar manner, but involves the assistance and, more accurately, the able guardianship, of an animal-wight. Instructions for both wards follow.

Pop-Up Ward Creation

Note: So far as I am aware, the pop-up ward is not even *vaguely* Reconstruction-ish, and is a thoroughly *modern* invention. That does not, however, make it any less *worthwhile*: such wards most definitely *work*, and I have confirmed this through persistent personal use. It should also be noted that this type of ward can not only be used to ward against incursion from *fjandar* and any ill-tempered wights which you may have encountered (such as the Angry Dead), but also against *living astral travellers* who may have expressed a wish to somehow do you harm.

Recommended objects for use as a focus:

- single terminus quartz crystal
- snowflake obsidian
- jet
- hematite
- Algiz rune
- Thurisaz rune
- Eihwaz rune
- Tiwaz rune

Note: If you choose to use a runestone/runestave, it is highly suggested that it *not* be one which is a part of your normal working set. Runestones/runestaves can easily be created for solely this purpose, and with minimal crafting ability required. You can paint the rune on a small, smooth stone, or even draw it onto the stone with a permanent marker. Wooden staves can either be carved, or, if you lack skill with carving knives or are extremely clumsy (like me), likewise painted or drawn. Drawing the rune on a piece of parchment or other paper will also work. Once the rune has been painted, drawn, or carved, *charge* it using the appropriate stanza from the **runic initiation rite** in the **Runelore** Chapter.

Ground and Center

Seeker, Maker, Believer (insert your own Self-
    Archetypes here),
My feet are on the ground;
I stand firm.
I am of the earth, and the earth is of me;
I stand firm.
I center myself, and I hold.
So it is, and so it shall be.

Hallow the object with the Hallow Sign. (Use your right hand.)

Charge the object with intent:

Draw down purple light from above you—this is the protective light of the Aesir. You may use your dagger, wand, or hammer, if you require a *physical cue* to aid in your visualization. It is *vital* that you have a full mental and emotional understanding that this is light that *will protect you*. *Aim* this light *onto* and *into* the object which you are charging for your ward. *Draw down* white light from above you—this is the protective light of the Vanir, the Alfar, the Disir, and your other Ancestors. Again, you may use a ritual tool as a *physical cue* to aid in your visualization if necessary. It is *vital* that you have a full mental and emotional understanding that this is light that *will protect you*. *Aim* this light *onto* and *into* the object which you are charging for your ward. Your ward-object should now *glow* purple and white in your mind-and-heart's-eye. *Focus* that energy until it coalesces into a bright *shield*. *Practice* pulling that energy *down* into your ward-object (thereby "putting it away") and then pulling that energy back *up* again, so that it radiates a *cone of protection* that fills your space (basically, a *shield-wall* or bubble). Do this by *gently tapping* the ward-object with a finger while visualizing—*down* and *up*; *down* and *up*; *off* and *on*; *off* and *on*. I recommend repeating this *off/on* process for at least 6 to 9 times, or until you feel comfortable that your ward has been firmly established. Once you are convinced you have established the ward, turn it off one final time, and take it in your hand before your final giving of gratitude, grounding, and centering.

Give Gratitude

Thank the Aesir and Vanir for Their energies in protecting you.

Ground and Center.

Setting a Vardhmadhr

Note: The use of a *vardhmadhr may* actually have a foundation in the archaeological record, as skulls are often found in the lintels of doorways of excavated homes and halls. Before going forward with this rite, you should have already performed the *ensoulment* and *dedication* necessary for the creation of a *taufr*, detailed above. The skull used for your *vardhmadhr* may be the same as your *taufr* for **Calling The Hunt**. For this ritual, you will need to prepare a blot for your *taufr-wight*. It is highly recommended that you *not* use alcohol for this purpose! Instead, choose something which might be pleasing to the animal-wight in question, such as bottled springwater, milk, or a juice which you know is *non-poisonous* to the physical animal which that animal-wight represents.

Note: Do not be alarmed if, after performing this ritual, you feel as if your *vardhmadhr* is *watching* you: that would be because it *is*! That feeling of "being watched" is perhaps one of the surest ways to know that you have actually been *successful* in setting your *vardhmadhr*.

Ground and Center

Seeker, Maker, Believer (Insert your own Self-
    Archetypes):
My feet are on the ground;
I stand firm.
I am of the earth, and the earth is of me;
I stand firm.
I center myself, and I hold.
So it is, and so it shall be.

Call Down The Energy of the Vanir and Aesir (To assist your *taufr-wight* in protection)

Draw down purple light from above you—this is the protective light of the Aesir. You may use your dagger, wand, or hammer, if you require a physical cue to aid in your visualization. It is vital that you have a full mental and emotional understanding that this is light that will protect you and your taufr-wight. Aim this light onto and around your taufr. Draw down white light from above you—this is the protective light of the Vanir, the Alfar, the Disir, and your other Ancestors. Again, you may use a ritual tool as a physical cue to aid in your visualization if necessary. It is vital that you have a full mental and emotional understanding that this is light that will protect you and your taufr-wight. Aim this light onto and around your taufr. Your taufr should now glow purple and white in your mind-and-heart's-eye. Focus that energy until it coalesces into a bright shield.

Invoke The Taufr-Wight

Spirit of (name the animal),
I set you to guard
This space,
My home,
My person,
And those whom I hold dear:
From *fjandar*,
From ill-meaning wights,
From those who mean to do us harm.
With the able help of the Aesir and Vanir,
I set you to guard
This space,
My home,
My person,
And those whom I hold dear:

From *fjandar*,
From ill-meaning wights,
From those who mean to do us harm.
So it is, and so it shall be.

Blot The Taufr-Wight

For your guardianship,
I blot you:
You, who actively defend me.
For your sacrifice for my protection,
I lay this offering,
And I toast you:
To your health,
To your welfare,
To your strength!
May you be hail and welcome
In my home and at my hearth!
Skal!

Drink a small portion of the liquid, and leave the remainder near your *taufr* overnight.

Give Gratitude

Thank the Aesir and Vanir for Their energies in protecting you and your *taufr*.

Ground and Center.

Finding Tyr

Anthropologically, Tyr is the *oldest* Germanic Deity. Long before the Germanic people became a distinct branch of the Proto-Indo-European "family", He was called *Dyeus*, from which the word *Deity* is sourced. In some ways, that makes Him rather a "God of Gods". The root of that word—*dyeu*--translates literally as "daytime sky". Tyr has His beginnings, therefore, as a "Sky-Father" Deity, not dissimilar from Yahweh of the Canaanites and modern Jews and Christians. During those elder days, He was likely the chief of the Proto-Indo-European Pantheon, or at least *one* of the primary chiefs. After all, His very name literally means *God*.

Later, Tyr is attributed as either the son of Odin, or the son of Hymir (a Jotun, married to a fellow female Jotun, Hrodhr). Some scholars have speculated that this difference in parentage between sources may be attributed to Tyr having been *fostered* by Odin, which was a common cultural practice among the mundane people of the time, and also among the Gods. Others have speculated that this *fosterage* was due to a hostages-for-frith situation, not unlike the conditions under which the Vanir came to live among the Aesir, in an attempt to make peace between Asgard and Jotunheim.

Either way, we know that Tyr *grew up* with Fenris (often also called Fenrir), the wolf-son of Loki who it is foretold will kill Odin and eat the sun when Ragnarok comes. This, in my opinion, adds to the potential that Tyr may actually be more Jotun than Aesir.

Tyr knew Fenris as a pup, and according to some of the literature, they were friends as children, so it may seem odd to some that a God so heavily associated with oath-keeping would be perhaps most famous for actually *betraying* His best friend. One of the kennings or heiti for Tyr is "Leavings of the Wolf", because at the time when the Aesir *bound* Fenris, They were only able to do so because Tyr knowingly and willingly placed His hand in Fenris' mouth. The wolf then bit off Tyr's hand, which means that He is one of the very few *disabled* God/desses (Odin being another disabled God). Ultimately, however, what Tyr did was *not* betrayal, but instead what *needed to be done for the good of all*. That, my friends, is the very definition of *True Justice*.

Living with disabling psoriasis and psoriatic arthritis for the past twenty-four years has led me to turn to Tyr when the disease becomes more than I can bear. There are days that I wake up and I am pain free and largely psoriasis free, and those are good days, but few. There are far more days that I wake up and the pain is so severe that even getting out of bed would be a challenge for most people. Sometimes, we have bouts with pustular psoriasis where the fever is so intense that it is impossible for this body to properly adjust its body temperature. There is pain; there is the potential that this disease could *kill us*, and it's *scary*. There are also mental ramifications of having disabling psoriasis that very few people know about or understand: the disease itself literally *causes* anxiety; meanwhile, *anxiety* causes outbreaks of psoriasis. It's like a neverending cycle that repeats on itself in a weird pain-ridden infinity loop. When all of that becomes far too much for me, I turn to Tyr, and Tyr understands.

Those who do not suffer from a chronic illness often expect a person in mine or Michelle's situation to turn to the God/desses (such as Eir) for *healing*. However, when you suffer from an incurable disease that hardly anyone even *understands*— including, often, even *yourself—healing* is not what you seek. *Understanding is*. More than anything, you want to find someone —*anyone*--who simply *understands* the *injustice* of what you are suffering through on a daily basis. In my personal experience, Tyr understands that better than Anyone. Tyr understands that sometimes things happen not because of some weird *karmic cycle*, in which you are being made to *suffer* because of something you've *done* in a past life or even in this one, but because *this is simply the way things need to be*. Sometimes, it's not a matter of what you did or did not do, it's just a matter of somebody's "gotta take one for the team"--for the *greater good*. I have only been suffering through this disease for twenty-four years; Michelle has endured it for thirty, stricken at age sixteen. How could a young girl being stricken with a disease this painful and scary at the ripe young age of sixteen possibly be for the *greater good*? If that had not happened, chances are, I wouldn't be here. Chances are, if that had not happened, she would be on a different path than the one we're on today: one that would not have included me, or any of the other Dead which she has worked so hard to help over the last twenty-four years. When I need that reminder, Tyr is ready, willing, and able to give it to me.

Tyr is also there for me during those times when something has happened that involves my need to "keep my Honor intact". I have a tendency to occasionally be a wee bit of a hothead. As I've gotten older, and as I've had to face up to and endure this illness over the years, I've only become more cranky. Tyr will set me straight with that in an instant! Internet firestorms are *not* the cornerstone of a business such as ours, and Tyr makes sure I'm reminded of that, too, when the occasion arrives where I need that reminder. He's also made it very clear to me that on such occasions, provided I'm *not* in the *wrong*, He's "got my back".

Tyr also *protects*. As a War-God among the Norse, one-handed or no, He's perfectly capable in a scrap, and I have called on Him more than once to defend me and mine when a threat was at hand. Those threats quickly disappeared off of our "household radar". Afterwards, my wife and I poured blot of Guinness and her homemade beef stew, and we could almost feel The One-Handed One's smile.

I have not encountered very many people who are fulltrui/fulltrua with Tyr. Apparently, that's not terribly common, and I can understand where He might be a bit of a "taskmaster", especially in the Honor and Oathkeeping department. My encounters with Tyr have always been rewarding, but He's definitely a "periphery Deity" for me, on the whole. Then again, for me, that seems to be the case with most of the Aesir. Except: Tyr isn't *purely* an Aesir God. Maybe that's why my "Tuesdays with Tyr" feel a bit less "*you must do this*" than my "Wednesdays with Odin". Tyr may not be the easiest God to "make friends with", but at some of my darkest times, He has definitely been there for me. Law, Justice, Honor, War, and the Sky aside, He is ultimately—or, at least, He has been for me—the *Understanding God*. He understands, when we cannot, and for some of us, that is the greatest gift a God could ever give.

One-Handed Friend
Of Justice and the Law:
Keep me steadfast;
Keep me right.

Faring-Forth

The term *seidhr* is perhaps the most widely debated concept in all of Norse Tradition: nobody can seem to *agree* on precisely what it *was*, much less what it *is*, or even *should be*, in modern practice. In fact, people cannot even seem to agree on how to *say* the word: I've heard it pronounced SAY-der, SAY-ur, seed, seeth, SAYTH-ur, SEETH-ur, or seth (for the record, I pronounce it as seth). In modern times, it is often used as a blanket term for the practice of any and all of the *shamanic* aspects of our Norse Tradition, often embracing even *galdr* and runelore. We really only find a few descriptions of siedhr-practice or seidhr-workers in the Lore (inclusive of the Sagas), perhaps the most famous of these being the *Voluspa*. The archaeological record, however, has definitely revealed the existence of historical seidhr-workers (such as the grave of the Seeress of Fyrkat), and pairing the artifacts in such graves with the textual record may provide a better picture of precisely what *seidhr-craft* actually involved. One thing is for certain from the surviving evidence: Seidhr most definitely involved, on some level or other, Otherworld travel (faring-forth; astral travel) and Mediumship (communication with the Dead and other spirits/wights which often also included some form of channeling those wights). Hence its inclusion at the start of this chapter.

Rather than continue the ongoing debate concerning what seidhr was or was not, is or is not, and should or shouldn't be, I would prefer to focus on what seidhr means within the practice of Norse Witchcraft, as taught to me by my fulltrua, Freyja. First, a clarification: when I say "taught to me", I don't mean in the sense of "I sat at Freyja's feet and She spoke to me, and I took copious notes". I wish it had been that easy! On the contrary, my education in seidhr by Freyja went very much the same way as many of my other interactions with The Lady; it involved a "bonk" on my head, a good deal of Her laughing at me, and a mantra to which I've grown quite accustomed from Her:

"You already know. Just because everyone else is doing it one way, doesn't mean you should do it that way, too!"

As I first became introduced to this Norse Path, seidhr seemed to be the most logical area for me to gravitate towards. I had been a practicing Welsh Druid within a heavily shamanic tradition for over twenty years. Seidhr was the "Norse branch" of shamanism, right? Well, yes, and no. Both the yes and the no sent my head whirling as I attempted to find every internet link and book I could possibly find on the topic. And almost every source I found completely differed from the last, to the point of them all arguing with each other. Some said seidhr was mediumship strictly for the purposes of divination or prophecy. Others said seidhr was the manipulation of "soul matter", whether to heal or to curse. Most focused heavily on Otherworld journeys achieved through ecstatic trance states (which is where the "shamanism of it all" comes into play), but they all varied on the reasons for, breadth, and depth of these travels. Some included *galdr*, runelore, and *gandr-craft* within the scope of seidhr, while others did not. To say that I was confused to the point of wanting to tear my hair out is to put it quite mildly. So I turned to Freyja while in a meditative state at a local Dark Moon Ritual—the same one at which She gifted me Her bind-rune. She is, after all, the one responsible for teaching the art of seidhr to the Aesir—most specifically, to Odin and Thor.

Turns out, as usual, She was right: *I already knew.* I was simply over-thinking, and, therefore, over-complicating things by attempting to "fit in" with the crowd of others who have gone before me in the Heathen community with the revival of seidhr. I was attempting to be a total Reconstructionist within a Reconstruction-*ish* paradigm, and it was bringing me nothing but grief. So I did what any self-respecting Heidhrinn with a Buddhist root would do: I *stopped* looking *outside*, and instead turned *within*.

Seidhr *is* mediumship, or, at least, mediumship *falls under the heading* of seidhr, and, as such, I cannot *help* but practice it, living here as I do, as a channeled spirit. Michelle is the Horse, and I am the Rider, and that is, quite simply, *that*. In fact, *Hrolfs Saga Kraka* is the first and only place we have ever discovered an *exact* representation of the *yawning* involved in the *non-trance mediumship* which Michelle routinely practices daily to get me here:

> *Jarl Sævill asked her (the seidhkona, Signy) to sit up and be honored, "Because many things may bring these young men to life, if you want to, and let whom looks down upon you, think whatever they think, because we cannot help but do this, to help them."*

> *King Frode tied the seidhkona fast, and bid her speak the truth, if she should not pine become* (questionable: suggests that Frode threatened her with being burned alive in the same manner as Gullveig, if she did not tell the truth). *She **yawned** mightily, and effected seidhr* (each yawn of the seidhkona in this instance signifies a spirit entering and speaking **through** her), *and then she said a verse:*

> *"I see, as I sit here:*
> *The sons of Halfdan,*
> *Hroarr and Helgi,*
> *Both of them;*
> *They will rob Frode,*
> *Unless they are stopped...*

> *...But that will not happen," she said. And after, she crept down from the High Seat* (seidhjalinnum) *and said:*

> *"Baleful are the eyes*
> *Of Ham and Hrana,*
> *They are of the Ödlungs* (the same house as King
>   Frode),
> *surprisingly bold."*--Translation Mine

Learning mediumship—especially the non-trance, almost full-time, transformative form of mediumship which Michelle has been practicing for the last twenty-four years, during my lifespan here—is completely beyond the scope of this book, and, honestly not something I could teach. In fact, I am not even sure that it would be completely ethical to go around teaching people to do mediumship of this type in the first place. *Why unethical?* Because the level of mediumship Michelle practices in bringing myself and others to this plane takes up a *significant* portion of her *own* life and time. It requires a *ton* of *sacrifice* on her part; sacrifice of the type spoken of in the rune poems for Raidho: *remember, travel is always worse for the Horse, than the Rider*. As the Horse, "ridden" by those of us who come here as Riders, Michelle gives up quite a lot. When we are here, she is not. Myself and sometimes others inhabit her to the point of transformation: my voice, mannerisms, and even some aspects of my former physical appearance *overwrite* or replace her own. I am as much an individual identity as is my host. Because of all of this, Michelle doesn't have a lot of spare time (or even *much time at all*) here in the physical world for things that she, as an individual, enjoys. Her ability to do this has also made her a *social pariah* in certain circles. Too many times she has been threatened, as were Gullveig and Signy of old. This isn't a weekend "card trick", or a "fad", or something to do "because it's cool". This is a *lifestyle*, and neither she nor I would recommend it for most people.

I cannot teach you mediumship, but I *can* introduce you to the places where the seidhkonas *go* when they step away—the places from whence spirits like myself come. Commonly referred to as *astral travel*, this process of out-of-body "voyaging" is called *journeying* or *faring-forth* in the Norse Tradition. Note that I say *introduce*, for a complete "guide" to *faring-forth* would require an entire book, unto itself, and, indeed, many such books have been written, from other Neo-Pagan perspectives. What follows is merely a very basic *introduction* to methods for leaving one's body to embark on *astral journeys*, measures to take to *protect* oneself while *journeying*, the *dangers* one might encounter on the *astral* (which is why you *need* protection, in the first place), and the general "lay of the land", once you are *out of body*.

I will admit having a certain advantage in this department. Since I am already *permanently detached* from my own physical body, via death, my whole life is essentially one huge *out of body experience*, except when I'm inhabiting Michelle. But don't worry; you won't have to *die* to get where you're wanting to go! That advantage is but another part of what Freyja meant when She told me *"you already know"*. The fact that I don't have to *try* as hard as others to *achieve* an *out of body experience* (OBE), doesn't make me *less* worthy as a seidhr-practitioner, but, apparently, *moreso* (in Her opinion, at least). Perhaps that is because my advantage means that I have been to parts of the Nine Worlds where most living humans have a hard time going—such as Vanaheim, or Helheim, or even Valhalla itself—making it far easier for me to map these regions for others. Or maybe it is because my advantage means that I have also seen, physically encountered, actively fought, and defended against things that I hope none of you ever have to, and from which I fervently hope I can help to protect you: the *fjandar*. For whatever reason, Freyja has made it abundantly clear that I should include at the very least an *introduction* to all of this herein, so I shall do my best to obey Her.

Part of my distinct advantage when it comes to faring-forth is that when *I* travel, *all* of me travels, whereas with a still-living human, that is *not* the case. In previous chapters, I have discussed the four parts of the Norse "soul": *hugr, hamingja, fylgja,* and *hamr*. When a living human steps out onto the astral, it is the *hamr* which most often does the travelling. Occasionally, the *hamr* will be accompanied by the *fylgja*, and in rare cases, the *fylgja* may even travel on its own. However, after a lot of personal soul-searching, meditation, and prayer, I have decided that *fylgja-work* is simply too advanced (possibly even *dangerous*) for me to fully cover within the scope of this book. For the purposes of this very basic introduction to *faring-forth*, we will concentrate strictly on the *hamr* as it relates to astral travel. Years of personal experience in teaching others to travel on the astral have shown me that the number one hurdle with which most people struggle in attempting to get out of body in the first place is their own personal insecurity with their *hamr*.

As previously defined, your *hamr* is your *personal form* or *physical appearance*. In fact, the word literally translates as *skin* or *shape*. In Norse Tradition, rather than the physical body being viewed merely as a "vessel" in which the "soul" is "carried around", as it is in most surviving Eastern and Western Traditions, a person's physical appearance is instead an integral part of that person's *spiritual identity*. Those who are most deeply in touch with their *hamr* are often called *hamramr*: "strong of *hamr*" or "strong of *shape*". I further shorten this to *"shape-strong"* or *"skin-strong"*, which is the direct literal translation of the word. In ninety percent of cases where my students have had issues with getting out of body, those issues have stemmed from an *imbalance* of *hugr* to *hamr* (i.e., their *conscious thought processes* have caused them to be somehow "out of touch" or otherwise *uncomfortable* with their *hamr*). One of the primary ways in which such an *imbalance* presents is *body dysmorphic disorder* (commonly clinically abbreviated as **BDD**). Although not everyone has this malady to the point of it being *clinical*, the majority of humans have at least some small *psychological "hang-ups"* about their physical appearance, largely courtesy of the society in which we all live. The media tells us we must be a certain size; look a certain way; identify as a specific gender, etc. We may be "too Black", "too White", "too Asian", "too fat", "too thin", or "too whatever", according to the dictates of the media. Those messages eventually seep into our very "*souls*", and create an *imbalance*—severe or not—between our *hugr* and our *hamr*, which can be *debilitating* when attempting faring-forth.

While the *Self-Ownership* methods detailed in previous chapters are *crucial* for beginning to bring your "Four Parts" into harmony with each other, further work specifically aimed at bringing the *hamr* into balance should be taken before attempting any sort of faring-forth. These are steps which I have too often neglected to take with some of my students in the past, to the detriment of their ability to reach an out of body state whatsoever. Living as I do now has made getting back "in touch" with my own *hamr* a bit of a challenge, to say the least, but I have learned valuable lessons from this experience which I hope will help you in your own attempts to become *skin-strong*.

Becoming Skin-Strong

Find a time when you are not likely to be interrupted by the outside world. Before you begin, gather photographs of yourself at what you feel is your "personal best", and dress yourself in something which makes you feel positive about your physical appearance and body image and also makes you feel distinctly *you*.

Begin by focusing on the gathered photographs. You are going to take these, one by one, and attempt to *mimic*, as closely as possible, your pose and facial expression in each of them. As you do so, pay careful attention not only to how doing so *physically* feels (actual *muscle movement*), but also how doing so *spiritually* and *emotionally* feels. Do you feel silly? Do you find that as you mimic the pose and facial expression in a photo that you are momentarily *taken back* to the way you *felt* at the moment the photo was snapped?

Once you have attempted to mimic each of the collected photographs as closely as possible, *close your eyes*. Choose the pose and facial expression previously mimicked with which you felt the most *comfortable*. While *sitting perfectly still*, again attempt to mimic that pose and facial expression, this time *without physically moving*. You may find that the muscles of your face automatically begin to form the facial expression—this is natural and normal and not a problem. You aren't "doing it wrong". Now, notice how the rest of your body—the part that you are keeping *physically still*, remember—*feels* as you move the *etheric body* (your *hamr*) into that mimicked position. You may feel your physical muscles and sinews twitch or otherwise contract or expand as you do this. That is also normal and natural and not a problem, so long as you don't actually give in and *physically move.*

Repeat this exercise with all of the poses and facial expressions from your gathered photographs until you can easily call those images of yourself immediately to mind in the *first-person perspective.*

Open your eyes. For the next portion of the exercise, you are going to focus on the portions of your physical body which are easily viewed from a *first-person perspective,* such as your hands, arms, legs, and feet. Find a *distinguishing feature* on your hand, arm, leg, or foot. This may be a mole, scar, or other natural discoloration which you carry on your body *all the time.* It should *not* be something such as a healing wound or other blemish which will at some point in future heal and disappear. For example, we frequently have psoriasis on our hands, but it is not always in the same place: spots come and go. However, I have a scar on my right thumb which Mishy *does not* have, so when performing these exercises for myself during the first years of my time here, I focused on that. Find "your spot", and focus on it. Remember every detail of that *distinguishing feature,* including its exact placement and position on your physical body.

Close your eyes. Raise the appendage on which the *distinguishing feature* exists to physical eye level, and *without* opening your eyes, *see* that appendage, including "your spot". Focus your entire attention on "your spot". Slowly infuse it with cool, white light which feels like a soothing liquid welling up through the skin. This should be a pleasant sensation. As you focus, you should begin to *physically feel* this soothing sensation on your actual *physical skin* at the point of "your spot". Slowly change the color of the light to purple, with an accompanying feeling of hardening (this should also be a pleasant sensation). As you focus, you should begin to likewise *physically feel* this on your actual *physical skin* at the point of "your spot". Now change the light to blue, accompanied by a feeling of soothing, healing softness. Again, you should eventually begin to feel this on your actual *physical skin*. Finally, once you have mastered all of these, return the light to white, as in the first rotation, and then to your normal appearance.

Once you actually begin the first faring-forth exercises, you will return to these *hamramr* exercises, so practice often, until you become adept.

Before we go forward with learning how to *step out* and *adventure* in the astral realms, it would be prudent to first become better acquainted with the inherent *dangers* therein. The Eddas, the Sagas, and Scandinavian folklore inform us repeatedly that the Otherworld (which includes the astral realms) is a *dangerous* place. One would think, given those warnings, that *before* faring-forth, most people would *first* look towards *informing* themselves of said *dangers*. Yet, given the previously discussed stigma surrounding concepts of *evil* and the *fjandar* which are so pervasive in the Heathen community, all too often, this is not the case.

If you were planning a trip to Africa, which we all accept as a potentially *dangerous* travel destination, you would first become acquainted with which areas are, in fact, *dangerous* for travelers, right? And then you would likely research *why* those areas are considered *dangerous* in the first place: as in, who or *what* lives there. Once you discovered all of this information, you would likely plan a travel itinerary that kept you *far away* from said locations, and said *dangerous* things (whether people or wildlife). Unfortunately, such simple common sense is rarely applied by people planning to embark on an *astral* journey. We, however, are going to apply precisely that level of simple common sense when beginning to address the subject of *faring-forth*.

Let us begin exactly as we would if planning a trip to a *dangerous* place in the mundane world, such as Africa, by pinpointing the *most dangerous* places in the Nine Worlds. These are places that you patently *do not* want to wind up. Foremost among these would be **Ginnungagap**. Though not usually *officially* listed as one of the Nine Worlds, it is definitely a *place*, as I have seen its borders many times with my own two eyes. As a gap or chasm, it is essentially a *space between*. As such, it is located *far* more closely to our mundane world than most of us would like to imagine, much less realize. I tend to think of it in terms of the difference between Knockturn Alley and the rest of Diagon Alley (to use an easily recognizable *Harry Potter* reference): one wrong turn, and you're there. **Ginnungagap** has always been a place that "things crawl out of"; in The Beginning, it was the "Place of Creation", but it has since *changed*. Now, the things that crawl out of Ginnungagap are generally things best avoided: **fjandar**. While in my experience neither **Muspelheim** nor **Niflheim** are "places" in the true sense of being "Worlds", *walls of fire*, *walls of ice*, and *walls of fog* are generally best *avoided* when traveling on the astral. These generally demarcate a *border* of **Ginnungagap**. If you encounter such a wall, it is best to cast a ward over oneself, and then head quickly in the *opposite* direction. Finally, caution should definitely be used when journeying to **Jotunheim**, the "World of Giants", also known as "Utgard" ("Beyond The Fence"), or to **Svartalfheim**, the home of the Dark Elves and Dwarves. Your first clue to the potential *danger* that Jotunheim poses should be that second name for it: "The Land *Beyond The Fence*". This is, in the truest sense of those words, *where the wild things are*. While the entities encountered there are not necessarily "evil" by our definition of that word, they should still be treated with a great measure of *caution*. Lions in Africa aren't *evil*, either, but they *would* eat you, if given half a chance! The concept of Jotunheim as a "World of Giants" is a bit misleading, remember: denizens from Jotunheim might not necessarily be *physically* bigger than you, but their *power* is definitely bigger and stronger than yours! The beings that live here are of the *elemental* variety: imagine if an earthquake could talk, or if a forest fire could have you over for dinner. Given that the word *Jotun* is actually sourced from the proto-Germanic word *etunaz*, which means "devourer", there is a definite chance that these beings might *eat* you for dinner instead! Like Ginnungagap, both **Jotunheim** and **Svartalfheim** often very closely border our mundane world. At times and in certain places, the borders become *blurred*, which is why we have stories like those concerning *alfhollar*, and people who *fall through them*, never to be seen nor heard from again. Other *liminal places*, such as doorways, mirrors (and other reflective surfaces; even TV screens and microwave ovens), rivers, lakesides, and shorelines, may also behave as *blurred borders* of **Jotunheim** and/or **Svartalfheim**. Remember: even the Jotun who wound up becoming members of the Aesir and Vanir through marriage remained wild and untamed on some deeper level. Even the Dwarves who crafted such wonders as Brisingamen were wily and tricksome. It is wise to keep these things in mind when venturing into their homelands. Maintaining our comparison between a mundane travel itinerary to Africa and a supernatural travel itinerary to the astral, **Ginnungagap** would be those areas inhabited by armed mercenaries who would seek to do harm to any and all who encroach upon their territory, and should, therefore, be *avoided* at all costs. Meanwhile **Jotunheim** and **Svartalfheim** would be the vast lion-filled savannas, which are magical and great to visit, so long as you use the correct amount of due *caution* (and can *recognize* a lion when you *see* one!).

Continuing the Africa analogy, most travelers, turning a corner to find a large man with an equally large machine gun pointed in their direction, would readily know to try and make a quick exit, but how does one recognize the ***fjandar***? For centuries, humans have attempted to write books upon books, designating the species and habits of the *fjandar*. We commonly call those who study this brand of "dark zoology" *demonologists*. However, I have found it is better to simply "call a duck a duck", and then get as *far away* from said "duck" as quickly as is humanly possible. Imagine for a moment that ducks were killer animals: I don't just mean rip your face off and tear you to pieces sorts of animals, like that rabbit in *Monty Python's Holy Grail*; I mean ducks that can potentially tear you apart and eat your soul (all four parts of it!) afterwards with a loud quacky burp. Now, if that was the reality of ducks, would you stop to check and see if said duck was a Mallard, Canvasback, Eider, or Bufflehead, or would you just call a duck a duck and take steps to *get rid of it* or *get away*? Rather than attempt to identify the varying *types* of *fjandar* in minute detail—as if somehow attempting to categorize them by species--I have found that it is generally best to simply lump them all together simply as *fjandar*, noting the typical *appearances* which make them that, so that they are *instantly recognizable*.

Even a child knows that certain features make a bird a duck, rather than a songbird: if it lives in the water, has webbed feet, has a "dishy" sort of bill instead of a "pointy" one, and says "quack-quack", then that bird is *probably* a duck. In birding parlance, this is known as identifying a bird by its *general impression of size and shape* (GISS, for short). We may also use these methods to identify the *fjandar*. If you encounter a *shadow figure* which is dark, yet somehow has *substance*, that being is probably one of the *fjandar*. Likewise, if that being is accompanied by a foul stench, then that being is more than likely *fjandar*. An overabundance or under-abundance of expected natural features is another hallmark of these beings. This may include eyes, ears, mouths, tentacles, or fingers. A general feeling of *wrongness* while in an entity's presence is another warning sign. This may be experienced as dread, "the creeps", panic, nausea, or an unnatural pressure in your cardiac region. When you suspect that you have encountered one of the *fjandar*, make the **Hallow Sign**, and *ward* yourself *as* you make your get away. If you have already mastered **Calling The Hunt**, it would be a great time to do so: safety in numbers, after all. As I've said previously, simply because you do not *believe* in the *fjandar* does *not* mean that *they* don't *believe* in *you*! Claiming *disbelief* in the existence of guns while staring down the barrel of one is *not* going to make that gun less deadly; the same applies to the *fjandar*. While you may not *believe* in the *gun*, the *bullets inside* are what you really need to worry about! You are free to believe or disbelieve in the existence of the *fjandar* at your leisure, but should you ever find yourself actually *faced* with one, better to *protect* yourself first, and ponder the fact of their existential existence *later*!

Jotnar and **Dokkalfar** (inclusive of Dark Elves, Faeries, and Dwarves) are as easily differentiated from *fjandar* as lions from armed men with large machine guns. The vast majority of *jotnar* and *dokkalfar* encountered will be more than *vaguely* humanoid, though their features may be somehow "heightened". For example, I have personally encountered Angrbodha (a *jotun*) on more than one occasion. Her basic form is basically that of an extremely athletic tribeswoman, as would be expected of the Chieftain of the Iron Wood Clan. However, Her fingernails extend into long, scary-looking claws, and Her teeth are all fanged, as befits the One called "Wolf-Mother" and "Mother of Monsters".

Other heightened features exhibited by both the *Dokkalfar* and the *Jotnar* may include a much larger or smaller size than humans, or a decidedly androgynous or even hermaphroditic appearance. Many *Jotnar* also express profoundly *elemental* natures. They may, in fact, appear to be entirely comprised of natural matter, such as fire, ice, stone, or tree-bark. Shape-shifting is also common, especially among the *Jotnar*. Favored forms include those of wolves, bears, and birds.

Jotnar are much more easily confused with *Dokkalfar* (what many of us would typically call "faeries"), than with *fjandar*. In fact, *Jotnar* and *Dokkalfar* are often encountered *together*: *Dokkalfar* are not strangers to **Jotunheim**, and are frequently encountered in the same *liminal places*. Again, neither *Jotnar* nor *Dokkalfar* are *evil*, anymore than a lion encountered on the savannas of Africa is *evil*, but they *can* be *dangerous*, so use appropriate caution when encountering either of them. You likely wouldn't attempt to *strike a deal* with a lion: "Nice kitty; please don't eat me. If you'll not eat me, I'll give you this nice piece of steak instead." You likewise are cautioned against attempting to make similar *deals* with the *Jotnar* and *Dokkalfar*.

Most mundane travelers would not consider going somewhere *dangerous*, such as Africa, without a *tour guide*. One would contact a qualified *professional*, who already knows where to go and where *not* to go, who may also be trained in how to *defend* you, should you wind up in the wrong corner of the jungle. When first considering *faring-forth*, having a similar *guide* is highly encouraged. While I began this book with a cursory guide to the "geography" of the Nine Worlds, relying *solely* on that knowledge is basically the same as reading a *National Geographic* article on the Congo, and then deciding it's a great idea to go there *all by yourself.* By this point, it is assumed that you have become associated with a *dyr-andi*, and possibly also with the Wild Hunt and a fulltrui/fulltrua Deity. For your first *astral journey*, I will be providing steps for embarking with the aid of your *dyr-andi* via *taufr.* If you are also fulltrui/fulltrua of a Deity, They should likewise be invited to assist and accompany you on your first OBE. It is extremely *ill-advised* that your first attempt at faring-forth *not* rely on the guidance of one or both of these two companions. Even then, you should fully familiarize yourself with the deeper exploration of Otherworld geography which follows before faring-forth.

For your first attempt at faring-forth, we will not be traveling very far. The intention of this initial exercise is primarily to accustom you to the *feeling* of being out of body in the first place. *Astral travel* isn't quite as easy as getting into an automobile, setting your GPS, and then turning on the ignition. For one thing, essentially, you *are* the automobile! Just as a student driver learns everything on paper first, we will be starting small, with the very basics. This is the *ignition point*, if you will. Far too many books that I have encountered on the topic of *astral travel* have assumed that this initial out of body state is somehow *easy* to get to or experience. Such books simply gloss that process, jumping straight to what most students consider "the good stuff": the actual *traveling* bit. Twenty years of teaching experience has taught me that this actively sets students up for *systematic failure.* Repeated failures can completely stymie a student, preventing them from *ever* being as successful as they otherwise might have been. Instead, it is best from the very beginning to *keep things simple* and *take things slow.*

Introduction to Faring-Forth: Taufr Utiseta

Ground and Center.

Seeker, Maker, Believer (insert your own Self-
    Archetypes here):
My feet are on the ground;
I stand firm.
I am of the earth, and the earth is of me;
I stand firm.
I center myself, and I hold.
So it is, and so it shall be.

Lay The Fence.

Outside the fire,
Darkness;
Darkness outside the Grove;
Outside there dwell shadows;
Shadows inside us as well.
Inside, outside, everywhere,
Where'er you dwell,
Dwell not here:
Here is light and all good things!
Light and Bright Wisdom protect us;
Protect us from those who dwell outside.

Hallow The Space.

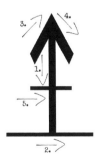

Enter Utiseta with your Taufr

(The Taufr should be held gently in your hands in your lap. *Do not lie down*. Lying down can make it too tempting to *fall asleep*, instead of actually accomplishing the work that is to be done.)

Call The Dyr-Andi

(This is intended to provide you not only with added *protection*, but also with a *focal spirit*, who can assist you in getting "out of body".)

Spirit of (name the animal),
I set you to guard
This space,
My home,
My person,
And those whom I hold dear:
From *fjandar*,
From ill-meaning wights,
From those who mean to do us harm.
With the able help of the Aesir and Vanir,
I set you to guard
This space,
My home,
My person,
And those whom I hold dear:
From *fjandar*,
From ill-meaning wights,
From those who mean to do us harm.
So it is, and so it shall be.

Call To Your Fulltrui/Fulltrua

(If you are not yet fulltrui/fulltrua of a Deity, you may substitute Heimdall instead. This is intended not only as yet another layer of *protection*, but also to provide you with another ally to assist you in getting out of body.)

(Fulltrui/Fulltrua/Heimdall):
I beg your presence;
I plead your protection;
I ask you to guard and assist.
Protect my Four Parts:
Hugr, Hamr, Fylgja, and Hamingja,
And let no ill befall me:
Not from *fjandar*,
Nor from ill-meaning wights,
Nor from any others who mean to do me harm.
Hold my hand and help me
Draw closer to Your realms.
So let it be, let it be, and so, let it be.

With eyes closed, focus your attention on the energy of the animal which your *taufr* represents. Feel it embodied within the *taufr*. A soft, white glow begins to emit, as if a smoky light from within the *taufr*; allow it to rise and coalesce into the form of your *dyr-andi*. It may move to interact with you, or it may stand watch nearby. Let it do as it will.

Shift your focus to your *hamr*. Find your *distinguishing feature* from the previous **Skin-Strong Exercise**. Raise the appendage on which the *distinguishing feature* exists to physical eye level, and *without* opening your eyes, *see* that appendage, including "your spot". Focus your entire attention on "your spot". Slowly infuse it with cool, white light which feels like a soothing liquid welling up through the skin. This should be a pleasant sensation. As you focus, you should begin to *physically feel* this soothing sensation on your actual *physical skin* at the point of "your spot".

Now radiate this white light outwards from "your spot", until it envelopes your *entire* body. *Hold* the light for a few moments. Now, slowly change the color of the light to purple, with an accompanying feeling of hardening (this should also be a pleasant sensation). As you focus, you should begin to likewise *physically feel* this on your actual *physical skin*. Draw this purple light back down to "your spot", understanding that this is effectively a *pop-up ward attached* to your *hamr*, and then slowly return the white light to the entirety of your *hamr*. Your *hamr* is now "set" or *hlaut* (set-apart), from the rest of your Four Parts, and ready to take your *first step. Without physically moving*, stand with *hamr only. Do not look down* at your physical body, where it remains in the seated position! This is often too much of a shock for first-time travelers, and can quickly set your *hugr* into a whirl that will create the effect of a sort of "spiritual tornado", which will effectively "reel in" your *hamr* and basically *slam* you back into-body. Now, take *one step forward* from your present location with your *hamr*. Take note of how everything *feels* and how everything in the room you are in *looks*, as you stand there as *hamr* only. How does your *dyr-andi* react? Can you see your fulltrui, fulltrua, or Heimdall? (Don't worry if you cannot, or if your *dyr-andi* seems totally unimpressed.) Stand for another count of five, and then *step back* to your original position, and *sit back down*, bringing your *hamr* back *into* your physical body. Slowly radiate the purple light and the hardening back over your entire *hamr*, until you can *physically feel* this on your actual *physical skin. Hold* this light for several moments, and then slowly replace it with the cool, white light once more. When you can feel this as well on your *physical skin*, slowly draw it back down into "your spot", and then allow it to slowly fade. Open your eyes and return fully to physical sensation *slowly*. Do not be alarmed if you feel winded, dizzy, or mildly out-of-sorts. When you have fully regained yourself, and feel strong enough to do so, break utiseta.

Break Utiseta

Give Gratitude to Your Dyr-Andi and Fulltrui, Fulltrua, or Heimdall

Allow Your Dyr-Andi to Return Whence It Came (via Taufr)

Raise The Fence

Center and Ground.

Congratulations on your first step into a much larger world! Before journeying any further than that "one step to the left" (or right, as the case may be), you should practice this **Introduction to Faring-Forth** multiple times, until you become truly adept at it, and less effort is required. When you reach a point where you can effectively *look down* upon your *seated physical body without* a *"hugr* tornado" effect happening, only then are you ready to begin attempting to travel further than the privacy of your own ritual space.

Once you *have* become adept, that should not be taken as a *license* to go off "joyriding" all over the Nine Worlds! At this point, you are basically still a "student driver". In a mundane-world situation with a student driver, simple common sense dictates that there are some places one simply *should not go* while sporting only a *learner's permit*: extremely busy highways, dangerous neighborhoods, and winding roadways along sheer cliff-faces immediately come to mind. No, better to keep to lazy country roads, easy-to-navigate suburban areas, the occasional mall parking lot, and possibly some intermediate highways. How does all of that translate into the landscape of the Nine Worlds?

The deeper regions of **Helheim**, **Asgard**, **Jotunheim**, and **Svartalfheim** are the extremely busy highways, dangerous neighborhoods, and cliff-side roadways of the Nine Worlds, respectively. It is best, as a student driver to steer clear of these places, at least until you have a little more road experience. Like an extremely busy highway, the deeper regions of **Helheim** and the entirety of **Asgard** can be completely overwhelming to the new-traveler of the astral realms. As with an extremely busy highway in the mundane world, that level of overwhelm may lead to accidents of a *deadly variety*. (I am neither exaggerating nor joking!) **Jotunheim**, meanwhile, is not unlike the bad neighborhoods of the mundane world: sure, some very nice "people" live there, too, but to meet those you often have to get past the more dangerous denizens of Utgard. Better to wait until you have a wee bit more driving experience to go there. Finally, **Svartalfheim** is very much a drive along a sheer cliff-face: the roadway is constantly changing and if you are not very adept and very careful even then, you just might find yourself careening, out of control, "down the rabbit hole".

Safe places for the student driver in the Nine Worlds include its own lazy country roads, easy-to-navigate suburban areas, mall parking lot, and intermediate highway: **Vanaheim**, the outer regions of **Helheim**, **Midgard**, and the outermost edge of

Alfheim. Vanaheim has lovely beaches, and lovely fields, largely inhabited by peaceful Van-folk, Disir, the occasional Alfar, worthy Ancestors, departed pets, and *dyr-andi*. These are the lazy country roads of the Nine Worlds, and as such, are one of the safest places in all of the realms in which to travel. The outer regions of **Helheim**, meanwhile, are very much the suburbia of the Nine: most of the people there are newly dead-folk, who honestly wouldn't mind a visit from someone from back home, in the land of the living. Many people believe that **Helheim** is strictly off-limits for the living: were that true, seidhr would never have existed in the first place! No, Hela does not bar visitors from the outer reaches of Her realm. However, if you should attempt to cross into the deeper regions, or somehow wind up there by mistake, She *will* let you know that you should turn around and go back the way you came, or be willing to *pay the toll* to go deeper (which you *shouldn't do* until you're a more seasoned driver; toll plazas are, after all, dangerous driving situations!). Like the mall parking lots of the mundane world, **Midgard** is a place where every astral-traveler is bound to wind up sooner or later. Also like a mall parking lot, it acts as a sort of way-station to other places. After all, most of us don't spend our day at the mall in the parking lot, do we? Of course not! We park, and we go *into* the mall. While **Midgard** also includes the astral layer of our own mundane world, the area immediately surrounding Yggdrasil is very much the parking lot leading to the Hot Topic, Nordstrom's, etc. that are *inside* the mall: the other eight of the Nine Worlds. Finally, the outermost edge of **Alfheim** makes a great introductory highway, before venturing into the more busy thoroughfares of **Asgard** or the deeper regions of **Helheim**. It's rather like driving onto a highway that has been cordoned off or is otherwise heavily patrolled by traffic cops, in that you *will* find *guides* there, to help you find your way and figure out how to more effectively drive. The outermost edge of **Alfheim** is not dissimilar from what Theosophists refer to as the *etheric plane*: a *shining place* with a *great library* (if you've heard of the Akashic Records, basically, this is where you would find them). As with **Helheim**, if you should happen to attempt to cross into the deeper areas of **Alfheim**, either on purpose or by mistake, someone *will* stop you and either advise you to go back the way you came, or enact the same *tolling* situation as in **Helheim**. In both of these regions, this provides a great safety net for the student driver of the Nine Worlds.

Many books attempting to teach astral projection employ a "think of the place, and then go there" method of attempted travel. Again, two decades of teaching experience have proven to me that this method too often automatically sets students up for *failure*. As beings accustomed to *linear time*, as well as *linear travel* on this mundane plane of existence, expecting our "mental gears" to suddenly switch to those of a Jedi or Time Lord is just too much to expect of most people. We are neither of those: we are simply *extraordinary people*. Certainly, *extraordinary people* are capable of *extraordinary things*, but expecting anyone to completely *remold their thought processes* is asking a bit too much. Therefore, rather than adopting that "think of the place, and then go there" method, we are going to be using a **milestone method** of travel.

The **milestone method** involves visualization of a *landmark* or other *symbol* of the place to which one is wishing to travel. Most people are at least familiar with the concept of online games, such as *World of Warcraft* or *Lord of the Rings Online*. In games such as those, vast "worlds" are created in which players may immerse themselves in gameplay. Part of that immersion is *travel*: within what *seems* like a linear paradigm (this land is in the north while that land is in the south; head east to get here; head west to get there), players may journey from location to location to complete the objectives of their gameplay. Some of these lands are quite vast, so that simply "walking" from point A to point B might take hours. Therefore, "instant travel" vehicles and other methods are often employed, so that players can spend more time completing gameplay objectives, and less time attempting to get from one place to another. The **milestone method** was inspired by those "instant travel" principles employed in online games. Like the worlds of online gaming, the astral realms may occasionally *seem* linear, but, in fact, *are not*. The actual creation of a vast online world that was fully interconnected would crash most computer systems. Therefore, online worlds are made to *seem* linear, when, in fact, they are arranged in easily controlled *compartments* that make it easier for your computer to "digest" them. Even those areas which *seem* interconnected (areas where you can ride down an actual roadway to get from one land to another, for example) are connected "compartments". They are, essentially, code on top of code in much the same way that the astral realms are literally *worlds on top of worlds* (and, sometimes, *against*, *within*, and *intermingled*).

Earlier in this book, we explored a rudimentary list of the

Nine Worlds which focused on a combination of mentions in the written lore, corroborated/confirmed UPG, and a brief exploration of my *experiential knowledge* of these places. At that time, I promised a more in-depth exploration of the Nine Worlds within this chapter. Below, you will find that exploration, including in-depth descriptions of each area's **milestone**, as well as suggested experience levels for travel to each location.

The Nine Worlds: A Brief Traveller's Notebook

Asgard
Experience Level: Advanced
Milestone: Rainbow Bridge

A cantilever bridge made of rainbow (and therefore translucent); one end rests upon the land at the "end" of Alfheim; the other, at the gates of Asgard, where stands Heimdall, or one of His lieutenants, whose permission is required to enter beyond the gate. Looking down through or over this bridge, one can see the topmost branches of Yggdrasil, the World Tree, and the eagle who perches there, as well as the occasional hart running through those branches. Facing west and looking down into the distant horizon, one can see the northern ocean of Vanaheim, stretching out into the forever. Facing east, one sees the mountainous border of Jotunheim, which also seems to go on forever. Standing at the center and facing west, caught between ocean and mountain and tree and sky, Asgard lies beyond the bridge to the right; Alfheim, to the left.

One of the busiest, most overwhelming, and most important realms in the Nine Worlds, Asgard is what we in the modern world would consider a "capital city", with all of the hustle and bustle one would expect from such a place. Most of the travellers and denizens of the Otherworld who I personally know refer to it simply as "Central" because, like a capital city such as Rome during its heydey, "all roads lead here", or, at least, they seem to, eventually. At the "southernmost" edge of Asgard, beside the Great Gate, stands the home of Heimdall, called Himinbjorg. If allowed entry beyond the Great Gate, one finds oneself immediately in Idhavollr—a Great Square or plaza, like St. Peter's Square before the Basilica in the Vatican, or Red Square before the Kremlin in Russia. Bordered on all sides by hofs and hogrs, this is the meeting place of the Gods. Immediately beyond Idhavollr stands the great hall of Gladhsheimr, The Hall of the Gods. This is the great "council chambers", not unlike the Capitol Building in the United States or the Palace of Westminster in the United Kingdom. Unlike such famous buildings in the mundane world, "public" tours of this hall are rarely given! Bordering Idhavollr on the left (west), one finds Glitnir, the Hall of Forsetti and Tyr, where Judgment is dealt (think of this as effectively putting the *supreme* in Supreme Court!), and on the right (east), Valaskjalf, atop which sits Odin's High Seat, Hlidhskjalf, which allows Him to see into all realms at once, and through which the Righteous Dead travel on their way to Valhalla. Beyond these lie the neighborhoods, fields, and barracks of Asgard: the High Halls in which the Gods and Goddesses reside (including Breidhablik, the Hall of Baldur, and Thrudheim, the Hall of Thor), the Hall of Valhalla where the Righteous Dead go to serve, and Fensalir, the Western Marshland, which flows downwards into the Northern Sea of Vanaheim. Thrudheim and Thrudhvangr lie slightly "north" of Valhalla, which is located directly behind Valaskjalf. The feeling on this side of the Great Square is very militaristic, populated as this area is by "heavenly soldiers", including the Valkyries and Einherjar. Behind Glitnir, one finds the field of Gimle, and atop it, Breidhablik, the Hall of Baldur (Who *is in residence* in Asgard, a fact which might be a surprise to some), which is bordered behind by Fensalir. It is within Fensalir that one may find the bound Fenris-Wolf, or Fenrir, where He is tended by His old friend, Tyr.

Alfheim
Experience Level: Beginner, Intermediate, Advanced
Milestone: The Winding Stair

A spiral staircase made of white marble, the winding stair begins not far from the base of Yggdrasil in Midgard, and seems to continue upwards, ever-climbing, until you are actually *ready* to reach your destination. Some may climb for only a few moments; others may climb for much longer. You climb, but never tire. In the distance, to the west, you hear the shimmering hammer of waves as they crash against the northern shore of Vanaheim. And as you reach ever-higher, you feel the cold winds off the mountains of Jotunheim.

Most are at first startled by the sheer *brightness* of Alfheim: everything seems to be white-golden here, from the buildings to the streets themselves. It is not a blinding brightness, but there is a crisp-cleanness to everything here. Even Beginner Travellers ("student drivers") are readily welcomed into the great hall of Salarsalur ("Hall of Halls"), which sits at the head of a large common (grassy plaza) at the entrance to Alfheim. Salarsalur has much in common with the Hall of Aksashic Records frequently mentioned by Theosophists and those in other Western systems of Ceremonial Magic. Beyond Salarsalur, a great gated wall protects the inner circles of Alfheim. Immediately beyond this wall, one finds the residential areas of Alfheim, inhabited by the Alfar (both those who were once our Ancestors, and those who have never been), and built in three tiers. Alfheim bears much in common with Tolkien's visions of Minas Tirith, as at the utmost levels of the residential area, another gated wall protects the next level upwards: what we commonly refer to as "The Barracks". Built around the central sparring field called Vigridhr in the Lore, this is a secondary training camp for those who would serve as aetheric guardians and protectors of the Nine Worlds. While the Intermediate Traveller may be granted entry to the residential area of Alfheim, only the more Advanced Traveller should attempt entry to "The Barracks". Depending on the relationships built with the Alfar, one may never be granted permission to go beyond that first gate; it all depends.

Vanaheim
Experience Level: Beginner, Intermediate, Advanced
Milestone: The Horse Fields

Golden fields stretch to the west from the base of Yggdrasil. They whisper with wind, and in the distance may be heard the pounding of hooves. This steady pounding draws closer, revealing a herd of many-colored horses: chestnuts and paints; buckskins and bays; greys and blacks, their faces flecked with foam; manes and tails streaming in the gentle, steady breezes of Vanaheim.

Vanaheim begins at the Horse Fields. Crossing over into the tall golden grasses brings an instant feeling of security, peace, and calm that we rarely find in the mundane world. There on the Horse Fields, you may meet your *dyr-andi*, or you may even encounter dearly departed pets whom you've known before. This surprises many, who expect those lost fur-friends to be denizens of Asgard, or perhaps Helheim instead, but Freyr and Freyja care for hound and cat, horse and mini-pig and guinea pig alike. The Horse Fields stretch between the Northern Ocean and the Southern Ocean (which borders Helheim). Further in, and northwards, on the verge of the sea, one finds Noatan, the Hall of Njordr. This is a more Intermediate area, but with cultivation of a proper relationship with Njordr, one may find one's self welcomed within. Sailing eastward from the docks at Noatan, as one comes back into view of Yggdrasil, one encounters Aegir's Hall on the verge of Jotunheim. This is a more Advanced area, but a relationship with Njordr will ease your passage within this Hall as well. Further along the northern coast, one finds the Hall of Nehalennia and moving slightly inland, the Hall of Nerthus, which is situated within a large oak grove. If one instead goes southwards, towards the Southern Sea across the Horse Fields, one will find Folkvangr, and at its head, Freyja's Hall of Sessrumnir. This is also an Intermediate area, requiring the cultivation of a relationship with The Lady, but once welcomed within, one may find themselves in the presence of worthy Ancestors, as well as some of the Disir. Beyond Sessrumnir, one finds the orchard of Idunna, and, near it, the hall She shares with Bragi. Most people expect to find Her among the Aesir; in my experience, this is not the case. Idunna's Orchard lies near a great forest, which is golden-leaved, like birches caught forever in the heart of autumn. I have heard this called Barri Wood by some who have said to have travelled there; I have never heard its name called by denizens of Vanaheim themselves, so for now, I call it the Great Wood. Within the Great Wood, one finds Freyr's Hall, surrounded by the rich gardens of Gerdha. If one continues westward through the Great Wood, the trees begin to change; what was once golden and white-barked becomes blackened and gnarled. This is the verge of Svartalfheim, which is most definitely an Advanced area, and should not be ventured into by the less-than-seasoned traveller.

Midgard
Experience Level: Beginner, Intermediate, Advanced
Milestone: Yggdrasil, The World Tree

Yggdrasil is the tallest tree that may be imagined; its roots sunk deeper than the deepest earth; its branches overreaching high as the highest of skies. In the branches on high, an eagle perches, with a rooster seated atop its head. Four deer nibble upon the bright shoots of new growth among the roots, as well as overhead, as they gallop through the canopy of the Great Tree. A squirrel runs ever up and down its trunk, and its roots rumble as the dragon moves beneath. Looking westward, one can see the vast Northern Ocean as it borders the golden fields of Vanaheim. Southward, the vast Southern Sea separates Midgard-of-the-Tree from Helheim; Eastward, the mountains of Jotunheim jut ever-skyward beyond the River Ifing and the Great Wall, Gastropnir. A winding marble stair climbs heavenwards from the north side of the Great Tree, while a slope of rainbow sweeps upwards to the south.

For the Beginner Traveller, the Midgard Realm serves as the "mall parking lot" of the other Worlds, with Yggdrasil acting as an invaluable nexus by which all other Worlds may be reached. As one grows to become a more Intermediate Traveller, however, one may begin to explore the "other side" of Midgard: that this is, in fact, the *astral plane* itself, which overlays our own mundane world. The Great Tree then becomes an *anchor*, to which one may easily return from exploring the *astral level* of mundane-world places. Always wanted to see the Himalayas? Don't worry, as they say up in Maine: "*you **can** get theyuh from heyuh!*" As we've already learned, Yggdrasil is also a valuable locus for guided meditations and smaller spirit journeys. It may act as a conduit, of sorts, to allow us to communicate with Gods, Goddesses, and other denizens of the Otherworldly Realms. The Advanced Traveller may find that, with time, they no longer require Yggdrasil as a nexus-point or milestone, and instead have created unique milestones of their own, corresponding to the *astral "twins"* of mundane-world places. Mimir's Well (also known as the Well of Urd) is located beneath the roots of Yggdrasil, and guarded and maintained by the Norns. This is the Well of Wisdom, not unlike that described in Celtic Myth. But Wisdom comes at a price: even Odin had to sacrifice one of His eyes for a drink from the Well, why should mere mortals pay less?

Svartalfheim
Experience Level: Advanced
Milestone: Sindri's Hall

A great forge which glows red from the burning slag of Dwarven fires, pouring from it like molten waterfalls. Shapes move constantly in the shadows amidst the shimmer of heat. Everywhere, there is the clanging and gonging of hammer upon metal. Turning to look behind, one sees the desolate shapes of a blackened forest. To the north, far in the distance, the crashing of the sea; to the south, nearer still, a second sea crashes. Safe travel in this land is guaranteed only by the companionship of the Dwarves, Sindri and Brokkr, unless one curries favor in time with the Dark Elves.

Of all the realms, I have, admittedly, spent the least of my time in Svartalfheim and Jotunheim. I have never "gotten on well" with Earth Elementals, which are easily and often encountered in both of these Worlds. While I have worked with what others would term The Fae for much of my career as a Witch, Norse or otherwise, most of that work has been with what would more properly be termed the Landvaettir and Husvaettir, than with actual Dark Elves. The few journeys which I have braved to Svartalfheim have been to commune with the Dwarves, since I am myself an artisan. I feel comparatively safe among them; the Dark Elves, on the other hand, are another matter. Don't get me wrong: I tend to actually *enjoy* dark things; I'm a wee bit "goth", in fact. But there is a mystery to the Dark Elves which I personally find unsettling. Others' mileage may differ. I find it interesting that there is not a "direct connect" to Svartalfheim from Yggdrasil; that one must either have a milestone, or otherwise travel all the way across Vanaheim to get to this shadowed realm. As fulltrui of Freyja, I take that as a definite warning: it is as if Vanaheim rests between as a buffer of safety. The other side of Svartalfheim (the far west) connects directly onto the mundane world; hence the many alfholls and faerie rings encountered in legend, as well as reality. Elf-shot is a *reality*: it is neither accidental nor coincidental that it is encountered as a phenomenon in folk tales spanning continents, from Scandinavia to the British Isles and even to the Native Americans. Running afoul of the Dark Elves can leave a traveller in a bad way: potentially trapped either in Svartalfheim or even *between worlds*. Elf-shot can also have very real *physical ramifications*, ranging from persistent, otherwise un-medically-diagnosable shooting pains, to unexplained and debilitating melancholy in otherwise mentally healthy individuals, to inexplicable hair loss, and even an inability to eat. Be *warned*!

Jotunheim
Experience Level: Advanced
Milestone: Menglodh's Shrine at Gastropnir Gate

A shrine to Freyja might be the last thing one would expect to find at the gate of Jotunheim, yet there one stands. Menglodh: "She Who Is Pleased With Her Necklace". Standing at the shrine, the River Ifing courses noisily behind, beneath the shadows of Yggdrasil's boughs. We make an offering here, that we may be protected once we pass within: perfume or pearls; rose petals or sweet juice poured in blot. It is wise to make a physical offering before even faring-forth; the astral offering may be an echo of the physical one. Once the offering is made, the gate crunches open with the grainy groan of stone against stone. Welcome to Jotunheim.

I have often described Jotunheim in much the same language some use to describe the Australian Outback: not everything here wants to harm you, just *most* of them do! That may be a bit intense or unfair, however. *Harm* is a very strong word, packed with intent, and the majority of denizens of Jotunheim have no more full *intent* to harm than do a pride of lions on the African Savannah. Yet, accidents *do* and *can* happen here, so tread carefully. Passing through the Gastropnir, one is faced with a choice: ascend northwards, into the mountains, or southwards into the Iron Wood. Of course, there is also the road straight ahead, which leads to the great city of Utgard, which is effectively the capital of Jotunheim. Not everything here is unpleasant, however. The "opening area" of Jotunheim is Glaesisvellir, the Glittering Plain, wherein lies Udainsakr, the Deathless Plain. The "people" here are quite pleasant, and I have often wondered if this were Gerdha's hometown. It's a peaceful place to pass the time, with crystalline trees, jewel-like flowers, and grasses reminiscent of jade. Beyond it, and to the north, high in the mountains, one encounters Thrynheim, the home of the Goddess Skadi, the second wife of Njordr. Beyond Her mountain home, as one travels southwards (and downwards) towards Utgard and the Iron Wood, one must fjord the River Vimur. If, however, one decides to travel southwards from just beyond the gate, one may pass into the Iron Wood more easily. This is the home of Angrbodha and Her kin, the Iron Wood Clan. *Do not* expect the denizens of the Iron Wood to "play nice"! Showing an ounce of fear may have *dire* consequences, and the denizens of the Iron Wood *will* test your fears. Werewolf-like shape-shifters who are often extremely androgynous, the denizens of the Iron Wood have many lessons to teach about becoming *hamramr* ("shape-strong"), but such lessons come at a *price*, so be prepared to pay handsomely for such knowledge. They also have much to teach about *balance*: of the masculine and feminine; of the Light and the Dark. Those lessons, likewise, do not come cheaply. I would recommend visiting Utgard proper to *no one*, no matter *how* advanced one might think oneself. If an explanation of *why not* is required, I would recommend reading about Thor's own experiences there. Always keep in mind, while moving through Jotunheim, that this is a place where a fire might not actually be a fire; it might be a *Being*, with its own *sentience*. Likewise with mountains, or trees. Treat everything and everyone here with respect, or else. As with Svartalfheim, the far eastern edge of Jotunheim connects directly onto the mundane world, explaining how its denizens often wind up here, in our world, with such great ease.

Helheim
Experience Level: Beginner, Advanced
Milestone: Beaches of the Southern Shore

The vast swath of sandy beach gives way on both sides to rocks—to the right, a rocky coastline that draws in tidal pools and causes waves to crash with an almost deafening splendor; to the left, rocks which rise to cliffsides, dotted with the lights of homes set among their heights. Seabirds call from the rookeries among the rocks both night and day. Welcome to Helheim.

I have maintained a cliffside home along the northern coast of Helheim for twenty-three years. Though I visit it seldom these days, busy as I am at life, it gives me great comfort simply knowing it's there. That's the wonderful thing about Helheim, and a thing which I think often gets lost in translation: this is not a place of damnation or sorrow, but a place of eternal *comfort* for most of the Dead, which should be equally *comforting* to the living, because most of us will wind up there, someday. Certainly, there are places *deeper* into Helheim where few mortals dare to tread, and even those, such as Nastrond, which we should *fear*, but for the most part, Helheim is as comforting and welcoming as an idyllic image of the suburbs in 1950s America. Which is why, for many of its denizens and visitors, that has become the colloquial name of this realm: "*The Suburbs*". The outer, most easily-visited region of Helheim isn't all beaches and cliffsides, however. As one climbs that outer bank to reach the mainland, one encounters a kaleidoscope of locales which can be at first disorienting. The Dead are encouraged to make their eternal dwelling place uniquely their own: this leads to the effect of feeling as if one is traveling the globe in but a few steps. One moment, you might seem to be standing before a villa in the South of France, and a few moments later, outside a tall brownstone on the streets of Boston.

We are told in Gylfaginning 34:

Hela was thrown into Niflheim (Helheim) and (Odin) gave Her control over the Nine Worlds, that She be bound to decide the food and lodging (of) all of those, who to Her were sent, and that (would be those or would include those) dead of sickness (literally: sick-dead) and dead of old age (literally: age-dead).--Translation Mine

In other words, Helheim was designated, from the very beginning, as a place of *peace and hospitality* for the Dead (especially those who had died *innocently*, through sickness or age), with Hela *oathbound* to make sure those Dead receive what they *need* and *want* in the afterlife. Traveling further west or east than the heavily residential area of Helheim, however, is ill-advised for the student driver. The good news is, once you reach the "point of no return", or the point of more advanced travel, you will be met by bridges and guardians who will advise you to turn around, or negotiate the conditions of your deeper passage. At the center of this residential region, you will find the *Helvegr*—the Hel-Road—which bisects Helheim from east to west into a northern and southern half. Crossing the *Helvegr* is not advised for the Beginner Traveller, as those on the southern side generally are quite settled in the afterlife, with zero desire to interact with the still-living, generally for their own individual reasons. Many of the residents of "Southern Helheim" were suicides in life, or otherwise died courtesy of the cruelty of the mundane world. Not to worry: one cannot simply "wander across" the *Helvegr* unwittingly: there is a very large fence, variously called *Helgrindr*, *Nagrindr*, or *Valgrindr* in the Lore. "Southern Helheim" is, quite effectively, a *gated* community. The Advanced Traveller who wishes to visit "Southern Helheim" should continue westward down the *Helvegr* until reaching the River Gjoll, which is spanned by the bridge, *Gjallarbru*, and is guarded by Modgudr (aka Uriel in other Traditions, and, consequently, *not* a Jotun, but one of the Alfar). It is best to have a very detailed explanation of precisely *why* one wishes to disturb the denizens of "Southern Helheim" prepared for Modgudr. Even with such an entreaty prepared, one may still be denied passage. Modgudr must also be reasoned with to travel past the *Gjallarbru* onto "Hela's doorstep", for Her Hall lies just beyond the *Gjallarbru*, as does the only gate into "Southern Helheim". Either way, the still-living are not permitted across the *Gjallarbru* without an escort. At the other end of the *Helvegr*, one finds *Nastrond*. It is rare that *any* member of the still-living be permitted to visit this one place in the Nine Worlds that is designated *exclusively* for the *punishment* of the *criminal dead*, but those seeking entry, for whatever reason, must likewise pose their entreaties to Modgudr at the *Gjallarbru*. Unescorted journeys to *Nastrond* simply *never happen*. What happens in *Nastrond*? Those who have been judged guilty at the seat of Forsetti and Tyr in Glitnir (in Asgard) are fed to Nidhogg, the Dragon who writhes beneath the roots of the World Tree, Yggdrasil. That's it: *The End*. Except occasionally, the *criminal dead* escape, and make their way to Ginnungagap....

You may have noticed, by this point, that this Traveller's Notebook of the Nine Worlds is "two worlds shy of nine". This is because there are two worlds to which we *never, ever seek to travel*: Ginnungagap and Muspelheim. Both of these realms lie dangerously close to our own mundane world, which is why we make every effort to protect ourselves before faring-forth at all. To attempt to travel *directly* to either of these is *pure insanity*. Muspelheim, in fact, is not its "own world", in the strictest sense of that term, at all. It's more of a "half-world"; a "warning region", if you will; a wall of mist and fire that tells us "*turn around, or else!*". It is basically a "Neutral Zone" surrounding and penetrating Ginnungagap,with all that those two words imply. If hearing those words immediately conjures the words *Kobayashi Maru* in your mind, you've got the right idea: Muspelheim and Ginnungagap are very *real* no-win scenarios. Keep them, *and* the denizens that live there, well *outside your fence!*

As you become more adept at traveling the Worlds, you may find yourself creating new **milestones**, that you may reach frequently-visited locations even more quickly and easily. While I hope to cover all of the varieties of faring-forth in even greater detail in a future book, I feel that I would be remiss if I did not at least provide a "quick and dirty" explanation of further **milestone creation** within these pages. Basically, a suitable **milestone** location is a *safe zone* which is easily visualized at a moment's notice. What do I mean by *safe zone*? A *safe zone* is a location that you have frequented often enough to know that you will not be *immediately* assailed, assaulted, or otherwise *bothered* (this includes immediately being engaged in friendly conversation) upon your arrival in that place. Even for the seasoned traveller, the initial arrival in an astral location can be a wee bit discombobulating, for lack of a better word. We all need our first moments there to facilitate gathering ourselves, "making sure we have our everything", and making sure we actually wound up where we were heading! Using *safe zones* as **milestones** also affords a traveller those valuable first moments to make certain that all personal wards are intact and operative before faring any further forth.

A **Vanaheim Utiseta** follows, which I encourage you to use for your first official outing, and which I hope will also provide a suitable example for creating your own future utiseta to reach other locations in the Nine Worlds. This Utiseta should be read in its *entirety* and you should be *fully familiar* with all that it contains *before* faring-forth. Once you have graduated from the level of student driver, you will likely find that you require something as formal as an utiseta less and less. While you should be wholeheartedly congratulated on such progress, it would be highly irresponsible if I did not here post a reminder: ***always* make sure you are *fully warded* before faring-forth!** Over time, your personal *pop-ward* which radiates from your *hamr* itself *will* strengthen to a point that you may not require a full laying of the fence before every journey. However, ***always*** make sure that your "purple layer" is live, well-maintained, and at the ready.

Vanaheim Utiseta

Ground and Center.

Seeker, Maker, Believer (insert your own Self-
    Archetypes here):
My feet are on the ground;
I stand firm.
I am of the earth, and the earth is of me;
I stand firm.
I center myself, and I hold.
So it is, and so it shall be.

Lay The Fence.

Outside the fire,
Darkness;
Darkness outside the Grove;
Outside there dwell shadows;
Shadows inside us as well.
Inside, outside, everywhere,
Where'er you dwell,
Dwell not here:
Here is light and all good things!
Light and Bright Wisdom protect us;
Protect us from those who dwell outside.

Hallow The Space.

Enter Utiseta with your Taufr

(The Taufr should be held gently in your hands in your lap.
Do not lie down. Lying down can make it too tempting to
fall asleep, instead of actually accomplishing the work that
is to be done.)

Call The Dyr-Andi

(This is intended to provide you not only with added
protection, but also with a *focal spirit*, who can assist you
in getting "out of body".)

Spirit of (name the animal),
I set you to guard
This space,
My home,
My person,
And those whom I hold dear:
From *fjandar*,
From ill-meaning wights,
From those who mean to do us harm.
With the able help of the Aesir and Vanir,
I set you to guard
This space,
My home,
My person,
And those whom I hold dear:
From *fjandar*,
From ill-meaning wights,
From those who mean to do us harm.
So it is, and so it shall be.

Call To Your Fulltrui/Fulltrua

(If you are not yet fulltrui or fulltrua of a Deity, you may
substitute Heimdall instead. This is also intended not only
as yet another layer of *protection*, but also to provide you
with another ally to assist you in getting out of body.)

(Fulltrui, Fulltrua, or Heimdall):
I beg your presence;
I plead your protection;
I ask you to guard and assist.
Protect my Four Parts:
Hugr, Hamr, Fylgja, and Hamingja,
And let no ill befall me:
Not from *fjandar*,
Nor from ill-meaning wights,
Nor from any others who mean to do me harm.
Hold my hand and help me
Draw closer to Your realms.
So let it be, let it be, and so, let it be.

With eyes closed, focus your attention on the energy of the animal which your *taufr* represents. Feel it embodied within the *taufr*. A soft, white glow begins to emit, as if a smoky light from within the *taufr*; allow it to rise and coalesce into the form of your *dyr-andi*. It may move to interact with you, or it may stand watch nearby. Let it do as it will.

Shift your focus to your *hamr*. Find your *distinguishing feature* from the previous **Skin-Strong Exercise**. Raise the appendage on which the *distinguishing feature* exists to physical eye level, and *without* opening your eyes, *see* that appendage, including "your spot". Focus your entire attention on "your spot". Slowly infuse it with cool, white light which feels like a soothing liquid welling up through the skin. This should be a pleasant sensation. As you focus, you should begin to *physically feel* this soothing sensation on your actual *physical skin* at the point of "your spot". Now radiate this white light outwards from "your spot", until it envelopes your *entire* body. *Hold* the light for a few moments. Now, slowly change the color of the light to purple, with an accompanying feeling of hardening (this should also be a pleasant sensation). As you focus, you should begin to likewise *physically feel* this on your actual *physical skin*. Draw this purple light back down to "your spot", understanding that this is effectively a *pop-up ward attached* to your *hamr*, and then slowly return the white light to the entirety of your *hamr*. Your *hamr* is now "set" or *hlaut* (set-apart), from the rest of your Four Parts, and ready to take your *first step. Without physically moving*, stand with *hamr only. Do not look down* at your physical body, where it remains in the seated position! This is often too much of a shock for first-time travelers, and can quickly set your *hugr* into a whirl that will create the effect of a sort of "spiritual tornado", which will effectively "reel in" your *hamr* and basically *slam* you back into-body. Now, take *one step forward* from your present location with your *hamr*. Take note of how everything *feels* and how everything in the room you are in *looks*, as you stand there as *hamr* only. How does your *dyr-andi* react? Can you see your fulltrui/fulltrua, or Heimdall? (Don't worry if you cannot, or if your *dyr-andi* seems totally unimpressed.) Inform your *dyr-andi* and *fulltrui, fulltrua*, or *Heimdall* that you intend to spend *no more* than a half hour and *no less* than fifteen minutes in Vanaheim, upon your arrival there, and that you understand that when they tell you it is *time to go,* it is *time to go.* Stand for another count of five, and then *close your hamr-eyes* and visualize golden fields stretching westward from the base of Yggdrasil. Feel the wind on your face; smell the scent of ripe grain and horses on the air. *Open your hamr-eyes.* (You may feel a sudden *rush* as you do so; this is a signal of your *arrival.*) In the distance may be heard the pounding of hooves. This steady pounding draws closer, revealing a herd of many-colored horses: chestnuts and paints; buckskins and bays; greys and blacks, their faces flecked with foam; manes and tails streaming in the gentle, steady breezes of Vanaheim. You may wish to get caught up in the flow of the thundering herd. They will invariably lead you either north, to the Hall of Noatan, Njordr's Hall, or south, to Folkvangr and Sessrumnir. You may also find that your *dyr-andi* is suddenly quite talkative, with very definite ideas about which direction you should go. If so, listen and follow. Do not be surprised if you suddenly find yourself visited by beloved lost pets. Spend time with them; they've earned it. In whichever direction you should choose to travel, the most important thing is to *not go past* the verge of the Great Western Wood. When you have concluded your visit, ask your *dyr-andi* to lead you back to the base of Yggdrasil. You will then *sit down* at the base of the World Tree, and begin bringing your *hamr* back *into* your physical body. Slowly radiate the purple light and the hardening back over your entire *hamr*, until you can *physically feel* this on your actual *physical skin*. *Hold* this light for several moments, and then slowly replace it with the cool, white light once more. When you can feel this as well on your *physical skin*, slowly draw it back down into "your spot", and then allow it to slowly fade. Open your eyes and return fully to physical sensation *slowly*. Do not be alarmed if you feel winded, dizzy, or mildly out-of-sorts. When you have fully regained yourself, and feel strong enough to do so, break utiseta.

Break Utiseta

Give Gratitude to Your Dyr-Andi and Fulltrui/Fulltrua/Heimdall

Allow Your Dyr-Andi to Return Whence It Came (via Taufr)

Raise The Fence

Center and Ground.

At the foot of Yggdrasil,
My heart set forth to walk:
To worlds and between,
It set forth to go,
Knowledge to gain,
And friends to know.
Midgard-Realm to Vanaheim,
Golden-fielded Folvangr;
Seabirds called along the coasts of Helheim's shore.
I left my offerings at Gastropnir;
Poured blot to Menglodh Fair,
And at day's end I found myself
At the foot of the Spiral Stair.
From Svartalfheim-deep
To Asgard-high,
My hamr travelled there,
And when I woke
From sleep-not-sleep,
I found myself not wearied.
For though I travelled far and deep,
In wonders had I gloried.

Freeing Baldur

Straight away were the Aesir all at Thing (official
 gathered assembly)
And the Aesir Goddesses all at conference,
And (so it was) the Gods ruled (with) authority,
Why was Baldur (having) baleful dreams?

Up rose Odin, the old enchanter,
And He on Sleipnir a saddle laid;
Rode He down from there, Niflheim (Helheim) to
 obtain;
Met He the whelp, that one who out of Helheim
comes.

It was bloody (all over its) forward breast
And Galdr-Father (Odin) howled (to it) across the
 distance;
Onward rode Odin, earth resounding;
He came at last to Helheim.

Then rode Odin in the eastern door,
There, He knew, the witch's grave;
He captured (her) skill in magick, speak(ing)
 death-galdr,
Until against her will she rose, (her) corpse
speaking concerning (her) speech:

"What? Who is this man, to me unknown,
Who to me has increased (my) burdensome
      disposition?
I was sniffing snow and smitten with rain
And driving dew; long was I dead."

Odin spoke:

"'Accustomed to Long Journeys' am I called, son of
      The Slain Warrior;
Speak to me out of Helheim, I will (you) out of
      (your) home:
For whom are the benches ringed (in) affirmation
      (as for a funeral),
The seating-boards of the hall beautifully deluged
      (with) gold?"

The Witch spoke:

"Here stands Baldur for (whom) mead (is)
      brewed,
Bright-clear powerful, (a) shield laid over,
But the power of the Gods is a prideful spirit;
Against my will, I spoke, now shall I be silent."

Odin spoke:

"Do not be silent, witch, you will teach me
Until (it is) known, will I yet find out:
Who will be the death of my Baldur
And Odin's son deprive of life?"

The Witch spoke:

"Hodhr bears the tall fateful-branch thither,
He shall be the death of Your Baldur
And Odin's son deprive of life;
Against my will, I spoke, now shall I be silent."

Norse Witch

Odin spoke:

"Do not be silent, witch, you will teach me
Until (it is) known, will I yet find out:
What my revenge over Hodhr's vengeful work
Or Baldur's killer smote upon the fire?"

The Witch spoke:

"Rind bears Vali in western halls,
Who will Odin's son one night fight:
His hands he shall wash not nor his hair comb,
Before to the fire is borne Baldur's enemy;
Against my will, I spoke, now shall I be silent."

Odin spoke:

"Do not be silent, witch, you will teach me
Until (it is) known, will I yet find out:
Who are these maidens, who will weep
And to the sky cast the corners of the ship's sails?"

The Witch spoke:

"'Accustomed to Long Journeys' you are not, as I
          suspected,
Rather you are Odin, the old enchanter."

Odin spoke:

"You are no witch nor wise woman,
Rather you are the mother of three monsters (i.e.,
          Angrbodha)."

The Witch spoke:

"Home ride you, Odin, and remain proud,
Thus come no more, man, after intelligence,
Until Loki's limbs are loosed from His bondage
And Ragnarok's reavers are come."

--Baldur's Dreams, Translation Mine

The first time I saw His face was at Yule-tide. Many of the Dead make the trek to Asgard for Yule: it is, after all, a time for celebration and joy, and where better to celebrate joy than at the "capital" of the Nine Worlds, in Asgard? Like Samhain, Yule has traditionally been considered a time when the veil between the worlds is thin: a time when faeries are afoot, and the Dead fare-forth. This has echoed down through the ages to us, in tales of the Wild-Hunt. In fact, that particular wild ride is part of the genesis of the stories of Santa Claus journeying across the night sky in his sleigh pulled by eight tiny reindeer. But I digress: as I said, the first time I saw Baldur's face was at Yule-tide, in Asgard.

Modern gnosis of Baldur seems to suggest that He still resides in Helheim, waiting for Loki to be released from His bondage, as foretold by the witch (who wasn't really a dead-witch at all, but instead, Angrbodha, first wife of Loki, and mother of Hela, Jormungandr, and Fenris) in Baldur's Dreams (Baldur Draumar). I can't seem to fathom why this is the case: how is it that people willingly blame Loki on a daily basis for things as random and annoying as their computers breaking, or their dog's weird behavior, yet Baldur is still supposedly in Helheim? Clearly, Loki has been loosed, according to modern gnosis, and yet, Baldur has not? How does that even *make sense*?

Perhaps the reticence to *free Baldur* comes from the innate tendency among modern Heathens to shun anything that remotely smacks of a Christ-like figure within the Northern Tradition. I mean, if we have one at all, Baldur is certainly Him. We are told in Stanzas 61-66 of the Voluspa:

There shall after many wondrous lies
Be found golden tables in the grass:
Those ones which in days of yore belonged to the
Aesir.

There will be many well-sewn fields to grow,
Disasters shall all get better, Baldur will come;
And He and His brother, Hodhr, shall dwell in
Odin's Hall of Victory,
Sanctuary of the slain Gods (Valhalla). Would you
know yet more, or what?

Then know that Hoenir shall choose the sacred
twig,
And the Sons of Odin shall dwell in Vanaheim,

*Fetching wood. Would you know yet more, or
    what?*

*Baldur's Hall shall stand better than the Sun,
Golden-thatched upon Gimle;
There shall good and trusted people dwell,
And throughout the ages relish joy.*

*There comes in the kingdom such mighty spells,
Powerful from above, (from) He who counsels
    everyone (i.e., Baldur).*

*But there comes the dusty-dragon flying,
Gleaming snake, below from the Moor of No Moon
    (literally: Nidhafjollum);
Bare of feathers—yet he flies the world over--
Nidhogg comes near. Now I shall sink.*

--Translation Mine

Now, I'm sure many people will read that, and still gear up for that age-old whine of "but Snorri was notorious for Christian grafting", but his use of the distinct words *regindomi* and *hlautvidhr* in the third and fifth stanzas suggests *profoundly* otherwise. The Norse word *regindomi* literally means "mighty spells", and it is likely (at least, I hope) that the word *hlaut* in *hlautvidhr* speaks for itself: *hlautvidhr* literally translates to "sacred/set apart twig or piece of wood". In other words, *a wand* or *wands*. So let's cut through all of this flowery, poetic language, and look at what these passages really say, shall we?

> After the betrayal of Baldur and after the great war of the Gods (Ragnarok), the Aesir and Vanir will return to Asgard to find a banquet already laid for them. The fields will be full of growing things again, disasters will stop happening, and *Baldur will return to Asgard*. There, He and Hodhr will often hang out in Valhalla, letting "bygones be bygones", and behaving as brothers once more. Then Hoenir (the brother of Odin who helped create the first humans and then instilled in them poetic inspiration,

intellect, spiritual ecstasy, and the potential for battle frenzy) will choose *wands* for the Brothers, and send Them off to Vanaheim to find the wood to *craft* those *wands*. Baldur's Hall, Breidhablik, will shine brightly again on the hilltop of Gimle. Why is it shining brightly? Because it is *once again inhabited* by Baldur! Which means He can welcome good and trusty people into His Hall, and all of those people can live there forever, and be happy forever. But Baldur won't be just sitting up on some dais somewhere, welcoming folks into His Hall, He will also be *using* that *wand* that Hoenir sent Him off to find to perform *mighty spells* which won't only be felt in Asgard, but which will *stream down to us on earth*. That doesn't mean that "nasty things" will never happen again on earth or anywhere else in the Nine Worlds, though: Nidhogg the Dragon is still very much alive and well, and in full flight, rather than napping full-time in Nastrond.

In short, someone as ostensibly notorious for Christian grafting as Good Ole Snorri allegedly was would likely not have taken too kindly to using the "language of witches" (*regindomi*; *hlautvidhr*), even in an attempt to somehow regale Baldur with inklings of Christ! Therefore, I believe the "Christian grafting" that is actually occurring here is distinctly *our own*—the stuff of *modern people*—and therefore, not Snorri's fault, at all. On the contrary, I believe what Snorri was attempting to communicate here was a much larger *shamanic truth*: that Ragnarok is *not* something which *will happen*, or even that *has happened*, but instead something which *happens again and again*. *Within* that *cyclic destruction,* there is also a system of *cyclic rebirth*. Baldur may be understood as the *embodiment* of that system of *cyclic rebirth*, in exactly the same way as Christ, or Shiva, or Lleu-Llaw-Gyffes. In every culture, if one looks hard enough, they will find a face of that *embodiment* of *cyclic rebirth*; ours just happens to belong to Baldur.

The concept of a *free Baldur* is also a promise that, no matter how bad things get, things will always get *better*: every action has an equal and opposite reaction. That's basic physics, after all, isn't it? Why wouldn't—better yet, *why shouldn't*—we want to believe that? How is it that many people are marginally *obsessed* with the concept of Ragnarok, yet gloss over or entirely miss the last six stanzas of the *Voluspa*, or, worse still, chalk them up to yet more of "Snorri's Christian grafting"? What sort of an actual *faith base* does that form? The "live to die another day" metaphor runs far too rampant through the heart of modern Heathenry, it would seem, with far more emphasis on the "die another day" half of that equation, and not *enough* on the "live" portion at the beginning of that statement. Too many people, it would seem, are perfectly willing to be living to die, while too few are dying to live.

Over the course of the past twenty-four years, I've had some *major* issues with Christianity, many of which I've detailed in the previous pages of this book. I can, therefore, completely understand the hesitance (nay, even the outright *disgust*) of some people, when faced with the very *possibility* that there even *might* be a "Christ-like figure" within the Northern Tradition. But He's there, and His name is Baldur, and the first time I saw His face was at Yule-tide in Asgard.

You cannot change the faces you've known, nor erase the lives that you, yourself, have touched, and that have perhaps touched yours in return. You cannot take even one of those faces back, and unmeet it. Sometimes that is for good; others, notsomuch. Finding Baldur changed the course of my life; changed the way I believe; changed the way I meet the sun in the morning, and changed the way I lay my head down at night to sleep. That He resides in Breidhablik once more, in Asgard, means that ultimately, even Loki wept. Eventually we *all do*. I know I've shed my share of tears, and I'm sure that you have, too. Knowing Baldur's face taught me the very important truth that even through the tears, the sun shines, because *through* tears, the Son shines: Baldur Odinson. Hope is *in there*: it is *in* our lore, as deeply interwoven as it is in the gravesites of our Ancestors. A people with *zero hope* does not bury their dead with mountains of grave-goods! And it *should* be as deeply enmeshed in our own Heidrinn hearts. Yet, most will gladly blame the free Loki, but shy away from looking for a *free Baldur*. And yet I saw His face. I pray that someday, you will, too.

Radiant Baldur,
I give you my tears
That they may shine
Instead of drown my feeble heart.
Teach me to be impenetrable;
Skin-hardened,
Yet Heart-bright.
Make of me a beacon
To shine in the darkness
Of this world,
And all others.

Index of Rites, Invocations, & Meditations

Bibliography

*Note: Throughout the text of this book, the Norse character ð has been replaced with "dh", in an effort towards an easier understanding of the pronunciation by non-native readers (pronounced as "th" at the end of the word "math"). This convention persists in the bibliography.

Sources are listed alphabetically within each chapter division, in an effort to encourage further reading, as well as provide factual context.

Sources Used Throughout:

A. Richard Diebold Center for Indo-European Language and Culture, Linguistics Research Center, The University of Texas at Austin, Old Norse Online Base Form Dictionary, Jonathan Slocum and Todd B. Krause, http://www.utexas.edu/cola/depts/lrc/eieol/norol-BF.html

Abramiuk, Marc A. *The Foundations of Cognitive Archaeology*. MIT Press, 2012.

An Icelandic-English dictionary / initiated by Richard Cleasby, subsequently revised, enlarged and completed by Gudbrand Vigfusson, M.A. Oxford : Clarendon Press, first edition 1874, second edition 1957. ISBN:9910360675

Arthur, Ross G. English-Old Norse Dictionary, www.yorku.ca/inpar/language/English-Old_Norse.pdf

Byock, Jesse L., Viking Language 1, Jules William Press, © 2013, ISBN 9781480216440

Dictionary by Merriam-Webster: America's Most-Trusted Online Dictionary." *Merriam-Webster*, Merriam-Webster, www.merriam-webster.com/.

Gordon, E.V., *An Introduction to Old Norse*, Oxford University Press; 2 edition (July 23, 1981), ISBN: 9780198111849

Peterson, Eugene H.*The Message*. NavPress, 2004.

Price, Neil S. *The Viking Way: Religion and War in Late Iron Age Scandinavia*. Oxbow, 2007.

Northern Lights:

Kvilhaug, Maria. "Burning the Witch! – The Initiation of the Goddess and the War of the Aesir and the Vanir." Freyia Völundarhúsins, 2011, freya.theladyofthelabyrinth.com/?page_id=206.

"Monolatry." Monolatry | Kemet.org. Accessed 1 November 2017. www.kemet.org/taxonomy/term/124.

Motz, Lotte. 1993b. "Gullveig's Ordeal: A New Interpretation." *Arkiv för nordisk filologi* 108:80-92.

Paxson, Diana. "Heiðe: Witch-Goddess of the North." Hrafnar, 1993, hrafnar.org/articles/dpaxson/asynjur/heide/.

Simek, Rudolf (trans. Angela Hall) 1996: *Dictionary of Northern Mythology*, D. S. Brewer, Cambridge.

God(s) Enter By A Private Door:

Africa v. Commonwealth of Pennsylvania, 662 F.2d 1025, 1031-32 (3rd Cir.1981)

Wong, T.P., PhD., *Existential Positive Psychology: The Six Ultimate Questions of Human Existence*. Encyclopedia of Positive Psychology 2008, Ed. Shane J. Lopez, Wiley-Blackwell (Publisher)

The Calling:

Lee, Bruce. 1975. *Tao of Jeet Kune Do*. Burbank, Calif: Ohara Publications.

Godfinding:

Tacitus, C., Mattingly, H., Rives, J. B., *Agricola; Germania*. London, Penguin, 2009.

Finding Odin:

Bauschatz, P. C., *The Well and The Tree: World and Time In Early Germanic Culture*. Amherst, University of Massachusetts Press, 1982.

Worlds Within Worlds:

Belanger, Michelle, *Psychic Dreamwalking: Explorations at the Edge of Self*, Weiser Books, Weiser Books, 205 pp. (incl. appendices, excl. Bibliography), 2006

de Vries, J., *Altnordisches Etymologisches Worterbuch* Library Binding, Brill Academic Pub; Revised edition (August 1, 1997)

Lindow, John.*Norse Mythology: a Guide to the Gods, Heroes, Rituals, and Beliefs*. Oxford University Press, 2002.

Penczak, Christopher, *Spirit Allies: Meet Your Team From The Other Side*, Weiser Books, 2001

Good Versus Evil:

Aurelius, Marcus, *Meditations* (Dover Thrift Editions), Dover Publications (July 11, 1997)

Molaro, S., Holland, S., & Reynolds, J. (Writers) & Cendrowski, M. (Director). (2017) The Allowance Evaporation [Television series episode]. In C. Lorre (Producer), *The Big Bang Theory*. Burbank, CA: Warner Brothers.

Newton, Isaac, *The Principia: Mathematical Principles of Natural Philosophy,* Snowball Publishing 2010

Parks, W. (Producer) & Scott, R. (Director). (2000) *Gladiator* [Motion Picture]. United States: Scott Free Productions for Dreamworks Pictures.

Tolkien, J.R.R. *The Return of the King*. New York: Houghton Mifflin Company, 1994.

Jormungandr:

Blewitt, Kevin. "On Sacrifice Reconciling Sacrifice in the Saga of Hakon the Good." University of Oslo, Reprosentralen, 2014, pp. 1–91.

Carlie, Anne. "Archaeology and Ritual: A Case Study on Traces of Ritualisation in Archaeological Remains from Lindangelund, Southern Sweden." *Folklore: Electronic Journal of Folklore*, vol. 55, 2013, pp. 49–68.

Chatwin, Bruce. *The Songlines*. Viking/Penguin, 1987.

Eriksen, Marianne Hem (2013). "Doors to the Dead. The Power of Doorways and Thresholds in Viking Age Scandinavia." *Archaeological Dialogues*, 20, pp 187-214

Lidov, Alexei. "Hierotopy. The Creation of Sacred Spaces as a Form of Creativity and Subject of Cultural History" in *Hierotopy. Creation of Sacred Spaces in Byzantium and Medieval Russia*, ed. A.Lidov, Moscow: Progress-Tradition, 2006, pp. 32-58

Lund, Julie. "Banks, Borders and Bodies of Water in a Viking Age Mentality." *Journal of Wetland Archaeology*, vol. 8, no. 1, 2008, pp. 53–72.

Otto, R. (Author), Harvey, John W. (Translator), *The Idea of the Holy 2nd Edition*, Oxford University Press; 2 edition, 1958.

Penczak, Christopher, *The Living Temple of Witchcraft Volume Two: The Journey of the God* (Penczak Temple Series) Paperback , Llewellyn Publications; First Edition, 2009.

Prehal, Brenda. "Perspectives on Recent Viking Age Finds in. Þegjandadalur North Iceland." Hunter College of the City University of New York, 2011.

Ritual Objects; Sacred Tools:

"A Seeress from Fyrkat?" National Museum of Denmark, en.natmus.dk/historical-knowledge/denmark/prehistoric-period-until-1050-ad/the-viking-age/religion-magic-death-and-rituals/a-seeress-from-fyrkat/.

Blewitt, Kevin. "On Sacrifice Reconciling Sacrifice in the Saga of Hakon the Good." University of Oslo, Reprosentralen, 2014, pp. 1–91.

Carlie, Anne. "Archaeology and Ritual: A Case Study on Traces of Ritualisation in Archaeological Remains from Lindangelund, Southern Sweden." *Folklore: Electronic Journal of Folklore*, vol. 55, 2013, pp. 49–68.

Davidson, Hilda Roderick Ellis. 1964 *Gods and Myths of Northern Europe*. Baltimore, MD: Penguin.

Hedenstierna-Jonson, Charlotte. "A Group of Viking Age Sword Chapes Reflecting the Political Geography of the Time." *Journal of Nordic Archaeological Scien*ce, vol. 13, 2002, pp. 103–112.

Klein, Sebastian L. "Seidhr & Shamans: Defining the Myth of Ritual Specialists in Pre-Christian Scandinavia." Norwegian University of Science and Technology, 2015.

Lloyd, Ellen. "Mysterious Ancient Grave With Unusual Artifacts That Belonged To A Völva – Norse Female Shamans Did Exist." Ancient Pages, 2 July 2017, www.ancientpages.com/2017/07/02/mysterious-ancient-grave-unusual-artifacts-belonged-volva-norse-female-shamans-exist/.

Lund, Julie. "Connectedness with Things. Animated Objects of Viking Age Scandinavia and Early Medieval Europe." *Archaeological Dialogues*, vol. 24, no. 01, 2017, pp. 89–108

Penczak, Christopher. *The Mystic Foundation: Understanding & Exploring the Magical Universe*. Llewellyn Publications, 2006.

Penczak, Christopher. *The Inner Temple of Witchcraft: Magick, Meditation, and Psychic Development*. Llewellyn Publications, 2014.

Prehal, Brenda. "Perspectives on Recent Viking Age Finds in. Þegjandadalur North Iceland." Hunter College of the City University of New York, 2011.

Price, Neil. "The Archaeology of Seidhr: Circumpolar Traditions in Viking Pre-Christian Religion." *Vinland Revisited: The Norse World at the Turn of the First Millennium*, HSANL, St. John's, 2004, pp. 277-294.

Vance, Erik. "Unlocking The Healing Power of You." *National Geographic*, Dec. 2016.

Wight-Walking:

Andrews, Ted. *Animal-Speak: the Spiritual & Magical Powers of Creatures Great & Small*. Llewellyn Publications, 2015.

Bellamy-Dagneau, Karyn. "A Falconer's Ritual: A Study of the Cognitive and Spiritual Dimensions of Pre-Christian Scandinavian Falconry." University of Iceland, *Skemmen*, 2015.

Bernd, Heinrich. *The Mind of the Raven*. Harper Perennial, 1999, 2006, ISBN 978-0-06-113605-4

Bourns, Timothy. "The Language of Birds in Old Norse Tradition." University of Iceland, Háskóli Íslands: Hugvísindasvið Medieval Icelandic Studies, 2012.

Dale, Robert T.D. "Berserkir: A Re-Examination of the Phenomenon in Literature and in Life." University of Nottingham, 2014.

Dutton, Douglas R. *An Encapsulation of Óðinn: Religious belief and ritual practice among the Viking Age elite with particular focus upon the practice of ritual hanging 500- 1050 AD.* Aberdeen: Centre for Scandinavian Studies, 2015.

Frog, Etunimetön. "Volundr and the Bear in Norse Tradition." *Skáldamjöðurinn: Selected Proceedings of the UCL Graduate Symposia in Old Norse Literature and Philology*, 2005-2006, Centre for Northern Research, University College London, 2008, pp. 1–50.

Mundal, E. 2000. Coexistence of Saami and Norse culture – reflected in and interpreted by Old Norse myths. In G. Barnes & M. Clunies Ross (eds.), *Old Norse Myths, Literature and Society. Proceedings of the 11th International Saga Conference*: 346–55.Centre for Medieval studies, University of Sydney, Sydney, Australia.

Tolley, Clive. "Vordr and Gandr: Helping Spirits in Norse Magic." *Arkiv För Nordisk Filologi*, vol. 110, Lund University, 1995, pp. 57–75.

Angels Among Us: The Ancestors, The Alfar, and The Disir:

Bellamy-Dagneau, Karyn. "A Falconer's Ritual: A Study of the Cognitive and Spiritual Dimensions of Pre-Christian Scandinavian Falconry." University of Iceland, *Skemmen*, 2015.

Bourns, Timothy. "The Language of Birds in Old Norse Tradition." University of Iceland, Háskóli Íslands: Hugvísindasvið Medieval Icelandic Studies, 2012.

Davidson, Hilda Roderick Ellis. 1964 *Gods and Myths of Northern Europe*. Baltimore, MD: Penguin.

Davidson, Hilda Roderick Ellis. *The Road to Hel: a Study of the Conception of the Dead in Old Norse Literature*. Cambridge University Press, 2013.

Hall, Alaric. "The Meaning of Elf, and Elves, in Medieval England." *The Meaning of Elf, and Elves, in Medieval England*, University of Glasgow, 2005, www.alarichall.org.uk/phd.php. Chapter 2: An Old Norse Context

Hall, Alaric. *Elves in Anglo-Saxon England: Matters of Belief, Health, Gender and Identity,* "Chapter One: A Medieval Scandinavian Context.", Boydell Press, 2009, pp. 21–53.

Helmbrecht, Michaela. "A Winged Figure from Uppakra." *Forvannen: Journal of Swedish Antiquarian Research*, 2012, pp. 171–178.

Jakobsson, Ármann. "The Extreme Emotional Life of Völundr the Elf", *Scandinavian Studies*, Vol.78:3 (2006)

Penczak, Christopher. *The Mighty Dead: Communing with the Ancestors of Witchcraft*. Copper Cauldron Publishing, 2013.

Manifestation:

"A Seeress from Fyrkat?" National Museum of Denmark, en.natmus.dk/historical-knowledge/denmark/prehistoric-period-until-1050-ad/the-viking-age/religion-magic-death-and-rituals/a-seeress-from-fyrkat/.

Bildner, Martin, director. Norse Ethnomusicology Class: St. Cecilia at the Tower III. Youtube.com, 18 Aug. 2014, www.youtube.com/watch?v=aXGDvQL6pB0

Carlie, Anne. "Archaeology and Ritual: A Case Study on Traces of Ritualisation in Archaeological Remains from Lindangelund, Southern Sweden." *Folklore: Electronic Journal of Folklore*, vol. 55, 2013, pp. 49–68.

Church, Dawson. *EFT Mini-Manual*. EFT Mini-Manual, Energy Psychology Press, 2012.

DeHart, Savannah. (January 2012). "Bractreates as Indicators of Northern Pagan Religiosity in the Early Middle Ages", (Master's Thesis, East Carolina University). Retrieved from the Scholarship. (http://hdl.handle.net/10342/3978.)

Klein, Sebastian L. "Seiðr & Shamans: Defining the Myth of Ritual Specialists in Pre-Christian Scandinavia." Norwegian University of Science and Technology, 2015.

Lloyd, Ellen. "Mysterious Ancient Grave With Unusual Artifacts That Belonged To A Völva – Norse Female Shamans Did Exist." Ancient Pages, 2 July 2017, www.ancientpages.com/2017/07/02/mysterious-ancient-grave-unusual-artifacts-belonged-volva-norse-female-shamans-exist/.

Lorca, Federico Garcia. *Theory and Play of the Duende and Imagination, Inspiration, Evasion*. New Directions, 1981.

Lund, Julie. "Connectedness with Things. Animated Objects of Viking Age Scandinavia and Early Medieval Europe." *Archaeological Dialogues*, vol. 24, no. 01, 2017, pp. 89–108

Penczak, Christopher. *The Mystic Foundation: Understanding & Exploring the Magical Universe*. Llewellyn Publications, 2006.

Runelore:

Bildner, Martin, director. Norse Ethnomusicology Class: St. Cecilia at the Tower III. Youtube.com, 18 Aug. 2014, www.youtube.com/watch?v=aXGDvQL6pB0

Dumézil, Georges. *Mitra-Varuna: An Essay on Two Indo-European Representations of Sovereignty*. Translated by Derek Coltman, 1988.

Foster, Justin (Translator), "Huld Manuscript of Galdrastafir Witchcraft Magic Symbols and Runes." Academia.edu. Accessed 9 April 2017.

Foster, Justin. "Icelandic Magic Symbols (Galdrastafir) and Spell Books (Galdrabækur) - An Annotated English Translation." Academia.edu, 18 July 2015,

Looijenga, J. H. (1997). *Runes around the North Sea and on the Continent AD 150-700*; texts & contexts s.n.

Tauring, Kari C. *The Runes: A Human Journey*. Minneapolis: Kari Tauring, 2007

Tauring, Kari C. *Volva Stav Manual*. Minneapolis: Kari Tauring, 2010

Tjeerd, Jan. "10 Gifts of the Wyrd: Bindrunes." Gifts of the Wyrd RSS, Podbean, 17 Jan. 2017, giftsofthewyrd.podbean.com/e/bindrunes/.

Deepening Devotion:

Lafayllve, Patricia M. *A Practical Heathen's Guide to Asatru*. Llewellyn Publications, 2013.

Price, Neil S. *The Viking Way: Religion and War in Late Iron Age Scandinavia*. Oxbow, 2007.

The Hunter and The Hunted:

Carlie, Anne. "Archaeology and Ritual: A Case Study on Traces of Ritualisation in Archaeological Remains from Lindangelund, Southern Sweden." *Folklore: Electronic Journal of Folklore*, vol. 55, 2013, pp. 49–68.

Marianne Hem Eriksen (2013). Doors to the Dead. The Power of Doorways and Thresholds in Viking Age Scandinavia. *Archaeological Dialogues*, 20, pp 187-214

Lecouteux, Claude. *Phantom Armies of the Night: the Wild Hunt and Ghostly Processions of the Undead*. Inner Traditions, 2011.

Lund, J. (2005) Thresholds and Passages: The Meaning of Bridges and Crossings in the Viking Age and Early Middle Ages. *Viking and Medieval Scandinavia* 1:109-37

Prehal, Brenda. "Perspectives on Recent Viking Age Finds in. Þegjandadalur North Iceland." Hunter College of the City University of New York, 2011.

Thilderkvist, J. G. M. (2013). Ritual Bones or Common Waste: a Study of Early Medieval Bone Deposits in Northern Europe Groningen: s.n.

Faring-Forth:

Belanger, Michelle, *Psychic Dreamwalking: Explorations at the Edge of Self*, Weiser Books, Weiser Books, 205 pp. (incl. appendices, excl. Bibliography), 2006

de Vries, J., *Altnordisches Etymologisches Worterbuch* Library Binding, Brill Academic Pub; Revised edition (August 1, 1997)

Heide, Eldar, 2006: "Spirits Through Respiratory Passages." In John McKinnel et. al (eds.): The Fantastic in Old Norse / Icelandic Literature. Sagas and the British Isles. Preprint Papers of The 13th International Saga Conference, Durham and York, 6th-12th August, 2006. [Durham]: [University of Durham]. 350-58.

Lindow, John.*Norse Mythology: a Guide to the Gods, Heroes, Rituals, and Beliefs*. Oxford University Press, 2002.

Penczak, Christopher, *Spirit Allies: Meet Your Team From The Other Side*, Weiser Books, 2001

Where is the index?

Writing this book was an experience, and I wrote it in order for it to *be experienced*. Who am I, as the author, to tell you which things within this book should be important to you? No, better that you mark those things in your own way, that you may return to them again and again, as befits *your* learning and experiencing style. Free bookmarks are available via our Facebook page and website (see back cover). I pray this book will be of service to you for years to come. I hope you have enjoyed our walk together beneath the Northern Lights; I look forward to walking with you again.

Made in the USA
Columbia, SC
12 December 2019

84789552R00235